Gender, Diversity and Trade Unions

Globalisation and diversity are requiring organisations to rethink their priorities, methods and practices. This book is the first to bring together research on gender, race, ethnicity, sexuality and disability and the growing intersection between trade unions and social movements. In this collection, leading researchers examine the debates and developments on gender, diversity and democracy in trade unions in eleven countries.

The topics covered include:

- Theory and practice of self-organising in trade unions, with case studies from the UK, Canada and Italy
- Strategies of gender democracy in unions in the new South Africa and in reunified Germany
- Issues of sexual politics and sexuality in traditional heterosexual 'male' union domains in Australia and Canada
- Women in the formal and informal economies and trade unions of India
- Issues of class, gender and race/ethnicity in Sweden and Malaysia
- Renewal of American unions through organising and equity strategies

Offering an authoritative basis for comparative analysis, this book is essential reading for researchers, teachers, trade unionists and students of industrial relations and equal opportunities, along with all those concerned with ensuring that modern organisations reflect and represent the needs and concerns of a diverse workforce.

Fiona Colgan is a Senior Research Fellow in Employment Studies, the Director of the Centre for Equality Research in Business and the MA Employment Studies and HRM Programme Leader at the University of North London. She researches and writes on gender and organisation and trade unions, democracy and equality. Her previous publications include a co-edited book with Sue Ledwith, *Women in Organisations: Challenging gender politics*.

Sue Ledwith is the Course Director of the MA Women's Studies at Ruskin College. She also runs a regular 'round table' with trade union women and female academics. She researches and writes about women in organisations, especially trade unions. In addition to co-editing *Women in Organisations* (1996), she is joint editor of *Women and the City: Visibility and voice in urban space* (2000).

Routledge Research in Employment Relations

Series editors: Rick Delbridge and Edmund Heery
Cardiff Business School

Aspects of the employment relationship are central to numerous courses at both undergraduate and postgraduate level.

Drawing from insights from industrial relations, human resource management and industrial sociology, this series provides an alternative source of research-based materials and texts, reviewing key developments in employment research.

Books published in this series are works of high academic merit, drawn from a wide range of academic studies in the social sciences.

Gender, Diversity and Trade Unions

International perspectives

Edited by Fiona Colgan and Sue Ledwith

London and New York

First published 2002 by Routledge
11 New Fetter Lane, London EC4P 4EE

Simultaneously published in the USA and Canada
by Routledge
29 West 35th Street, New York, NY 10001

Routledge is an imprint of the Taylor & Francis Group

Typeset in Baskerville by Keystroke, Jacaranda Lodge, Wolverhampton
Printed and bound in Great Britain by Biddles Ltd, Guildford and
King's Lynn

British Library Cataloguing in Publication Data
A catalogue record for this book is available from the British Library

Library of Congress Cataloging in Publication Data
Gender, diversity and trade unions: international perspectives / edited by
Fiona Colgan and Sue Ledwith.
    p. cm.
  Includes bibliographical references and index.
  1. Women labor union members—Case studies. 2. Women employees—Labor
unions—Case studies. 3. Labor unions—Case studies. 4. Diversity in the
workplace—Case studies. I. Colgan, Fiona. II. Ledwith, Sue.

  HD6079 .G46 2002
  331.4'7—dc21   2001058173

ISBN 0–415–23021–7

In memory of John Colgan who always made the
world a better place to be

In memory of Nick Hughes

Contents

Tables

Contributors

Bianca Beccalli is Full Professor of Sociology and Director of the Centre for Gender and Women Studies at the University of Milan, Italy. She has worked and published on Italian unionism, working time, equal opportunities and feminism.

Mhinder Bhopal is a Senior Lecturer in the Centre for Equality Research in Business at the University of North London. He has published on the impact of US MNCs on Malaysian trade unionism, and other pieces exploring the relationships between colonialism, multinationals, trade unions and ethnicity. He is co-author of a forthcoming special edition of the Asia Pacific Business Review focusing on the impact of the Asian Crisis in South East Asia.

Monica Bielski Michal is a doctoral candidate in the School of Management and Labor Relations at Rutgers University, USA. Her ongoing research topics consider issues of identity and sexual diversity within the American labour movement.

Linda Briskin is a Professor in the Social Science Division and the School of Women's Studies at York University, Canada. She has both an activist and a scholarly interest in the documentation and development of feminist strategies for change. She has published widely on women and unions.

Dorothy Sue Cobble is a Professor in the School of Management and Labor Relations at Rutgers University, USA, where she teaches history, women's studies and labour studies. She has published extensively and her first book, *Dishing It Out: Waitresses and Their Unions in the Twentieth Century* (1991, University of Illinois) won the Herbert Gutman Book Award.

Fiona Colgan is a Senior Research Fellow in Employment Studies and the Director of the Centre for Equality Research in Business at the University of North London, UK. Her research interests include trade union democracy, equality and social movements and trade union organising and diversity. She has co-edited two books with Sue Ledwith.

Suzanne Franzway lectures and researches in women's studies and sociology at the University of South Australia, where she is an executive member of the

Research Centre for Gender Studies. She is Chairperson of the Management Committee of the Working Women's Centre, South Australia and has a long-standing involvement in union women's forums. She has published *Sexual Politics and Greedy Institutions: Union Women, Commitments and Conflicts in Public and in Private* (2001, Pluto Press, Australia).

Geraldine Healy is Reader in Employment Relations and Director of the Employment Studies Research Unit in the Business School of the University of Hertfordshire. She has published widely on industrial relations, women and work.

Rohini Hensman is active in the trade union and women's liberation movements. She belongs to the Union Research Group, Bombay, which is a constituent of the Trade Union Solidarity Committee, a coordination of independent unions. She is also a member of Women Working Worldwide, a network of women workers' groups in several countries.

Gerald Hunt is an Associate Professor in the School of Business at Ryerson University, Canada. He has published extensively on minority issues in organisations including *Labouring for Rights: Unions and Sexual Diversity across Nations* (1999, Temple University Press).

Gill Kirton is Senior Lecturer in HRM and Industrial Relations in the Centre for Equality Research in Business at the University of North London. She has a long-standing interest in equality issues and has published articles on women's roles in trade unions.

Sigrid Koch-Baumgarten is Associated Professor, Free University of Berlin in the Department of Political and Social Sciences. Her main fields of research are German Communism, the German political system and German and international trade unionism including gender questions.

Sue Ledwith works at Ruskin College, Oxford, where she runs the MA in Women's Studies, and also a regular 'round table' with trade union women and women academics. She formerly wrote the women's pages for the print union SOGAT '82, and now researches and writes about women and organisations, especially trade unions.

Rianne Mahon is Director of the Institute of Political Economy and Professor in the School of Public Administration and the Department of Sociology and Anthropology at Carleton University, Canada. Mahon has published numerous articles and chapters on unions in Sweden and Canada. She has recently co-edited (with Sonya Michel) a book on gender and welfare state restructuring, through the lens of child care.

Guglielmo Meardi is Lecturer in Industrial Relations at the University of Warwick. His main field of research is comparative labour relations, with a focus on Eastern and Southern Europe.

Patricia Todd is a Senior Lecturer at the University of Western Australia. She has published many articles on Malaysian Labour and is co-author of *Trade Unions in Peninsular Malaysia*. She has also recently researched and published for the ILO. Her PhD thesis, due to be published soon, is an investigation of Australian MNCs in Malaysia. She has a special interest in Malaysian and South East Asian Industrial Relations.

Malehoko Tshoaedi is an MA graduate from the university of Witwatersrand in Johannesburg, South Africa. She became involved with the project on women and trade unions in 1997 when she was studying and doing a research internship with the Sociology of Work Unit (SWOP, a research unit based at Witwatersrand university within the Sociology department). Since 1999, she has worked as a researcher for an independent research organisation, Fafo, Institute for Applied Social Science, focusing mainly on labour markets and trade unions in Southern Africa. She is currently pursuing a PhD degree on women's studies.

Claire Williams is Professor of Sociology at Flinders University in Adelaide, South Australia where she teaches the sociology of work, industrial sociology, occupational health and safety and the sociology of emotions. Most of her academic work has involved a close association with trade unions particularly the Australian Flight Attendants Association (AFAA).

Preface

This is a book born of globalism. Its subject matter, the dynamics of gender and diversity challenges to trade unionism, is being reshaped by the forces of global capital. Although globalisation is seen largely as malevolent, it does also offer important opportunities for international labour solidarity and the exchange and development of innovative strategies. Also the book itself has been an outcome of academic globalism. We would especially like to thank all the contributors for the many stimulating discussions and debates electronically and in person in the various parts of the world where we have been able to meet and network over the period of the book's development. It is with very many thanks indeed to all of them for their interest and willingness to participate in this project, and their patience in dealing with our many requests and queries. The contributions come from ten different countries, and although there are some patterns and similarities, there are also wide differences both in approach and content. Grasping and making sense of all these has been a daunting task, and we hope that we have been able to do credit to the authors and that they think it has been a worthwhile project.

Together, we offer accounts from around the globe, of the gender and diversity politics of trade unionism, an assessment of the present state of play, and of the potential for its future shape. It is noticeable that the majority of the contributions are from the industrialised West. We think that this is the result of a praxis which reflects the state of activity within unions around the politics of gender and diversity relations, together with the state of academic inquiry about democracy, equality and the forms and character of trade unions. Since some of the academics contributing to the book also work collaboratively with unions, and are active in unions and other political and community organisations, maybe this is not surprising.

Perhaps it is also to be expected that the studies in the book are focused in two main cultural blocs, which represent the oldest and longest-established labour traditions of the Western capitalist world, the Anglo and the European. These are also important sites of second wave feminism, and more recently of developing social movements. Recently too feminism has reinvigorated research in the field, and extended the traditional scope of inquiry in industrial relations. These cross-overs and links are important because as observed and experienced by many of us, the academic industrial relations tradition is still largely peopled by men (Forrest 1993; Pocock 2000; Wajcman 2000) and there have also been too few points of contact between social movements such as the women's movement and the labour movement (Muir and Franzway 2000).

We do also recognise that this book is to some extent a product of what Yuval-Davis (1997) calls 'Westocentric' academic thought, although, as she acknowledges, the 'non-dialogue' between women from the 'first' and 'third' worlds in the 1970s and 1980s gave way in the 1990s to a greater sensitivity among white Western feminists to issues of difference and 'multi-positionality' (1997: 118). Although we are not all white and not all from the 'first' world, most of us are. Yet we also come from a range of different industrial relations, academic, feminist and social movement traditions and positions. We hope that sufficient issues are raised to engage and speak to the diversity among trade union men and women as well as those active within a range of social movements.

References

Forrest, A. (1993) 'A view from outside the whale: the treatment of women and unions in industrial relations', in Briskin, L. and McDermott, P. (eds) *Women Challenging Unions: Feminism, Democracy and Militancy*, Toronto: University of Toronto Press.

Muir, K. and Franzway, S. (2000) 'Editorial – sexual politics and trade unions', *Hecate* 26, 2: 4–8.

Pocock, B. (2000) 'Analysing work: arguments for closer links between the study of labour relations and gender', *Journal of Interdisciplinary Gender Studies* 5, 2: 10–26.

Wajcman, J. (2000) 'Feminism facing industrial relations', *British Journal of Industrial Relations* 38, 2: 183–201.

Yuval-Davis, N. (1997) *Gender and Nation*, London: Sage.

1 Tackling gender, diversity and trade union democracy

A worldwide project?

Sue Ledwith and Fiona Colgan

Introduction

This is a book about moves towards new forms of trade union democracy – initially aimed at addressing the gender democratic deficit, although as workforces and union memberships across the world become increasingly diverse, so more demands are placed on unions to deliver on new, inclusive diversity and equality agendas.

In the modern world, the developed world, or the first world, in newly industrialising countries, and in formal labour markets in developing countries, trade unions are the main, established sites of collective solidarity in the search for improved terms and conditions of work and employment protection. However, increasingly these institutions of traditional, male, working-class, blue-collar trade unionism are in crisis. In the developing world there is particular anxiety about the capabilities and the future of the trade union movement (Thomas 1995). Globalisation and restructuring have changed the landscape of work and workforces both within and across countries and continents, and trade union membership has been in free fall in many countries as established constituencies have disappeared. At the same time groups organised around ethnicity and race are reshaping societies, upsetting old assumptions and challenging established systems of power (Cornell and Hartmann 1998). Challenges from young, lesbian and gay and disabled workers are also questioning the status quo. Trade unions have been unable, unwilling, and slow to recognise and exploit the membership potential of these new workforces. Primary among these are women, who by the start of the twenty-first century make up half of the global workforce and are diverse in terms for example of class, race, ethnicity, age and sexuality. Women workers are increasingly seen as the saviour of trade unionism. Yet women are only 1 per cent of trade union governing bodies worldwide (ILO/ICFTU 1999).

Dissatisfied with this situation, and nowadays in a better position of numerical strength, demands from women and minority groups for visibility and voice have been gathering momentum. Since the 1960s and second wave feminism, it has been women who have led the challenge to traditional, male trade union government. In addition the US civil rights and the South African anti-apartheid movements, and subsequently the lesbian and gay and disability movements have ensured that other oppressed groups, principally minority ethnic and racial groups, lesbian and gay members, and disabled members have also been demanding their places and voices in institutions of organised labour.

Academic subjects have also been transformed by feminist contributions, and in many countries academic life has in large part experienced a paradigm shift as a result (Evans 1997: 46). We agree with Anne Forrest (1993), Barbara Pocock (2000) and Judy Wajcman (2000), however, that in the field of industrial relations, although feminism has reinvigorated research and extended the traditional scope of inquiry, the white masculine tradition has meant an over concentration on the institutions and structures of industrial relations and a neglect of the social processes which gender organisational logic, culture and structure. The increasing integration of gender, race, disability, lesbian and gay politics and analysis into the discipline, plus critical contributions from wider social movements and the growth of masculinity studies is central to extending analytical perspectives, scrutinising and challenging traditional narratives and discourses, and refocusing the epistemology. Attempting to draw on these developments in order to bring together the theory and practice of industrial relations and the study of gender, race, sexuality and disability has become a project for many of us who work in the field.

Aims

In this book we aim to do three things. First we want to bring together debates and developments about women, gender and diversity in trade unions in order to develop an international perspective, or perspectives, on the reshaping of trade union democracy.

Second, using empirical studies from a range of countries and cultures we hope to make it possible to identify and assess structural and cultural developments in trade unions as they respond to new labour market conditions and challenges to traditional forms of unionism from increasingly diverse agendas among the membership.

The third aim is to offer a site for the voice of gendered and diversified trade union activism. To do this we present where possible, the social processes of debate, challenge and change, the dynamics of gender and diversity in union politics through the lenses and voices of activists themselves.

Rather than attempt a strictly comparative approach, our method in this first chapter is to identify common themes and issues across the cases studies, and to explore the differences and similarities between them. Models of change are never wholly transferable across cultures and industrial relations systems, but there is plenty of room for cross-cultural adaptation and the borrowing of ideas and innovative practice.

Organisation of the book

We start with the global questions. Linda Briskin's chapter provides an account of the equity project in Canadian unions; confronting the challenge of restructuring and globalisation. She revisits key strategies used by Canadian women and assesses their relevance to building resistance to the forces of globalisation and restructuring. Rianne Mahon also situates her analysis within the global paradigm. She discusses how the impact of global capital has weakened the corporate state in Sweden, the tensions between the male dominated 'export sector' and the female dominated services sector and what effects this is having on class and gender relations in the main blue-collar union the LO. Both these chapters also explore the union relations of gender and race. The fourth chapter which is framed by globalisation is by Patrica Todd and Mhinder Bhopal. They examine how the recent rapid economic development of Malaysia has impacted on labour relations of ethnicity, race and gender, especially since much of the expansion was reliant on female labour in the low-skill, low-wage electronics based export sector. The chapter from India follows. In writing of the complex and fragmented relations of gender, caste and religion, Rohini Hensman has adopted both a global outlook, and a discussion based on six case studies of women's relationship with trade unions in both the formal employment sector and the informal sector – where women dominate.

The next group of chapters come from Europe. Bianca Beccalli and Guglielmo Meardi trace women's relationship with their unions in Italy since 1945, and since, as they say, there is a shortage of gender analysis in Italian industrial relations, this is a welcome contribution. They draw on case study research about union gender policy in Milan with Italy's two largest unions, the CGIL and the CISL, and also look at how the unions have responded to increased immigration. In the following chapter, Sigrid Koch-Baumgarten asks whether the German trade union model has yet changed from homogeneity to heterogeneity. She surveys the recent history of women in German unions in the light of reunification and also with the increasing presence of migrant workers. Fiona Colgan and Sue Ledwith present findings from their detailed research with women in the UK print union The Graphical Paper and Media Union (GPMU), and women, black, lesbian and gay and disabled self-organised groups in the public service union UNISON. As UK unions have responded to membership decline through merger, these groups have seen opportunities to tackle the democratic deficit in UK unions through forms of semi-autonomous organising, or self-organisation. Also from the UK, Geraldine Healy and Gill Kirton consider how ideology and solidarity among professional teachers in the National Union of Teachers (NUT) and highly qualified women trade union activists in the Manufacturing, Science and Finance union MSF are both different and similar to that of women in more traditional unions, and how this agenda is carried forward by the women within the union hierarchy and structures.

Malehoko Tshoaedi explores gender democracy in the new South Africa. Her findings are of disappointment. Whereas women and men worked side by side when forming and developing their unions under apartheid, freedom and political power has resulted in the reassertion of male hegemony. Tshoaedi discusses the significance of gender processes and politics within the trade union movement of the new South Africa.

In the USA, where trade union membership has haemorrhaged, Dorothy Sue Cobble and Monica Bielski Michal look at how after decades of pushing for cultural and institutional change in US labour unions, the impact of women's efforts is increasingly being felt. They argue for a positive gender partnership in the remaking of American unions and a reframing of bargaining issues towards more inclusive and collaborative projects encompassing diversity based on class, gender, race, and sexuality. The following chapter by Gerald Hunt is an account of the progress made in Canada by unions in supporting and taking forward lesbian and gay rights. He shows how it has been possible to build lesbian and gay activism by making alliances with and building on the example of women's union organising which arose through the women's movement of the 1970s. He highlights the subsequent contribution of the labour movement to campaigning to help achieve legal and constitutional gains on lesbian and gay rights.

The two final chapters are both from Australia. From complementary perspectives they each address and analyse the sexual politics and hegemonic masculinity which underpin gender relations in trade unions. Suzanne Franzway puts the sex as well as the gender back into the trade union debate as she examines some of the ways that women unionists are confronted by dilemmas of sexual politics, and how they handle the pleasures and dangers of gaining and exercising power. Claire Williams explores masculinity and sexuality through the voices of trade union men who articulate gay and green (environmental) discourses that challenge taken-for-granted masculine norms in the timber, meat and health sectors. She provides new insights into the structuring of gender and sexual politics in trade union life.

Trade union democracy, gender and diversity

Trade unions are political organisations whereby representative democracy is seen to be achieved through elections of leaders, checked by balances between the powers of elected executives and delegates and appointed officers which aim to ensure that the interests of all the members are met. In this regard, democracy implies equality. The extent to which trade unions are democratic in practice has been a source of much debate within the industrial relations tradition. This has focused on the key concerns of the relationship between representative and participative democracy, and the balance of power between members and their officials and whose power prevails (Fosh and Heery 1990). Here, Michels' 'iron law of oligarchy' is often invoked to show how leaders in political organisations acquire and retain a relative influence which is then used against the interests of the membership as the leadership seeks to protect its position of privilege. Writers have sought to identify counter-vailing tendencies, especially through forms of participatory democracy whereby challenges are mounted by 'outsider' groups and factions, rank and file grass-roots activism, and shop stewards' movements (Lipset *et al.* 1956; Hyman 1975; Hemingway 1979; Fairbrother 1984). In discussing these balances of interest within unions, traditional analysis has been slow to address those of gender or race, or other membership diversities even though as Hyman (1994, 1996) has pointed out, most unions have 'typically been biased in the composition of their officials and activists towards relatively high-status, male, native-born, full-time employees' (1994: 121).

The debate thus far has been informed by a class-based analysis and subsequent critiques from feminist and race studies. This book seeks to draw on the growing number of studies which consider the interplay between class, gender and race. This is now supplemented by the research concerning sexuality, democracy and equal rights (Herman 1994; Rayside 1998; Rahman 2000) and lesbian and gay activism within trade unions (Colgan 1999a; Hunt 1999; Humphrey 2000). The other developing area of research concerns the links between the wider disability movement and trade unions (Campbell and Oliver 1996; Hales 1996; Humphrey 1998). The book is thus titled *Gender, Diversity and Trade Unions.* We acknowledge that the term 'diversity' has acquired 'political baggage' but in deciding to use it in this book we follow Noon and Ogbonna (2001) in reclaiming diversity purely as a 'neutral descriptor of variation within the workplace'. The contributors have interpreted 'diversity' as appropriate given the ways in which the term is understood and addressed currently by the labour organisations studied within each chapter.

Class

The unifying ideology of trade unionism has been based on the notion of class solidarity. However although the tendency has been for class to be articulated within a Marxist analysis of antagonistic relations between two main opposing classes, labour and capital, in both theory and practice, as it suits, class becomes both fixed and flexible; what Hyman has referred to as the 'incoherence of class' (2001: 32). In traditional trade union analysis, class has been symbolised by the male working-class, blue-collar worker. In reality this has never been a homogeneous group, exemplified instead by a hierarchy of labour with craft workers (exclusively male) at the top and the unskilled (mixed sex) at the bottom. In the early period of industrialisation each was organised into different unions, focused on their own sectional interests, and this formulation has endured. As Hyman observes, 'competitive sectionalism has most commonly been the hallmark of trade union action' (2001: 31). As a result of restructuring, professional and white-collar service sector unionism has been the most recent interest group to emerge – a sector where women dominate. Recognising the salience of the proletarianisation and embourgeoisement debates, these are significant developments for trade union relations of gender and class. Healy and Kirton's chapter illustrates how among professional and highly qualified trade union women activists, an individual instrumental career orientation can coexist with a commitment to both professional and trade union values of collective solidarity. Moreover, within the superordinate goal of gender equity their complementarity enhances union solidarity.

As feminist and diversity studies and analysis develop, it becomes clearer how what Hyman (2001: 30) describes as the 'paradox of collective organisation that simultaneously unites and divides workers' is no longer solely about concepts of class. Cobble and Michal suggest in their chapter that the question is not whether class or gender or race should be given priority, 'but whether it will be finally understood that workers come in all sizes and shapes, and there is no *one* class identity or consciousness because there is no *one* worker. A new and vibrant working-class politics can be built but only when no one *particular* experience is taken as *universal*'.

Patriarchy, gender regimes, sexuality and hegemonic masculinity

Feminist analyses of patriarchy show how the power relations of gender structure the overall subordination of women and the dominance of men. Recently the term has tended to give way to the concept of gender regimes on the basis that, as Walby comments, patriarchy always exists in articulation with other social systems. She identifies six interrelated regimes, or structures of patriarchy in which men dominate, oppress and exploit women. These are: household production, patriarchal relations in paid work, patriarchal relations in the state, male violence – including sexual harassment, patriarchal relations in sexuality, including homophobia, and in cultural institutions such as education, religion, the media (1990, 1997: 6). Clearly these are not fixed, nor universal, and the forms they take will be contingent on interrelated structures of culture, politics, social relations, economics and history. These interrelations are especially well illustrated by Hensman in the chapter from India. There, the inseparability of gender politics in the spheres of domestic relations, work relations, and those with male violence is exemplified, particularly for vulnerable women in the informal sector where constitutional rights are relatively meaningless and employment rights do not exist.[1]

Feminist analysis has also blown away the cover of gender neutrality and the notion that organisations are a-sexual (Pringle 1988; Acker 1990; Mills and Tancred 1992; Alvesson and Billing 1997). The studies by Hearn *et al.* (1989) concerning the sexuality of organisations built on and further opened the door to research on a range of topics including sexuality and the labour process, sexual harassment, men's sexuality and women's sexuality. Lesbian and gay studies have added to this literature by focusing on the experiences of lesbians and gay men and the inequalities based on sexuality within organisations (Oerton 1996; Humphrey 1999). Masculinity studies have made further important contributions. Connell (1995) identifies a three-fold model of the structuring of gender, whereby he distinguishes relations of power, relations of production, and relations of cathexis (emotional attachment). These cover similar ground to Walby's six gender regimes. In Connell's model, gender power relations are about the structuring of patriarchy. Gender divisions in paid and domestic work and which structure the unequal and gendered economic consequences through concepts such as the family wage, result from gendered production relations. Relations of social attachment and sexual desire, and the central role they play in the gendering of organisational life raise political questions such as whether or not sexual practices are consensual or coercive. He stresses that in feminist analysis of sexuality these have become 'sharp questions' about the connection of heterosexuality with men's position of social dominance.

From this analysis, and using Gramsci's notion of hegemony as a cultural dynamic by which a group claims and sustains a leading position in social life, Connell has developed the concept of hegemonic masculinity. Hegemonic masculinity becomes a configuration of gender practice which guarantees the dominant position of men and the subordination of women. It is a cultural dynamic, a 'historically mobile' relationship which may vary in time and place with cultural specificity, and the resulting pattern of social relations is always contestable. Within its overall framework, Connell identifies specific gender relations of dominance and subordination between groups of men – heterosexism and homophobia. We would add that there is also the possibility of such relations between groups of women, and in her discussion of sexual politics in this book, Franzway comments on how little attention is paid in the literature to sexual diversity among women. Connell points out that masculinity is also constructed in relation to race. Thus white men's masculinities are constructed not only in relation to white women, but also to black men and gay men. At any given time one form of masculinity rather than others is culturally exalted.

These analyses are having an impact on the study of trade unions (Briskin and McDermott 1993; Cobble 1993; Pocock 1997). Reconceptualisation of trade union democracy has become a gendered, sexualised and racialised project. For example, in their research with particular UK unions, while McBride (2001), Colgan and Ledwith (2000, 2002), and Healy and Kirton (2000) have been putting gender back in, Colgan (1999b) and Humphrey (2000) have been raising the issue of sexuality and Humphrey (1998) that of disability and trade unions. Healy and Kirton (2000) emphasise that women's constituency can act as a countervailing faction against male oligarchic leadership. They conclude that the resulting continual opposition does seem to constrain the dominant gendered oligarchy. They also point out though, that reassertion of oligarchic tendencies ensure that gendered change is evolutionary rather than transformative.

The resulting 'democratic deficit' for women and other minority groups has wider implications and is intimately related to these memberships' position in the workforce. A crude, but potent measure of this is the gender pay gap, which internationally, even for similar jobs, still averages between 20 and 30 per cent. This is in part an outcome of the absence of women from collective bargaining in the majority of unions (Colling and Dickens 2001; ETUC 1999). A recent international survey found that only a third of unions had a policy for the participation of women in collective bargaining teams. (ILO/ICFTU 1999).

Race and ethnicity

Cornell and Hartmann (1998) in discussing the differences and relationships between ethnicity and race suggest that ethnicity is based on self-consciousness, on shared beliefs in common descent, memories or legends of a shared historical past and a cultural focus on symbols which rate as the 'epitome of their peoplehood' (Schermerhorn in Cornell and Hartmann 1998: 19). Racism they describe as a more 'slippery' concept, as less benign than ethnicity, although the two cannot be neatly divided, and both are bound up in power relations and conflicts over scarce resources such as jobs or status. Race typically has its origins in assignment by others, whereas ethnicity may have similar origins, but frequently originates in assertions of group members themselves. Race is based on the psuedo science of biological distinctiveness, which they suggest owes more to history and social construction – especially European colonialism – than to any physical or biological basis.

Wets (2000: 2) discussing the attitudes of trade unions towards immigrants and immigration in Europe comments that although unions may commit themselves verbally in varying degrees to internationalist worker solidarity, in practice this tends to become subordinated to the national state and national arena, and increasingly in Europe regionalism has become an important rallying point. Like the other categories we are dealing with here, race is culturally determined, and in Western systems, whiteness, itself a racial category, is privileged over others. Race forms a powerful and persistent group boundary through forms of constructed 'arbitrary closure' (Yuval-Davis 1997: 119) and the use of assigned essentialist characteristics as expressive means of exclusion and control. Stuart Hall describes the work of racism as being 'directed to secure "us" "over here" and "them" "over there"', to fix each in its appointed place (Hall and duGay 1996). Whatever the source of minority ethnicity however, traditions of class and national identity combine to exclude and control minority groups. Ethnicity and race are seen as having a 'striking potency' as bases of collective identity and action (Cornell and Hartmann 1998: 12). It seems that when such groups launch an active claim for access and entry to closed institutions, what previously may have been a benign institutional tolerance of ethnic difference, slides into an antagonistic racist response.

In the countries represented in this book it is evident that there are a number of different categories of ethnic minorities. There are indigenous peoples in Canada, Australia and the USA for example, who have been oppressed by the incoming dominant majority, usually white. Until 1993 this was also the case in South Africa, although there the dominant white group was the minority and thus the majority was oppressed by the minority. There is little contemporary research available in Australia about Aboriginal and Torres Strait Islander workers, although it is argued, reports Franzway, that union support for these workers has been, at best, equivocal. Currently what is termed 'reconciliation' with the indigenous groups by the white majority is politically disputatious, although now in some unions there are officers and groupings specifically to represent their interests. In the USA the domination by slavery of the black by the white population has a unique historical significance. Its legacy, the civil rights movement, has been the main engine for development of black consciousness and collective action and has been a significant model for social movement organisation both in America and abroad. Elsewhere minority ethnic groups are mainly the result of immigration, and there are many variations in time-waves, groups of immigrant peoples, and geography. Early phases of immigration as a result of previous colonial relations have been significant in the UK, and Australia and Canada. In Europe there has been migration from Mediterranean southern countries to the more prosperous north, while the most recent migrant waves have resulted from the break up of the USSR, the Eastern European bloc including former Yugoslavia, and the opening up of China. Economic immigration, flight from conflicts and political expulsions in south east Asian countries have also impacted on for example Australia and Britain. Forms of indentured immigrant labour have been an important presence in Germany and Malaysia. On the Indian continent caste, religion and multiple ethnic groupings present complex hierarchies.

The range of analyses from contributors in this book offers the opportunity to observe the forces at work in these domains and the interrelationships between them. We suggest that study of the cultural and social processes involved in the dynamics of class, gendered, sexualised and racialised hegemonies can help explain the oligarchic tendencies involved in structural practices of closure, exclusion, demarcation and segregation in trade unions.

Strategies of challenge and resistance – a conceptual framework

To help to do this we have developed a conceptual framework. This is now outlined, and then we move on to discuss it in relation to the analysis in the chapters that follow. As already indicated here, and in the chapters in the book, traditional trade unionism as characterised by patriarchal, working-class, organisation is being challenged externally by the forces of global restructuring and internally by the groups of workers which it has marginalised.

To help understand the fluid social processes of challenge and resistance to these hegemonic and oligarchic forces we draw on approaches from industrial relations, sociology and organisational theory. In Witz's analysis of patriarchy she utilised neo-Weberian concepts of exclusion, inclusion, demarcation, closure and power to develop a model of gendered strategies of exclusionary and demarcatory closure (1992). From an industrial relations perspective, similar ground has been covered by Penninx and Roosblad and others in relation to immigrants (Roosblad 2000). This analysis can be expanded to include a broader conceptualisation of racial and ethnic groupings. Three main dilemmas are identified for trade unions in considering their position in relation to immigration and immigrant workers. First, do unions resist immigration and immigrants, or cooperate with governments and employers, and if so under what conditions? Second, once immigrants are in the country/labour market should unions assimilate them as part of the working class or exclude them from membership? Third, if trade unions consider immigrants as potential members, should they defend their general interests as workers, emphasising the collective stake in working-class interests while disregarding differences in material and cultural positions, or should they develop specific policies and structures to address their particular concerns at the risk of upsetting the indigenous workers?

From these sources we have developed a framework which is concerned with both traditional trade unionism's strategies of closure, and challenge and response to these. The model is not fixed. Particular strategic forms in different countries will always be mediated by and be contingent on external factors such as labour market positions, employer approaches, government ideology and strategy, legal rights and industrial relations systems. Six closely related and often overlapping systems are identified: exclusion, demarcation, inclusion, usurpation, transformation and coalition.

Exclusion

Traditional trade unionism has applied oligarchic and hegemonic strategies of resistance and closure to outsiders such as women, part timers, and minority ethnic groups, in order to secure and maintain cultural and class homogeneity and access to resources and rewards. Exclusionary strategies are adopted in order to protect against the threat of dilution by undermining core pay and conditions and fear of strike breaking. These practices give rise to the dual concepts of the male breadwinner and the family wage.

There are strong parallels with exclusionary practices in relation to immigrants. Virdee (2000) discusses how in the postwar period large numbers of Caribbean workers were encouraged to move to work in Britain's new welfare state and Asian immigrants moved into the country's manufacturing sector. Through examples of industrial disputes where white trade unionists resisted the employment of black workers, or insisted on a quota system, he shows how parts of the white working class actively colluded with employers in restrictive practices of racist exclusion in key sectors of employment. Thus exclusion may also be achieved through collusion between capital and organised male labour against 'dilution' by women, unskilled, and 'outsider' racial and ethnic groups. Responses by these groups have often been to organise separately, but they have then run the risk of being denied resources by predominant union organisations.[2]

In the last quarter of a century, in the developed world, trade union practices of total exclusion have largely broken down as closed systems such as pre-entry closed shops in craft unions have been swept away by a combination of technological, economic, social and political change. Nevertheless exclusion of women, ethnic groups, disabled and lesbians and gay members from union leaderships and power elites continues today. For example, a recent survey by the European TUC of its affiliates in twenty-eight countries found a serious under-representation of women in trade union decision-making, particularly in positions of responsibility and leadership, and in collective bargaining (1999). Employers and/or the state may also practise exclusion both of trade unions altogether, and of women from particular spheres. Such practices include marriage bars for working women, and legal restrictions on women working in certain occupations such as mining and seafaring, and night working. Absence and silence are also potent motifs, and the suppression and stigmatisation of lesbians and gay men through cultures and practices of hetero-sexism and homophobia have been effectively employed in exclusionary projects.

While total exclusion is no longer practised in trade unions in any of the countries represented in the chapters in the book, there is evidence of a range of exclusionary and demarcatory practices, and gender and diversity challenges to these. Exclusion of women from the formal employment sector through discriminatory employment practices in India is of central and increasing importance as this also means exclusion from legal employment rights and trade union organisation. These difficulties have driven women into autonomous organising, often outside trade unions, through women's non-governmental organisations (NGOs), and into leading the way in organising across caste and religion, work, community and family, cross-organisational and cross-nationally. Similar exclusionary practices can be seen in Malaysia, where for example, temporary migrant labour is prohibited by the government from joining unions, and the government supports employer antagonism to trade unions in the export driven electronics sector where many women work. Once again NGOs have moved in to fill the gap left by trade unions providing advice and support to these women and migrant workers (Committee for Asian Women 1995).

There is evidence across the chapters of systemic exclusion from internal positions of trade union power in every country. Perhaps the most extreme example is from South Africa, notwithstanding the impressive commitment to equality within its constitution. Tshoaedi describes how once trade unions gained political power post-apartheid, women leaders found themselves being pushed aside and sidelined from senior and leadership posts through processes of homosocial closure.

Demarcation

Demarcation and segregation occur when total exclusion gives way to entry by marginalised groups, for example through external forces such as labour market restructuring, employer strategies, or statutory rights. Then, traditional trade unionism seeks to contain and regulate the participation of outsider or minority groups through the creation and control of boundaries. Usually these are already well established through gendered and racialised labour market segregation and hierarchical occupational segmentation, which become replicated within trade unions, again sometimes through strategies of collusion.

Thus low paid workers in low status jobs, usually women and members of ethnic and racial minority groups, may also be held in low esteem in their unions, and find themselves excluded from power elites and institutions of collective bargaining. If they do succeed in taking on union positions, they may find it difficult to participate in union circles where closure techniques are used such as excessive jargon, rigid constitutional rules and procedures, meetings in 'smoke filled rooms' in inhospitable environments and at times of day which are difficult for those with family responsibilities. For those whose employment status is precarious it may also be risky to take time off work for trade union activities. In addition, strategies of traditional hegemonic masculinity, such as sexual and racial harassment and homophobia, are prime techniques for policing demarcation lines between insiders and outsiders and keeping the latter in their place. Writers have discussed how in the UK, where it was not possible to exclude, then quota systems restricting the numbers of black workers were agreed with employers (Wrench and Virdee 1996). As a result these workers came overwhelmingly to occupy a position at the bottom of the British class structure (Virdee 2000: 210).

Demarcation practices may vary in detail in each of the country case studies, but they do show similar patterns. In South Africa, within unions women are routinely segregated into secondary positions and excluded from union power elites and collective bargaining. In Italy, Beccalli and Meardi report that among the job specifications of paid union officer work are being on call, and job mobility. While women find they are required to uphold these requirements, their male colleagues are able to ignore them. Koch-Baumgarten discusses how German unions restricted women's political participation by corralling them in special women's structures without power or status, and excluding women from the union power elites. In Germany into the 1980s, and in the UK in the print union the GPMU, for example, male executive members remain responsible for the work of women's departments. In these forms, separate organising has been described as 'ghettos to keep women quiet, ineffective, and talking only to themselves' (Briskin 1993: 94).

Hegemonic masculinity is explicitly brought into play as part of the systems of control and demarcation through sexual politics. The moral question of women and men working together, historically important in the West, is still employed in a number of countries, for example Malaysia where patriarchal and religious forces opposed women doing paid work outside of the home, especially under foreign male authority. Cobble and Michal identify how the labour movement in the USA helped men achieve 'manhood' through traditional sexual practices built on deeply embedded gender norms at work. These arguments are extended by Williams in her discussion of how masculinities and emotion work maintain hegemonic heterosexual masculinities within Australian trade unionism in the meat, timber and health industries – through a particular form known as 'Mate'-ism'. Key among these practices is sexual harassment, which Franzway identifies as being deeply and centrally implicated in the development and maintenance of traditional patriarchal trade unionism. In almost every chapter in the book practices of sexual harassment appear as a core and contentious issue in trade union gender relations. In the USA and Italy for example, unions have shunned this issue leaving women to take up cases without the active support of their unions and being forced to turn for help to outside women's organisations. In Italy and Sweden, the unions have also been happy to leave lesbian and gay and disability issues to lesbian and gay and disabled campaigning organisations. Where unions have taken on the issue of sexual harassment, they have often been pressed to do so as a result of internal union cases which have reached to the heart of union sexual politics.

In Germany, special departments were established in some unions to deal with the particular problems and interests of migrants. This form of affirmative action reserves space and resources for education, anti-racist publicity, and negotiating non-discrimination works agreements in leading companies. Elsewhere, for example in Malaysia, demarcation remains strong among ethnic groups. Ethnic hierarchies are also important in India, where oppressed groups such as Dalits (formerly Untouchables) and Muslims are excluded from mainstream society. In the formal sector, trade union leadership is dominated by caste Hindu men.

Inclusion

Here two strategies can be identified. *Contested inclusion* whereby inclusion or assimilation within the existing systems and structures is sought, campaigned for and negotiated by excluded/minority groups. Second, the dominant union group may *invite inclusion* for material and/or ideological reasons such as membership growth, union solidarity, or democratic ideals. In practice the two often operate together. For example women have long been actively campaigning and negotiating for inclusion in unions. Simultaneously, the forces of globalisation, restructuring and demographic change in labour markets have led to huge losses among male (mostly) trade union memberships, and it has become clear to trade unions that women are their main source of membership and renewal. As a result, new strategies of recruitment and organising are being developed by trade union movements across the world. Recruitment into membership is the first step. More complex, more radical and more vigorously contested is inclusion into mainstream decision-making structures, power elites and top positions of power.

In the current period, at the start of the twenty-first century, strategies of inclusion are possibly the main challenges facing union movements. It can be seen from the discussion below and in more detail in the case study chapters, that these are all currently practised in trade unions in various forms in different countries and different situations. In some, challenges from outsider groups have progressed as far as the next strategy, usurpation.

As already outlined in this chapter, increasing the membership of women, young workers, migrant workers and those from previously marginalised ethnic and racial backgrounds has become a major objective of trade union renewal in a growing number of countries. Contrary to previous conventional union wisdom, the workers keenest to join unions are those who have most to gain; the marginalised and oppressed – women and those from other diversity groups. Many of the organising breakthroughs in the USA in the 1990s have been among women, particularly women of colour and immigrant women, in the hotel and healthcare sectors. In the UK, analysis of the increase in union membership during 2000, found that it was mainly accounted for by women part-time workers (LRD 2001).

Unions in Anglophone countries where restructuring and employer antagonism have been central to membership losses, have developed increasingly sophisticated strategies of organising, recruitment and retention, and have drawn on one another's experience to do so. Australia's *Organising Works* campaign, initially modelled on developments in the USA, helped lead to the British TUC's *Organising Academy*, which in turn linked up with New Zealand unions, and was one of a number of Anglo labour movement initiatives recently studied for a new Australian project: *unions@work* (ACTU 1999). These 'new unionism' projects are primarily geared to addressing the membership crisis. In the UK this is seen for example as 'a trade unionism for the new insecure world of work' (TUC 1997). However, it is one thing to organise new members into membership. It is another to retain them, and it is yet another again to move members beyond instrumental membership and into ideological and practical collective commitment to union solidarity.

Strategies designed to move towards inclusive internal union democracy take two main trajectories:

- *autonomous* or *separate organisation* and *special structures* – forms of affirmative action – for previously oppressed and marginalised groups working as constituency groups; and

- *mainstreaming*[3] – inclusion and integration of representatives from such groups into mainstream structures and decision-making positions.

Both of these increasingly coexist and interrelate, with for example representatives and delegates from diverse constituencies taking up positions in the mainstream. Both strategies have been driven principally by women and other minority groups themselves. Among the responses triggered have been resistance and opposition both direct and indirect, from traditional trade unionism (both male and female) which has often interpreted such entrism as a threat to class solidarity and as usurping male privilege. Increasingly, however, unions' espoused formal positions have been to welcome and include diversity and to develop structures to support it. In doing so, institutional organised labour has begun to move towards what Cockburn (1989, 1991) has described as a longer, transformative agenda of equality politics in trade unions.

Separate organising has already been referred to in the discussion of exclusion and demarcatory strategies by trade unions. It can also be used in a more positive sense and here we move to consider this more positive and proactive approach to self-organisation. The debate around separate organising was first opened up by Briskin (1993, 1999), and she has argued that its success depends on maintaining a balance between autonomy and integration. The dangers of autonomy include ghettoisation, outlined above, and those of integration resting on a deficit model which suggests that it is women who are the problem and need changing, and that they are poorly equipped to take on leadership roles because they lack skills and self-confidence (Briskin 1993: 96). What Briskin has described as a proactive politic of separate organising is now becoming the preferred choice of marginalised groups (Colgan and Ledwith, 2002).

Separate organisation can be seen as a goal, as an end in itself and as a way of building an alternative community. Such groups may organise outside of mainstream trade unions altogether. Alternatively, groups may organise semi-autonomously within trade unions. Self-organisation may also be an interim strategy in preparation for mainstreaming self-organised group interests and transforming union cultures and structures. Autonomous organising by groups of women teachers in Canada (Briskin 1993), and in New Zealand (Street 2001) have been important models of transformational feminist change.

Two main strategies of self-organisation are of significance here; *social creativity* and *social change* (Colgan and Ledwith 2000). Strategies of social creativity involve the development of individual skills, self-confidence, and possibly of political consciousness. If and when these combine collectively into a group consciousness they may (or may not necessarily) develop further into a strategy of social change. Strategies of social change seek to bring about actual change in material circumstances and objective social relations between groups such that marginalised groups may improve their position and their access to resources in relation to those of existing power holders. Examples of social creativity strategies are illustrated in the Indian chapter in particular, where women reported high levels of empowerment as a result of women-only organising, even though their material gains were low.

Healy and Kirton's professional and highly qualified trade union women were committed to both types of strategies, seeing them as complementary. The same was the case for women in Italy and Sweden. Colgan and Ledwith (Chapter 8) and Hunt (Chapter 12) show the further development of self-organisation for black/ethnic minority, lesbian and gay and disabled members and their importance as locations in which to gain self-confidence and build political strength. The evidence from the UK is assessed in an appraisal of the utility of self-organising and the balance between autonomy and integration.

Much of the ground for these developments was laid in the 1970s, when the rise of second wave feminism either influenced or directly connected with an upsurge in political activism and labour movement politics. Hunt, for example records the presence of informal lesbian groups at Canadian union women's conferences and national congresses of the time. In the UK, there was a significant shift in union attitudes towards inclusivity of black workers as a reaction against the extreme right stirring up racist feelings, and combating racism has become an important feature of many British trade unions' work (Virdee 2000: 218). In European countries while elements of institutional[4] racism clearly remain within trade unions, their positive recent strategies on immigrants has largely been as a response to the rise of the far right and neo-Nazism.

In India, the impetus for women to organise autonomously was their marginalisation by male dominated unions. Hensman charts the formation and rapid spread of women's wings especially in banking and in mineworking and shows how the women's movement also bridged the formal/informal sector divide. This reflects the indivisibility of domestic and production gender relations, so women members of workers' families were included in campaigning across issues of housing, sexual harassment, alcoholism and domestic violence.

Cobble and Bielski discuss how in the early 1970s American women, especially in white-collar and professional jobs such as clerical work and flight attendants, broke away from the male-dominated unions and formed their own. This became an interim separatist strategy for changing the gendered norms of their occupation, such as pressures to 'appear forever young, slim and sexually alluring', to end sexploitation and gain control over compensation for their sexual and their emotional labour. In Italy and Sweden, it was women in the metal (car workers') unions who pioneered women's separate organising, although they met strong resistance from the traditions of working-class solidarity, especially, in Italy among communists in the CGIL union.

In the USA nearly a quarter of the workforce was made up of minority ethnic groups in 1999. American women from ethnic minority groups, mainly African-American and Latina, have been rapidly joining unions, especially from the sectors unions have traditionally labelled as difficult to organise; home healthcare workers, and service workers in the hotel industry. In the UK too, there is evidence of a similar inclination among women, particularly Afro-Caribbean women, for joining unions. Agency among these groups is high, and there is considerable autonomous organising among racial and ethnic minorities both within the labour movement and across civil rights and community groups.

Ethnic and racial inclusivity is also illustrated by the progressive attitude of the Canadian Auto Workers' challenge to an 'increasingly mean-spirited and at times openly racist attitude towards immigrants and refugees' in Canada. Other inclusionary initiatives during the 1990s relate to indigenous and well-established minority ethnic groups. As in Britain this was the outcome of years of organising by anti-racist activists. The main aim of these strategies is to integrate – not assimilate, and Swedish trade unions have also recently moved in this direction. German trade unions have not only had to cope with reunification but also with recent increases in refugee immigration. Here strategies have changed from assimilation to special treatment, with departments being established to deal with the particular problems and interests of migrants, and to develop works council agreements.

In Italy, ethnic minorities have also become a trade union issue since the 1980s, but unlike unions in many other countries, Italian unions moved directly to a strategy of supporting immigrants, such as promoting various laws for undocumented immigrants and supporting their rights in the wider society including those of migrant prostitutes (ILO-ICFTU 1999: 119).

More recent still have been developments in separate organising among lesbian and gay members and members with disabilities. The Canadian Labour Congress (CLC) is described by Hunt as the world leader in the field of sexual diversity initiatives – which are limited to a few developed countries. While these developments are strongest in the public sector trade unions, it is possible to chart increasing shifts towards inclusion in private sector unions. Colgan and Ledwith outline similar development in the UK, where for example, the Trades Union Congress (TUC) has moved from running a women's conference, since 1925, to organising a black members' conference and a lesbian and gay workers' conference in the 1990s. In 2000 it established a conference for disabled members.

Australian unions meanwhile remain reticent about developing rights and policies and practices for lesbian and gay men. Franzway comments that creative strategies are required to tackle such issues in unions. The Gay and Lesbian Members (GLAM) of the Australian Services Union are a pioneering group in these areas.

The weakest area of change has been for workers with disabilities although some progress is now evident in the UK. Even in Canada, the labour movement has taken a minimalist position, focusing mainly on the legal responsibilities of unions.

Usurpation

This is where a subordinate group mobilises through strategies of social change to challenge the dominant group, and succeeds in changing the structure of positions and balance of leadership between the groups. An example of a successful strategic challenge here would be the achievement of proportional or quota representation of women and of minority ethnic or racial groups or lesbian and gay and disabled trade unionists in union structures. Since usurpation strategies are about altering the balance of power between groups, of replacing men with women, white members with black, and so on, they may be fiercely resisted, once again through discriminatory exclusionary and demarcatory practices. Where it is effective however, usurpation may lead to strategies of change and transformation.

When unions adopt policies and practices for increasing women's representation such as proportionality, reserved seats or self-organisation, the common response from traditional unionism is antagonistic. As Tshaoedi comments, in South Africa, the closer to the centre of male power basis women's challenges go, the more vigorously they are rejected. Opponents of radical interventionist affirmative actions such as women's quotas, claim that these are tokenistic and anti-democratic since those elected are not truly representative of the membership. A related argument is made on the basis of union ideology of unity and solidarity, claiming that separate structures are divisive. In Sweden, women and men in the *Landsorganisation i Sverge* (LO) sought to prioritise a policy of class-based solidarity, mainstreaming gender equality issues while campaigning for work/life balance and 'family friendly' state and employer policies to apply to both men and women workers. Paternalistic arguments are also used. In South Africa it is men who raise the fear that women will be marginalised by their separatism, while women point out that it is precisely by organising on their own that they will be able to develop strength. In India, Germany, the UK, the USA, Canada and latterly in Sweden too, women activists all strongly supported women's structures as essential to maintaining a critical mass of women to advance a feminised trade union agenda. However, in Italy, Beccalli and Meardi report a form of malaise concerning these structures particularly among younger women. In the UK, when proportionality was introduced for women in UNISON, it reversed the existing gender power balance among members elected to positions at all levels of the union, giving rise to varying forms of opposition.

To try to avoid such problems, some unions have expanded the total number of elective seats on mainstream decision-making committees and conferences in order to *add* women, and avoid women being seen as displacing men. Colgan and Ledwith discuss how in the UK the male dominated print union, the GPMU, has done this, with some success.

As traditional work opportunities for men have declined, there has been a rise among women entering white-collar and professional male bastions such as the law and management so usurping male privilege. The exclusionary and demarcatory responses of closure have been described in detail by Anne Witz in her study of health workers (1992). There has been surprisingly little research into union practice among the increasing number of women in these professions, and their attachment to trade union principles and practices. So we are pleased to be able to include the chapter by Healy and Kirton, which explore these. Their findings show how women's occupational and professional skills such as literacy and advocacy together with their experiences of working in mainly male milieux, equip them for the masculine world of trade unions. Elsewhere we have discussed four styles of political behaviour women may adopt in homosocial organisations: wise, clever, innocent and inept (Ledwith and Colgan 1996). Among the union women in Healy and Kirton's studies, the professional and highly qualified women union activists could be seen as using wise behaviour – which entails accurate reading of organisational mores and acting with integrity. Wisdom is no guarantee of success however.

Franzway comments that women do not fail in their efforts to change sexual politics simply because their strategy is flawed. If relations of male domination shape women's subordination, then successful challenges to that domination are likely to be strenuously resisted. In addition, since recognition of sexual difference strikes at the heart of class-based heterosexual masculine hegemony, it is also to be expected that where heterosexism is strong, lesbians and gay men will experience most difficulties. Among the chapters here, it is seen that resistance in South African and Australian unions has often been strong, and in Canada and the UK progress on lesbian and gay rights has not been achieved in unions without opposition.

Transformation

Transformation involves a wider range of structural and cultural organisational change such as extensive and innovative diversity structures and a reallocation of union resources, whereby representing the interests of diversity groupings becomes central to campaigning and collective bargaining agendas. Transformative strategies may involve autonomous organising by diverse groups as a source of empowerment and as a site from which to challenge and to bring about change. Strategies of collaboration with existing power holders might also be pursued in search of formulae for transforming union structures and cultures. Or both. Again, such measures are also likely to set up resistance, triggering discriminatory exclusionary and/or demarcatory tactics. Counter-pressure may also involve seeking to work together more widely with forces outside the union(s), and to seek alliances and coalitions.

There is much evidence in the chapters in the book of increasingly assertive and dynamic groups representing women, ethnic and racial groups, lesbian and gay groups, and in a few cases, disabled members organising, and pursuing trans-formative strategies. It is clear that these pioneers have changed union cultures and structures and in some cases have moved into situations with transformative potential. Women and minority groups are on the whole keen to link with union mainstreams, but on their terms, and increasingly they have resisted assimilation. The form and character of these new unionisms is varied, but in all the chapters from the developed world there are accounts of special structures for women and in some cases minority groups, and these are clearly significant as sites of social creativity and social change. There are fewer accounts however of quotas/proportionality for women or minority groups on key committees and bodies in the union hierarchies. While special structures may serve as sites for transforming and empowering their constituents, it is a harder task to reach the core power structures and attempt to change and transform them. Oligarchic tendencies reassert themselves.

In Germany, the opportunities offered by the fluidity following reunification was a boost to women's membership, especially from former east Germany, where strategies for women and diverse groups moved towards more inclusionary – although nevertheless, contested – approaches. These initiatives are mainly in service sector and professional unions, and in some, women have managed to expand their power base, manage their own budgets, and even have a right of veto.

With its wide-ranging, inclusive strategies the Canadian union movement must be a model of transformational change, both within internal union democracies, and in the wider engagement with the state and more broadly across union and social movements. In the USA, workers are generally seeking involvement at work, a less combative trade unionism, and, as in the UK, a form of collective protection that gives them job security and advancement and responds to their emotional as well as their economic needs. The drive is to rethink traditional models, especially among professional workers. For example, the organising model being rolled out in the Anglophone countries is also about equipping activists to take on decentralised bargaining, which offers opportunities for new forms of community-based organising (Mantsios 1998).

Material terms and conditions at work form a crucial test of whether or not new approaches are delivering for women and those from other marginalised groups. If we look at the gender pay gap in the countries represented in this book, reported by the contributors, then the gender union project does not look strong. The smallest gap is 11 per cent, in Sweden, where trade union density remains at around 80 per cent overall and 83 per cent for women. The largest pay gap among the case studies is in Malaysia, where trade union organisation is poor and women are marginalised. Certain conditions are important for improving women's pay. In industrialised economies the corporate state, government equality frameworks, centralised systems for pay determination, social partnership, and high trade union density and collective bargaining, are all institutions which are known to make a difference (Rees 1998; Rubery *et al.* 1999). In the USA for example, where trade union density is around 14 per cent only, union women earn over a third more than non-union women.

Universal measures such as improving low pay generally will always help women and marginalised ethnic groups. In Britain the introduction of a National Minimum Wage in 1999, which impacted mainly on women and ethnic minorities, led to a narrowing of the gender pay gap to 18 per cent. It had stuck at around 20–5 per cent for over twenty years. Across the chapters, however, the authors comment that women and diversity members are not present at bargaining tables. Lack of access to inner circle power positions in unions means that they will rarely be involved in setting bargaining agendas. A creative exception is the participative bargaining agenda setting among Harvard university staff in the USA discussed by Cobble and Bielski.

Gender and diversity projects do fare better however when considering qualitative bargaining outcomes. Canadian unions have negotiated solid gains such as child care benefits for parents, and the right to paid leave following workplace harassment. Most countries represented in the book report wide-ranging policies and in some cases, collective agreements which provide for equality and non-discrimination, the right not to be sexually harassed, and increasingly, commitment to work–life balance policies and practices. Campaigning around violence against women is gathering momentum in several countries, from Canada to the UK, to India. These gains provide the basis on which to build broader-based demands, for example mainstreaming gender into union bargaining across the board. As already mentioned, this is an important strategy among European trade unions. The real challenge however is to move such progressive policies into practice. Too often they remain at that level without the means or the will at workplace level for unions to take on and demand that policy becomes practice.

Coalition

Here the diverse constituencies within unions make links internally, across union movements, as well as alliances with external organisations such as community groups, NGOs, social movements, political groups, campaigns and so on. Strategies of coalition enable the movement beyond the narrow interests of sectoral and sectional organised labour towards a framework of rights (Sen 2001), and is especially important for women and members of racial, ethnic and sexual minorities where such groups are weak. In developing countries, for example, in the informal economy especially, those who attempt to organise may face intimidation, threats and violence and sometimes even murder (Committee for Asian Women 1995; ILO/ICFTU 1999). Also often excluded from trade unionism are agricultural, domestic and migrant workers, especially in Export Processing Zones. Women particularly remain marginalised and highly vulnerable to discrimination and exploitation and thus family poverty is perpetuated (Ledwith and Colgan 2001). The Platform for Action of the Fourth World Conference on Women at Beijing in 1995 was a rallying point for international women's networking. It also called for recognition of collective bargaining as a right and an important mechanism for the promotion of gender equality (ILO/ICFTU 1999).

Coalition strategies are increasingly being led by social movements and diverse groupings, within, across and outside trade unions. Unions are starting to recognise that their unity no longer rests solely on a central class ideology, but on a more pluralist form of alliances and coalition politics. In her discussion of the problems women's diversity poses for the labour movement and for the notion of 'sisterhood', Yuval-Davis (1998) argues that feminist and trade union politics should now incorporate the notion of 'women's positionings' into their agendas by developing 'transversal' coalition politics. Thus women (and men) in different constituencies may be rooted in their own membership and identity, but at the same time be prepared to shift into a position of exchange with those with different memberships and identities. Within unions, this was always to some extent possible for different occupational and sectoral constituencies; what is now required is that this be extended to the self-organised constituencies through new union democratic structures, coalitions and alliances (Colgan 1999a).

In the USA, as Cobble and Michal show, the women's movement and African-Americans have been working across civil rights and labour unions since the 1960s and current organising campaigns in the US seek to build on and extend their coalitions and alliances with community and campaigning groups (Mantsios 1998). For example, in 1997 the USA Pride at Work organisation (PAW) affiliated with the main trade union confederation, the AFL-CIO, following more than twenty years of work by gay and lesbian union members. Hunt makes the point that the

Canadian Labour Congress's success in rolling out lesbian and gay rights was due to 'networks, networks, networks' over nearly thirty years.

Among unions which have become adept at reaching out to use the courts to test for and extend the rights of their diverse membership, are those in Canada, and the UK. In Europe, the European Union's social agenda has become a significant focus of gender mobilising, and has developed a solid body of women's legal rights (Pillinger 2000). Mainstreaming has become a strong organising basis, and increasingly unions are working across countries and through federal union organisations to carry forward work on gender equality to ensure that all aspects of union work and employment include a gender dimension as a matter of course. At the turn of the new century, the paramount concern has been work–life balance, and public sector unions especially have been developing innovative practices in partnership with employers whereby union members themselves are centrally involved in planning, negotiating and organising change. Long-standing forms of collaborative work between unions in developed and developing countries on gender and women's rights are also spreading. Partnerships and twinning arrangements organised around gender issues are growing. Often focusing on education and training these are frequently initiated and resourced wholly or partly by union organisations such as the Public Services International (PSI) which then roll out training and campaigning at local level within the unions and forge alliances with NGOs and political and community groups.

Reaching out further, Briskin is especially keen to see unions build on such developments in order to realise the global potential for international labour and feminist alliances. Here she is very much in accord with women in the developing world. For example, Hensman discusses how Indian women are benefiting from alliances and coalitions with NGOs and Women Working Worldwide, based in the UK and linked with women workers' groups in several Asian and Central American countries. In Malaysia examples include Tenaganita, a multi-ethnic women workers' organisation which has taken up the cause of migrant labour and sex workers. In the absence of teeth with which to implement important international codes of conduct and ILO conventions, these forms of self-help are crucial.

Can we draw conclusions?

So how can we assess the current state of play in projects of gender and diversity trade union democracy? It is clear from the extensive and detailed evidence in the contributions here that in all these countries, to a greater or lesser degree, traditionalism continues to coexist with innovation, and even with transformation. Is the glass we raise to toast union equality endeavours half full, or is it half empty? This is a discussion we often have with trade union equality activists. Are advances being made towards a new trade union democracy? How far does the resistance encountered mean two steps forward and one back?

From the review of gender and diversity trade union democracy projects in the countries in this collection there are some patterns which emerge. In terms of internal union democracy favourable conditions seem to be:

- where traditional blue-collar, male working-class trade union membership has plummeted and trade union futures are seen to be under threat;
- in feminised unions (i.e. those where women are in the majority of membership);
- in public sector unions;
- among white-collar, service sector and increasingly, professional and highly qualified workers – many of whom are women;
- where there is a critical mass of women, led by a vanguard of feminist women and equality activists pursuing strategies of social change and transformation in adversarial industrial relations systems;
- autonomous or self-organisation and separate structures for women;
- in turn, where these have been built on by other diversity groups, based on race, sexuality, age and disability;
- coalitions and alliances within own unions with 'modernisers', the 'left', the 'mainstream'; and
- learning from, and transversal working across civil and human rights and social movements.

These conditions then provide the basis and springboard for external work, especially strategies of social change in terms of collective bargaining outcomes, conferment of legal and social benefits from the state, and wider transnational alliance formation with social movements, international labour organisations, campaign groups and NGOs.

Binary analysis however has also shown that within each of these conditions there are negatives as well as positives, and that as labour movement democracy projects proceed, they also set up resistance. Against the weight of such oligarchic tendencies and hegemonic gender processes, change is slow and much remains to be done. Perhaps the most significant achievement is altogether both broader and more important – the dynamic of creativity that emerges out of oppression and marginalisation.

The history of creativity and innovation arising from challenge to, conflict with and deviance from hegemonic structures, systems and ideologies is long and celebrated. So it is within labour movements. Marginality is not merely a symptom of oppression, it is also a site of critique, creativity and a launching pad for challenge, change and transformation (Ledwith and Manfredi 2000). From the evidence presented in this book, there also seems to be an inverse relationship between the strength of exclusion and that of the response among women's and other equality seeking groups within trade unions. The more adversarial and exclusionary the industrial relations experience, the more innovative and creative the response. These are important strategies to bring to labour movements in crisis.

The decline of traditional, sectional trade unionism, makes it inevitable and necessary that unions adapt to their new environment. There is some debate about whether or not union regeneration is possible at all, but if it is, through what processes and what forms may it subsequently develop? In his optimistic assessment and using a model of mobilisation, collectivism and long waves theory, Kelly claims that the classical labour movement is more likely to be on the threshold of resurgence than in terminal decline (1998: 1). Kelly concentrates on process, whereas other studies are more concerned with form.

A more realistic assessment we would suggest is Hyman's view that: 'Despite familiar stereotypes of trade unions as "overmighty subjects", the reality is that even the most cohesive and strategically sophisticated of workers' collective organisations can only partly offset the structured imbalance of power which confronts them' (1994: 128–9). In discussing the future of (European) trade unionism, he identifies five emerging models: narrow and exclusive representation along the lines of the pre-industrial guilds; providers of services to workers as individuals, company unionism along Japanese lines, social partnership, and populist campaigning akin to the social movement model. Hyman suggests that if trade unions are to reassert their relevance there has to be a radical shift of emphasis, one which embraces the concept of a network of citizenship associations which gives voice to all those faced by insecurity (2001: 176). The evidence from and discussions among the contributors to this book, point to agreement with Hyman that the future of trade unionism rests on its capacity to construct a global project around which can be built alliances to render partially contradictory interests sufficiently convergent (Freyssinget in Hyman 1996: 55). We see the contributions in this book pointing to the social movement model, whereby somehow the traditional tensions between the representation of sectional interests and those of social mobilisation can be balanced. A 'loose-tight' fit. The reconciliation of competing interests is especially important in the global context, and for those weaker groups in the developing world. Whether it is achievable is another question.

Notes

1   For an extended, fictionalised account see Rohini Hensman 1990.
2   There is an historical literature about women's unions in the nineteenth and early twentieth centuries. See Drake 1984; Boston 1987; and Davis 1993 for example.
3   The term 'mainstreaming' usually refers to gender mainstreaming. The European TUC (1999) describes it as, rather than being restricted to adopting a catalogue of measures, it aims to 'infuse a preoccupation with equal opportunities into all trade union decision-making processes, so that the gender question is incorporated wherever decisions are made. In this way it becomes a permanent subject for discussion and negotiation within trade union organisation' – especially in training and in collective bargaining. Teresa Rees (1998: 194) describes it as entailing a paradigm shift in thinking towards the development of policy and practice. It requires being able to see the ways in which current practice is gendered in its construction, despite appearing to be gender-neutral. The essence of mainstreaming is that equal opportunities thinking is integrated into the policy development process from the beginning. It is, she says, a long-term agenda.
4   'Institutional racism' has recently been defined in the UK as the 'collective failure of an organisation to provide an appropriate and professional service to people because of their colour, culture or ethnic origin. It can be seen or detected in processes, attitudes and behaviour which amount to discrimination through unwitting prejudice, ignorance, thoughtlessness, and racist stereotyping which disadvantage minority ethnic people' (Macpherson 1999: 28).

References

Acker, J. (1990) 'Hierarchies, jobs, bodies: a theory of gendered organizations', *Gender and Society* 4, 2, June.

Alvesson, M. and Due Billing, Y. (1997) *Understanding Gender and Organizations*, London: Sage.

Australian Council of Trade Unions (ACTU) (1999) *unions@work: The Challenge for Unions in Creating a Just and Fair Society*, Melbourne: ACTU.

Boston, S. (1987) *Women Workers and Trade Unions*, London: Lawrence and Wishart.

Briskin, L. (1993) 'Union women and separate organizing', in Briskin, L. and McDermott, P. (eds) *Women Challenging Unions: Feminism, Democracy and Militancy*, Toronto: University of Toronto Press.

—— (1999) 'Autonomy, diversity and integration: Union women's separate organizing in North America and Western Europe in the context of restructuring and globalization', *Women's Studies International Forum*, 22, 4: 543–54.

Briskin, L. and McDermott, P. (eds) *Women Challenging Unions: Feminism, Democracy and Militancy*, Toronto: University of Toronto Press.

Campbell, J. and Oliver, M. (1996) *Disability Politics*, London: Routledge.

Cobble, D. (ed.) (1993) *Women and Unions: Forging a Partnership*, Ithaca, NY: ILR Press.

Cockburn, C. (1989) 'Equal opportunities: the short and long agenda', *Industrial Relations Journal* 20, 4, Autumn: 213–25.

Cockburn, C. (1991) *In The Way of Women: Men's Resistance to Sex Equality in Organizations*, London: Macmillan.

Colgan, F. (1999a) 'Moving forward in UNISON: lesbian and gay self organisation in action', in Hunt, G. (ed.) *Laboring for Rights: Unions and Sexual Diversity Across Nations*, Philadelphia: Temple University Press.

—— (1999b) 'Recognising the lesbian and gay constituency in UK trade unions: moving forward in UNISON?', *Industrial Relations Journal* 30, 5: 444–63.

Colgan, F. and Ledwith, S. (1996) 'Women as organisational change agents', in Ledwith, S. and Colgan, F. (eds) *Women in Organisations: Challenging Gender Politics*, Basingstoke: Macmillan.

—— (2000) 'Diversity, identities and strategies of women trade union activists', *Gender, Work and Organization* 7, 4: 242–57.

—— (2002) 'Gender and diversity: reshaping union democracy', *Employee Relations*, 24: 2.

Colling, T. and Dickens, L. (2001) 'Gender equality and the trade unions: a new basis for mobilisation', in Noon, M. and Ogbonna, E. (eds) *Equality, Diversity and Disadvantage in Employment*, Basingstoke: Palgrave.

Committee for Asian Women (1995) *Silk and Steel: Asian Women Workers Confront Challenges of Industrial Restructuring*, Hong Kong: Committee for Asian Women.

Connell, R.W. (1995) *Masculinities*, Cambridge: Polity Press.

Cornell, S. and Hartmann, D. (1998) *Ethnicity and Race: Making Identities in a Changing World*, Thousand Oaks, London, New Delhi: Pine Forge Press.

Davis, M. (1993) *Comrade or Brother?: The History of the British Labour Movement (1789–1951)*, London: Pluto Press.

Drake, B. (1984) *Women in Trade Unions*, Virago reprint of 1920 first edition, London: Labour Research Department.

European Trade Union Confederation (1999) *The "Second Sex" of European Trade Unionism*, Brussels: ETUC.

Evans, M. (1997) 'Negotiating the Frontier: women and resistance in the contemporary academy', in Stanley, L. (ed.) *Knowing Feminisms*, London: Sage.

Fairbrother, P. (1984) *All Those in Favour: The Politics of Union Democracy*, London: Pluto Press.

Forrest, A. (1993) 'A view from outside the whale: the treatment of women and unions in industrial relations,' in Briskin, L. and McDermott, P. (eds) *Women Challenging Unions: Feminism, Democracy and Militancy*, Toronto: University of Toronto Press.

Fosh, P. and Heery, E. (eds) (1990) *Trade Unions and Their Members: Studies in Union Democracy and Organization*, Basingstoke: Macmillan.

Hales, G. (1996) *Beyond Disability: Towards an Enabling Society*, London: Sage.

Hall, S. and duGay, P. (1996) *Questions of Cultural Identity*, Thousand Oaks, London, New Delhi: Sage.

Healy, G. and Kirton, G. (2000) 'Women, Power and Trade Union Government in the UK', *British Journal of Industrial Relations* 38, 3, September: 343–60.

Hearn, J., Sheppard, D.L., Tancred-Sheriff, P. and Burrell, G. (1989) *The Sexuality of Organization*, London: Sage.

Hemingway, J. (1979) *Conflict and Democracy: Studies in Trade Union Government*, Oxford: Clarendon Press.

Hensman, Rohini (1990) *To Do Something Beautiful*, London: Sheba Feminist Publishers.

Herman, D. (1994) *Rights of Passage: Struggles for Lesbian and Gay Equality*, Toronto: University of Toronto Press.

Humphrey, J. (1998) 'Self organise and survive: disabled people in the British trade union movement', *Disability and Society* 13, 4: 587–602.

—— (1999) 'Organizing sexualities, organized inequalities: lesbians and gay men in public service occupations', *Gender, Work and Organization* 6, 3: 134–51.

—— (2000) 'Self organisation and trade union democracy', *Sociological Review* 48, 2: 262–84.

Hunt, G. (1999) *Laboring for Rights: Unions and Sexual Diversity Across Nations*, Philadelphia: Temple University Press.

Hyman, R. (1975) *Industrial Relations: A Marxist Introduction*, London: Macmillan.

—— (1994) 'Changing trade union identities and strategies', in Hyman, R. and Ferner, A. (eds) *New Frontiers in European Industrial Relations*, Oxford: Blackwell.

—— (1996) 'Changing union identities in Europe', in Leisink, P., Van Leemput, J. and Vilrokx, J. (eds) *The Challenges to Trade Unions in Europe: Innovation or Adaption*, Cheltenham: Edward Elgar.

—— (2001) *Understanding European Trade Unionism: Between Market, Class and Society*, London: Sage.

ILO/ICFTU (1999) 'The role of trade unions in promoting gender equality and protecting vulnerable women workers', First report of the ILO-ICFTU Survey.

Kelly, J. (1998) *Rethinking Industrial Relations: Moblization, Collectivism and Long Waves*, London and New York: Routledge, LSE.

Labour Research Department (LRD) (2001) 'Union density steady again', *Labour Research* 90, 8: 7.

Ledwith, S. and Colgan, F. (1996) *Women in Organisations: Challenging Gender Politics*, Basingstoke: Macmillan.

Ledwith, S. and Manfredi, S. (2000) 'Balancing gender in higher education: a study of the experience of senior women in a "new" UK university', *The European Journal of Women's Studies* 7: 7–33.

Ledwith, S. and Colgan, F. (2001) 'Unions need women: women need unions', *International Union Rights: Working for Equality* 8, 1, March.

Lipset, S.M., Trow, M.A. and Coleman, J.S. (1956) *Union Democracy*, Glencoe: Free Press.

Macpherson, Sir W. (1999) *The Stephen Lawrence Inquiry: Report of an Inquiry Into the Matters Arising from the Death of Stephen Lawrence*, London: HMSO.

McBride, A. (2001) *Gender Democracy in Trade Unions*, Aldershot, Brookfield USA, Singapore, Sydney: Ashgate.

Mantsios, G. (1998) *A New Labor Movement for the New Century*, New York: Monthly Review Press.

Mills, A.J. and Tancred, P. (eds) (1992) *Gendering Organizational Analysis*, London: Sage.

Muir, K. and Franzway, S. (2000) 'Editorial – Sexual politics and trade unions', *Hecate* 26, 2: 4–8.

Noon, M. and Ogbonna, E. (2001) 'Introduction: The key analytical themes', in Noon, M. and Ogbonna, E., *Equality, Diversity and Disadvantage in Employment*, Basingstoke: Palgrave.

Oerton, S. (1996) 'Sexualizing the organization, lesbianizing the women: gender, sexuality and 'flat' organizations', *Gender, Work and Organization* 3, 1: 25–37.

Pillinger, J. (2000) 'A-typical workers and trade union membership and activism: the experience of the public service unions across Europe', paper for *Women, Diversity and Democracy in Trade Unions*, Oxford Women's Studies Network/ESRC Seminar, Oxford.

Pocock, B. (ed.) (1997) *Strife: Sex and Politics in Labour Unions*, St Leonards NSW, Australia: Allen & Unwin.

—— (2000) 'Analysing work: arguments for closer links between the study of labour relations and gender', *Journal of Interdisciplinary Gender Studies* 5, 2: 10–26.

Pringle, R.(1989) *Secretaries Talk*, London: Verso.

Rahman, M. (2000) *Sexuality and Democracy: Identities and Strategies in Lesbian and Gay Politics*, Edinburgh: Edinburgh University Press.

Rayside, D. (1998) *On the Fringe: Gays and Lesbians in Politics*, Ithaca, NY: Cornell University Press.

Rees, T. (1998) *Mainstreaming Equality in the European Union*, London: Routledge.

Roosblad, J. (2000) 'Trade union policies regarding immigration and immigrant workers in the Netherlands (1960–95), in Wets, J. (ed.) *Cultural Diversity in Trade Unions: A challenge to class identity?*, Aldershot: Ashgate.

Rubery, J., Smith, M. and Fagan, C. (1999) *Women's Employment in Europe: Trends and Prospects*, London: Routledge.

Sen, A. (2001) 'Work and rights', in Fetherlolf Loutfi, M. (ed.) *Women, Gender and Work*, Geneva: International Labour Office.

Street, M. (2001) Survival of the Fittest: Women and Trade Unions in New Zealand, unpublished paper.

Thomas, H. (ed.) (1995) *Globalization and Third World Trade Unions: The Challenge of Rapid Economic Change*, London: Zed Books.

TUC (1997) *Partners for Progress: Next Steps for the New Unionism*, London: Trades Union Congress.

Virdee, S. (2000) 'Organised labour and the Black worker in England: A critical analysis of postwar trends', in Wets, J. (ed.) *Cultural Diversity in Trade Unions: A Challenge to Class Identity?* Aldershot: Ashgate, ch. 9.

Wajcman, J. (2000) 'Feminism facing industrial relations', *British Journal of Industrial Relations* 38, 2: 183–201.

Walby, S. (1990) *Theorising Patriarchy*, Oxford: Blackwell.

—— (1997) *Gender Transformations*, London: Routledge.

Wets, J. (ed.) (2000) *Cultural Diversity in Trade Unions: A Challenge to Class Identity?*, Aldershot: Ashgate.

Witz, A. (1992) *Professions and Patriarchy*, London: Routledge.

Wrench, J. and Virdee, S. (1996) 'Race, poor work and trade unions', in Ackers, P., Smith, C. and Smith, P. *The New Workplace and Trade Unionism: Critical Perspectives on Work and Organization*, London: Routledge.

Yuval-Davis, N. (1998) 'Beyond differences: women, empowerment and coalition', in Charles, N. and Hintjens, H. *Gender, Ethnicity and Political Ideologies*, London: Routledge.

2 The equity project in Canadian unions

Confronting the challenge of restructuring and globalisation

Linda Briskin

Restructuring and regional integration raise new challenges for equity practices in Canadian unions, and for mobilisation strategies both inside unions and in the workplace. This chapter opens with a brief profile of union density and sectoral unionisation patterns, outlines new forms of competition, and highlights the importance of unions integrating equity into their responses to restructuring and globalisation.

The second section of the chapter argues that, in the current context, the risk that equity concerns will be marginalised has increased dramatically. It revisits the key strategies used by Canadian women unionists – representation, redefining union issues and expanding the collective bargaining agenda, separate organising and constituency building, and establishing alliances and coalitions across unions, with social movements and across borders. It assesses their relevance to building resistance to globalisation and restructuring.[1]

Unions, competition and equity

> We will take the message to Ottawa that we want jobs, not unemployment and attacks on the unemployed; that we want fair trade, not free trade/NAFTA [North American Free Trade Agreement]; that we want good public services, not attacks on public sector workers; that we want child care, not child poverty; that we want equity and equality, not discrimination and inequality; that we want a social and economic agenda based on fairness, not an agenda dedicated to multinational corporations at the expense of the rest.
>
> (Bob White, then president of the Canadian Labour Congress (CLC) in his letter calling for a major demonstration, 12 March 1993)

Despite the politics of the Canadian Labour Congress (CLC), the major umbrella organisation of Canadian unions,[2] and despite the adoption of equity policies and practices in many unions, women and other marginalised workers continue to be disproportionately disadvantaged by processes of restructuring and globalisation. For example, in her analysis of the Office and Technical Employees' Union

(OCTEU Local 378) at British Columbia Hydro from 1944 until 1993, Creese (1995: 146) found that, even though the union 'had an active Women's Committee throughout the 1980s, achieved gender parity on the union's Executive Board, and elected its first (feminist) woman president in 1984 . . . women still fared worse than men in the process of corporate restructuring'. Creese's research underscores the central dilemmas facing Canadian unions.

Privatisation, deregulation, increasingly hostile neo-liberal states, 'global' employers, wage competition across national boundaries and increasing corporate rule are challenging the very foundations of unions. The 'labour accord' based on good faith bargaining, systems of job control by unions, legal compliance on the part of business, and the 'neutral' role of the state are all disintegrating (Adams 1989; Panitch and Swartz 1988) forcing the Canadian union movement to reconceptualise its politics, strategies and allies. At the same time, the declining commitment of both provincial and federal governments to workplace employment equity, to the funding of advocacy groups, and to the needs of what are now dismissively labelled 'special interest groups' are heightening the politics of radical individualism and repositioning unions as a key vehicle of resistance.

In the current context, unions need to organise the unorganised to maintain union density. They also need to develop innovative organising strategies to address the changing labour market. Work reorganisation, especially homework and casualisation, poses a great challenge; for example, between 1975 and 1993 the number of part-time jobs jumped 120 per cent (CLC 1997a: 21). See Tables 2.1 and 2.2.

The decline in unionisation rate for men can be traced to the shift of employment from the heavily unionised male-dominated goods-producing industries to the less-unionised service industries (Mainville and Olineck 1999). Not surprisingly, these shifts have led to a changing balance of union membership in the public and private sector. In fact, public employees constitute 42 per cent of total union membership although they only account for 18 per cent of the paid workforce (Akyeampong 1997). Gender is also significant: the majority of unionised men are in the private sector and the majority of unionised women in the public sector (CLC 1997a: 9). See Table 2.3.

Table 2.1 Women's workforce participation, Canada 1999/2000

Labour force category	*Percentage*
Labour force who are women	45.9
Private sector labour force who are women	42.9
Public sector labour force who are women	58.8
Part time labour force who are women	69.7
Full time labour force who are women	40.5

Sources: Statistics Canada 1999 and 2000.
Notes
The term 'labour force' includes those seeking work. Canadian data uses the term 'workforce' for those employed.

Table 2.2 Trade union density in Canada

	Women %	Men %
Public sector	71.9	68.6
Private sector	12.8	22.5
	1966 %	*2000 %*
Total percentage men	38.4	31.1
Total percentage women	15.9	29.6
Total	30.8	30.4

Sources: Akyeampong, 1997, 1998 and 2000; CLC, 1997.

Table 2.3 Union membership, by sex and sector

	Women %	Men %
Public sector	64.3	24
Private sector	35.7	76
	1967 %	*1997 %*
Total percentage women	20	80
Total percentage men	45	55

Sources: As for Table 2.2.

Unions must also organise the 'organised' to deepen commitment to unions. At the same time, unions increasingly face the task of representing the interests of diverse constituencies of workers based on race, ethnicity, gender, age, sexuality, ability and First Nations status whose claims to citisenship inside unions have been consolidating, and who are rapidly becoming a larger proportion of the unionised workforce.[3] In fact, 86 per cent of the growth of union membership since 1972 was among women (Jackson and Schellenberg 1998: 21). Visible minority and aboriginal workers and those with disabilities currently make up a total of 14 per cent of unionised workforce (CLC 1997a: 50–1). It was estimated that by the year 2000, 85 per cent of the new workforce entrants would be women, visible minorities, people with disabilities and aboriginal people (Yalnizyan 1998: 28). See also Tables 2.3 and 2.4. Organising the multiple constituencies of unionised and un-unionised workers, many of whom have traditionally been marginalised, will undoubtedly be central to the long term survival of the Canadian labour movement.

Competition is also increasing among workers: inside workplaces, between the unionised and un-unionised, and from workers moving from the manufacturing to the service sector, and across national boundaries. Such competition is at the heart of restructuring and globalisation and it, too, is a gendered and racialised phenomenon. For example, given the decline in employment in the primary and manufacturing sectors which have traditionally been dominated by male workers,

Table 2.4 Women's membership in the ten largest Canadian unions, 2000

Union	Total	Women	Percentage women
Canadian Union of Public Employees (CUPE)	485,000	291,000	60
Canadian Auto Workers (CAW)	220,000	49,600	22.5
Food and Commercial Workers (UFCW)	210,390	102,040	48.5
United Steelworkers of America (USWA)	190,000	28,500	15
Public Service Alliance (PSAC)	146,560	80,610	55
Communication, Energy and Paper Workers (CEP)	144,320	26,150	18
International Brotherhood of Teamsters (IBT)	100,170	17,170	17
Fédération des affaires sociales (FAS)	96,970	72,730	75
Service Employees International Union (SEIU)	90,000	72,000	80
Fédération des syndicats de l'enseignement (CEQ)	80,920	55,660	68.7

Source: Survey done in collaboration with Canadian labour organizations by Workplace Information Directorate, Human Resources Development Canada, May 2000. Unpublished data.

the focus has shifted from women seeking 'male' jobs to men competing for women's jobs (see, for example, Fox and Sugiman 1999).

Unions need to strategically reposition equity from the margin to the centre, and reinvent solidarity to address its complexity in a global context. In fact, the ideology of 'taking labour out of competition' has always provided the economic foundation of the union movement (Parker and Gruelle 1999: 71). However, the notion of a generic worker with a homogeneous and self-evident set of interests has, more often than not, informed the commitment of union solidarity, now contested not only by women's organising inside and outside the unions, but also by the corporate agenda itself. Abstractly calling for solidarity or seeking a common denominator like class will not suffice to address the realities of diversity and the new competitive forces. Nor will it strengthen the union movement. Solidarity now must mean 'unity in diversity', that is, addressing discriminatory practices inside unions and workplaces based not only on gender but also on race, ethnicity, citizenship, ability, age and sexuality.

This argument is particularly significant for Canada where the importance of diversity cannot be over-estimated: racial and ethnic diversity, regional diversity, language diversity, all of which are framed within the context of debates about Quebec as a distinct society and about the right of First Nations peoples to self-government. In fact, in legal and policy contexts, 'equity' has a difference-sensitive meaning (from the important 1984 Abella Commission on *Equality in Employment*). It is used to acknowledge that sometimes equality means ignoring differences and treating women and men the same, and sometimes equality means recognising differences and treating women and men differently. Equity then refers to what is fair under the circumstances (also called substantive equality). This understanding of equity informs the following discussion.

This chapter, then, rejects the 'narrative of eviction' in 'mainstream accounts of the global economy . . . [which] proceed as if these dynamics are inevitably gender-neutral' (Sassen 1998: 82). Rather, it seeks a narrative of inclusion not only for self-evident social justice reasons but also because, in contrast to the claims for neutrality, race, gender, age and citizenship are deeply inscribed in the corporate politics of competition. Now more than ever, unions need to link the struggles around diversity and equity inside unions and in workplaces to the realities of restructuring and globalisation. At both a strategic and analytic level, equity and restructuring cannot be separated (Briskin 1994). The Canadian Auto Workers takes up this perspective directly:

> With this increasing gap between rich and poor, between Northern countries and those in the South, there is a parallel growing polarization based on class, race, gender, sexual orientation and ability. . . . Our challenge is . . . to ensure that the corporate agenda of polarization and division does not permeate our union. To do this we need to actively struggle against the scapegoating of any disadvantaged groups by continuing to advance our human rights and women's programs.
>
> (CAW 1999: 92–3)

Strategies for ensuring equity inside unions

Restructuring and new forms of competition provide the frame within which to explore the equity practices of Canadian unions. Undoubtedly, the negotiation of diversity inside unions is a task made more salient and more difficult by the deepening exploitation of racial and gender differences by corporate capital, and the increasing silence of the state on equity issues. In the current context, then, the danger that the concerns of women and other equity-seeking groups inside unions will be marginalised has increased dramatically. In response, union equity strategies must proactively challenge the neo-liberal invocation of patriarchal and individual-istic values for workplaces and households, and build solidarities across diversities, with the un-unionised, and across national boundaries.

Union women have taken significant initiatives around representation, redefining union issues, expanding the collective bargaining agenda, separate organising and constituency building, and developing alliances and coalitions across unions and with social movements. As a result, unions have changed the way they do their work, and moved towards greater inclusivity and more democratic practices (Briskin 1998). This section outlines some successes and examines the relevance of these strategies to maintaining and extending equity for all marginalised groups in the current context.

Representation

In order to broaden representation and inclusion at all levels of union leadership and work, unions must examine the culture of privileges, perks, hierarchies and euro-centricity which mirror aspects of corporate structures and have no place in organizations fighting for equality.

(CLC 1997b: 12)

Concerns about representation have been a major focus in Canadian unions. Many unions and federations now have affirmative action policies that designate or add seats on leadership bodies for women in an attempt to address their under-representation in top elected positions. This process began in 1983 when the Ontario Federation of Labour (OFL) broke new ground by amending its constitution to create five affirmative action positions on its executive board. Undoubtedly, these strategies have increased women's participation in top leadership. In fact, White (1993: 105) reports that 'Of the ninety-five executive seats held by women in these organizations, fully thirty-nine of them (41 per cent) are affirmative action positions. Without them, the representation of women on these labour central executives would fall from 28 to 18 percent'.

The focus on top leadership may make invisible local and informal leadership by women, thereby exacerbating women's low status in unions, and reproducing traditional patterns of organisation and male domination (Briskin 1999a). However, the increase in leadership representation by women and minorities does help to ensure that unions take account of their concerns. In fact, Penni Richmond from the CLC Women's and Human Rights Department reports that the presence of 'outsiders' on the CLC Executive has 'changed the issues raised, changed who gets to hear what we talk about, and changed rank and file perception of who has power; in fact, it has put the discussion of power itself on the agenda' (Telephone Interview, 12 Oct 1994).

The increased awareness of representational issues has had effects in other areas: employment equity for union staff; affirmative action seats on union Executive Boards for visible minorities, and gays and lesbians; and equity representation in education courses. For example, the CLC constitution was amended in 1992 to include two seats for Visible Minorities on the CLC Executive Council, and in 1994 a Visible Minority Vice President. At the OFL Convention in 1997, a position on the Federation executive for an out lesbian or gay trade union vice-president was adopted – a Canadian first. Members of equity-seeking groups are pushing unions to be proactive in ensuring their visible representation at all levels.

Redefining union issues / expanding the agenda of collective bargaining

Over the last two decades, Canadian women unionists have successfully pressured unions to take up issues of childcare, reproductive rights, sexual harassment and violence against women, pay equity, and employment equity among others. Around each of these issues, union hierarchies questioned the legitimacy of unions addressing such issues. With each victory, the boundaries of what constitutes a legitimate union issue have shifted, the understanding of what is seen to be relevant to the workplace has altered, and the support for social unionism has increased.

A dramatic case in point is the increasing union involvement, with active support from top leadership, in the broad issues around violence against women. These campaigns go well beyond a focus on employer harassment or even co-worker harassment, and many have successfully integrated issues around racial harassment and violence. For example, the material for the campaign against domestic violence by the United Steelworkers of America (USWA) says: 'Our society, based on unequal wealth, status, opportunity and power is a breeding ground for abusive behaviour. Because of their lack of economic and political power, women are especially vulnerable to acts of violence. Doubly disadvantaged women – women with disabilities, lesbians, Aboriginal and visible minority women are doubly vulnerable to acts of violence' (quoted in Fonow 1998: 118).

These shifts in the understanding of what constitutes a union issue, have had impacts not only on union policy but also on the collective bargaining agenda. Half of workers covered by major collective agreements now have the protection of a formal sexual harassment clause (up from 20 per cent in 1985); 60.5 per cent of major collective agreements contain a non-discrimination clause; 27.6 per cent have pay equity (equal pay for work of equal value) clauses (up from 5.4 per cent in 1985), and 11.8 per cent have affirmative action clauses (up from 5.9 per cent) (Jackson and Schellenberg 1998: 18).

The Canadian Auto Workers (CAW), a key private sector union, has also negotiated some pioneering language.[4] Recently, they bargained a child care benefit which offers parents a subsidy for each child registered in licensed, *non-profit* childcare up to a maximum of $2000 a year (Nash 1999). In some workplaces, CAW locals now have women's advocates in the workplace trained to deal with women's concerns around violence, harassment or any other form of discrimination; and anti-discrimination and human rights training for membership, union leadership and front line management personnel. They have also developed language for and won protection against discipline procedures for women who lose time at work as a result of an abusive family situation (Nash 1998). In another example, the Canadian Union of Public Employees (CUPE) (Local 1), the largest public sector union in Canada, negotiated the right to leave work with full pay if members are harassed, thus expanding the notion of occupational hazard, and health and safety (Ross 1999).

Despite such gains, women's issues are susceptible to marginalisation. For example, Creese (1995: 163) reports that, in Office and Technical Employees' Union (OCTEU Local 378) at British Columbia Hydro, 'for the most part women's issues continue to be seen as secondary, as issues affecting half of the membership, while traditional issues are presumed to affect all members in the same way. As currently defined, special women's issues are bound to be sidelined during economic restructuring and concession bargaining'.

In order to protect against the potential peripheralisation associated with 'women's issues' and to resist the pressures to strategise about economic restructuring through a gender-neutral lens, it is critical to *gender* union issues. Gendering issues means a move from an identification of a women's platform of concerns to a recognition of the gender implications in all issues (sometimes called 'gender mainstreaming'). This has started to occur in discussions on restructuring, seniority, health and safety, and telework. Second, issues need to be scrutinised for their impact on diverse groups of women. For example, discussions of family benefits increasingly reject traditional definitions of 'family' that exclude gay and lesbian couples. Such scrutiny highlights diversity and provides the ground for bridge-building among diverse groups of women unionists, and for alliances with marginalised male workers.

Separate organising and constituency building

For almost three decades in Canada, union women's committees, and educational programmes and conferences organised by and for women, have played a key role in politicising women and producing them as a vocal constituency. Women have organised in response to male domination, patriarchal cultures, and hierarchical organisational practices in unions that have indisputably marginalised women and their concerns (Briskin and Yanz 1983; Briskin and McDermott 1993). Evidence suggests a growing acceptance and legitimation of separate and self-organising, at least in the public discourse of unions, and increasing formalisation of structures to facilitate it. Just a sampling: the constitution of the Canadian Auto Workers (CAW), a union with 20 per cent female membership, mandates women's committees and human rights committees at all levels of the union, has offered annual national women's conferences until 1999 when it shifted to regional women's conferences to reach out to more women members. The three Maritime Federations of Labour (Nova Scotia, New Brunswick and Prince Edward Island) organised a women's conference with the Theme 'Rise Up! Act Up!' in April 2000.

Women's separate organising has also provided an important precedent. Increasingly women and men of colour, lesbians and gay men, and native peoples are organising separately inside the union movement, often through Human Rights and Rainbow Committees, Aboriginal Circles and Pink Triangle Committees. For example, CUPE established a Rainbow Committee in 1988 to address issues affecting racial minorities and Aboriginal peoples, and in 1991 a Pink Triangle Committee which works towards eliminating homophobia and heterosexism and promoting the human rights of lesbian, gay and bisexual members (CUPE 1997).

Separate organising has also modelled alternative union practices. Traditionally, separate organising among women has been overly associated with the 'separate from whom' (men) rather than with the equally important 'separate from what' (bureaucratic and hierarchical organisational practices). However, since men's power, privilege and leadership combine with traditional organisational forms to exclude and disadvantage women, the practice of women's separate organising has challenged both. Women's committees have utilised more inclusive, flexible and responsive structures, and developed vocal constituencies which have challenged leaderships to be accountable, and unions to be more democratic and participatory (Briskin 1990, 1993).

The CLC National Anti-Racism Taskforce which was established in response to years of organising by anti-racist activists also used democratic and inclusive organising practices through regional consultations across the country involving both union and non-union members (CLC 1998: 9). The Taskforce was 'conceived of as one very important piece in the process of building grassroots activism so that real change can happen' (CLC 1997b: 1). In fact, the discourse of alternative forms of organising is gradually being integrated into the labour movement. For example, 'We must respect the existing models of self-organising by equality seeking groups and adopt new models for radical community activism and networking which would build on existing labour organising models' (CLC 1999b).

Undoubtedly, separate organising has increased women's commitment to unions. Now, continued and expanded constituency organising of women and other marginalised workers, *especially at the local level*, may offer a vehicle for politicising workers about the links among the work process, restructuring and competitiveness, and for bridging what might be a growing gap between the national and local politics of the Canadian labour movement.

In this regard, Waddington (1999: 3) highlights the importance of 'union articulation', that is, the relation among different levels of union organisation, and between workplace and union. A recent Canadian study on unions and restructuring (Pupo *et al.* 1998: 4) identifies a gap between 'an increasing commitment, albeit sometimes merely rhetorical, to social movement unionism and social democratic politics at the top . . . and a resurgence of what appears to be a micro corporatist variety of business unionism at the bottom'. What the authors call 'neo-feudalism' emerging in response to workplace reorganisation encourages 'local leaders and members [to] strategically align themselves with their managements as their first line of defense within a precarious work arrangement' (p. 49).

Ross (1999: 8) explores the problem of articulation in CUPE, a union with strong traditions of local autonomy. She recognises that local autonomy has made it difficult to implement equity policies developed at the provincial and national level. Given the trend identified by Pupo *et al.* (1998), these problems may well increase without proactive intervention.

At the same time, equity seeking groups are expecting more from unions on the shop floor. The Human Rights Director of the OFL speaks bluntly to this dilemma:

> The problem has shifted from the top to the bottom. How are these policies going to be implemented down on the shop floor? Local leadership are resisting it. Yet people of colour on the shop floor, perhaps even more than before, are expecting change.
>
> (Quoted in CLC 1997a: 102)

Experience in Canada has demonstrated that unions can help to reconcile the competing interests of diverse groups of workers and build a stronger union movement by taking account of difference (often expressed organisationally through separate organising) rather than abstractly calling for solidarity. The 1994 CLC Policy Statement, 'Confronting the Mean Society', speaks directly to this point:

> Equality seeking groups have strengthened our movement, bringing new ideas and perspectives into the practice of unionism. The diversity that is now present

in our unions has not divided the labour movement: on the contrary, it has energised us and brought many more committed people into our activist cadre.

(CLC 1994a: np.)

Positioning separate organising

Those committed to women's empowerment in the unions raise strategic questions about whether separate organising leads to ghettoisation or marginalisation of women's concerns. There are two key issues: how to position women's separate organising or any social justice organising within the institutional map of the union; and what kind of working structures most effectively bring equity-seeking groups together.

The success of any separate organising initiative, especially in the face of potential marginalisation, depends upon maintaining a strategic balance between autonomy from the structures and practices of the labour movement, and integration (or mainstreaming) into those structures (Briskin 1993). Autonomy measures support fundamental revisioning of union practices. They prevent political marginalisation and the dissipation of the radical claims for inclusivity and democratisation often embedded in such initiatives. They offer a vehicle for women (and other equity-seeking groups) to assert their rights (to full time work at a living wage, to social welfare measures, health care, to protection against violence) in opposition to the trajectories of current economic and political policies. They also provide the context for building alliances between equity-seeking groups and progressive social movements.

Integration into union structures prevents organisational marginalisation, and creates the conditions for both resource allocation, and gendering union policy and strategy. Integration measures, which ensure that women are strategically placed in union structures, will help deter the unions from accommodating the conservative values which coexist with and support restructuring. Integration strategies help ensure that equity consciousness is widespread and that the responsibility for equity is borne by the entire union. This has been a central feature of the anti-racist work in Canadian unions. For example, the aim of the CLC National Anti-Racism Task Force was 'to integrate anti-racism work at all levels of the labour movement ranging from research and organizing to changing internal union structures and process to encourage the active involvement and leadership of Aboriginal people and people of colour' (CLC 1998: 9).

The evidence of the last 20 years suggests that separate organising is a critical vehicle to agitate for union transformation, to ensure voice for the disadvantaged and to resist the marginalisation of equity issues, and simultaneously to organise constituencies of workers both to challenge and defend unions. In the current context, separate organising may offer a critical space in which to politicise rank and file membership about work reorganisation. For such organising to be successful, however, both autonomy and integration measures are necessary (Briskin 1999c).

Separate organising and diversity

The CLC clearly understands that sexism, racism, ableism, and heterosexism share common roots. We acknowledge that we can change attitudes and behaviour if we stand united; we know we will fail if we allow ourselves to be divided. We believe that we can be unified without uniformity and that we can celebrate our diversity without divisiveness. We will strive to achieve a truly inclusive union movement that is representative of all its members (CLC 1994b).

In Canada, the recognition of difference – not only based on gender but increasingly on race, sexuality, ability, region, language, and the acknowledgement of relative privilege have been gradually integrated into union discourse. In fact, in the last decade, there has been a remarkable development of union policy on racism, homophobia, sexism and newly on ableism. Despite the fact that such policies are not necessarily fully operationalised in the daily life of unions, without a doubt the passing of each policy has involved widespread education and mobilisation. They certainly provide a window into the politics of the Canadian labour movement.

The CLC Anti-Racism Task Force is described as 'historic' – the first time that the labour movement has been involved in documenting the experiences of Aboriginal Peoples and People of Colour. The Framework for Action in their report focused on 'Racism and Unions' with recommendations about internal structural change, internal union democracy, education, research, communications strategy and organising. It also developed a set of recommendations about 'Racism in our Communities' focusing on employment, immigration, education, housing, political process, legal system, media and environmental racism and health, and inter-national issues.

The following anti-racism initiatives by its member unions are reported: active standing committees; resolutions and policy statements at conventions; awareness material and courses; constitutional clauses prohibiting discrimination; workplace anti-racism education programme delivered to mixed groups of employers and managers by union trained workers; contract compliance programmes requiring organisations doing business of $20,000 or more to adopt a specific anti-racism and anti-discrimination policy; employment equity plans; staff members with specific anti-racism responsibility; and building alliances with Aboriginal People and People of Colour communities, among others (1997b: 16). Following the Taskforce, the 1999 CLC Constitutional Convention adopted a Statement on Fighting Racism:

> The future of workers of colour, Aboriginal workers and the labour movement are linked because as a working class movement we can not separate the exploitation of working people from the exploitation of women, Aboriginal Peoples and People of Colour. . . . We must work with Aboriginal Peoples and People of Colour in the fight to address the disproportionate impact of government fiscal and economic policies on their communities. . . . We must assume a commitment to fight all forms of multiple oppression faced by workers of colour or Aboriginal workers who are women, gay, lesbian, young persons or persons with disabilities. . . . A commitment to fighting racism and upholding

human rights should be integrated into every oath of office taken by elected union officers.

(CLC 1999b)

There has also been an upsurge in organising among gay and lesbian union activists, increasingly supported by the union movement. In May 1994 delegates at the CLC convention overwhelmingly endorsed a major policy paper on sexual orientation. Since that time, the CLC organised the 1997 Solidarity and Pride Conference which attracted over 350 activists and was the first pride conference world-wide to be officially sponsored by a trade union movement (Genge 1998). In 1998 it sponsored 'A Solidarity and Pride Conference' in cooperation with the Alberta, Saskatchewan and Manitoba Federations of Labour. In 1999 the OFL sponsored the 'Labour Behind the Rainbow' conference, and the CLC is currently preparing a position paper on transgendered and transsexual workers. Individual unions are also taking initiatives. For example, the CAW (1999: 97) has negotiated same sex benefits, adopted the 'Working with Pride' policy statement, and used their national union voice to demand that both provincial and federal governments amend all necessary legislation to provide protection from discrimination on the basis of sexual orientation. They have future plans to expand sexual orientation caucuses, incorporate workshops on sexuality issues in their human rights and women's conferences and make their family programme fully accessible to same sex partners.

On the issues of disability, the labour movement has mostly focused on the legal responsibilities of unions, like the duty to accommodate. Penni Richmond of the CLC notes that 'the activism part has hardly been developed' (quoted in Garcia-Orgales 2000: 22). The CLC offered its first course on disability awareness in 2000.

Despite these advances, in the current conjuncture of sharp attacks on unions and working people and an intensified need to build coalitions, a significant concern is whether separate organising produces strategic fragmentation among various equity-seeking constituencies, and increases the possibility that the legitimately diverse agendas of various groups will be played off against one another.

Paradoxically, past experience in Canada suggests that union women's separate organising has often been instrumental in raising issues of other marginalised groups. Women's committees and conferences have offered a venue where race and racism, and sexuality and homophobia were first addressed, and continue to be raised. White's study of Canadian unions concludes: 'Issues of race or disability or gay/lesbianism were often first raised within women's committees or women's conferences, because these forums were more accepting of the problems and more prepared to deal with them' (1993: 232). Hunt (1997: 806) confirms this point in his overview of Canadian union initiatives around sexuality. In his three detailed case studies, he found that gay and lesbian activists 'found their strongest allies within women's committees'. Yet such support was not offered without struggle. Ann Newman of the Ontario chapter of the American Coalition of Black Trade Unionists recalls a fight at one OFL convention to retain the position of human rights director which was not supported by the women's committee. 'To speak out on human rights issues' was seen as something that 'would take away from the women's issue' (Gordon 2000: 24).

Separate organising can also facilitate different constituencies coming together and demonstrate that solidarity can be built on a foundation of diversity. For example, Messing and Mergler (1993) examine the links established between health and safety committees and women's committees in Quebec which led to the consideration of previously ignored women's occupational health issues.

Despite the importance of vehicles to coordinate cross-constituency organising, some calls for mainstreaming involve folding women's committees into human rights or social justice committees/departments which would then attempt to simultaneously address the diverse needs of various constituencies. For example, coincident with celebrating the twenty-fifth anniversary of the Status of Women Committee of the British Columbia Teachers' Federation in March 1998, a resolution to amalgamate the Status of Women Committee into a larger Social Justice Committee passed by a tiny margin: 334 votes for and 322 votes against. Those who argued against the motion feared that integration 'will dilute and make invisible the voices of women' (BCTF 1998: 8), a concern I share. I would argue that a critical foundation for such mainstreaming is deeply embedded constituency organising to highlight the specificity of voices, and to ensure that the voices of the most marginalised will be heard (Briskin and Newson 1999).

Building alliances and coalitions across unions and with social movements

> We need to break down false barriers between unions and community groups and integrate both in organising campaigns, education and international solidarity work.
>
> (CLC 1998: 24)

For several decades, Canadian women's organising has embraced alliances and coalitions across political current, sector and institution in order to bring women together from unions, political parties, and community based groups to cooperate nationally, provincially and locally (Colley 1983; Egan and Yanz 1983; Antonyshyn *et al.* 1988; Kome 1995; Ash 1996). The most successful formal expression of this, but by no means the only one, is the National Action Committee on the Status of Women/Comité Canadien d'action sur le statut de la femme (NAC), a bi-national (includes Quebec), bilingual umbrella organisation of over 700 member groups which celebrated its 25th anniversary in 1997. This cooperation has meant that trade union women work with community based feminist groups, both to build coalitions around key issues such as childcare and pay equity, and to pressure the union movement to respond to the feminist challenge. Trade union women, in turn, have had an important impact on the politics and practices of the Canadian women's movement, weakening the tendency towards individualistic solutions and introducing (and reintroducing) a class perspective (Briskin 1999b). Coalition strategies both respond to and highlight the significance of diversity in the Canadian context, that is, they represent a recognition of power dynamics and an organisational alternative to homogeneous organisations that tend to silence marginal voices.

Several recent innovative initiatives are worthy of note. In June of 1995, after a year of intense planning, three branches of the 10-day Québec Women's March Against Poverty converged on the National Assembly in Québec City to join 15,000 supporters. This March was initiated by the Fédération des femmes du Québec, and organised by more than 40 groups including unions, anti-poverty groups, immigrant groups and women's organisations. The March was quite a success: in response to their nine demands, the Québec government agreed to raise the minimum wage; to introduce a proactive pay equity law; to deduct child support payments automatically; to set aside 5 per cent of social housing for poor women and five places for every 15 in non-traditional trades; to reduce the length of sponsorship for immigrant women; to allocate money to the 'social economy' to generate jobs; to extend basic employment standards to those on workfare; and to freeze student fees (Nadeau 1995).

Building on this initiative, NAC and the CLC sponsored a national women's March Against Poverty 'For bread and roses, for jobs and justice' in May and June of 1996. Caravans travelled to Ottawa from both the west and east coast stopping in over 100 communities. The March ended with a two-day women's 'Tent City' and a protest rally of over 40,000 women at Parliament Hill which demonstrated against the right wing corporate and government agenda. 'The diversity represented in the march was truly amazing and it reflected the joint leadership of labour and the women's movements. One couldn't have done it without the other' (CLC 1997a: 65).

The Canadian union movement was actively involved in building the World March of Women launched on 8 March 2000 and culminating on 17 October 2000, the International Day for the Elimination of Poverty. This worldwide activity endorsed by over 200 countries and 2200 organisations was initiated by the Fédération des femmes du Québec modelled on their successful 1995 March. Its goals were to eliminate poverty and violence in women's lives. Ethel LaValley, Ontario Federation of Labour (OFL) Secretary Treasurer commented, 'The world mobilization of women is a profound project of international solidarity'. The fifth Biennial OFL Convention in 1999 voted in favour of supporting the World March and underscored the need to ensure that 'the work reflects the demands of women of colour, women with disabilities, lesbians, aboriginal women and women living in poverty'. In Vancouver, the March committee was co-facilitated by the British Columbia Federation of Labour Women's Rights Committee and the National Action Committee on the Status of Women. The CLC also devoted considerable resources to the March and hired a staff person to foster coordination inside the labour movement, and between the labour and the women's movement (*Women's Rights Bulletin* of the Ontario Federation of Labour Women's Committee [Feb 2000], and *Sisterhood*, the women's bulletin of the British Columbia Federation of Labour).

Crossing borders: transnational alliances

> As corporate concentration leads to larger and larger employers and international trade agreements expose workers to ever increasing insecurity, unions around the world are looking for ways to pool their strength to meet the new challenges.
>
> (Alberta Federation of Labour 1999: 42)

The globalisation of production, the mobility of capital and competitive wage bargaining are clearly redefining the significance of national boundaries for unions and putting transnational solidarity firmly on the agenda. Unions increasingly see the need to move across national boundaries to build alliances and cooperate with workers in other countries in order to limit the power of capital. Wells (1998: iii) argues that unions now recognise that 'the choice is between internationalism and a new feudalism built around workers' micro-corporatist loyalty to "their" firms'. He calls for a 'transnational coordinative unionism that combines participatory mobilization at the local union and community levels with strategic coordination at national and international levels'.

Such new cross-border alliances emerge from shared economic realities. Although women in the North, South and East experience restructuring in divergent and asymmetrical ways, undoubtedly they also face a common set of problems. The successful struggle to improve conditions in the El Salvador plants that produce clothes for the GAP (a large, trendy clothes, chain store) is an example of such transnational work. A joint campaign was undertaken in the US and Canada by unions and popular organisations, and in El Salvador by workers who put their jobs and often their lives on the line. The goal was to force the GAP to establish and enforce a code of conduct to improve working conditions, and to extend the right to unionise to workers in the free trade zones. The campaign used the power of Western consumers and the vulnerability of clothing retailers to public criticism. But it was also about protecting employment standards in the West, challenging deregulation, and preventing maquiladora working conditions from moving north. (In Ontario sweatshops, women are now commonly forced to work for less than the minimum wage.) A common goal infused this coalition work – to 'pressure retailers and major labels to take responsibility for the conditions under which their clothing is produced' in both industrialised and developing countries, and a shared recognition of the impact, although asymmetrical, of the GAP's working conditions on workers in both the North and the South (Jeffcott and Yanz 1997).

In 1998, the CLC launched a 'Break the Sweat' campaign against the sweatshops in Canada and in countries such as China, Indonesia and Vietnam servicing Nike, Woolworth, Disney Corporation and Hyundai in cooperation with the Global March Against Child Labour. They designated 1 May 2000 as a day of international solidarity and mobilisation and argue that 'local solidarity and global solidarity are inextricably connected' (CLC 1999a). In 1999 the CLC pledged to make equality for women and marginalised groups a priority in all aspects of international work 'since women everywhere are seeing advances they achieved driven back by economic conservatives and religious fundamentalism'. In the Middle East and

South America, the CLC works with labour centrals to hold seminars on women and leadership, fighting sexual harassment, and changing union structures to include women and organising women workers (CLC 1999a).

The politics of transnational labour solidarity are clearly moving away what Wells (1998: 3) refers to as the 'fraternal tourism of labour elites' and towards a social justice perspective. In fact, McNally (1998: 32) argues that anti-racist perspectives need to be central to the politics of workers' movements. As an example, he points to the protectionism of workers in the developed countries which is often accompanied by racist depictions of Third World workers. McNally concludes that effective working-class resistance to global capital involves internationalism at home by way of campaigns which defend migrant workers (immigrants, refugees and undocumented workers), and which demand world-wide mobility rights for labour.

Interestingly, the CAW in its 1998 Brief on the Report of the Immigration Legislative Review Advisory Group takes such a progressive view on these issues. In their opening preamble, they say: 'We have witnessed in this country an increasingly mean-spirited and at times openly racist attitude towards immigrants and refugees. Through our CAW policies and through extensive educational programs, we have made every effort to challenge these attitudes within our membership' (p. 1). Their Brief goes on to support government funding for settlement services, immigration from the South, recognition of same sex partners in the immigration profession, a reduction of sponsorship to decrease the dependency of immigrant women, for labour standards and rights for temporary foreign workers, for greater protection for refugee claimants, and finally for an amnesty for all undocumented persons currently living in Canada. They conclude: 'Neo-liberalism and the global agenda of capital are creating refugees as rapidly as the actions of ruthless despots in individual countries or regions. . . . Canadian government policy should be driven by the values of higher good, and not the vagaries of the bottom line.'

The coalition work among women which began in the 1970s has redefined both the ideology and practice of union solidarity, and now challenges the competitiveness and individualism at the core of the corporate and state agenda. Perhaps more than any other single strategy, coalition building, nationally and transnationally, will be critical to the resistance which must be mounted against corporatisation, workplace restructuring, changing state forms, decommodification and globalisation.

Conclusion

The inextricable links between equity inside unions and workplaces, and the new economic and political realities are creating both crisis and possibility for Canadian unions. Changing patterns of competition among workers call for new forms of solidarity which take account of diversity. Key transformation strategies continue to include representation, redefining union issues and expanding the collective bargaining agenda, separate organising and constituency building, and establishing alliances and coalitions across unions and across borders. Under the pressures of globalisation and restructuring, which mobilise diversity based on age, citizenship, gender and race to divisive ends, such strategies are gradually shifting away from the margins of union activity.

The current context repositions unions as critical sites of opposition not only to corporate rule and workplace reorganisation but also to the neo-liberal state. Despite the hostility of neo-liberal states, Wood (1998: 11–12) makes a sustained argument for the continuing relevance of a politics directed at the state which she sees as the '*main agent* of globalisation' and complicit in 'capital's anti-social purposes'. Indeed, she argues that 'capital [is] being forced to rely on the state to create the right conditions for accumulation'.

Undoubtedly, the organising of women and other marginalised groups has traditionally focused on the Canadian state. Certainly state-sanctioned and initiated equality policies have represented important successes. However, the state has also co-opted women's organising, reproduced patriarchal and heterosexist family forms, policed reproduction and sexuality, and disproportionately addressed the needs of some women over others. Currently, labour market deregulation and declining government support for social programmes and equality policies are undermining Canadian political traditions which have supported state intervention, thereby increasing the importance of pressuring rather than relying on the state. A strengthened union movement and extra-institutional organising in progressive social movements represent important sites from which to make demands on, and simultaneously decentre the state.

Unions also offer one of the few arenas to counter both the ideological onslaught supporting 'competition', and the neo-liberal promotion of radical individualism which is weakening citizenship rights and the tolerance for making special claims on the basis of difference or systemic discrimination (Brodie 1995: 57). Constituency organising and coalition building model a proactive alternative to this individualism.

In Canada, then, the unions may be the decisive arena for organising by equity-seeking groups. They are now a key player in the women's movement. However, this did not happen without resistance; indeed, the movement of union women has struggled for almost 30 years to make this a reality. Resituating equity from the margin to the centre will undoubtedly revitalise the unions but also depend upon sustained cross-sectoral organising and cooperation.

Acknowledgement

This research was funded by the Social Sciences and Humanities Research Council of Canada (SSHRC) and the Faculty of Arts at York University. I would like to thank Walter Giesbrecht, the data librarian at York, Nicole Boudreault of the Workplace Information Directorate of Human Resources Development Canada, and Cara Banks and Krista Scott-Dixon for their work as research assistants.

Notes

1 Since Canada has multiple union movements – at the local, provincial, regional and national levels, this one chapter cannot do justice to them. It does use examples from across the country in order to make visible this diversity; however, the goal is not an exhaustive documentation but rather a thematic presentation of interventions, struggles and victories which avoids generalising and thus falsely homogenising. This discussion aso relies heavily on documents from the Canadian Labour Congress (CLC) which have been used as models by many provincial federations and many member unions. The whole of the Canadian labour movement, however, does not necessarily espouse such progressive positions. Constraints of length also mean that the somewhat unique character of the labour movement in Quebec is not addressed.
2 The CLC is the largest central labour body in Canada and is composed of about 85 national and international unions representing about 2.2 million workers (CLC 1997b: 98). The so-called international unions are America unions (affiliated with the American Federation of Labor (AFL-CIO)) which have branches in Canada.
3 Although unionised, teachers and nurses have traditionally not belonged to central labour bodies. However, in recent years, both groups have started to join the CLC. Undoubtedly new demands and new tensions will surface as a result of this increase in professional workers.
4 The CAW has approximately 220,000 members. Since 1985 when it broke away from its 'international' parent, the United Auto Workers, it has doubled in size through mergers and new organising.

References

Abella, R. (1984) *Commission of Inquiry on Equality in Employment*, Ottawa: Supply and Services Canada.

Adams, R. (1989) 'North American industrial relations: divergent trends in Canada and the United States', *International Labour Review* 128: 47–64.

Akyeampong, E. (1997) 'A statistical portrait of the trade union movement', *Perspectives* 9, 4: 45–54.

—— (1998) 'The rise of unionization among women', *Perspectives*, Statistics Canada catalogue No. 75-001-XPE: 30–43.

—— (2000) 'Unionization – an update', *Perspectives*, 12, 3: 1–29.

Alberta Federation of Labour (1999) *Now More than Ever: An Examination of the Challenges and Opportunities Facing Alberta Unions in the 21st Century*, Alberta.

Antonyshyn, P., Lee, B. and Merrill, A. (1988) 'Marching for women's lives: the campaign for free-standing abortion clinics in Ontario', in F. Cunningham, S. Findlay, M. Kadar, A. Lennon and E. Silva (eds) *Social Movements Social Change: The Politics and Practice of Organizing*, Toronto: Between the Lines.

Ash, S. (1996) 'More cuts, few benefits', *Kinesis* (Dec–Jan).

—— (1998) 'BCTF [Bristol Columbia Federation of Teachers] vote a step backward', *Kinesis* (July/August).

Briskin, L. (1990) 'Women, unions and leadership', *Canadian Dimension* 24: 38–41.

—— (1993) 'Union women and separate organizing', in Briskin and McDermott.

—— (1994) 'Equity and economic restructuring in the Canadian labour movement', *Economic and Industrial Democracy* 15, 1: 89–112.

—— (1998) 'Gendering union democracy', *Canadian Woman Studies/les cahiers de la femme* 18, 1: 35–8.

—— (1999a) 'Feminisms, feminization and democratization in Canadian unions', in K. Blackford, M. Garceau and S. Kirby (eds) *Feminist Success Stories/Célébrons nos réussites féministes*, Ottawa: University of Ottawa Press.

—— (1999b) 'Unions and women's organizing in Canada and Sweden', in L. Briskin and M. Eliasson (eds) *Women's Organizing and Public Policy in Canada and Sweden*, Montreal: McGill-Queen's University Press.

—— (1999c) 'Autonomy, diversity and integration: union women's separate organizing in North America and Western Europe in the context of restructuring and globalization', *Women's Studies International Forum* 22, 5: 543–54.

Briskin, L. and McDermott, P. (eds) (1993) *Women Challenging Unions: Feminism, Democracy and Militancy*, Toronto: University of Toronto Press.

Briskin, L. and Newson, J. (1999) 'Making equity a priority: anatomy of the York strike of 1997', *Feminist Studies* 25, 1: 105–18.

Briskin, L. and Yanz, L. (eds) (1983) *Union Sisters: Women in the Labour Movement*, Toronto: Women's Press.

Brodie, J. (1995) *Politics on the Margins: Restructuring and the Canadian Women's Movement*, Halifax: Fernwood Publishing.

Canadian Auto Workers (CAW) (1998) *Brief on the Report of the Immigration Legislative Review Advisory Group*, Ottawa.

—— (1999) *Past Gains, Future Challenges: Mobilizing for the New Millenium: Report to the 1999 Collective Bargaining and Political Action Convention*, Toronto.

Canadian Labour Congress (CLC) (1994a) *Confronting the Mean Society*, Policy Statement 20th Constitutional Convention, May.

—— (1994b) *Sexual Orientation Policy Paper*, Ottawa.

—— (1997a) *Women and Work: A Report*, Ottawa.

—— (1997b) *Challenging Racism: Going Beyond Recommendations. Report of the CLC National Anti-Racism Task Force*, Ottawa.

—— (1998) *'No Easy Recipe': Building the Diversity and Strength of the Labour Movement – Feminist Organizing Models*, CLC Women's Symposium.

—— (1999a) *Global Solidarity*, Policy Statement from the 22nd Constitutional Convention.

—— (1999b) *Statement on Fighting Racism*, 22nd Constitutional Convention.

Canadian Union of Public Employees (CUPE) (1997) *Working Together to Achieve Equality*, Ottawa: CUPE.

Colley, S. (1983) 'Free universal daycare: the OFL takes a stand', in Briskin and Yanz.

Creese, G. (1995) 'Gender equity or masculine privilege? Union strategies and economic restructuring in a white-collar union', *Canadian Journal of Sociology* 20, 2: 143–66.

Egan, Carolyn and Yanz, Lynda (1983) 'Building links: labour and the women's movement', in Briskin and Yanz.

Fonow, M. (1998) 'Women of steel: a case of feminist organizing in the United Steelworkers of America', *Canadian Woman Studies/les cahiers de la femme* 18, 1: 117–22.

Fox, B. and Sugiman, P. (1999) 'Flexible work, flexible workers: the restructuring of clerical work in a large telecommunications company', *Studies in Political Economy* 60: 59–84.

Garcia-Orgales, J. (2000) 'Breaking barriers: disability awareness and rights', *Our Times* 20–7.

Genge, S. (1998) 'Solidarity and pride', *Canadian Woman Studies/les cahiers de la femme* 18, 1: 97–9.

Gordon, S. (2000) 'Ann Newman and the Coalition of Black Trade Unionists', *Our Times* 22–9.

Hunt, G. (1997). 'Sexual orientation and the Canadian labour movement', *Relations industrielles* 52, 4: 787–809.

Jackson, A. and Schellenberg, G. (1998) *Unions, Collective Bargaining and Labour Market Outcomes for Canadian Women: Past Gains and Future Challenges*, Ottawa: Canadian Labour Congress Research Paper #11.

Jeffcott, J. and Yanz, L. (1997) 'Bridging the GAP: exposing the labour behind the label', *Our Times* 24–8.

Kome, P. (1995) 'Common front de-Kleins cutbacks,' *Herizons* (Spring).

Mainville, D. and Olineck, C. (1999) *Unionization in Canada: A Retrospective*, Statistics Canada: Catalogue No. 75-001-SPE. Ottawa.

McNally, D. (1998) 'Globalization, trade pacts and working class resistance', *Socialist Studies Bulletin* 53: 22–37.

Messing, K. and Mergler, D. (1993) 'Unions and women's occupational health in Quebec', in Briskin and McDermott.

Nadeau, D. (1995) 'For bread and roses', *Kinesis* (July/August).

Nash, P. (1999) 'Ring in the new millennium with a national child care program', *Toronto Star*, 8 October.

—— (1998) *CAW Women's Bargaining Agenda*, Canadian Auto Workers, 16 October.

Panitch, L. and Swartz, D. (1988) *The Assault on Trade Union Freedoms*, Toronto: Garamond.

Parker, M. and Gruelle, M. (1999) *Democracy is Power: Rebuilding the Unions from the Bottom Up*, Detroit: A Labor Notes Book.

Pupo, N., Wells, D. and White, J. (1998) 'Service workers under neo-feudalism: unions, restructuring and the hotel sector', paper presented at the meetings of the World Congress of Sociology, 30 July.

Ross, S. (1999) 'Gender and structure in the Canadian Union of Public Employees', Speech presented to the CUPE Ontario Women's Conference, unpublished.

Sassen, S. (1998) *Globalization and its Discontents*, New York: The New Press.

Statistics Canada (1999) *Labour Force Survey: Annual Averages*, Ottawa.

—— (2000) *Women in Canada: A Gender Based Statistical Report*, Catalogue No. 89-503-XPE, Ottawa.

Waddington, J. (1999) 'Situating labour within the globalization debate', in Waddington, J. (ed.) *Globalization and Patterns of Labour Resistance*, London: Mansell Publishing.

Wells, D. (1998) *Building Transnational Coordinative Unionism*, Kingston: Industrial Relations Centre, Queen's University.

White, J. (1993). *Sisters and Solidarity: Women and Unions in Canada*, Toronto: Thompson Educational Publishing.

Wood, E. (1998) 'Labor, class and state in global capitalism', in E. Wood, P. Meiksins and M. Yates (eds) *Rising from the Ashes? Labor in the Age of 'Global' Capitalism*, New York: Monthly Review Press.

Yalnizyan, A. (1998) *The Growing Gap: A Report on Inequality Between the Rich and Poor in Canada*, Toronto: Centre for Social Justice.

3   Sweden's LO

Learning to embrace the differences within?[1]

Rianne Mahon

This chapter focuses on the LO (*Landsorganisation i Sverige*), the peak organisation of blue-collar workers, as a way of providing insight into the way 'difference' is dealt with among Swedish unions.[2] Throughout the twentieth century, LO stood at the centre of the powerful Swedish union movement. It exercised leadership not only *vis-à-vis* its own unions but also the white-collar unions, especially those affiliated with the Tjänstemännens Centralorganisation (TCO). While by the end of the century, LO's hegemony had been undermined by a variety of developments, the choices that it and its affiliates make continue to be of central importance for the Swedish union movement as a whole.

Although the focus is on contemporary developments, this chapter begins with an analysis of the way LO dealt with 'difference' in the postwar period, the Swedish LO and its partisan ally, the Swedish Social Democratic Party (SAP) recognised the importance of alliances with other subaltern[3] forces. Considerable attention has been focused on the postwar construction of a 'wage earners alliance' with white-collar employees. The LO also recognised that other differences,[4] notably gender and ethnicity, could undermine solidarity and acted to neutralise[5] these by developing programmes designed to encompass working women and immigrants in its project. Nevertheless, LO only begrudgingly recognised 'difference' as its aim was to incorporate these groups into the working class. There were limits, too, to the depth of the 'wage earners' alliance with white-collar employees.

The second part of the chapter examines the crisis of LO's hegemony. In the 1990s, LO had to grapple with mass unemployment and an employer-led drive to establish a 'flexible' labour market, in an ideological context marked by an ascendant neo-liberalism. While these and other changes have undermined its position within the Swedish union movement, they have also opened LO to new ways of thinking about the place of women and immigrants within the unions. While this represents a promising development, it will be argued that it is not enough. LO has also to learn how to reconstruct 'wage earner' solidarity on firmer foundations or the employers may succeed in driving a wedge between the male-dominated industrial unions and the service sector unions where women and immigrants now predominate.

The analysis throughout draws on documentary material, including the web-sites of the leading Swedish papers and the unions. These are supplemented by selected interviews with trade union activists[6] as well as appropriate secondary sources.

LO and Swedish unions in the golden age

During the golden age of the Keynesian welfare state, the Swedish unions stood as the exemplar of labour strength and innovative capacity and LO stood at the centre of the Swedish union movement. Throughout the golden age, the rules of collective bargaining followed the Saltsjöbaden accord between LO and SAF (the Swedish employers' association). Moreover, the LO and SAF agreement set the parameters not only for LO's affiliates and their locals, but also for the white-collar unions. Under these conditions, LO was able to pursue its policy of solidaristic wages bargaining with considerable effect. In politics, LO's special relationship with the governing social democratic party afforded it an opportunity to shape government policy and several key policy innovations came from LO's research office.[7] Yet even in the golden age, LO faced potential challenges that required it to deal with class, gender and ethnic differences. This section will examine how it responded to these, beginning with a brief outline of the changes in the labour market and LO's membership.

Changing labour markets, new workers

During the postwar boom, blue-collar workers remained the major group in the labour market but structural change steadily increased the proportion of white-collar workers. The continued predominance of the blue-collar workforce, moreover, could not hide important changes within that group itself. Although the prototypical worker represented by LO was understood to be male and ethnically Swedish, this was becoming increasingly outdated. Already in 1960, 43 per cent of Swedish women between the ages of 25 and 54 were in the labour market. By the end of the 1970s, that figure had jumped to 64 per cent (LO 1992: 6). Women's rising labour force participation rate has been felt within the LO as its unions have been quite successful in organising women. By 1975, 67 per cent of blue-collar women workers were organised and by the 1990s the organisation rate for women was actually higher than it was for men (LO 1999a: 91). Yet, as the majority of women work in public and private services, the incorporation of women into the ranks of LO was uneven. Fully 80 per cent of the largest LO union, the Municipal Workers Union, are women whereas for the second largest (and long the leading) union, the Metal Workers, the figures are almost the reverse.

While ethnic and religious homogeneity is often cited as a factor contributing to Sweden's high rate of unionisation, this too began to change significantly in the postwar years such that immigrants now constitute 10 per cent of the population. Immigrants make up a larger share of LO members (20 per cent) in part because they are over-represented in blue-collar occupations. Whereas Swedish women were drawn into the service sector, the majority of immigrants in the 1950s and 1960s – both men and women – found industrial jobs. Immigrants have been drawn into the private service sector, and, since the 1970s, the public sector as well. This too is reflected in union membership. Thus whereas during the 1950s and 1960s immigrants were over-represented in industrial unions like the Metal Workers, today it is unions like the Hotel and Restaurant Workers and the Cleaners unions. The largest numbers, however, are in the two biggest unions, the Municipal and Metal Workers unions.

The sources of immigration changed too. In the 1950s, two-thirds of immigrant workers were from other Nordic countries and the majority of these came from Finland (Hammar 1988). In the 1960s, there was substantial immigration from Yugoslavia, Greece and Turkey (Knocke 1997). The virtual halt to recruitment of workers from abroad in the 1970 has meant that most immigrants since then have come as refugees, usually from non-European countries. By 1995, one-third of the foreign-born population were from countries in Latin America, the Middle East, Africa and Asia.

LO and its unions were quick to understand the need to neutralise the potential threats to their strength on the labour market which these changes posed. They responded in somewhat different ways to each of these challenges. In each case, their strategy contributed to forging the solidarity required to maintain their position within Swedish society and politics. While LO organised a significant share of women and immigrants, white-collar workers had their own unions.[8] Yet many of them also came to support the LO's social democratic project. The reforms LO and its unions supported did much to mitigate not only class but also gender and racial/ethnic inequalities. They did not, however, eliminate them. In part this reflects the very strength of the forces generating inequality in capitalist societies. It is also, however, indicative of limitations in the way the unions understood these relationships.

Alliance among the subaltern classes

Solidarity within the working class and between it and other subaltern classes was always central to the LO's project. Thus the social democratic reforms of the 1930s were made possible by, and helped to cement, an alliance with the farmers' party. The 'Rehn-Meidner' strategy, named after the two LO economists who developed it, sought to improve the terms of the tradeoff between full employment and price stability and thus to maintain wage earner solidarity. Critical to the new alliance of wage earners were the social policy reforms of the 1960s in which Beveridge style flat rate programmes were supplemented by a variety of income-related social insurance schemes. High quality public services similarly appealed to white- as well as blue-collar workers.

The establishment of conditions favouring a new collectivity of wage earners did not, however, eliminate the distinct identities of the classes comprising it. Although many white-collar workers supported the social democrats, TCO and SACO have held to their official policy of non-partisan alignment. Moreover, the white-collar unions had their own collective agreements, patterned along different lines (Mahon 1994). This allowed the employers to reinforce the status divisions established in the Fordist production process between 'mental' and 'manual' labour (de Geer 1992: 122).

Tensions between blue- and white-collar collectivities surfaced in the late 1960s and early 1970s. The wave of wild cat strikes that marked this period expressed, in part, a sense of injustice stemming from a bargaining structure that operated to the disadvantage of blue-collar workers, especially the more skilled (Swenson 1989: chapter 3). At the same time, the growing cadre of white-collar unions was no longer content to let the LO-SAF agreement set the parameters. New white-collar bargaining cartels emerged to challenge LO in the public and private sectors. To some extent the 1970s labour law reforms addressed their common interests as classes subordinated to capital in the production process. While these reforms marked significant gains for blue- and white-collar workers, they left the division between them intact.

Gender: from housewife–mother to wage earner–parent

Class was not the only basis of difference that the LO sought to neutralise. In the early years, LO and its social democratic project was biased in favour of the male breadwinner household (Jenson and Mahon 1993; Hirdman 1994). Unlike their sisters in many continental European countries, Swedish social policies supported women both as citizens and as mothers (Sainsbury 1994). Although little was done to assist those women who combined parenthood and wage work, married women's right to work was officially recognised (Hobson 1993). From the 1960s on, moreover, a set of changes was introduced giving real meaning to this hitherto abstract right. In the debates that opened the way to the dual earner family, the LO was not the leading force but it played an important role.

Wage policy

By the early 1960s LO had become increasingly concerned that projected labour shortages should largely be met by drawing married women into the labour market (Kyle 1979). Women were not, however, to be a source of cheap labour. Thus in the early 1960s, LO reached an agreement with SAF on the abolition of separate (and lower) women's wages. When it became clear that this had done little to close the gender wage gap, LO was prepared to do something about this – but not in the name of gender equity. Rather, in the interests of all low wage workers, it pushed a version of solidaristic wage bargaining, emphasising special increments for the lowest paid.

LOs' solidaristic wages bargaining strategy did contribute to lower wage differentials among full time male and female workers. Some thirty years on, however, women remain over-represented among the low paid full time workers. Thus 54 per cent of full time women blue-collar workers are considered low paid vs 16 per cent for their respective male counterparts (LO 1999a: 103 Diagram 5). As many as

50 per cent of LO women and 30 per cent of TCO women had part time jobs vs 9 and 6 per cent respectively of the unions' male membership (LO 1999a: 102). Behind these figures lie two important facts: the high degree of segregation in the Swedish labour market, with women, for the most part, in the lowest paid occupations and branches; and the failure to achieve the feminist-humanist vision of shared parenting, shared work.

Reconciling work and family

LO took up the demand for public day care but the argument was cast in ways that obscured gender differences. LO refused to identify with the 'bourgeois feminism' that was seen to dominate the sex roles debate of the 1960s. It was, however, prepared to fight for day care as part of the broader class struggle. The expansion of public social services like day care were favoured as 'anti-capitalist' to the extent that they expanded collective, at the expense of private, consumption (Hirdman 1998: 268). More importantly, day care was seen as something for the working-class family – a way to compensate for the advantages bestowed by class origin (LO 1969: 11).

The focus on the working-class family reflected LO's view that equality of the sexes took second place to class equality (LO 1969: 13). LO was not entirely closed to the 'sex roles' debate, however. Although it was careful to take its distance from the 'highly educated, professional women' whose concerns allegedly shaped the debate, it did adopt the feminist-humanist ideal of shared parenthood. This was reflected in its early support for the idea of adding 'parental' to maternity leave (LO 1969: 50). The party's Equality Commission, in which LO participated, took a similar stance. Thus the way was paved for the 1972 adoption of what remains the most advanced parental leave legislation.

In the 1970s, young socialist feminists in the Swedish Social Democratic Women's League (SSKF) took up the demand for the six-hour day for all as an important step towards realising the feminist-humanist idea.[9] Implementation of the six hour day promised to redefine the work norm from one based on the male breadwinner pattern, to one where both men and women had dual roles, as parents and as wage earners. LO, however, consistently ranked the six-hour day below other 'more important' goals. Thus instead of a commitment to move towards the six-hour day for all, parental leave legislation was amended to give the parents of young children the right to reduce their working hours to six hours until the children are older. Thus women are the ones who take the lion's share of parental leave (over 90 per cent) and this is especially true of LO families. Blue-collar women have also tended to 'choose' part time work as a way of coping with their dual roles as mothers and as workers.

LO was not, however, prepared to accept the more radical position articulated by the younger Swedish socialist feminists. The latter dared to put the system of sexual oppression on par with class exploitation and thus struggle to change gender relations was seen as equal the class struggle. For LO, class clearly took priority over other differences:

a policy for equity between men and women must . . . form part of a general policy for equality between all people. Women in different social classes are not equal. It is the worst placed women who are most affected by the lack of equal opportunity. Working-class women have more in common with men from the same social class than they have with highly educated, well-placed women.

(LO 1976: 10)

'Equal opportunity' of the sexes was seen as, at best, a component of the larger struggle for class equality. As we shall see, this position would be challenged in the 1980s by a new generation of working-class feminists. The crisis of the union movement would give them a chance to make gains that eluded their sisters.

Separate organising?

Debates about how to understand and deal with gender were also reflected in the sphere of union organisation. From 1947 to 1967, LO (reluctantly) recognised gender difference in the form of a distinct Women's Council. The existence of 'special organisations' was understood by local and national leadership – at that time, predominantly male – to conflict with the principle of shared class interests. As one of the opponents of a special women's ombudsman put it, 'It is not appropriate to deal with this question as a special women's question within the union movement; we must not distinguish between men and women when it comes to organising' (cited in Waldemarsson 1998: 12). Those who spoke for a women's council had to show that they respected that principle. As Sigrid Ekendahl, LO's first woman's ombudsman, put it: 'women do not want to lay the basis for any special organisation, but only want to create an enlightened cadre of women union members who, I would like to underline, can work together with men to carry out the union's work' (cited in Waldemarsson 1998: 14). A special council was needed fully to integrate women into the union.

In the end, the LO leadership was prepared to make an exception because women posed a problem: they were less inclined to join unions and when they did join, rarely became active (Waldemarsson 1998: 17–19). The Women's Council aimed to fix those problems. It arranged special women's courses and organised special lecture series and study circles. A network of women's committees was established under the wing of local LO organisations. While many remained hostile to 'special organisations', where they were established women's participation in union activities rose significantly (Waldemarsson 1998: 32–9).

The change in 1967 from Women's Council to Family Council – a move recommended to the Executive by the Women's Council (Waldemarsson 1998: 255–60; Hirdman 1998: 258) – was in line with the feminist-humanist ideology of that time.[10] This form of feminism was more palatable to LO than the 'man hating' variant allegedly carried by young feminists in the 1970s. Yet the embrace of this vision failed to come to grips with the fact that it had yet to come into existence, especially in LO families. The closure of the Women's Council also meant the abolition of the special women's committees at the local level and this virtually destroyed the links the Council had worked to establish among LO women (Hirdman 1998: 362). Women's involvement in official union work also declined. Nothing was done to change this until 1979, when the threat posed by the bourgeois government's equal opportunity legislation forced LO to set up a committee to look into the question. The latter's report to the 1981 congress mused about whether the union's formal meeting forms might put women off, a theme which would later become an important part of LO discourse on women and youth. Innovative forms for involving women would not, however, be developed until the 1990s, a point to which we shall return.

Race-ethnicity: equality, freedom and partnership

Since the early nineteenth century, Swedish national identity had been imagined as one founded on religious, linguistic and ethnic homogeneity. Yet, in the postwar period, Sweden eschewed a guest worker policy for one that recognised the right to settlement (with one's family) and later moved to embrace a form of multiculturalism based on the principles of equality, freedom of cultural choice and partnership.[11] In answering the question of why Sweden began to 'reimagine' itself in ways more typically associated with countries of classical immigration, Castles and Miller emphasise the values and policy legacies of Swedish social democracy (1998: 248). More emphasis needs to be placed, however, on the active role played by the unions, with LO in the lead.

LO and immigration policy

Right from the beginning, the LO unions sought to make the newcomers part of the working class and they were well placed to make sure it happened (Hammar 1988: 12). In 1947 the first bilateral agreements were signed to recruit non-Nordic workers and in 1948 the new labour market board (AMS), on which the unions were well represented, assumed responsibility for negotiating the agreements. Thus the unions were in a position to ensure that immigrants were to be paid at the same rate as their Swedish counterparts (Knocke 1997). The AMS agreements also included a clause specifying that immigrant workers join and remain union members throughout their stay. In 1965 this clause was replaced by SAF's agreement with LO that employers recommend that the immigrants join the union.[12] The unionisation rate among immigrants has thus matched that of Swedish workers from the beginning.

In the 1960s, the LO unions began more actively to push for recruitment of Swedish women, rather than immigrants, to fill projected labour market shortages. The latter were considered less expensive as immigrants require housing, then in short supply. LO also argued that immigration allowed employers to fill bad jobs rather than modernising their activities. It thus undermined the unions' economic strategy (Hirdman, 1998: 192–4). With AMS support, LO pressed the government to limit immigration and in 1967, possession of a work contract, a work permit and housing were made mandatory prior to immigration. When this proved insufficient to limit immigration, and as unemployment rose in the early 1970s, LO counselled its unions no longer to go along with the granting of work permits. As Hammar notes, 'when the local unions thereafter said no, the national unions said no and AMS said no, no further work permits were granted and the flow of foreign workers ceased . . .' (1988: 11).

LO did, however, support the Swedish government's generous stance *vis-à-vis* refugees which saw Sweden receive the highest number of asylum-seekers (mainly from Third World countries) relative to population size, of all Western European countries (Castles and Miller 1998). In addition, LO unions, with the Metal Workers in the lead, raised concerns about the lack of Swedish language instruction. In 1970, LO concluded an agreement with SAF requiring 200 hours of Swedish language instruction, of which the employers paid the first sixty hours. The Metal Workers Union insisted that this was not enough: the basic minimum should be 240 hours and the entire cost should be paid by the employers. This was, in fact, the position that the government adopted when the legal right to Swedish language instruction during work hours was introduced in 1973 (Knocke 1997: 17).

Immigrants within the unions

While in the 1960s, LO replaced its Women's Council with the gender neutral Family Council, it was in this period that 'difference' as it concerned immigrants was being recognised. Yet just as with the early Women's Council, recognition was reflected in an understanding of immigrants as problematic. This understanding included awareness that immigrants were not being treated equally and were over-represented in low wage, low skill, dead-end jobs, with high rates of work-related injuries. The problems, however, were attributed to the immigrants, not to discriminatory practices within Swedish society, including the unions.

Language difficulties were seen as part of the problem, which the unions addressed by securing the right to Swedish instruction during paid working time. Yet this was not enough. The unions needed to reach their new members even before the latter became fluent in Swedish. As early as 1976 the Metal Workers began to produce special material on the meaning of union membership in Sweden for Finnish and Yugoslavian members. After the adoption of its 1979 Action Programme for Immigrants, LO and its affiliates started a quarterly journal, which comes out in several languages. Trade union courses began to be offered in major immigrant languages and, for smaller groups, interpreters are provided.

Immigrants are also seen to 'lack the social contact networks and the cultural frame of reference of those brought up and educated in Sweden' (LO 1991: 9). With the shift in migration from Nordic and North-Western European countries to the southern and eastern regions, moreover, the immigrants' cultural baggage is seen as more of a problem: 'a relatively large share of today's refugee immigration comes from countries where unions are an unknown concept or where they have a very different role than they have in Sweden. Many new refugees come moreover from countries lacking democratic traditions and ways of working, which many Swedes take for granted' (LO 1991: 8). To deal with this, the unions needed to teach immigrants the meaning of workplace rights as well as the responsibilities associated with membership in a democratic trade union movement.

The same strategy earlier used to motivate and educate women workers was adopted to deal with these problems too – the establishment, in the early 1970s, of a distinct Immigrants Council and a network of local immigrant committees. By 1979, almost half of the LO sections had immigrant committees and these were quite successful at increasing immigrants' participation. Nevertheless, LO's 1981 study of union activism confirmed that the unions were still being run largely by Swedish men (LO 1981). As Knocke notes,

> this model led to the paradoxical situation that immigrant related issues were integrated into the trade union programme, at the same time being organizationally separated from trade union concerns at large. Elected representatives at local workplace level or appointed officials on the higher echelons felt they had little support from other union people . . . Those working with immigrant issues . . . were simply too few. At union meetings, immigrant related questions were given low priority on the agenda, since neither responsibility nor knowledge were widespread among the members of the local union board.
>
> (Knocke 1997: 18–19)

LO began to acknowledge this problem as the 1980s came to a close. In the policy document prepared for its 1991 congress, it urged that 'Immigrant questions should be integrated in a natural way in the unions regular activities. It must be emphasised that all union stewards have the same responsibility for immigrants as for Swedish members and that union service to immigrant members is not something that rests only on the shoulders of those responsible for immigrants or immigrant committees. Thus immigrant and refugee questions should become a part of general union education' (LO 1991: 21). Instead of making immigrants' concerns part of the unions' main business, those who previously had responsibility for these issues were given additional tasks (Edam February–March 2000). And when the economic crisis hit, it was these other tasks which took priority.

Crisis and renewal

Cracks in the foundations of LO's position had already begun to appear in the 1980s, and these rapidly widened in the 1990s. LOs' decline certainly has had internal dimensions that have to be understood within the wider context of the employer-led drive to decentralise collective bargaining and the erosion of the Social Democrats' capacity to manage the national economy. These changes prompted the leaders of several of affiliates to call for a redefinition of LO's role. While their demands can be seen as a response to the employers' challenges, they have also contributed to a broader questioning of LO's moral authority and its capacity to lead the union movement. This followed on the heels of rank and file revolts against the trade union leadership in the 1980s and the decision by a growing number to exit or simply not to join in the first place. In the latter half of the 1980s, for the first time since the great strike and lockout of 1909, union density fell (Kjellberg 1998).

If the employer-led drive to decentralise bargaining helped to undermine LO's hegemony in this arena, internationalisation of the Swedish economy has added to the centrifugal forces within the union movement. The leading export branches (where the majority of men work) have become increasingly oriented to the international market, not only for sales but also for inputs. At the same time, the health of the Swedish economy is very much linked to performance in this sector, which has fuelled the argument that it is the export sector that must set the pace for the rest in collective bargaining. This has made it difficult to press the pay equity issue as most women work in the 'sheltered' sector where, it is argued, wages are to be restrained in the interests of maintaining Sweden's competitive position.

Globalisation also seriously exacerbated tensions in LO's relationship with the Social Democratic party. The relationship was under stress in the early 1980s. The adoption of the SAP's so-called 'third road' economic policy signalled that LO had lost its special position as a source of Social Democratic economic policy innovation (Pontusson 1992b: 317). Globalisation, especially in the form of financial liberalisation, meant that the Swedish Social Democrats found it increasingly difficult to find a formula that would allow them to manage an economy increasingly vulnerable to international developments. The various crisis packages cobbled together to grapple with this, in turn, only contributed to the alienation of Social Democratic voters, blue-collar and otherwise.

The full extent of the erosion of the tie between LO members and the party first became apparent in 1990 when support for the Social Democrats plunged and the party was voted out of office in 1991. The party's performance was even worse in the 1998 election, which followed the period of substantial cuts to social programmes by a Social Democratic government. Unlike 1991, however, when the party saw some of younger, mainly male LO members drawn to the right-wing populist 'New Democracy' party, in the 1998 election disgruntled LO voters looked to the Left Party. This support has held. On the eve of LO's Congress 2000, and despite the series of attacks on it by LO and party leadership, support for the Left party stood at 14 per cent – several percentage points above the unprecedented support it received in the 1998 election.

From 'working-class family' to equal opportunity

In the 1970s LO blended elements of the feminist-humanist vision with its core concern (class equality) with mixed results. On the one hand, issues which had previously received low priority because they were 'women's problems' became important components of the LO's agenda. On the other hand, the actually-persisting inequalities as between men and women tended to slip from view. The deepening crisis of the social democratic model, however, served to underline these differences and helped create an opening for LO to embrace the notion that the struggle for equality involved both class and gender.

Recognising that difference has meant inequality within the working class

Although unemployment hit men and women, women were more likely to have some form of temporary work than men. The rate of part-time employment increased for both men and women too but women continued to predominate among those with part-time work and the share of those involuntarily working part time rose. The attack on coordinated bargaining and wages solidarity has also had gendered effects. Thus the gap between men's and women's incomes began to widen again in the 1980s. Given the high degree of sex segregation in the Swedish labour market, the shift to branch-based bargaining also has very clear gender dimensions. Of particular importance here is the attempt to pull the male-dominated unions in the export sector into a cross-class coalition with 'their' employers, at the expense of the female-dominated public sector. Finally, women have been more directly affected by cuts to social expenditures because they rely on public transfers for a greater share of their income and because the domestic division of labour makes them more dependent on care services provided by the state.

By the time that these facts were becoming apparent in the latter half of the 1980s, LO was ready to recognise them. This was in no small part due to an earlier change in how gender relations were represented within LO – from family policy to 'equal opportunity'. This shift occurred in direct response to the passage of the equal opportunity law in 1980. LO and its affiliates were clearly concerned about the government's new Equal Opportunity Ombudsman, empowered to take the employers and the union before the labour court (Hirdman 1998: 370–4). For the most part, the unions had done nothing to follow up on the 1977 equal opportunity agreement between LO and SAF. Metall – a union in a very male dominated branch – was exceptional in this regard, establishing a post responsible for dealing with these issues as early as 1977. Following the 1981 congress, where equal opportunity was, in principle, accepted as one of the unions' central tasks, LO and its affiliates followed Metall's example. With the establishment of its own network of activists, LO internalised the potential for recognising inequalities as between the sexes and doing something about them.

Equal opportunity might have remained something of concern only to (certain) union activists at the workplace had it not been for the release of the report of the commission established to look at women's place in Swedish public life.[13] This government report made it clear that the issue of parity of the sexes was clearly relevant to the unions. Women were under-represented in the ranks of union officials and among the delegates at LO congresses. Thus at the 1981 congress, women constituted only 24 per cent of the delegates and the percentage had scarcely improved by the next congress in 1986 (Waldemarsson 1992: 94). Wage earner feminists within LO began to develop their strategy in response to the challenge.

They argued that women had saved the Social Democrats in the 1985 election – and that they could be LO's saviours too, if LO were prepared to change. LO and its affiliates had, however, to earn their support. Women, who now accounted for nearly half LO's membership, may have been ready to join unions in the past but they might not continue to do so if the unions continued to show 'a male-dominated profile in society and towards its members. Women, especially those who belong to the younger generation, have difficulty in feeling a sense of belonging to LO and sometimes even towards their own union' (LO 1987: 4). The document went on to lay out an ambitious long-term strategy for drawing women into union positions.

While there have been some significant setbacks, the women behind the new initiative have scored some important successes. Thus, for instance, in addition to arguing for new courses for women, they proposed that LO organise a series of seminars on women in the labour market. The lectures laid the basis for a major conference scheduled for International Women's Day in 1988, in the old industrial town of Borlänge – LO's first real conference by and for women. The Borlänge conference in turn helped to broaden the network, reaching out from the wage earner feminists within LO headquarters to women activists in the affiliates and local equity officers and establishing alliances with feminist work life researchers outside LO.

LO feminists also began to organise for the next LO congress in 1991. In this they were helped by the prominence given women in LO's new survey series, *Voices on the Union and Work*. *Voices* has become an important means of diffusing the broader wage earner feminist argument that women members are central to the union movement's renewal. A new working group of LO women produced an important background document, *Class and Sex* (LO 1990). Here, for the first time, 'equal opportunity' for the sexes was defined as essential to the broader struggle for (class) equality. And, although LO women were 'lowest down on the class ladder', the struggle for equal opportunity was seen to include solidarity with white-collar women for inequality of the sexes cut across class lines.

Parity within the unions

The 1991 Congress also marked a breakthrough for LO women in another sense. When it became clear that the vast majority of the representatives would, again, be men, the equal opportunity officer organised to ensure that women would be very visible. Thus four of five on the panel chairing the congress were women; all marshals were women; and women artists were features at the special evening of entertainment. Nor was this all 'show'. At the Congress, pay equity was accepted as a union goal and LO's statutes were at last amended to make parity of the sexes, at all levels of the organisation, a central objective. LO's equal opportunity officer played a key role in securing these and other changes.

At the 1991 congress, too, LO made two decisions regarding its contribution to the SAP's coming election campaign that had a longer term significance. First, it voted funds to establish the 'girls' league. The league was initially intended only to last for the election campaign but feminists within LO persuaded the leadership to keep it alive for some years. With 11,000 members across the country, the league became an exemplar of the new, unconventional way of organising that earlier studies had argued for. Although it has since been disbanded, it played an important part in mobilising LO women to become active in their unions and in politics at the local level. Unafraid to resort to unconventional tactics like street theatre, it functioned as one of the most visible bases of grassroots union mobilisation against the unpopular policies of the Conservative-led government (Briskin 1999). The 1991 congress also voted funds to establish a special pre-election publication that formed the basis for a new LO magazine, *Clara*. Directed especially at younger working women, *Clara* also outlasted the election and, for most of the decade, played an important part in LO's broader campaign to regain the initiative from SAF in the struggle for the hearts and minds of Swedes. It offered a lively blend of everyday issues and more typical union concerns but even the latter were presented in a new, more engaging way.

On the issue of parity within LO, the gains have taken longer but there have been some, especially at the top (see Table 3.1). Between 1988 and 1993, LO invested 15 million crowns in various projects designed to achieve internal parity. In 1988, Lillemor Arvidsson became the first woman to head a LO union; by 2000, three LO unions had women leaders, two of these (the Municipal Workers Union and the Retail Workers Unions) are among the three largest. Parity was achieved at the top early in 1994 when a younger woman member from the Municipal Workers Union, Wanja Lundby-Wedin, became vice-president. The results of the 1994 survey were disappointing, however. While women were 'more than ever willing' to take on union tasks, the percentage of women active in the unions had actually fallen since 1988, while the number of LO men had rising by nearly one-fifth (*LO Tidningen*, 27 May 1994). The slow progress could, in part, be attributed to cutbacks or hiring freezes imposed by tough financial times, especially at union headquarters, but it also reflected resistance. Metall's former secretary (now LO vice-president), Ulla Lindquist, noted the angry response of some of Metall's local officials to the new form of meetings that replaced the old regional bargaining councils (LO, 1994a).

Yet LO was now strongly committed to achieving parity and feminists within LO were able to persuade the board to approve a new action plan designed to achieve parity by 1998 – LO's one hundredth anniversary. Thus it was agreed that the number of women representatives at congresses must equal their share of the membership. LO agreed to employ women when vacancies arose until an equitable representation of the sexes, in headquarters and at the section level, had been reached. Finally those in charge of nominating committees are to be given training towards these ends. Although this stopped short of imposing a mandatory quota, the effort has borne fruit. Within LO, women's share of union posts now nearly matches their share of the membership (46 per cent). At LO's Congress 2000, Lundby-Wedin was confirmed as LO's first woman president. Success has not bred complacency, however. LO is developing a network for younger women employed by the unions to help them to reach leadership positions. The congress also approved a motion requiring LO and its affiliates to include the results of their efforts to achieve parity in their annual reports.

Table 3.1 Proportion of women in senior positions in ten largest LO unions (31 December 1997)

	SKAF	Metall	SEKO	Handel	Byggn.	Industri	Transp	Livs	Hotel and rest	Trä
Total membership	633,567	422,874	189,531	173,183	139,292	98,700	73,086	61,532	61,334	57,390
Women in membership	511,151	88,053	60,874	123,026	1528	40,154	11,509	25,416	41,908	11,048
Women as percentage of membership	80.7	20.8	32.1	71.0	1.1	40.7	15.7	41.3	68.3	19.3
Women as percentage of union congress delegates 1998	66.5	17.3	23.0	67.6	0.4	40.1	18.5	27.5	65.3	15.1
Women as percentage of i.e. TU board*	69.2	13.3	22.2	70.0	0	38.5	9.1	45.5	53.3	18.2
	9/13	2/15	4/18	7/10	0/10	5/13	1/11	5/11	8/15	2/11
Women as per cent of national full-time officers	44.2	9.5	17.6	30.3	0	14.3	0	0	55.5	0
Women as percentage of regional full-time officers	28.6	3.9	0	40.6	0	7.4	8.5	20.0	43.5	7.0

Note
* Only ordinary board members.

Pay equity

In addition to parity, in 1991 LO made pay equity one of its objectives in collective bargaining. In the past, women disappeared among other low-waged workers, whose lot LO and its unions sought to improve through solidaristic wages bargaining. This policy did much to narrow the gender wage gap, as we have seen. With the erosion of coordinated bargaining in the 1980s, however, the gap began to widen and this did not go unnoticed. A group of women associated with all three trade union centrals began to work together to document the way 'sex determines wages' in a way that cuts across collar lines. Their report mounted a strong argument for the revaluation of women-dominated jobs across the labour market. As the government moved to strengthen the Equal Opportunity Ombudsman's powers of initiative, feminists within LO seized on the opening this provided to make pay equity part of LO's agenda.

At the 1991 congress, LO agreed to prepare a policy to support the revaluation of women-dominated jobs before the 1993 bargaining round. In fact, LO did not play a coordinating role in that round but the Municipal Workers Union and its white-collar counterparts carried the banner of pay equity. In the preparations for the 1995 bargaining round, however, LO seemed to have worked out an agreement that would constitute the first step towards evening out differentials across the labour market. Thus all affiliates were to secure a special 'women's pot' which would vary with the proportion of women in the bargaining area. This would accelerate the process of *de facto* revaluation by giving a greater share of the room for increases to women-dominated branches and occupations. Thus, for example, Metall's members would get only 20 per cent of the pot while the Municipal Workers would get 80 per cent, reflecting the proportion of women among their membership.

The idea of a special women's pot was not uncontroversial. As then leader of Metall argued, redistribution to the women-dominated sector would make it difficult for the export sector to recruit the younger workers it needs. More broadly, redistribution challenges the pace-setting function of the export sector. Nevertheless Metall was prepared to support the inclusion of a women's pot. Eight months of internal negotiations came to naught, however when three unions – the Paper Workers, the Retail Workers Unions and the Transport Workers – all refused to give their consent.

The failure in part reflects the difficulty of persuading some of the unions to accept special measures for 'women', especially when these include white-collar and semi-professional workers like nurses, rather than the low-paid in general. Yet LO also failed because it had failed to move along with its affiliates, and develop a new relationship with TCO and SACO. As the leader of one LO affiliate argued, 'LO wanted to direct the wage setting process for the whole labour market this year but this was the last time. We need to work more closely with the white-collar workers even, in the planning stage'.[14] Most of LO's affiliates are working with their white-collar counterparts at the branch level. LO has not kept pace. Ironically then, it is LO's identification as working class, rather than its ability fully to embrace the broader wage earner identity, that currently stands in the way of an effective push for gender equity.

Race-ethnicity: from paternalism to mutual recognition

If 1991 marked a breakthrough point for women within LO, immigrants would have to wait. To be sure, the 1991 congress received the new Action Programme drawn up at the request of the 1986 congress but its perspective on immigrants remained paternalistic. By the late 1990s, however, LO seemed ready to see their role no longer as 'civilising' new members from 'less advanced' countries, but as promoting a 'mutual process where both Swedes and immigrants meet in dialogue' (LO 1998). LO's deepening understanding of ethnic-racial diversity has, in part, been sparked by developments external to the unions. It took activists within the unions themselves, however, to bring the point home.

Class inequality assumes an ethnic profile

Even before high unemployment became a general problem in the 1990s, the rate of unemployment was visibly and stubbornly higher among immigrants than Swedes (LO 1999c: 41 Table 3.3). In the 1990s, however, the gap really grew, especially for those coming from outside Europe. Nor have the children of immigrants, many of whom born and educated in Sweden, fared much better. Once again, the situation is worse for those most visibly 'different', i.e. those from Latin America, Africa and Asia (Schröder and Vilhelmsson 1998). Those who have come since the law changed in 1972 not only face a higher chance of being unemployed. They are also over-represented in low skilled jobs and jobs that offer limited opportunities for development (Wadensjö 1997: 209–10). They are also the most likely to have temporary jobs and jobs with high rates of work injury (Wadensjö 1997: 206 and 208).

Racism, and the xenophobia on which it feeds, has also been a force. Thus small, local racist parties began to appear in the 1980s (Castles and Miller 1998). Although the latter remain small, their anti-immigrant message finds a certain resonance in a country that has long understood itself as ethnically, linguistically homogeneous. The appearance of neo-Nazi groups in continental Europe during the 1990s encouraged similar groups in Sweden. Their isolated acts of violence had had little effect, especially when they targeted foreigners, until the assassination of a young Swedish trade unionist, Björn Söderberg, in October 1999. Söderberg had blown the whistle on a local union leader's membership in a neo-Nazi group.

The surfacing of racist sentiment, in turn, inspired government action. In 1986, the Social Democrats established an anti-Discrimination Ombudsman (DO). In 1987, a new commission, headed by the popular leader of Metall, was established to examine ways of combatting racism and xenophobia. Only in 1994, however, was discrimination at the workplace and in the labour market made illegal. Like the original equal opportunity law, the new legislation put the onus on the individuals concerned to prove discrimination. The government did, however, threaten legislation in line with the more proactive stance of the current equal opportunity law, if the labour market parties failed to promote workplace diversity. Accordingly, in 1997, unions and employer associations in the public and private sectors concluded an agreement on 'Diversity in the Workplace' and established a Council for Ethnic Diversity a year later. The latter has not, however, become an effective force, in large part because the employers have continued to resist proposals which 'infringe on the freedom to hire'.

Diversity and collective bargaining

Little had been done to implement the modest proposals for integration coming from the 1991 congress as attention focused on the sudden surge in unemployment and on defence against the Conservative-led government's attacks on the foundations of union power (Meidner and Mahon 1994). The passage of the new legislation, however, helped to turn the unions' attention to these issues. In 1995 LO appointed a senior person to deal with these issues and a new committee was established, with representatives from the key unions.[15] It is this group which oversaw the preparation of the important new document, *Diversity* (LO 1998).

Diversity breaks with the paternalism of the 1991 document. Rather than seeing immigrants as people with poor Swedish language skills and inappropriate cultural baggage, the problem is now understood as discrimination. Nor does responsibility rest solely with employers: the labour movement itself shares some of the blame: 'when they (immigrants) try to do something about their situation, they soon discover that all the democratic routes for change in politics, the union and the firm are closed. Immigrants are strongly under-represented in all decision-making fora in Sweden. This has hurt many immigrants' trust in democracy and the unions' (LO 1998: 10). The answer is integration – no longer defined simply as the freedom of cultural choice, while existing in an unchanged Swedish milieu. Rather, 'For the individual immigrant, integration means that one learns the language and the way the new society functions, that one enters the labour market and participates in the life of the society – at the same time as one maintains one's own language and culture. Yet integration also means that all who live in Sweden learn tolerance and an open attitude towards others, and learn to value and respect differences. Integration is also a mutual process in which all are participants' (LO 1998: 13).

Diversity was prepared to aid the affiliates and union locals in making the most of the opportunities provided by legislation and collective agreements. The handbook discusses how to recognise that discrimination exists – in hiring, wages, access to training, promotion and layoff procedures. It also makes it clear that harassment on the grounds of ethnicity as well as sex, is not acceptable. At the instigation of the new DO appointed in 1998, each of the unions has established an anti-discrimination contact person. This lays the basis for the kind of network that earlier developed among trade unionists dealing with equal opportunity.

Diversity within union ranks

It is not only work life, but also union representation that must change, however. The unions have to ensure that immigrants (and their children) are represented within their ranks. Many of the methods for achieving this are not new. Thus *Diversity* calls for courses and study circles oriented to immigrants but now these are to begin from the participants' knowledge. All union stewards, moreover, need education on integration questions. Their training needs to focus on combating discrimination in wages and working conditions as well as ways of encouraging immigrants to take an active part in the work of the union. Nominating committees are singled out for attention (LO 1998: 49). LO's new integration officer has also surveyed all local LO units to find out which are active on these issues. She also aims to get LO to incorporate race-ethnicity into broader surveys, like *Voices*, which has proved so effective in making the case for 'class and gender'.

Several of the unions have developed their own action plans. Just as in the 1970s, the Metal Workers Union has taken the lead. In addition to measures such as developing more open meeting forums and the formation of local action plans for engaging immigrants, Metall has encouraged the establishment of links with immigrant associations. The Municipal Workers Union has also developed an impressive plan. Its new strategy was given a high profile kickoff where representatives from locals across the country heard the union president and the Integration Minister underscore the importance of work on integration. This was but the first of a series of seminars that brought those involved in local projects together on a regular basis, providing new 'ammunition', ideas and energy. The union helped to fund local projects and has published a report on how the issues were tackled in Östergötland, one of the more innovative projects. Nor is integration treated as a side issue. It has become part of the union's main business. Thus for instance, the Municipal Workers' main project – 'Job Hunt' – sought out immigrants as local project leaders. The Municipal Workers was also one of the few unions that went out of its way to ensure that its representatives to LO's Congress 2000 reflect the age, sex and ethnicity of its membership (*LO Tidningen* 25.2.00).

The most important new development, however, occurred while *Diversity* was in preparation. In 1997, a new Network for Immigrant Union Activists (FAI) was established. In some respects, FAI is like the 'girls league'. Both differ from the earlier women's and immigrants committees in that they are informal (but sanctioned and funded) organisations within, and cutting across, the formal organisational structures of the unions. Unlike the league, however, FAI includes not only LO members but also activists within TCO and SACO. Together with LO's 'Idea Debate' group,[16] FAI has organised an important series of seminars on discrimination, racism, 'integration' and the unions' role. It organises courses for immigrants, through the trade union school at Runö where, in fact, the network got its start. It also speaks out for immigrants in public debate as well as participating in the consultation process on new legislation. It sees its role as not simply to support and encourage immigrants to become more active in their unions. It is there to give immigrants their own voice. FAI, in other words, enables immigrant workers to become active subjects, articulating their own needs, wants and dreams – within the common movement.

The assassination of Björn Söderberg further heightened the profile of integration questions. Already in *Diversity* LO had enjoined its affiliates to add an anti-racist clause to their statutes but when Söderberg blew the whistle on the neo-Nazi leader of a Retail Workers local, only two unions – the Hotel and Restaurant Workers and the Industrial Workers – had done so. A few local LO sections had become engaged in a systematic anti-racist work. Many, however, had done little prior to the assassination. Söderberg's assassination however galvanised the union movement. The entire LO leadership signed a public statement signalling their commitment to a long-term anti-racist campaign. LO highlighted the issue in its May Day celebrations. A 'map' of racist hot-spots across the country is being prepared, so resources can be targeted where they are most needed.

The assassination played such a role because it transformed the issue from a 'small question', seen of direct concern only to a minority, to one that struck at the core of union values. Thus, reflecting on why so little had been done to follow up on the 1996 resolution calling on the unions to take up an active struggle against racism and neo-Nazism, LO vice-president Inga-Lill noted, 'we thought that it was only a question of integration and did not recognise that it poses a real threat to democracy. I think that we defined the question too narrowly. The union must also defend democracy' (*LO Tidningen* 22.10.99). In other words, the threat to democracy is more readily understood as a threat to all, not just immigrants. The anti-racist struggle could, of course, draw energy and resources away from the struggle against the more mundane, but even deeper rooted, practices of discrimination in work life and in society at large. The network of activists that has developed within the union movement understand, however, that it can also provide an opening and they are prepared to use this to further the integration agenda. As Acchiardo notes, 'violence and threat are terrible but there is also discrimination in everyday life with which we must work parallel with the anti-racist struggle' (*LO Tidningen* 8.10.99).

Conclusions

In the golden age of Western labour movements, the Swedish LO was outstanding for its hegemonic capacity. It proved not only able and willing to form an impressive series of cross-class alliances but also to deal with other potential challenges to union solidarity by incorporating these too. Thus from the 1930s on, LO accepted women's right to work and, later, the need for special measures to support their organisation into unions and active participation as members. When it became clear that women were becoming an important part of the workforce, moreover, the Swedish unions embraced the feminist-humanist vision of gender equality and under this banner, acted forcefully to secure facilitating reforms. The unions also responded to the challenge of immigration, first by ensuring that immigrant workers enjoyed equality with their Swedish counterparts and then by pushing for special measures such as the right to Swedish language instruction on paid working time.

As impressive as these achievements were, they stopped short of a full 'reconciliation of the differences among the people'. Thus the efforts to form an alliance of white- and blue-collar workers into a new collectivity of wage earners was largely achieved through state policies that targeted the sphere of distribution. The old division between blue-collar workers and white-collar employees was kept alive not only in the Fordist division of labour but also by its institutionalisation within the union movement. LO was the union of blue-collar workers, the working class. This division in turn spilled over into the way that gender was dealt with. Thus LO was careful to mark its distance from the white-collar women who dominated the sex roles debate. And the struggle for gender equality was always subordinated to the struggle for class equality. It thus championed reforms in the name of the working-class family. Immigrants, too, were primarily members of the working class. To the extent that they had special problems, the unions were prepared to adopt special measures to help them become part of the Swedish working class.

While it proved more durable than most, the Swedish model of development has also gone into crisis and with it, the power relations on which it rested. As we have argued, however, the crisis also provided an opening for those within LO who argue for a deeper embrace of 'the differences within'. Thus wage earner feminists have made important gains: LO is now prepared to recognise that the struggle involves both 'class and sex'. Recognition of the reality of gender inequality came earlier than the recognition of discrimination and racism. The unions have, however, taken important steps to recognising that integration means establishing a dialogue, one in which both immigrants and Swedes are engaged in a process of learning and change.

Some progress has also been made towards putting the 'wage earner' dimension on firmer footing. At the branch level at least, LO unions have begun to work closely with their white-collar counterparts on a host of critical workplace and labour market issues. Unfortunately, however, the divide between has yet to be bridged beyond the branch level. Failure to do this will limit the unions' ability really to come to grips with the tendency towards labour market polarisation. It will also severely limit their ability to achieve gender and racial-ethnic equality for it is precisely women and immigrants who are the ones most adversely affected by growing inequalities in wages, employment security, training opportunities and work time.

One might ask whether LO's embrace of the (other) 'differences within' might not, in fact, make it more difficult for it to bridge the growing gulf between the male dominated unions in the export sector and the rest? After all, the large firms that dominate the export sector are trying to draw 'their' unions into a very different kind of cross-class alliance, one which pits this 'growth producing' sector against the 'parasitic' remainder. If the others can also be understood as 'different' on gender and racial-ethnic grounds, does this not make it easier for the industrial unions to join the employers?

The 'backlash' argument seems compelling but it fails to take into account the way that the industrial unions, too, have become involved in the struggle for gender and racial-ethnic equality. Of particular importance here is the Metal Workers Union. The latter was one of the driving forces behind the unions' solidaristic stance in the Fordist golden age. Yet we have also seen that it was one of the first LO unions to take up the struggle for equal opportunity, and even now it is recognised for its achievements in this regard. Metall was also a major force for immigrants' rights to adequate language instruction during working hours. It has remained ahead of many when it comes to 'integration'. And Metall remains the leading union within the industrial sector. In other words, 'backlash' is a possibility but only if the trade union centrals – and LO seems to carry more responsibility than TCO here – remain unwilling to make the moves necessary to establish the wage earner alliance upon new, more solid foundations.

Notes

1 An earlier version of this chapter was presented at the Twelfth International Conference of Europeanists, Chicago, 31 March 2000. The research was financed by a grant from the Social Science and Humanities Council of Canada. I would like to thank Ann Britt Hellmark for her research assistance, Bengt Abrahamsson for bibliographic support, and the Swedish Institute for Work Life Research. I would also like to thank Wuokko Knocke for her comments and for sharing her insights, as well as those whom I interviewed.

2 The LO and its 19 affiliates organise about 60 per cent of the unionised labour force but structural change has steadily increased the proportion of white-collar workers who have their own unions. The majority of the latter are affiliated with the TCO (*Tjänstemännens Centralorganisation*), while the smaller 'professional' unions are affiliated with SACO (Sveriges Akademikers Centralorganisation). Together, LO, TCO and SACO organise about 85 per cent of the labour force. In Sweden the growth of the service sector has been strongly associated with the rise in women's labour force participation rates.

3 The term 'subaltern' comes from the work of Antonio Gramsci and refers to classes and strata who do not form part of the dominant classes. In Sweden, it refers primarily to farmers and white-collar workers.

4 In addition to class, gender and race/ethnicity, disability and sexual orientation might also have been discussed here. The stories are likely to have had a lot in common with the ones told here in that, at one level, the Swedish labour movement (i.e. the Social Democratic Party and the LO) has long taken a relatively progressive stance and has funded national organisations representing (and run by and for) people with disabilities (Handikappförbundens samarbetsorgan) and homosexuals and lesbians (Riksförbunet för Sexuellt Lika Berättigande). This has by no means eradicated inequality and discrimination, however, and in the documents prepared for its Congress 2000, LO admits that more must be done by the union to combat such discrimination on the part of employers and in the movement itself (LO 1999a: 112–13). It would not have been possible, however, to provide an adequate political economy analysis of LO's response to all four of these. I therefore decided to concentrate on the three which touched the greatest number of wage earners – class, gender and race/ethnicity.

5 'Neutralisation' means taking action to prevent differences as between workers from being used by employers to 'divide and conquer'.

6 Those interviewed include: Lotta Grönblad, Hotel and Restaurant Workers Union; Elisabeth Brolin, who deals, *inter alia*, with gender questions at the Municipal Workers Union; Ann Sofi Hermannson, formerly with the Metal Workers, now with LO; Maria Paz Acciardo, responsible for race-ethnic integration questions at LO; Ingemar Lindberg, formerly in charge of the 'Idea debate' programme which plays an important part in the renewal process; Carlos Nunez Runo, one of the founders of the network of immigrants active in the unions (FAI); Margareta Wadstein, Ombudsman on questions of discrimination; and correspondence with Anita Edam, who is responsible for integration questions at the Municipal Workers Union. The interviews took place in the spring of 1999 and 2000.

7 The SAP was in office, at times with the support of other parties, from 1932 to 1976. It returned to office between 1982 and 1991 and again from 1994 to the present. LO and

the SAP form the two official wings of the labour movement – though there are also affiliated organisations representing women, youth and other groups.

8 While women have come to form around 45 per cent of LO's membership, they account for a larger share – approximately 60 per cent of TCO unions members. Conversely, LO has a larger share of immigrant workers.

9 LO's policy changes in the 1960s reflected, in part, the efforts of a small but influential group within LO, who formed part of 'Group 222'. The latter was an important network linking feminist activists within the Social Democratic, Liberal and Left parties, LO, TCO and the media together. Their feminist-humanism was considered insufficient by the more radical young feminists of the 1970s in the SSKF and small extra-parliamentary 'Group 8'. While LO could dismiss the latter, it could not ignore the SSKF, which formed part of the wider labour movement of which it too formed a part.

10 For the 1960s generation of Swedish feminists, including those in LO like Gertrud Sigurdsen and Per Holmberg, the replacement of the Women's by the Family Council reflected the goal not only of supporting women's right fully to participate in paid work but also men's right (and duty) to 'care'. And there was parity of men and women on the new Family Council, suggesting that men, too, were/should be interested in these issues. Hirdman argues it also reflected LO's increased interest in social policy as a means of pursuing class equality (1998: 259).

11 On Swedish immigration policy see Ålund and Schierup (1991), Castles and Miller (1998) and Knocke and Ng (1999).

12 Although this certainly helped to keep the rate of unionisation as high among immigrants as among Swedish nationals, the ease of organisation meant that Swedish unions often did little to encourage these new members to become active. See Knocke's important study of locals of the Factory and Municipal Workers unions (1986).

13 SOU 1987: 19 *Varannan Damernas Slutbetänkande från utredningen om kvinnorepresentation.*

14 These are the words of the then-leader of the State Employees' Union, as cited in *LO Tidningen* 28.4.95.

15 The core consisted of the Municipal Workers, Metall, the Retail Workers Union, Hotel and Restaurant Workers, the Cleaners and the Union of National Government Workers (SEKO). The core includes most of the important unions but a number that have a relatively high percentage of immigrant members – like the Industrial Workers (former Factory Workers and Textiles) Union and the Food Workers. The latter have become more active, especially the Industrial Workers, since the assassination of Söderberg.

16 Idea Debate is the intellectual ginger group within LO, which has carried on the task of winning back the ideological ground lost to SAF in the 1980s, originally assigned to the Justice Project. On the Justice Project and *Idedebatt* see Mahon (1999, 149–50).

References

Ahrne, G. and Clement, W. (1994) 'A new regime? Class representation within the Swedish state', in R. Mahon and W. Clement (eds) *Swedish Social Democracy: A Model in Transition*, Toronto: Canadian Scholars' Press.

Ålund, A. and C-U Schierup (1991) *Paradoxes of Multiculturalism: Essays on Swedish Society*, Aldershot: Avebury.

Åström, (1994) 'Delad makt och facklig demokrati', *Delad makt – kvinnor och facklig demokratisering* Samtal om Rättvis No. 19 Stockholm: Brevskolan.

Baude, A. (ed.) (1992) *Visionen om jämställdhet*, Stockholm: SNS.

Briskin, L. (1999) 'Unions and Women's Organizing in Canada and Sweden', in L. Briskin and M. Eliasson (eds) *Women's Organizing and Public Policy in Canada and Sweden*, Montreal: McGill-Queens.

Castles, S. and Miller, M. (1998) *The Age of Migration. International Population Movements in the Modern World*, 2nd edn, New York: Guilford.

Edam, A. (2000) 'Arbetet inom LO med invandrar och integrationsfrågor. Kommunals Integrations projekt', mimeo February/March.

Esping-Andersen, G. (1985) *Politics Against Markets: The Social Democratic Road to Power*, Princeton: Princeton University Press.

de Geer, H. (1992) *SAF i tio decennier*, Stockholm: SAF.

Hammar, T. (1988) 'Mellan rasism och reglering: Invandrings politikens ideologi och historia', *Arbetar historia* 46.

Hansson, S.-O. and Lodenius, A.-L. (1988) *Operation högervridning*, Stockholm: Tiden.

Higgins, W. (1996) 'The Swedish Municipal Workers' Union – a study in the new political unionism', *Economic and Industrial Democracy* 17: 2 167–98.

Hirdman, Y. (1994) 'Social engineering and the woman question: Sweden in the 1930s', in Rianne Mahon and Wallace Clement (eds) *Swedish Social Democracy: A Model in Transition*, Toronto: Canadian Scholars' Press.

—— (1998) *Med kluven tunga: LO och Genusordningen* Stockholm: Atlas.

Hobson, B. (1993) 'Feminist strategies and gendered discourses in welfare states: Married women's right to work in the United States and Sweden', in Seth Koven and Sonya Michel (eds) *Mothers of a New World: Maternalist Politics and the Origins of Welfare States*, New York: Routledge.

Jenson, J. and Mahon, R. (1993) 'Representing solidarity: Class, gender and the crisis of Social Democratic Sweden', *New Left Review* 201: 76–100.

Karlsson, G. (1990) *Manssamhället till behag?*, Stockholm: Tiden.

Kjellberg, A. (1998) 'Sweden: Restoring the model?', in A. Ferner and R. Hyman (eds) *Changing Industrial Relations in Europe*, 2nd edn, Oxford: Blackwell.

Knocke, W. (1986) *Invandrade kvinnor i lönearbete och fack*, Stockholm: Arbetslivscentrum.

—— (1994) 'Gender, ethnicity and technological change' in R. Mahon and W. Clement (eds) *Swedish Social Democracy: A Model in Transition*, Toronto: Canadian Scholars' Press.

—— (1997) 'Trade unions, immigration and immigrant workers: The case of Sweden', mimeo.

Knocke, W. and Ng, R. (1999) 'Women's organizing and immigration: Comparing the Canadian and Swedish experiences', in L. Briskin and M. Eliasson (eds) *Women's Organizing and Public Policy in Canada and Sweden*, Montreal: McGill-Queens.

Korpi, W. (1978) *The Working Class in Welfare Capitalism*, London: Routledge and Kegan Paul.

Kyle, G. (1979) *Gästarbeterska i manssamhället*, Stockholm: Liber.

LO (1969) *Fackföreningsrörelsen och familjepolitiken*, Stockholm: Prisma.

—— (1976) *Fackföreningsrörelsen och familjepolitiken: Rapport till LO Kongressen*, Stockholm: Prisma.

—— (1981) *Jämställdhet och solidaritet*, Stockholm: Prisma.

—— (1987) *Kvinnor i facket: en aktivitetsprogram för att få fler kvinnor i det fackliga arbetet*, LO.

—— (1990) Klass och Kön, Stockholm: Brevskolan.

—— (1991) *Invandrarpolitiskt Program*, LO.

—— (1992) *Röster om facket och jobbet*, Stockholm: Brevskolan.

—— (1994) *Röster om jobbet och facket*, Stockholm: Brevskolan.

—— (1994a) 'Är facket demokratiskt nog? Reportage om Rätteviseutredningens arbetssätt och andra exempel på facklig förnyelse', mimeo.

—— 1998) *Mångfald – en handbok för integration på arbetsplatsen*.

—— (1999a) *Frihet Tilsammans: LOs Demokratirapport om makt, medlemmar och möjligheter*, LO.

—— (1999b) *Röster om facket och jobbet: Synen på lönesättning och löneskillnader*, LO.

—— (1999c) *Invandrare på den svenska arbetsmarknaden: En delrapport från LO-projektet Ökad Sysselsättning*, LO.

Lundby-Wedin, W. and Hatt, G. (1998) *På spaning efter vänsterförnyelse*, Stockholm: Hjälmar and Jörgen.

Mahon, R. (1994) 'Wage-earners and/or co-workers? Contested identities', *Economic and Industrial Democracy* 15(3): 355–83.

—— (1996) 'Women wage earners and the future of Swedish Unions', *Economic and Industrial Democracy* 17(4): 545–86.

—— (1999) '"Both wage earner and mother": Women's organizing and childcare policy in Sweden and Canada', in L. Briskin and M. Eliasson (eds) *Women's Organizing and Public Policy in Canada and Sweden*, Montreal: McGill-Queens.

Martin, A. (1978) 'Dynamics of change in a Keynesian political economy', *State and Economy in Contemporary Capitalism*, London: Croom Helm.

—— (1984) 'Trade unions in Sweden: Strategic responses to change and crisis', in G. Ross *et al.* (eds) *West Germany, Britain and Sweden: Unions and Economic Crisis*, London: George Allen and Unwin.

Meidner, R. and Mahon, R. (1994) '"System shift" or, What future the Swedish Model?', *Socialist Review* 57–78.

Nermo, M. (1997) 'Yrkessegregering efter kön – ett internationellt perspektiv', I. Persson and E. Wadensjö (eds) *Glastak och glasväggar? Den könssegregerade arbetsmarknaden*, SOU: 137 (Swedish Government Inquiry).

Nyberg, A. (1997) *Women, men and incomes: Gender equality and economic independence*, SOU: 87 (Swedish Government Inquiry).

Olsen, G. (1994) 'Labour mobilization and the strength of capital: The rise and fall of economic democracy in Sweden', in R. Mahon and W. Clement, *Swedish Social Democracy*, Toronto: Canadian Scholars' Press.

Persson, I. (1990) 'The third dimension: Equal status between Swedish women and men', *Generating Equality in the Welfare State: The Swedish Experience* Oslo: Nordic University Press.

Pestoff, V. (1991) 'The demise of the Swedish model and the rise of organized business as a major political actor', paper presented at the Society for the Advancement of Socio-Economics, Stockholm.

Pontusson, J. (1987) 'Radicalization and retreat in Swedish Social Democracy', *New Left Review* 165.

—— (1992a) *The Limits of Social Democracy: Investment Politics in Sweden*, Ithaca: Cornell University Press.

—— (1992b) 'At the end of the road: Swedish Social Democracy in crisis', *Politics and Society* 20(3): 305–32.

Poulantzas, N. (1973) *Classes in Contemporary Capitalism*, London: New Left Books.

Rubery, J., Smith, M., Fagan, C. and Grimshaw, D. (1998) *Women and European Employment*, London: Routledge.

Sainsbury, D. (1994) 'Women's and men's social rights: Gendering dimensions of welfare states', in D. Sainsbury (ed.) *Gendering Welfare States*, London: Sage.

Schröder, L. and Vilhelmsson, R. (1998) '"Sverigespecifikt" humankapital och ungdomars etablering på arbetsmarknaden', *Ekonomisk Debatt* 26(8).

Streijffert, H. (1983) *Studier i den svenska kvinnorörelsen*, University of Göteborg: Department of Sociology.

Scott, H. (1983) *Sweden's Right to be Human: Sex Role Equality – the Goal and the Reality*, New York: ME Sharpe.

Stephens, J. (1979) *The Transition from Capitalism to Socialism*, London: Macmillan.

Swenson, P. (1989) *Fair Shares: Unions, Pay and Politics in Sweden and West Germany*, Ithaca: Cornell University Press.

—— (1991) 'Bringing capital back in, or social democracy reconsidered: Employer power, cross-class alliances and centralization of industrial relations in Denmark and Sweden', *World Politics* 43(4): 513–44.

Therborn, G. (1983) 'Why some classes are more successful than others', *New Left Review* 138: 37–55.

Therborn, G. (1986) *Why Are Some Peoples More Unemployed than Others?*, London: Verso.

Wadensjö, E. (1997) 'Invandrarkvinnornas arbetsmarknad', in I. Persson and E. Wadensjö (eds) *Glastak och glasväggar?*, SOU: 137 (Swedish Government Inquiry).

Waldemarsson, Y. (1992) 'Kontrakt under förhandling – LO, kvinnorna och makten', in Y. Hirdman and G. Åström (eds) *Kontrakt i kris*, Stockholm: Allmänna Förlaget.

—— (1998) *Mjukt till formen, hårt till innehållet LO: s kvinnorråd 1947–1967*, Stockholm: Atlas

Wikman, A., Andersson, A. and Bastin, M. (1998) *Nya relationer i arbetslivet*, Stockholm: Arbetslivsinstitut.

4 Trade unions, segmentation and diversity

The organising dilemmas in Malaysia

Patricia Todd and Mhinder Bhopal

Introduction

Malaysian trade unions operate in a political and economic environment in which ethnicity fuelled by ethno-economic divisions has dominated Malaysian political discourse. The economic development process that occurred rapidly over the past three decades focused on improving the position of the Malays whose socio-economic status was substantially less than that of the Chinese. Industrial development aimed to, and succeeded in, providing Malay waged work and business opportunities.

In comparison with the debates centred around ethnic difference in Malaysia, gender issues have received minimal attention from those exercising power. Yet much of the development was reliant on the utilisation of female labour in supposedly low-skill, low-wage electronics based export orientation. The percentage of manufacturing workers who were women increased from 28.1 in 1970 to 46.4 in 1990 before declining to 41.1 per cent in 2000 (6th Malaysian Plan; 8th Malaysian Plan).

Given the rapid industrialisation, urbanisation and growth of Malay labour and its increasing dominance of the trade union movement the main concentration of this chapter will be Malay male and female labour. By 2000, Malays constituted two-thirds of the total population and Malay labour had undergone the greatest transformation with its rapid incorporation into wage employment.[1] From constituting only 25 per cent of all employees in 1947, Malay workers increased to 48 per cent by 1980 and 52.4 per cent in 1995 (Jomo and Todd 1994; 7th Malaysia Plan). This paralleled their growing participation in manufacturing, from 29 per cent of all manufacturing employees in 1970 to 50.6 per cent in 1995 (see Table 4.1). This substantial change in the wage-paid workforce, from which unions draw their members, resulted in equally substantial change in the ethnic composition of the union movement. The percentage of Malay members grew from 21 in 1960 to 50 by 1980 and over 70 by 2000.

The changed composition of the wage-paid workforce and union movement is significant because for long it has been anticipated that the economic development of Malays would accentuate intra-ethnic differences and undermine structures of control premised on inter-ethnic difference which served to heighten intra-group solidarity. These perhaps economistic approaches, have possibly under-emphasised the salience of ethnic identity and the significance of the fact that Malaysia's industrialisation has occurred on the basis of a gendered division of labour resulting in unequal returns between male and female workers.

We argue, in agreement with many authors, that ethnicity hampered the development of class-based organisation amongst workers and that it has, indeed, seemed to divide Malaysian unions. Furthermore Malaysian unions have not been particularly successful in making themselves relevant to women workers, thus reducing their overall strength and relevance even further. However we are aware that this 'problem' is not confined to Malaysia. Trade unions' ability to respond to and utilise the multiple identities of labour has been viewed as generally weak, not least because unions have prioritised class over ethnicity and gender, often ignoring the significance of these other 'parts' of labour identity (Grint 1991: 250). Historically unions displayed a lack of interest in women and ethnic minorities although more recently, within the context of declining union strength and changing labour market participation, there has been greater recognition of the need to broaden their inclusion. Nevertheless, we believe that Malaysia as a patriarchal society in which ethnicity dominates virtually all socio-political and economic activity provides an interesting case study of the impact and interplay of class, ethnicity and gender on labour movements in multi-ethnic societies.

We begin our exposition with a brief overview of the Malaysian context and its relevance for Malaysian employment. We then proceed to outline and discuss the implications of the changing composition of the labour force, and the response of the state and labour movement to such change. To provide the broad coverage that we intend, our piece ends by exploring how issues of gender and ethnicity impact at workplace level. We conclude by arguing that issues of gender and ethnicity need to be transcended by the labour movement if it is to represent the voice of workers and overcome the historical fragmentation and divisions that have hindered Malaysian labour.

A short history of Malaysian labour – ethnicity, gender and class

In 2000 the Malaysian population was composed of 66.1 per cent Malays, 25.3 per cent Chinese and 7.4 per cent Indians (8th Malaysia Plan). Despite these apparently clear groupings there is as much difference 'within' as there is 'between' each ethnic group, depending on clan or caste origins as well as social class. Thus, despite easy theorising, it is important to note that in reality the picture is a complex mix of intra- and inter-ethnic group harmony and conflict (Husin Ali 1984). Nevertheless, Gomez and Jomo (1997) argue that many of Malaysia's problems are believed to stem from the multi-ethnic nature of the population. The ethnic divisions within organised labour and the broader Malaysian society were created and entrenched under colonial rule. Chinese and Indian workers were brought in to ensure a supply of low wage labour. They were employed in different occupations and industries under differing wages and conditions, making working-class unity difficult.

Since Independence in 1957, ethnicity has been the prime organising principle and basis of electoral mobilisation and competition in Malaysia. The main incumbent and opposition parties are largely organised on an ethnic basis. The government has also been antagonistic towards attempts to organise political groupings based on class, and the political focus has privileged ethnicity at the expense of other identities. In this sense the political domain has been rather conservative in as far as there has been lack of a sustained and deep challenge within the political sphere drawing upon non-ethnic, particularly class issues inherent in the social structure.

This ethnicisation of politics has had a significant impact on the development and strategies of the Malaysian labour movement. On the one hand, it has been unable to develop symbiotic links with political parties without undermining the horizontal basis of trade union solidarity; on the other, it has been unable to exert pressure through ethnically organised oppositional political parties, without the potential accusation of ethnic identification.

Aware that trade unions cannot remain outside politics, the Malaysian Trades Union Congress (MTUC) has produced a labour manifesto specifying the conditions under which the movement would endorse parliamentary candidates and particular political parties during elections, thereby avoiding being ideologically tied to them. This pragmatic approach has enabled the Malaysian trade union movement to maintain the integrity of its central role in promoting the labour interest. However, individual trade union activists and leaders have tended to be party political activists, with diverse affiliations to different but essentially ethnically based parties, which do not necessarily pursue a labour agenda. While the MTUC claims to be the only mass multi-racial organisation in Malaysia, cross-ethnic trade union identity has been undermined when 'pulling' integrative forces of labour identity are 'pushed' by the divisions resulting from ethnicity and attachment to ethnically based political parties.

Apart from the ethnicisation of politics, Malaysian labour has also had to contend with a post 1970 economic development process that has been portrayed ethnically. Politicians have used ethnic appeals to disguise class-based problems. Chinese wealth has been constantly contrasted with Malay poverty. Economic development goals – expressed in the affirmative action orientated New Economic Policy and the National Development Policy – became associated very specifically with the improvement of the economic position of the Malays. This ethnic discourse has served to mask intra-ethnic differences whereby there are wealthy elites amongst both the Chinese and the Malays and poverty is not confined to the Malays. Again, this has served to deter class-based action, as the economic goals of each ethnic group are seemingly (re)presented as different and, sometimes, in conflict.

The ethno-nationalistic basis of the affirmative action policies served the ruling coalition in so far as criticism of the incumbent political elites was, by association, a criticism of Malay rights and advancement. The success, however, of the Malaysian development process has increased the potential for class-based divisions to rise above those of ethnic identity, particularly amongst Malays. This is partly due to the fact that the benefits of economic development have flowed disproportionately to particular factions of the Malay political and business elite, a factor which has resulted in intra-Malay political conflict. At the same time, industrialisation has resulted in Malay workers becoming the majority of the industrial workforce and the union movement while previously they had been largely isolated from the industrial working class. These factors, in combination, have given rise to the potential for increasing intra-Malay economic and political competition.

Leaving aside issues of class, it would not be unfair to conclude that gender and women's issues have tended to arise within ethnic boundaries and to be subject to the hegemonic effects of ethnic identities in the political discourse (Chee and Ng 1997). While the superordinate goal of Malay economic advancement has been portrayed as gender free, in reality Malaysia has been gender dependent in the political and economic domain. Although women remain peripheral to the political discourses, the main political parties rely on women to mobilise female votes, which is not surprising given that half the membership of the ruling party is composed of women while they comprise less than one tenth of the parliamentarians (Ng and Kasim 2000). This may explain why, according to Ng and Kasim, there have been 'tokenistic' gestures to women's issues and why most parties maintain a women's wing.

The economy is, and has been, heavily dependent on utilising working women to provide a source of 'docile', low-cost, low-skilled labour to attract investment into the export orientated industries (Grace 1990; Kaur 1999). The issue of women and work has prompted some concern with Lim (1990: 5) asserting that the Islamic patriarchy opposed women undertaking waged work outside the home, and especially under foreign male authority. Debate and concern over the issue of 'loose morals' among young, single factory women has also been noted (Lie 2000). However, Malay tradition has not necessarily subordinated women and Kaur (1998) argues that in pre-capitalist Malaysia chores and harvest duties were shared within the household and that men and women performed most cultivation tasks as a family unit although cultural values gave women's roles and work less status than those of men.

Malaysia's integration into the international economy and the concomitant emergence of Malay male waged labour resulted in a redefinition of the role women performed in their households and communities. Commodity production was undertaken by men and domestic labour by women and ultimately led to the erosion of the position of women in Malaysian society. Lie (2000) has argued that in a traditional Malay village both men and women would own land and under customary law (*adat*) sons and daughters would inherit equal shares. Furthermore, the Malay village society allowed women freedom of action for economic activities and divorce and remarriage. Recent and past ethnographic accounts present Malay women as economic supporters and decision makers within their families. This author concludes that the reservation of public roles for men and a domestic role for women gained more acceptance with the Islamic resurgence of the 1980s; these 'new' ideologies were to a large extent directed at women, requiring them to maintain certain moral standards and religious duties in their families and in society at large. Nevertheless, it should be noted that the fact that women have both Islam and Malay traditions providing different systems of reference for rights and duties, may allow for manipulation and flexibility.

Thus, in summary, Malaysian labour has historically operated within a political and economic context in which ethnicity has been the predominant political discourse, which is reflected in the political and economic structures. Gender has been seemingly ignored at the altar of inter-ethnic competition despite the reality of gender being highly significant within both the political and economic spheres.

The changing composition of labour

This subsection considers the impact of Malaysia's industrial development upon the composition of the workforce and the union movement, both in terms of ethnicity and gender. Table 4.1 shows the changing occupational and ethnic distribution of labour between 1970 and 1995. Three important areas of change are reflected in the table: the nature of economic activity in Malaysia, the association of ethnicity with occupation and the distribution of Malay employment.

Malaysia's shift from the old to the new international division of labour has been dramatic as indicated by the fact that by 1995 the manufacturing sector accounted for 79.6 per cent of all exports. This transformation is evidenced in the changing composition of employment whereby in 1970 50 per cent of the paid workforce was in agriculture and 9 per cent in manufacturing, compared with 18 per cent and 26 per cent respectively by 1995. However, the manufacturing sector, like the earlier foreign investment in the primary sector, is highly concentrated in the production of electrical and electronic goods and particularly in the latter, indicating a continuing dependency on the metropolitan centres. Malaysia has become the third largest producer and largest exporter of semi-conductors in the world while the electrical and electronics sector alone accounted for 72.5 per cent of all manufactured exports in 2000 (8th Malaysia Plan). Despite the predictions of the flexible specialisation theorists of the return of first world capital to its home and market base, Malaysia has continued to receive substantial investments.

The association of ethnicity with industry still prevails although the degree of segregation has been declining since 1970. In 1995, Malay workers were over-represented in agriculture, utilities and services while the Chinese were over-represented in trade and commerce, finance and construction. Indian workers were concentrated disproportionately in transport, storage/communication, manufacturing and utilities. Given the industry basis of union organisation and the illegality of general unionism, individual unions in particular sectors tend to be dominated by a particular ethnic group (Jomo and Todd 1994), thereby conferring a *de facto* ethnic basis to union organisation, which has been downplayed by, but nonetheless significant for, the MTUC.

The most significant change, in terms of this discussion, has been the change in the distribution of Malay employment. For instance, in 1970 64 per cent of Malays were engaged in agriculture and 5 per cent in manufacturing; by 1995, the comparable figures were 21 and 25 per cent respectively. In absolute numbers manufacturing provided employment for just over 73,000 Malays in 1970, but

Table 4.1 Employment by occupation and ethnic group, Malaysia, 1970, 1990 and 1995 ('000)

Sector	1970					1990					1995				
	Malay	Chinese	Indian	Other	Total	Malay	Chinese	Indian	Other	Total	Malay	Chinese	Indian	Other	Total
Agriculture	922.3	292.9	131.7	5.0	1359	1179.9	251.6	131.9	174.6	1738.0	887.2	175.7	92.9	272.9	1428.7
	64	*30*	*46*	*19*	*50*	*33*	*12*	*23*	*43*	*26*	*21*	*7*	*14*	*39*	*18**
	67.9	*21.6*	*9.7*	*0.4*	*100*	*67.9*	*14.5*	*7.6*	*10*	*100*	*62.1*	*12.3*	*6.5*	*19.1*	*100***
Mining	13.3	37.1	4.6	0.3	55.3	19.2	12.1	3.4	2.3	37.0	23.8	8.5	4.7	3.7	40.7
	1	*4*	*2*	*1*	*2*	*.6*	*.6*	*.6*	*.6*	*.6*	*1*	*.4*	*1*	*1*	*1*
	24.0	*67.1*	*8.3*	*0.5*	*100*	*51.9*	*32.7*	*9.2*	*6.2*	*100*	*58.4*	*20.9*	*11.5*	*9.1*	*100*
Manufacturing	73.1	164.5	13.3	1.0	251.9	619.1	505.0	146.9	62.0	1333.0	1038.0	634.0	242.1	137.5	2051.6
	5	*17*	*5*	*4*	*9*	*18*	*23*	*26*	*15*	*20*	*25*	*26*	*37*	*19*	*26*
	29.0	*65.3*	*5.3*	*0.4*	*100*	*46.4*	*37.7*	*11.0*	*4.7*	*100*	*50.6*	*30.9*	*11.8*	*6.7*	*100*
Construction	13.0	43.1	3.6	0.2	59.9	148.0	217.8	24.5	33.7	424.0	252.5	281.6	33.0	92.3	659.4
	.9	*4*	*1*	*1*	*2*	*4*	*10*	*4*	*8*	*6*	*6*	*12*	*5*	*13*	*8*
	21.7	*72.0*	*6.0*	*0.3*	*100*	*34.9*	*51.8*	*5.8*	*7.9*	*100*	*38.3*	*42.7*	*5.0*	*14*	*100*
Utilities	9.5	3.6	6.4	0.3	19.8	33.0	4.7	8.0	1.3	47.0	51.1	6.5	7.8	3.7	69.1
	.6	*.4*	*2*	*1*	*.7*	*.9*	*.2*	*1*	*.3*	*.7*	*1*	*.3*	*1*	*1*	*1*
	48.0	*18.0*	*32.3*	*3.0*	*100*	*70.2*	*10*	*17*	*2.8*	*100*	*73.9*	*9.4*	*11.3*	*5.4*	*100*
Trade and Commerce	64.3	179.8	29.1	1.4	274.6	420.2	652.2	82.7	62.9	1218.0	488.6	674.5	85.0	79.7	1327.8
	5	*18*	*10*	*5*	*10*	*12*	*30*	*15*	*16*	*18*	*12*	*28*	*13*	*11*	*17*
	23.4	*65.5*	*10.6*	*0.5*	*100*	*34.5*	*53.5*	*6.8*	*5.2*	*100*	*36.8*	*50.8*	*6.4*	*6.0*	*100*
Transport, Storage/Comm.	41.5	39.1	16.7	0.7	98.0	148.0	92.9	45.1	16.0	302.0	210.6	118.2	48.3	18.2	395.2
	3	*.1*	*6*	*3*	*4*	*4*	*4*	*8*	*4*	*5*	*5*	*5*	*7*	*3*	*5*
	42.3	*39.9*	*17.0*	*0.7*	*100*	*49.0*	*30.8*	*14.9*	*5.3*	*100*	*53.3*	*29.9*	*12.2*	*4.6*	*100*
Finance	—	—	—	—	—	106.2	120.7	25.5	5.6	258.0	171.5	160.9	36.3	9.8	378.5
						3	*6*	*5*	*1*	*4*	*4*	*7*	*6*	*1*	*5*
						41.1	*46.8*	*9.9*	*2.2*	*100*	*45.3*	*42.5*	*9.6*	*2.6*	*100*
Services	223.9	173.5	66.3	8.9	472.6	859.8	318.0	102.6	48.6	1329.0	1021.6	339.5	112.6	90.7	1564.4
	16	*18*	*23*	*34*	*17*	*24*	*15*	*18*	*12*	*20*	*25*	*14*	*17*	*13*	*20*
	47.4	*36.7*	*14.0*	*1.9*	*100*	*64.7*	*23.9*	*7.7*	*3.7*	*100*	*65.3*	*21.7*	*7.2*	*5.8*	*100*
Misc.	74.1	55.6	14.3	1.2	145.2	—	—	—	—	—	—	—	—	—	—
	.5	*6*	*5*	*5*	*5*										
	51.0	*38.3*	*10.0*	*0.8*	*100*										
Total	1435.0	989.0	286.0	26.4	2736.4	3533.4	2175.0	570.6	407.0	6686.0	4149.9	2399.4	662.6	708.5	7915.4
	52.4	*36.2*	*10.5*	*0.1*	*100*	*52.9*	*32.5*	*8.5*	*6.1*	*100*	*52.4*	*30.3*	*8.4*	*8.9*	*100*

Sources: 6th, 7th Malaysia Plan; Jomo and Todd (1994).

Note: *indicates the proportion of ethnic group employment across sectors by year (to be read vertically); ** indicates the proportion of Malays, Chinese and Indians employed within the sector by year (to be read across).

over 1 million in 1995. The comparable figure for services, which together with manufacturing accounted for 50 per cent of Malay employment in 1995, are 224,000 in 1970 but just over 1 million in 1995 (7th Malaysia Plan 1996; Jomo and Todd 1994). Much of this change has come about due to the development of Malaysia's manufacturing sector. Between 1990 and 1995 almost 720,000 manufacturing jobs were created which added an additional 420,000 Malays into manufacturing employment accounting for almost 70 per cent of all new employment for Malays.

Another important consequence of the development of the manufacturing sector has been the growth of female participation in the industrial sector. Ninety five per cent of new manufacturing jobs created between 1980 and 1986/87 were taken up by women (Kaur 1999). Indeed it is common knowledge that the electronics workforce was composed mainly of rural Malay women (Wee 2000). This trans-formation in the position of Malay women raises significant issues for them not only in association with their own income but also in terms of occupational health and safety consequences. Thus, while in the early days young, single Malay women factory workers were expected to exit the labour market upon marriage and were therefore seen as temporary participants and secondary earners (Grace 1990), there are indications that this is changing and length of service is increasing. This, together with the facts that factory workers' income is used to support their families and that more and more continue working after marriage, undermine those who continue to argue that lack of women's participation in the union movement is a result of their transient employment status. Furthermore, women's exposure to chemicals in the modern factories where women semi-conductor workers have been reported to be suffering from cancers, miscarriages and birth defects owing to exposures to toxic chemical and gases (Corpwatch 1999) indicates a growing need to organise and ensure trade union involvement in the employment of such workers.

The labour movement is reflecting the relative and absolute change in the ethnic composition of the working population through increasing Malay dominance; over 70 per cent of trade union leaders and members are Malay, and 60 per cent of the MTUC general council is estimated to be Malay. This change in the ethnic composition of the labour movement is welcomed by the Malay President, but viewed with suspicion by the Indian contingent as the following quotations demonstrate:

> The bulk of the workers today are Malays, bumiputra-natives . . . in the early days of the labour movement there were not many Malay leaders. . . . What is significant and quite encouraging [is] the situation has changed as far as Malay leadership and trade unions are concerned. . . . Before it was an Indian majority. Now it's a Malay majority. It's a very good sign. They know what they are looking for, they no longer have to rely on the government, they can rely on their own resources. . . . There is a need for there to be Malay working-class leaders to make sure the balance is there . . . the only people who can fight are the Malay leaders.
>
> (Interview, MTUC President 1999)

In the last MTUC elections it was felt that the President wanted to push away all the Indians . . . [however] he needed [the General Secretary] because he was able to bring a lot of the Indian delegates into [his] camp, but the Indians are feeling very much pushed out.

(Interview, MTUC Research Officer 1999)

In contrast, the growth of female participation in the industrial workforce has had much less impact on the gender composition of the union leadership. For instance, in 2000 41 per cent of the membership of MTUC affiliated unions was female but of the 158 members of the general council 151 were males. There was only one woman amongst the 30 members of the executive committee of the MTUC and even that was a position reserved for the Women's Committee (Interview, MTUC Women's Committee 2000). This is partly explained by employer and state opposition to the unionisation of electronics workers (Grace 1990) but also due to the lack of inclusion by, and support from, the male-dominated union movement in terms of resources, training and solidarity. As the head of the Women's Committee stated:

[we] cannot trust the trade unions to look after gender issues . . . from my experience with the MTUC it's always the women's issues that comes last. It's not like Europe . . . at the moment, for me, it's not really progress because implementing a policy on gender is very, very difficult . . . even to organise a workshop for the MTUC is not easy. There are so many issues we face on gender issues, like between management and unions . . . we have to fight, even in the collective agreement, to put forward a childcare centre because the issues are secondary . . . even the females themselves say this is about welfare, welfare is not a negotiation right . . . We have insufficient resources, we are part-time . . . we need funds . . . we need power . . . we need the staff.

(Interview, MTUC Head of Women's Committee 2000)

State IR policy and Malay workers

The potential threat to Malay solidarity from a united labour movement has not been lost on the ruling elites of the Mahathir government. The government, rather than attempt incorporation has excluded labour from the export orientated developmentalist agenda through fragmentation and marginalisation, and the 1980's promotion of business orientated in-house unionism (Wad 1988; Jomo and Todd 1994; Wad and Jomo 1994; Kuruvilla and Arudsothy 1995). In the 1970s the state sought to control and limit the parameters of legitimate trade union activity, and arguably this was politically easier owing to the fact of a small Malay working class in these early development years. But as Malay participation in manufacturing increased the government switched to a policy of favouring in-house unionism to prevent the development of a mass class-based Malay union movement.

In-house unions were established within the newer government ventures (e.g. Petronas, Proton) and offered as an option within the electronics industry – areas in which high percentages of Malays were employed. American electronics employers in Malaysia, however, resisted any attempt to form unions – including in-house unions – within their enterprises leaving many, predominantly female, workers unorganised and vulnerable to state supported capital. Despite American multinational resistance to the issue of in-house unionism in the electronics sector, in 1996 the courts decreed that American attempts at union busting resulting in the eventual dismissal of twenty-four union activists was illegal and declared that the sacked unionists be reinstated (Bhopal 1997). After six years of legal battle conducted by the first electronics in-house union the state appears to be unable or unwilling to unconditionally back the anti-unionism of the American employers in this sector. Significantly the relative importance of US capital in the Malaysian electronics industry has declined as a result of the high levels of Japanese investment in the consumer electronics sector. The Japanese have been less opposed to enterprise type unionism (Abdullah 1992).

The in-house union policy aimed to create an enterprise based on a non-political business union model (Wad 1988; Wad and Jomo 1994). The unitarist assumptions underpinning the Malaysian Government's in-house unionism policy demonstrate a link beyond the workplace with a form of paternalism consistent with the discourse of Malay common interest and unity. While the objective of trade union solidarity and power, rather than the business focused fragmentation inherent in enterprise based unions, may explain the MTUC's opposition to such a model, Grace (1990) has suggested that women can be better served by such a structure. She argues that in the context of the patriarchal ideologies and structures of the society, Malaysian trade unions, like the wider political parties, have marginalised women from active involvement and trade union discourse. In general, male dominated trade unions have been accused of failing to provide the physical and psychological space for safety and confidence and underplaying the gender equality agenda. In light of this, localised in-house unions provide a potential for escaping male domination that is characteristic of larger national and industrial unions, and provide greater potential for female participation, particularly in the export industries and Free Trade Zones (FTZs) that employ significant numbers of women workers. It may also be more likely that the issues raised would reflect the needs of its predominantly women membership and thus enhance the prospect of a more gender sensitive bargaining agenda.

In its drive to prevent class organisation across or within ethnic groupings, the State has espoused a wider ideology of a common ethnic and national interest which supposedly clashes with that of labour in Western nations. The interests of the Malaysian (increasingly Malay) worker are pitted against the 'protectionist' tendencies of Western trade unions. The State has also attempted to distance workers from the principles of Western pluralist models by emphasising so called 'Asian values' of loyalty, hard work and docility prioritising the notion of nation and development before distribution. This was implicit in Prime Minister Mahathir's promotion of the 'Look East' policy of the 1980s:

> Look East means emulating the rapidly developing countries of the east in the effort to develop Malaysia. Matters deserving attention are: diligence and

discipline in work, loyalty to the nation and to the enterprise or business where
the worker is employed, priority of group over individual interests, emphasis
on productivity and high quality, upgrading efficiency, etc. . . .

(Quoted in Wad and Jomo 1994)

This stress on the need for an enterprise and work consciousness was not only aimed
at enhancing productivity and reduction of unit labour costs, through management
techniques such as TQM and a 'human relations' driven management style to
ensure managerial legitimacy, but also to meet the potential challenge from below.
A unitarist philosophy prevails, requiring workers to identify their interests as being
in common with capital and the State. However, the advocacy of the notion of
Asian values has additional implications for Malaysian women workers as such
a discourse could be used to reinforce the patriarchal structure whereby women's
place in the labour market is seen at best as transitory and secondary and, as
previously discussed, immoral. Indeed managerial control could be reinforced
by wider structures of patriarchal authority which may be accepted in as far as
the ability to earn also enhances independence and power within family structures
(Lie 2000).

Trade union diversity and Malay political structure

Inter-ethnic competition has been reinforced by The United Malay National
Organisation's (UMNO) role not only within the broader Malay community
but more specifically amongst Malay labour. UMNO, as the main Malay party, has
an organisational structure that permeates to the roots and branches of Malay
society (Singh 1998). It has 2.4 million members, out of a Malay population of
approximately 12 million. UMNO is perceived as the most powerful representative
and advocate of the Malay interest. In these circumstances, it is not surprising that
Malay workers have seen UMNO, rather than trade unions, as the first channel for
labour grievances (Mohamad *et al.* 2000). However, given the integration of local
and national UMNO leaderships into the developmentalist opportunities this is by
no means an effective channel for voice (see Ibrahim 1998). In addition, UMNO's
patriarchal structures serve to control Malay women workers who may be recruited
through the village headman and be expected to send remittances to supplement
family income. UMNO's extensive branch structure provides the potential for forms
of control based upon the surveillance and reporting capacity of an institutional
structure that is locally sensitive but at the same time nationally organised. UMNO
Wanita, the women's wing, is generally viewed as a middle-class, conservative
organisation with no progressive policies on working-class women.

   Thus the wider political discourse, including UMNO's claim to be the embodiment of Malay interest, has served to submerge debate over intra-ethnic inequality
and to undermine labour issues from being an integral part of the political agenda.
However, with the growth of a Malay labour force, in conjunction with increasing
exposure of the ruling coalition's largely self-serving behaviour, exposed by
recurrent intra-ethnic competition for economic rents (see Gomez and Jomo 1997),

such a position becomes less easily sustainable. The guardianship of the interests of Malay labour is being contested. Factional conflicts within UMNO (arising from disputes over control of resources) have resulted in the formation of breakaway organisations – Semangat '46 (the spirit of '46) in 1987 and Keadilan in 1998. Both groups have purported to be concerned to advance labour's interest.

The union movement has made minimal impact on UMNO's position as the primary protector of Malay labour's interest. The trade union movement has under-utilised, and at times marginalised, the multi-faceted nature of Malay identities by failing to question – or at worst accepting – the notion of Malay interest. However, given the sensitivity of this subject, issues of gender and class may well have been better used to undermine the disabling impact of the ethnicity discourse.

During the 1980s, in the culmination of conflict with the trade union movement, the government used ethnicity and nationalism in their attempts to discredit the union leadership by accusing the critical components as being anti-nation, anti-democratic and, therefore, anti-Malay. In the context of increasing divisions within UMNO, the State has adopted a more inclusionary approach towards the unions appealing to the union movement to become a 'partner' in Prime Minister Mahathir's decentralised, private sector driven concept of 'Malaysia Incorporated'. The conditions for the partnership are that the unions accept a business orientation in the workplace and assist in attracting inward investment. The strategy has not explicitly utilised ethnicity, but the target and goals are implicit – the incorporation of Malay working-class interests with capital and 'national' or 'Malay' interest, although the reality is one of inter-ethnic elite accommodation (Gomez 1999). This Malay interest is not only class but gender free, thereby avoiding division and elevating a manufactured national project. The government also sought to neutralise oppositional political forces within the MTUC by encouraging the more conservative Malaysian Labour Organisation to dissolve itself and rejoin the MTUC.

Thus ethnicity is being used by the ruling elite to disguise class based divisions within Malaysian society. But issues of ethnicity have also served to focus attention away from gender inequality within ethnic groups in favour of gender free inter-ethnic competition.

Limits of equal opportunities and affirmative action

Equal opportunity has been limited to the ethnic affirmative action policies of the government to enhance Malay employment and business opportunities. This has benefited many Malay businessmen, created a Malay professional class, and provided opportunities for waged work. However, the fact remains that there is a gendered division of labour amongst the working class. Malay males are concentrated in the capital intensive, import substitution sectors such as steel and automobile production while the women work in the export oriented FTZs involved in the production of electrical and electronic goods. Women comprise 55 per cent of the labour force in electronics, 56.8 per cent in textiles and 89.5 per cent in clothing (ILO 1996) – three of the industries implicated in the global division of labour (Dickens 1992). On the other hand, none of the production workers at the national car factory are women (Todd and Peetz in print). On average, men earn twice as much as women largely because of women's location in low wage activities and on lower rungs of the occupational hierarchy. Rather than reflecting any rational skills endowments, this outcome is a consequence of the patriarchal control of definition of skill levels and entry into senior occupational positions, which themselves are sustained by issues of societal power.

While the discourse relating to the female operators' tasks includes the demands for concentration, precision, dexterity and the capacity to suffer boredom in silence (see Grace 1990) these skills are treated as innate attributes rather than learned abilities. Nevertheless it has been reported that new young workers 'are delighted to be earning money and be independent of their families . . . [and] . . . see their employers as benefactors rather than exploiters' (Papachan 1994). This is also the experience of the MTUC Women's Committee, after their attempts to organise Motorola workers in the mid 1990s as the head of the MTUC Women's Committee explained:

> women in Motorola come from rural areas, and when they see the facilities, annual dinner, transport, overseas visits, and health care protection, they think they don't need a union to protect them, but they don't actually see what a union is for.

The organisation of women workers

This is not to say that women have not resisted, indeed there have been negotiations between unions and some companies to include sexual harassment clauses in collective agreements or to issue joint policy declarations. In a more informal way, however, dissatisfaction has been expressed through labour turnover. There have also been instances of mass hysteria, as a form of outburst of collective resistance among women factory workers although this has been expressed in cultural terms and attributed to spirit possession (Ong 1989). It is significant to note that formal action has also occurred and strikes and organising activities by women workers have been documented in companies such as Mostek (Chee and Ng 1997), Harris Semiconductor (Bhopal 1997), Motorola (Hamilton 1991) and Hitachi (*New Straits Times*, 15 June 1990). Despite the depiction of a young docile workforce, however accurate it may have been, there is change occurring with some studies showing that female electronics workers in FTZs are 'no longer young, single, nubile, mobile and relatively uneducated. Instead they are increasingly married, have a decent educational background and are a stable if not permanent workforce in the industry' (Mohamad and Ng 1997: 7). In this sense, the outlook for organisation as a potential issue is not necessarily as pessimistic as appears, due to the existence of employees with relatively long length of service and industrial experience. In the words of the male President of the Harris Advanced Technology Workers' Union:

they were a rural force when they came in twenty years ago and they were basically scared and they were beholden to authority even to the supervisor – whatever the supervisor says . . . it's the most important thing because he's the chief . . . the feudal mentality. But as time went along this changed. . . . Now it is the offspring of these interstate workers that is coming into the factory – they are urban females. They have a different consciousness; they don't have a sense of struggle. They don't feel that they are paid poorly, that the family is subsidising half in terms of accommodation and food, and whatever salary they earn is for their own expenditure. It is never easy to organize – then and now. Now the issues are different. Then organizing means those that are conscious go down to the grassroots and discuss and create an awareness, which is easy to accept because they are in a poverty stage. Now it's among themselves – a senior worker and a junior worker . . . a senior worker and union member who went through the struggle 20–25 years ago . . . [A] new worker comes in . . . wham . . . and they talk and have a higher success rate than in the 1970s . . . 'come here sister'.

Despite these actions the MTUC has made little headway in organising FTZ electronics workers, partly because the companies are resistant but also because MNCs tend to provide many welfare benefits and workers, with overtime, can earn better than average wages. This does not excuse the fact that issues of gender have been under-played and under-prioritised by a predominantly male trade union leadership, which has neglected the women's agenda in its policies and bargaining strategies (Grace 1990) and demonstrated a general bias against the involvement of women in unions (Malaysian Human Rights Report 1998). At a more micro level Sorvald[2] in her study of six Norwegian manufacturing companies in Malaysia, reported that fewer women than men were organised in trade unions. Her female respondents stated that 'men did not look after women's interests in the organisation, and therefore it was not worth being organised in a union'. Indeed women only occupied 5 per cent of leadership positions in 1990 (Jomo and Todd 1994). However, at Harris semi-conductor the bulk of operators are also Malay, with Malay females accounting for 90 per cent of the labour force and 91 per cent of the in-house union members. The executive committee of fifteen has ten women, the bulk of whom are Malay. In 2000 the union had achieved 70 per cent membership.

   In light of the above discussion it cannot be concluded that there is no desire for unionisation and organisation. Arguably there is a necessity for organisation as much of the work in FTZs is demand dependent and issues of job security are significant to ensure a future flow of necessary income. Furthermore Malaysia's changing position in the international division of labour has important implications for women factory workers labelled as unskilled and semi-skilled. The Asian Development Bank argues:

   Malaysian women . . . have been concentrated in low skill, labour intensive jobs requiring little training or previous experience, as a result they have the least bargaining power. . . . [As] Malaysia moves from labour intensive to more capital intensive forms of production female workers will be even less competitive . . .

(Asian Development Bank 1998)

Mohamad and Ng (1997: 13) argue that the emerging pattern is one of women workers being edged out by 'newly recruited and supposedly "qualified" male technicians'. However, it cannot be assumed or taken for granted that women factory workers will become uncompetitive for much depends not only on how labour market constraints affect management choice in these matters but what pressure can be brought to bear by the workforce themselves. Nevertheless, unionisation of the female dominated electronics sector remains minimal. The opposition to unionisation of electronics workers has been largely due to the preferences of particular multinationals in conjunction with the state desire to ensure a relatively compliant, low wage export oriented sector to attract inward investment, rather than the need to suppress Malay working-class organisation. The union movement itself resisted the formation of in-house unions in favour of a national union, which the Malaysian government has resisted. By 1996 the MTUC dropped its campaign for a national electronics union and thereby abandoned the previously significant effort to unionise this sector, which employs large numbers of women. Furthermore, the MTUC closed its hostel for FTZ workers in 1998 which was located near FTZ complexes, and was deemed too expensive to run. This hostel had been set up in part to develop union consciousness among new workers in these areas. This, possibly, indicates the degree of endurance and future commitment of the MTUC, to the organisation of FTZ workers in the face of adversity. In the absence of organisation and representation it would appear that the future of unorganised semi-skilled women workers will be left to managerial choice, dictated by the nature of labour markets rather than through worker attempts to shape managerial decision-making.

Finally, it is important to note the work of the many activists outside the trade unions, in the non-government organisations (NGOs). Examples include Tenaganita, a multi-ethnic women workers' organisation that has taken up the cause of migrant labour as well as sex workers and addressed such issues as AIDS; and Persatuan Sahabat Wanita Selangor (PSWS) which 'is a support group for women workers particularly for those who are not organised. The programmes of PSWS include education and training, community organisation, support for cases related to violation of employment laws and production of simple education material for women workers'. While such groups demonstrate the potential for broad based activism it is reported that Malay and Muslim women are generally absent from the more recent and generally radical women's NGOs (Ng and Leng 1996), and tend to be organised by UMNO, the dominant ruling political party. Mohamad (2000) argues that the radical and critical women's NGOs lack a constituency and mass base and are a location of last resort for those seeking assistance. However with the recent split within UMNO and the formation of Keadilan, led by the wife of the ex-deputy Prime Minister, aiming to pursue a more democratic agenda through a coalition with progressive factions there is a possibility that this may change.

Nevertheless, in these circumstances it is perhaps not surprising that the most well-known voice for Tenaganita, Irene Fernandez, has been the subject of lengthy court proceedings on charges of false reporting, which have the potential to expose and embarrass the government in revealing the treatment of illegal migrant workers in detention camps.

The micro level: the workplace

These ethnic and gender divisions of labour continue to prevail albeit they are becoming less sectoral and more organisational. In the managerial division of labour the Chinese dominate senior and middle managerial positions and their proportions decrease at lower hierarchical levels. Surveys of FTZ firms have found the Chinese to account for 75 per cent of all professionals. However, Malays tend to occupy the personnel management roles (see below; Smith 1994; Ibrahim 1998). Smith argues that the Malay personnel manager plays a key role as cultural interpreter, which is unsurprising given the high percentage of Malays at shop floor level. However, there is a danger that this denies how the personnel manager may act as an agent for capital (Legge 1995). The role of the Malay personnel manager can be viewed as that of ethnic buffer between labour and its 'foreign' employers, be they Malaysian Chinese or expatriates, defusing potential challenges to managerial control in what is an ethnically segmented internal labour market. Most studies of MNCs show that Malays and Indians are concentrated at supervisory and operator level (Abdullah 1992; Frenkel 1995; Sorvald; Todd 1994; Todd and Peetz forthcoming).

Table 4.2 demonstrates the ethnic and gender division of labour as reported by authors such as Sorvald and Abdullah (1992). The figures are derived from three electronics multinationals employing 6,190 workers reported in Abdullah's research. Malay females occupy the lowest grades while group leaders are disproportionately Chinese. At supervisory level there is a predominance of males with Chinese and Indians represented out of proportion to the national population. At operator level there are no males, and Malay females account for 55 per cent of all operators and 36 per cent of group leaders while the Chinese account for 21 per cent and 47 per cent respectively. Males are invariably employed at supervisor level and comprise 85 per cent of all supervisors with the Chinese most represented amongst this group.

Table 4.2 Ethnic and gender composition of labour – three electronics multinationals

	Malay		Chinese		Indian		Total	
	M	F	M	F	M	F	M	F
Operator	0	2859	0	1072	0	1253	0	5148
Group leader	0	285	0	374	0	132	0	791
Supervisor	76	14	81	13	57	10	214	37
Total	76	3158	81	1459	57	1395	214	5976

Source: Derived from Abdullah 1992.

There are other examples of more extreme ethnic division within the electronics industry. In one large American company Malay females accounted for 90 per cent of the operators and group leaders while the supervisors were mainly male and ethnically 50 per cent Malay, 50 per cent non-Malay (Interview with union organiser by Bhopal June 2000). At another large American electronics company, 70 per cent of the operators were Malay while 80 per cent of the officers were Chinese (Peetz and Todd forthcoming).

The range of influences upon the ethnic composition of each workplace is illustrated in the banking industry. Traditionally it has been an area in which the Chinese are over-represented and in a recent study of four Malaysian banks, 50 to 60 per cent of employees within three of them were of Chinese ethnic origin. But, in contrast, in the fourth bank 60 per cent of the employees were Malay due to the bank's closer links to the government and Malay community (Peetz and Todd in print).

While different ethnic groups are disproportionately represented at different levels, issues of gender, ethnicity and hierarchy interrelate. Thus Malay females, who form the majority of operator positions, are more likely to have a Chinese group leader than a Malay or Indian. Given their relatively low numbers it would seem that Chinese female operators are more likely to be promoted to the group or team leader level. The supervisory layer is predominantly male and is relatively multi-ethnic.

This ethnic division of labour has fuelled the communalism of Malaysia at the macro level but it does not necessarily have the same impact at the workplace, though this is not to deny that ethnicity is not relevant for management. There is little evidence that ethnicity is invoked by workers at workplace level, indicating that ethnicity is a latent, unexpressed but visible and important factor in workplace relations not least because of the discourse of Malaysian politics. However, this leaves the potential for the situational use of ethnicity to articulate grievances and make demands. For instance, Caspersz (1998) reports grievances over low pay levels being articulated as being the result of unequal promotions for Malays, leading to industrial action in an MNC. She also points out how Malay workers sought the removal of a 'Chinese' supervisor because of his 'attitude' towards them. Ibrahim (1998), albeit in a study of an indigenous company, also shows how conflicts over supervision can be expressed and articulated in ethnic terms. Smith (1994) reports how the Japanese managers resisted workgroup demands by arguing that a concession to one would be seen as favouritism by the other. Furthermore the substantive negotiating issues such as holidays, timing of bonuses and timing of negotiation deadlines all give rise to the potential for one ethnic group to feel that their interests have been compromised (Smith 1994).

The ethnic discourse also has the ability to obscure class relations so as far as material conflict of interest between workers of one ethnic group and managers and owners of another have the potential to be articulated in ethnic rather than class terms (Ibrahim 1998; Caspersz 1998). Smith (1994) reports how conflict between Malay workers and Japanese management was expressed in terms of the Japanese as Japanese rather than as managers. Indeed, ethnic articulation of grievances with managers has the potential to create ethnic divisions at workplace level. Ethnicity as a divisive force within the movement was noted by the MTUC '. . . [The] Labour movement is a multi-racial, multi-religious and multi-cultural mass organisation. Yet we cannot pretend that ethnic polarisation has not reared its ugly head in the movement . . .' (1994).

While ethnicity can divide class solidarity, this very fact has been used by management at workplace level, with a number of reports such as that already cited of managers resisting workgroup demands by arguing that concession to one would be seen as favouritism by the other. In other cases ethnicity can be used in undermining union organising campaigns. In one prominent US MNC anti-union tactics included appeals to intra-ethnic solidarity, out-grouping and use of ethnic disciplinary figures. Malay managers suggested Malay activists were being used and manipulated by the Indian union and were rebuked for having been 'used' by Indians 'when the Malays had always taken the leadership role in this country'. In the name of Muslim solidarity and self-organisation, the formation of non-union Muslim committees to channel grievances and enhance Muslim welfare and solidarity were proposed (Bhopal 1997).

An attempt was also made to use women to define boundaries (Allen 1994) and undermine organising efforts by combining issues of gender and ethnicity, by rumours of the sexual harassment of a Malay female member of staff by the Indian union president. At the most formal and company sanctioned level and during the period of the unionisation drive, an 'Ustaz' (Islamic religious teacher) was invited by the company to give two hour lectures on work ethics, as part of the company's Communication Helps Improve Productivity (CHIP) programme. Using the authority of platform, his religious position, and the implicit interaction of male religious authority figures with a predominantly female Malay and Muslim labour force, the Ustaz's speech was reputedly full of anti-union comments, resulting in the state publicly declaring that he was not acting in an official capacity.

Gender divisions within the Malaysian workplace have been perceived by some as providing the opportunity for enhanced management control. This is seen to emanate from the employment of Malay females as shop floor operatives in so far as the traditions of patriarchal Malay society subordinate them to male authority particularly in the public sphere (Lie and Lund 1991: 32). However, there is another undercurrent of independence and self-reliance (Lie 2000) and a history of equality in the sphere of work in pre-capitalist Malay society (Kaur 1999). It has been suggested that women factory workers are less willing now, compared to twenty years ago, to accept authority without question; this may be indicated by formal shows of resistance as indicated above and also by more informal means as indicated by the following comments from the HSSWU President:

> when you're under management and you are working an eight hour shift you are required to follow the instructions of a supervisor . . . they go through the motions of passing the time and they have their own unique way of turning this into a joke. For example, TPM – total productivity management – they call it *Tipu Punya Management*, Punya means type, Tipu means cheat – 'cheating type

of management'.[3] We have PMT meetings, this is where the managing director comes down and talks to them, and they turnaround and say *Pergi Minom Teh* – go drink tea. . . . They go along with it . . . this is a kind of resistance from the ground . . .

(Interview with union organiser by Bhopal June 2000)

Control may, however, also be enhanced because many female operators are recruited through a 'friends or family' policy and they make significant remittances to their families to assist with their subsistence (Arrifin 1994). Therefore, threats to job security and loss of unskilled jobs would have an effect beyond the individual worker concerned. The loss of employment would also threaten new found independence and valued identity (Caspersz 1998), much of which is centred around the place of employment in company sponsored sports and social events. Amongst the large FTZ employers there is a tendency to have beauty contests, sports activities, picnics, etc. – a ploy that may be particularly pertinent in enhancing worker cohesion and mutual support given the generally negative portrayal of women factory workers in Malaysia. This would indicate that, rather than a commonality of values, a coincidence of interest explains receptiveness to managerial control, in a context of the wider exclusion of these workers from trade union action and community embeddedness.

Interestingly, the gendered division of labour, combined with a recognition of common grievance, has the potential to give rise to inter-ethnic class alliances, indicating that ethnic identity can be secondary to issues of class as in the case of inter-ethnic union mobilisation. For instance, Bhopal (1997) reports on the inter-ethnic and gender unity in the face of management attempts to fragment both. Management had attempted unsuccessfully to utilise ethnic differences as a divide and rule strategy, as well as to make use of the interplay of ethnicity and gender by accusing some Indian male trade union activists of making improper and unwarranted advances to Malay females.

Finally, the use of temporary migrant labour has fuelled further divisions in some workplaces (Todd 1999). Apart from ethnic divisions, the government's prohibition on migrants' membership of unions has cut across class-based organisation. Their temporary migrant status further isolated them from other workers as well as making them vulnerable to greater levels of exploitation as illustrated in the following case. A large Japanese electronics company had been experiencing 90 per cent labour turnover in certain production areas where the working conditions were extremely uncomfortable in terms of heat and/or very low illumination. Management resolved their problem by recruiting Bangladeshi workers whose employment permits required them to remain with the company (Peetz and Todd forthcoming).

Conclusion

The above sketch indicates that ethnic, gender and class identities can mutually reinforce each other in solidaristic actions although they may, more often, cut across and fragment. Indeed the challenge for the labour movement is to develop a progressive agenda based on emancipatory politics that transcends, but does not negate, the identity issues of gender and ethnicity.

The Malaysian union movement, however, has had to develop within the context of ethnically based politics as well as very restrictive boundaries set by the state, fearful of a class based movement. Malaysia's economic development process has also been couched within ethnic discourse, disguising the class based outcomes. And until recently the union movement was associated with the smallest and least influential ethnic group, the Indians.

The situation is far from static. Malay labour has become much more integrated into the urban paid workforce with their increased employment in manufacturing, and the ethnic divisions associated with occupation have been decreasing. The economic development outcomes have heightened intra-ethnic differences, particularly amongst Malays as is reflected in the divisions which have emerged within UMNO. These developments have increased the potential for greater cross-ethnic identification of commonality of interest amongst labour. While there are examples within individual unions and workplaces of gender and class uniting workers across ethnic divisions, the broader union movement continues to suffer the disabling impact of the ethnicity discourse.

It could be argued that by virtue of Malaysia being a plural multi-ethnic society cross-cut by issues of gender and class, it has the potential to lead the way in the grass-roots diversity project, although these very attributes themselves can and have sewn the seeds of fragmentation and division by the elevation of particular identities. The question remaining for labour therefore, in the Malaysian context and elsewhere, is not only who they are and where they are from but also what they will become.

Notes

1   The focus of this chapter on Malay labour is in no way intended to deny the experience of Chinese and Indian workers. It should be noted, however, that Chinese employees have been disproportionately predominant in professional and managerial ranks and have played a minimal role in the union movement since the 1948 purge of the Malayan Communist party-backed unions. On the other hand, the plight of Indian workers is deserving of a separate story (see Ramasamy 1994): being a minority with little political power, their position has been perhaps the most neglected.
2   Date is unknown, although a reference is provided in the bibliography.
3   Tipu means deception, Punya means to possess/to have, thus this could also be taken to mean the deception that is possessed by management. Our thanks to Professor Michael Hitchcock at University of North London for this transliteration.

References

Abdullah, Syed R.S. (1992) *Management Strategies and Employee Responses in Malaysia: A Study of Management Industrial Relations Styles of US and Japanese Multinational Companies in the Malaysian Electronics Industry*. PhD Thesis. Cardiff: University of Wales.

Allen, S. (1994) 'Race, ethnicity and nationality: some questions of identity', in Ashfer, H. and Maynard, M. (eds) *The Dynamics of Race and Gender: Some Feminist Interventions*, London: Taylor and Francis.

Ariffin, Rohana (1989) 'Women and trade unions in West Malaysia', *Journal of Contemporary Asia* 19, 1: 78–94.

Ariffin, Jamilah (1994) *From Kampung to Urban Factories: Findings From the HAWA Study*, Kuala Lumpur: University of Malaya Press.

Bhopal, Mhinder (1997) 'Industrial relations in Malaysia – multinational preferences and state concessions in dependent development: a case study of the electronics industry', *Economic and Industrial Democracy* 18, 4: 567–97.

—— (forthcoming), *Asian Crisis: Malaysian Labour*, Asia Pacific Business Review, Special Edition: ASEAN Management in Crisis.

Caspersz, Donella (1998) 'Globalization and labour: a case study of EPZ workers in Malaysia', *Economic and Industrial Democracy* 19, 2: 253–86.

Corpwatch (1999) Global Semiconductor Health Hazards Exposed, accessed August 2000 at http: //www.igc.org/trac/corner/worlnews/other/206.html)

Dicken, Peter (1992) *Global Shift: The Internationalization of Economic Activity*, 2nd edn, London: Paul Chapman.

Frenkel, S. (1995) 'Workplace relations in the global corporation: a comparative analysis of subsidiaries in Malaysia and Taiwan', in Frenkel, S. and Harrod, J. (eds) *Industrialization and Labour Relations*, New York: ILR Press.

Gomez, T. (1999) *Chinese Business in Malaysia: Accumulation, Accommodation and Ascendance*, Richmond Surrey: Curzon Press.

Gomez, T. and Jomo, K.S. (1997) *Malaysia's Political Economy: Politics Patronage and Profits*, Cambridge: Cambridge University Press.

Grace, Elizabeth (1990) *Short-Circuiting Labour: Unionising Electronics Workers in Malaysia*, Kuala Lumpur: INSAN.

Grint, Keith (1991) *The Sociology of Work*, Cambridge: Polity Press.

Hamilton, F. (1991) 'Organizing at Motorola', *Women Organizing in Global Electronics*, London: Women Working Worldwide.

ILO (1996) *International Programme on More and Better Jobs for Women*, Geneva: International Labour Office.

Wee Siu Hui, A. (2000) The Malay female labour force in the electronics industry. Unpublished paper.

Husin Ali, Syed (ed.) (1984) *Ethnicity, Class and Development Malaysia*, Kuala Lumpur: Persatuan Sains Sosial Malaysia.

Ibrahim, Zawawi (1998) *The Malay Labourer: by the Window of Capitalism*, Singapore: ISEAS.

Jesudason, James (1989) *Ethnicity and the Economy – The State, Chinese Business and Multinationals in Malaysia*, Singapore: Oxford University Press.

Jomo, K.S and Todd, P. (1994) *Trade Unions and the State in Peninsular Malaysia*, Kuala Lumpur: Oxford University Press.

Kaur, A. (1998) *Women's Work: Gender and Labour Relations in Malaysia*. Working Papers on Asian Labour: Amsterdam. Accessed at http: //www.iisg.nl/~clara/clarawp (accessed January 2000).

Kuruvilla, S. and Arudsothy, P. (1995) 'Economic development strategy, government labour policy and firm level industrial relations practices in Malaysia', in Verma, A., Kochan, T. and Lansbury, D., *Employment Relations in The Growing Asian Economies*, London: Routledge.

Legge, K. (1995) *Human Resource Management: Rhetorics and Realities*, Basingstoke: Macmillan.

Chee Heng Leng and Ng, C. (1997) Struggling for change: Women's movement in Malaysia. Accessed at http//www.isiswomen.org/archive/articles/soc00004.htlm (June 2000) originally appeared in *Women in Action*, Isis International: Manila.

Lie, M. (2000) 'Two generations: life stories and social change in Malaysia', *Journal of Gender Studies* 9, 1: 27–43.

Lie, M. and Lund, R. (1991) 'What is she up to? Changing identities and values among women workers in Malaysia', in Stølen, Kristi Anne and Vaa, Mariken *Gender and Change in Developing Countries*, Oslo: Norwegian University Press.

Lim, L. (1990) 'Labour organization among women workers in multinational export factories in Asia', *Journal of Southeast Asia Business* 6, 4: 1–8.

Malaysia (1991) 6th Malaysian Plan 1991–1995, Kuala Lumpur: Economic Planning Unit.

Malaysia (1996) 7th Malaysia Plan 1996–2000, Kuala Lumpur: Economic Planning Unit.

Malaysia (2001) 8th Malaysian Plan 2001–2005, Kuala Lumpur: Economic Planning Unit.

Mohamad, M. (2000) *Whither the Women's Movement?* Aliran Monthly accessed April 2001 at http://www.malaysia.net/aliran/monthly/2000/04i.html. 15th June, 1990 (NST).

Mohamad, M. and Ng, C. (1997) 'Flexible labour regimes, new technologies and women's labour: case studies of two electronic firms in Malaysia', *Asian Journal of Womens Studies* 3, 1: 8–35.

Mohamad, M., Ng, C. and Tan Beng Hui (2000) Globalization, Industrialization and Crisis: The Coming Age of Malaysian Women Workers. Unpublished paper.

Ng, C. and Chee Heng Leng (1996) 'Women in Malaysia: present struggles future directions, *Asian Journal of Women's Studies* 2: 192–210.

Ng, C. and Kasim, Z. (2000), *Women and Politics in Malaysia*, highlights from Aliran Monthly accessed (9/6/2000) at http://www.malaysia.net/aliran/high9907.htp.

Ong, A. (1989) *Spirits of Resistance and Capitalist Discipline: Factory Women in Malaysia*, New York: State University of New York Press.

Papachan, S. (1994) *Malaysia Country Report*, accessed May 2000 at http://www.itcilo.it/english/actrav/telearn/global/ilo/frame/epzmal.htm

Peetz, D. and Todd, P. (forthcoming) Globalisation and Employment Relations in Malaysia, Geneva: ILO.

Rajah, Rajah (1993) 'Free trade zones and industrial development in Malaysia' in Jomo, K.S. (ed.) *Industrializing Malaysia: Policy, Performance, Prospects*. New York: Routledge.

Ramasamy, P. (1994) *Plantation Labour, Unions, Capital, and the State in Peninsular Malaysia*, Kuala Lumpur: Oxford University Press.

Singh, H. (1998) Tradition, UMNO and political succession in Malaysia, *Third World Quarterly* 19, 2: 241–54.

Smith, Wendy (1994) 'A Japanese factory in Malaysia: Ethnicity as a management ideology', in Jomo, K.S. (ed.) *Japan and Malaysian Development*, London: Routledge.

Sorvald, M. (date not known) Women and the Establishment of Norwegian Industry in Malaysia. Paper presented to 6th Annual Conference in the Nordic Association for South East Asian Studies.

Southall, Roger (ed.) (1988) *Trade Unions and the New Industrialisation of the Third World*, London: Zed Books.

Todd, P. (1994) 'Australian companies in Malaysia: Industrial relations implications of offshore investment', in Callus, R. and Schumacher, M. (eds) *Current Research in Industrial Relations*, Proceedings of the 8th AIRAANZ Conference, February.

—— (1999) 'The impact of foreign multinational corporations upon Malaysian employment relations – A study of six Australian companies manufacturing in Malaysia', *International Journal of Employment Studies* 7, 2: 1–23.

Todd, P. and Peetz, D. (forthcoming) 'Malaysian industrial relations at century's turn: Vision 2020 or a spectre of the past?', *International Journal of Human Resource Management*.

Trade Union News for Overseas (1959) No. 47, 2 February, London: TUC.

US Department of State (1998) *Malaysian Human Rights Report.*

Wad, P. (1988) 'The Japanisation of the Malaysian trade union movement', in Southall, R. (ed.) *Trade Unionism and the New Industrialization of the Third World*, London: Zed Books.

Wad, P. and Jomo, K.S. (1994) 'In house unions: looking east for industrial relations', in Jomo, K.S (ed.) *Japan and Malaysian Development*, London: Routledge.

Yun Hing Ai (1990) 'Capital transformation and labour relations in Malaysia', *Labour and Industry* 3, 1: 76–92.

Yin, Hua Wu (1983) *Class and Communalism in Malaysia*, London: Zed Books.

5 Trade unions and women's autonomy

Organisational strategies of women workers in India

Rohini Hensman

Introduction

The labour force in India is as diverse as Indian society itself, divided by gender, religion, caste, region, ethnicity, language and history. In this context, the issue of equality assumes extra importance, yet trade unions have failed to tackle it with the seriousness it deserves. This failure has had an adverse effect on all sections that suffer from discrimination, above all on women, and also on the movement as a whole.

This chapter looks at some examples of the ways in which women workers have organised successfully, and tries to assess how far these attempts go towards addressing the issues of discrimination and equality. It adopts a case study approach, looking at six cases from a diversity of locations: The All-India Chemical and Pharmaceutical Employees' Federation and its activities in Bombay, Maharashtra, in Western India; the Women's Wing of the All-India Bank Employees' Association which has branches throughout the country; The Chhattisgarh Mines Shramik Sangh and Mahila Mukti Morcha from Madhya Pradesh, Central India; the Navayuga Beedi Karmika Sangam in Hyderabad, Andhra Pradesh, Southern India; Sarba Shanti Ayog and Sasha based in Calcutta, West Bengal, in Eastern India; and the Self-Employed Women's Association (SEWA), based in Ahmedabad, Gujarat, in Western India. The absence of North India is not accidental; this is the region where women face the most brutal violence and oppressive patriarchal control, and organising autonomously is most difficult. I have also included material from a project sponsored by Women Working Worldwide to discover whether Codes of Conduct can help women workers in the garment industry, although this cannot count as a case study since the overwhelming majority of the women remain unorganised.

The chapter aims to show that while some progress has certainly been made, women and other disadvantaged sections remain marginalised in the labour force, and trade unions still fail to recognise the importance of tackling this issue. Finally, it argues that globalisation perhaps opens up possibilities of using new resources which might aid in the struggle for equality.

Research methods

The case studies draw on individual and group interviews/discussions with women workers, activists and organisers (at least ten, sometimes many more), carried out by myself, sometimes with various colleagues.[1] They also use whatever documentary material is available: collective agreements wherever they exist, court cases published in the Bombay Government Gazette and Maharashtra Government Gazette, and Annual Reports, leaflets, pamphlets and other publications by the groups being studied. My association with the pharmaceutical workers is an ongoing one, dating back to the early 1980s, and recent information is from male union activists; the association with the garment workers is also ongoing, but started much more recently (i.e. in 1998). The other cases were carried out by staying for some time in the places where they are located during the period 1994–6. A case study approach seemed the best way to do justice to the diversity of circumstances and strategies. It also provided a good opportunity to find out how the women themselves felt about their work and organisations.

Problems created by legislation and government policy

The concepts of equality and non-discrimination are not absent in India; the Constitution guarantees both. However, the legislative and policy instruments by which they are sought to be achieved have been sadly ineffective. The most serious attempt to eradicate discrimination has been made in the case of dalits (formerly 'Untouchables') or Scheduled Castes (SCs) and adivasis or Scheduled Tribes (STs). The practice of untouchability is illegal, and there are job reservations in the public sector as well as reservations of parliamentary and state assembly constituencies for SCs and STs. Yet the most blatant forms of discrimination are suffered by these sections, and even the degrading practice of untouchability still continues. There are two reasons for this. One is that the existing laws are frequently not enforced, and the other is that reservations by themselves are not an adequate means of achieving equality. They have ensured the emergence of a layer of educated, middle-class dalits and tribals, but have not prevented the vast majority of individuals from these categories being subjected to various forms of exclusion. Worse still, the reservations themselves are seen by other castes as a privilege unjustly confined to STs and SCs, rather than a measure to bring about social justice. In the case of women, there has been no policy of affirmative action in jobs, and there would undoubtedly be insurmountable obstacles to pushing any such measure through parliament. And even if it were possible to do so, such a measure would do little to counteract the persistent discrimination suffered by girls and women from birth to premature death: widespread female infanticide, deprivation of nutrition and health care, reluctance to invest in education because girls are regarded as *'paraya dhan'* (another's property), and so on, all of which ensure that women enter the labour force already at a disadvantage compared to men.

Within the labour force, they face further discrimination. The proportion of women workers in formal sector private industry fluctuates around only 10–12 per cent, and while the proportion is higher in the public sector, there too women are a small minority. For the small proportion of women in the formal sector, wages and benefits are relatively high, the Maternity Benefit Act, 1961, allows them to have three months' maternity leave with full pay from the employer, and where there are 30 or more women in the workforce, the Factories Act requires the employer to provide a creche for their pre-school children. However, occupational segregation limits the number of jobs available to them, and excludes most of them from the more skilled and better paid jobs (Banerjee 1985; Liddle 1988). Although in general large-scale employers observe the Equal Remuneration Act, 1976, which provides for equal pay for the same or similar work, the issue of work of equal value has not been addressed, and the skills involved in many jobs done by women tend to be unrecognised and unremunerated. Most seriously, the lack of any equal opportunities policy or legislation makes it very easy for employers not to extend formal employment to women at all, and they are increasingly taking this option, since in the formal sector women are more expensive (because of statutory maternity benefits and creche facilities) and less flexible (because of the prohibition on night work) (Hensman 1996c).

This leaves the overwhelming majority of women job-seekers with no option but to go into the 'informal sector'; for the purposes of this chapter, I have used this term to refer to all workers, both urban and rural, who are not covered by basic labour legislation, including unprotected workers (e.g. contract, temporary and casual workers) in large-scale production. The Indian Government's *Economic Survey 1997–98* estimated that the labour force was 397.2 million in 1997, with only 27.94 million in the formal sector. In other words, just 7 per cent of workers were in the formal sector, and a staggering 93 per cent in the informal sector. This is partly due to non-implementation of existing legislation, but mostly a result of the inadequacy of labour laws. For example, the Factories Act, 1948, which covers working conditions, health and safety, basic amenities like toilets, working hours, prohibition of child labour and night work for women, workplace creches, and much else, does not apply to workplaces with less than ten workers using electric power and less than 20 workers without electric power; similarly the Employees' State Insurance Act, 1948, providing for accident compensation and sickness and maternity benefits, does not apply to workplaces with less than 20 workers without power. This provides employers with a variety of ways to evade these laws: splitting up an establishment into smaller units which are supposedly independent of one another, employing large numbers of contract workers (on site) who are deemed to be employees of labour contractors and therefore do not appear on the payroll of the company, or subcontracting production to smaller workplaces. The Contract Labour (Regulation and Abolition) Act, 1971, forbids the employment of contract labour for work of a perennial nature, but the way this legislation has been formulated leaves gaping loopholes which have been exploited by unscrupulous employers, one of the worst of whom is the government itself.

The rationale behind the exemption of workplaces employing a small number of workers from most labour legislation is the argument that more employment will be created if labour costs are kept low, and this will relieve the problem of unemployment. Instead, the result has been a shift of employment from formal to informal workers and an overall deterioration in conditions rather than any expansion in employment, since such workplaces neither necessarily represent small capital nor employ labour-intensive technology (Banerjee 1981: 282–6; Holmstrom 1984: 110, 114, 151). Moreover, it has made trade union organisation to improve conditions in the informal sector extremely difficult. Splitting up a workforce between different production units or different employment statuses already creates problems for unions. But an even bigger obstacle to the organisation of informal workers is the fact that often they do not have a proper employment contract, and are not covered by provisions of the Industrial Disputes Act, 1947, which prevent arbitrary closure of the enterprise and provide redress for workers subjected to dismissal for trade union activities. Thus although workers in theory have the right to unionise, in practice this means very little, because employers can either dismiss individual workers who join a union, or close down an entire unit and reopen it with new, non-unionised workers, and there is no redress for workers who are victimised in this way. For women in the informal sector, exclusion from jobs perceived as being more skilled is exacerbated by lower pay for doing the same work as men. This has created whole sectors where employment is exclusively or predominantly female, homeworking being one (see Standing 1992).

There is also discrimination against other sections of the labour force. Dalits and tribals, most of whom are agricultural labourers, continue to work in atrocious conditions, sometimes as 'bonded labour' resembling conditions of slavery. Attempts to organise and fight for their rights are often met by the most brutal repression, including massacres of men, women and children. Muslims, a minority community frequently subjected to pogroms, are systematically discriminated against in the formal sector, including the public sector in which they do not have job reservations. Women from these sections face an extra hazard: the perception of their 'low status', usually shared by the police and sometimes even by judges, makes it possible for them to be raped with impunity. The feminist movement in India really took off from the protests against a Supreme Court judgement in 1979, acquitting a policeman who had raped Mathura, a sixteen-year-old tribal girl. Almost two decades later, the movement was galvanised again in the case of Banwari Devi, a low-caste social worker who was gang-raped by the high-caste men of a family in which she had prevented a child marriage. Functionaries of the ruling Bharatiya Janata Party felicitated the rapists publicly, and the judge acquitted them on the grounds that they *could not* have raped her – the implication being that a low-caste woman has no right to deny upper-caste men access to her body.

The relegation of the vast majority of women, along with SC, ST and Muslim men, to the informal sector – where union organisation is extremely difficult – means that these sections are seriously under-represented within existing unions, and the result has been that some women in the informal sector have been forced to organise autonomously. On the other hand, while most women workers in the formal sector are union members, their representation in the leadership is extremely low – in many cases nil – and this has led to a few cases where they have chosen to organise autonomously while still retaining membership of the union.

Fragmented unions, fragmented bargaining

Unions are as fragmented as the labour force. The national trade union federations are affiliated to political parties, and statistics are unreliable and hotly disputed. Data published in early 1997 show the position as follows: the All-India Trade Union Congress (AITUC), affiliated to the Communist Party of India (CPI): 938,486 members; the Indian National Trade Union Congress (INTUC), affiliated to the Congress Party: 2,692,388; the Hind Mazdoor Sabha (HMS) formed by the Socialists: 1,480,963; the Bharatiya Mazdoor Sangh (BMS), formed by the right-wing Rashtriya Swayamsevak Sangh (RSS) with the belief that the doctrine of class conflict is alien to the Indian ethos: 3,116,564; the Centre of Indian Trade Unions (CITU) formed by the Communist Party of India (Marxist): 1,775,220. There are smaller party-affiliated unions, such as the United Trade Union Congress (UTUC), the Hind Mazdoor Kisan Panchayat (HMKP), and the All-India Federation of Trade Unions (AIFTU), affiliated to CPI (Marxist-Leninist) splits from the CPI(M).

Apart from these, there are unions affiliated to regional political parties, public sector unions like the All-India Bank Employees' Association (AIBEA), unions run by professional leaders, a variety of independent unions like SEWA (Self-Employed Women's Association) and the Chhattisgarh Mines Shramik Sangh (CMSS), and employees' or workers' unions, run by the workers themselves and usually confined to a single workplace or company. It has been estimated that the proportion of unionised workers in party-affiliated unions fell considerably from around 60 per cent in the mid-1960s to around only 12 per cent in the 1990s (Bhattacharjee 1999: 22, 42). This implies that the proportion of unionised workers in independent unions, where the opportunities for women to be in leadership positions are marginally higher, rose correspondingly.

The Industrial Relations (IR) system is fragmented in other ways too. Except for some unions in the public sector, unions do not represent workers in an industry or occupation countrywide. In most cases, the bargaining unit is a single workplace, and attempts by unions to form federations across workplaces have usually been resisted fiercely by employers (Banaji and Hensman, 1990). The extreme degree of fragmentation has made it difficult for unions to work for wider social goals, such as social security, welfare, equality, and so on. But it is not just the IR system that is at fault. There has been a singular lack of attention to these issues from the movement as a whole, and a failure to challenge government policies creating a vast pool of unprotected workers. Most unions have confined their attention to the formal sector, and even where individual unions have been concerned about workers' rights in the informal sector, they have rarely been able to muster enough support from other unions to push through legal reforms which will strengthen them. The formation of the National Centre for Labour (NCL – an umbrella federation of informal sector unions) in 1995 was a step forward (Mukul 1995; Mani 1995), but was not accompanied by support from mainstream unions. Nor was the demand for equal opportunities ever seriously considered by the trade union movement, much less fought for. The leadership of the movement itself has been dominated by caste Hindu males, although there are exceptions among independent unions. Awareness that equality is a *trade union* issue has been sadly lacking; where the issue of equality has been raised, it has been by other movements – the women's and dalit movements, for example – and even by the state, but not by trade unions. This forms the context in which women workers have experimented with various forms of organisation.

The case studies

The case studies have been chosen to represent regional diversity as well as the diversity of circumstances, ranging from relatively well-paid and secure jobs in the public and private sector, through contract work in the public sector and homeworking in the informal sector, to those who have great difficulty in finding employment at all. Women workers have adopted different strategies in response to differing circumstances, and the issues tackled by these strategies tend to be varied, although common themes also emerge.

The All-India Chemical and Pharmaceutical Employees' Federation (AICAPEF)

This is a case where women workers who formed a significant proportion of a mixed union federation did not feel the need to organise separately, but led a struggle from within the federation. The issue was the removal of the marriage bar, widely practised at that time, but successfully challenged in this historic struggle.

The pharmaceutical companies which set up operations in and around Bombay from the 1940s onwards recruited young, single women in large numbers. Their workforces, generally literate, educated and ethnically mixed, attempted from the beginning to form unions; most of them did not seek affiliation with the party-linked national federations, but formed their own 'employees' unions'. For example, the Pfizer Employees' Union was formed in 1950. Within a few years, it had a woman president, Kamala Karkal: 'I was really nervous, because I didn't know anything! I had no experience of trade union work before. But they said, "Don't worry, we'll give you all the help you need." '[2]

The unions supported women's employment rights as they were then understood: the right to security of employment, equal pay, maternity benefits and childcare; indeed, when a federation of pharmaceutical employees' unions was formed in 1960, one of the first major actions it launched was an agitation against the marriage bar. Attempts by individual unions to challenge it legally had been defeated, with the courts seeing this practice as being part of management's prerogative to run an enterprise efficiently rather than an act of discrimination. So member unions of the Federation pooled their resources in order to appeal against unfavourable judgements in lower courts and pursue the case up to the Supreme Court.

Meanwhile, women workers conducted factory gate meetings, took out processions to the Maharashtra Legislative Assembly, and even demonstrated outside the homes of directors, shouting slogans like '*Hai, hai, kya hua? Shadi karna mana kiya!*'

(Hai, hai, what has happened? They have forbidden us to get married!), causing acute embarrassment to foreign directors by alleging in front of their neighbours that they were encouraging 'immoral traffic of female employees'. On 20 February 1965, they went on a one-day fast at Martyrs' Memorial, organised a huge procession, ceremonially burned a copy of the marriage clause, and threw the ashes in the Arabian Sea (Hensman 1988). Their activities certainly had an effect on public opinion, and final victory was won later in 1965, when the Supreme Court ruled in favour of the unions: a practice which had been accepted as legitimate was now seen to be discriminatory and unconstitutional.

The vibrancy of the women workers' activism can be attributed partly to the relatively democratic functioning of employees unions, which allowed for greater participation and leadership from women, and partly to the fact that the women were young and single at the time. But employers in many factories responded by ceasing to recruit women, and by the mid-1990s, women were a demoralised and shrinking minority. Philo Martin of Glaxo Wellcome, one of the very few women active in the agitation against the marriage bar who was still an active unionist in the mid-1990s, despite having a gross salary of 8084 rupees per month compared with only 84 rupees per month in 1960, could still look back and say, 'Those were the lovely days!'[3] By 2000, most of the women who were still employed were seeking voluntary retirement. With marriage, children and domestic responsibilities, women had dropped out of activism and leadership; only a handful who remained single or had supportive partners continued to be active, thus demonstrating the limitations of the earlier struggle, which took up neither the issue of equal opportunities in employment, nor issues of gender relations outside the workplace (cf. Rees 1992).

The All-India Bank Employees' Association (AIBEA)

This is a unique case where women formed their own wing in an all-India public sector union. The case is also notable for the breadth and radicalism of their demands.

The AIBEA is an All-India union formed in 1946. Of the approximately 8,500 members in the Bombay region, about 45 per cent were women in 1996, although in the whole of India women were only 15 per cent of the workforce in banks. Employment conditions are among the best available to women, with relatively high pay and allowances, reasonable working hours and a generous amount of paid leave. Women get equal pay for equal work and three months' maternity leave on full pay. The union was also demanding 21 days' paternity leave for male employees – a demand still pending in 2000.

One measure taken to involve women more actively was the reservation of some office-bearers' seats in the union, since 'normally, men didn't look at women as leaders'. This gave women a chance to get experience and standing as union leaders before contesting elections for the general posts. It was also evident that women participated more in their own programmes, as on International Women's Day, so it was decided to set up a women's wing. On 25–6 February 1996, the first All-India Women Bank Employees' Convention was held in Bombay, attended by almost

300 delegates from all over India. A procession they organised was joined by more women to make up the numbers to nearly 3,000.

In the convention, the point was made that it was extremely difficult for women to find time for union activities; 'as it is, they are doing two jobs – at work and at home – and to work for the union is like taking on a third job!' Speakers emphasised the need for sharing of household tasks between women and men. They acknowledged that men did play a role in nuclear families, but it was still far from being equal to what women had to do. A declaration issued by the convention drew a link between the different ways in which women are disadvantaged in society and resolved to combat all of them:

> In a male-dominated society, the women suffer from varieties of gender bias and repressive laws in all fields of life. Right from the moment of birth up to that of death, they suffer from severe handicaps in the fields of education, health care, child-bearing and rearing, laws relating to marriage, inheritance and also personal laws. . . . The convention calls upon all women employees as well as all male employees to stand up unitedly and fight against the exploitation of women in all forms at home or in office or in society . . .

A five-member committee of the women's wing of the AIBEA was elected at the conference, with the responsibility to struggle for women's interests as well as increase the involvement of women in union activities. Consequently, many more women did in fact get drawn into active participation; the convenor Asha Mokashi estimated that 'at least a hundred women can be mobilised overnight for any programme held by the Women's Wing'. Many women said they felt more comfortable in an all-women organisation, less inhibited in speaking out and taking inititative. Hence the women's wing provided an opportunity for the involvement of women who otherwise would not have participated actively in the mixed union. In September 2000 branches of the women's wing were flourishing in most parts of the country, especially the South, but not in the North, where they existed only on paper, and not as centres of autonomous women's activity.

Unlike the women in the pharmaceutical unions, these women *did* feel the need to organise separately, despite having a union which had won good employment conditions for them. This was basically due to the lack of women activists and leaders in the union. The success of the women's wing in mobilising women members as well as statements by the women themselves suggest the importance of separate organising for building up confidence and leadership skills. The demand for paternity leave, with its implicit recognition of a father's responsibilities in the home, as well as the call for the union to take up more general gender issues, indicate recognition of equality as a trade union issue, and an attempt to mainstream gender issues. The convention also took up the problem of discrimination and prejudice against minority communities, showing an awareness of the importance of combating other inequalities. While such efforts may be common in other countries they constitute a pathbreaking development in India.

The Chhattisgarh Mines Shramik Sangh (CMSS) and Mahila Mukti Morcha (MMM)

The MMM, like the women's wing of AIBEA, was formed mainly due to dissatisfaction with the relative marginalisation of women in the CMSS, but in other ways the two cases are very different. Firstly, these are mainly tribal, relatively uneducated women, who started out as contract workers with miserable wages and conditions. And second, the MMM was unusual in including women members of workers' families as well as women workers in its membership.

The CMSS was formed in 1977 in the public sector Dalli Rajhara manual, open-cast iron ore mines, with a membership of around 10,000 workers, and the charismatic leader Shankar Guha Niyogi. There was a high proportion of women miners – initially around 50 per cent – in the manual mines, where workers were hired through labour contractors and consisted of the local, rural and mainly tribal population. As mechanisation progressed, women were targeted by a variety of incentives to go in for early retirement, and some accepted these, so that the proportion of women declined. At the time the union was formed, however, around 4,200 of its members were women.

The CMSS raised wages substantially, and to some extent succeeded in bridging the divide between the formal and informal sectors, with the contract workers starting as informal workers (though in the public sector), but achieving a more formal status as they became organised. But the union did not confine itself to workplace issues. It also took up issues like housing and housing allowance for contract workers, sexual harassment of women workers, and struggles against alcoholism. Women played a leading role in this last campaign, seeing alcoholism as contributing to domestic violence, and also as 'putting an extra burden on women, who are left with the financial responsibility for supporting the family' (Sen 1995).

Women played an active and creative role in the new union, but once the initial stage of militant struggle was over, they began to slide back. If there was a rally or meeting in the afternoon, women had to leave it and go home by 6.00 p.m. This applied even to leading activists, because their menfolk did not help with domestic labour at all. Moreover, it became obvious that despite their active participation in union programmes, women did not get elected to leadership positions in proportion to their numbers in the union. Nor could the union handle problems like domestic violence. A discussion started among ten to twelve women and men about the reasons for these problems, and a separate women's organisation was suggested. This was the genesis of the Mahila Mukti Morcha (MMM), which was officially set up in 1981. The integration of workplace and community issues which characterised the CMSS was also an important feature of the MMM.

It was assumed that all women members of the CMSS would be members of the MMM, and all voted at the first meeting, at which a sixteen-member committee, including office-bearers, was elected; in addition, more than 500 other women from miners' families became members. The MMM took over the anti-liquor campaign, and also organised new campaigns for demands such as separate toilets for women at the bus stand, and punishment for hooligans harassing women at the cinema.

A group of about 100 women had a series of discussions analysing the reasons why women so rarely became union leaders. The equal sharing of housework was discussed and strongly supported. As other unions in the area were formed and came under the influence of the CMSS, the MMM too spread among the women workers and family members of workers in these unions.

Members of the MMM felt they had gained in confidence and dignity – in their own eyes as well as the eyes of male workmates, husbands and family members – by being part of an autonomous women's organisation and engaging in these collective struggles: 'We got strength – not only we, but our children also got strength when they saw their mothers could confront and deal with police and officials!' This made the experience a worthwhile one for them even if they suffered severe personal hardship as a consequence; as a victimised woman worker in Raipur put it, 'Since getting organised, we can speak back, we have dignity, we can even talk alone to the police. And our brothers and sisters work in better conditions. Never mind that we lost our jobs – we got courage as a result of organising.'

However, gender issues were not brought back into the mixed union, which was not challenged to take up problems like domestic violence and the unequal division of domestic labour as union issues. And although mechanisation, which was decimating women's jobs, was confronted by the union, they demanded a moratorium on the introduction of new technology rather than shorter working hours and an equal opportunities policy, and the practical outcome was limited. Consequently, by the mid-1990s the initial problem – lack of women in the union leadership – was made worse by the falling proportion of women in the workforce (Sen 1995).

The Navayuga Beedi Karmika Sangam

This is a case which is unambiguously in the informal sector: women homeworkers rolling beedis (Indian cigarettes). It is a good example of successful unionisation of women homeworkers, and illustrates the importance of legal rights even in the informal sector. An unusual feature is that the union organising the women is associated with a women's organisation which has taken up domestic issues that have an impact on the union.

The overwhelming majority of beedi workers are women homeworkers. Decentralisation of production enables employers to evade labour legislation, and the lack of any formal employer–employee relationship makes it easy for employers to get rid of workers who are seen as trouble-makers simply by denying them work. The women obtain their raw materials from an employer or contractor, roll the beedis at home, and return the finished product. Unlike most homeworkers, they do get minimal protection from the Beedi and Cigar Workers (Conditions of Employment) Act, 1966, which extends the definition of the employer–employee relationship to include contract workers and homeworkers. Along with the Minimum Wages Act, 1948, this is one of the few labour laws applicable to homeworkers.

The first struggle of the women homeworkers in Hyderabad was to be recognised as workers at all. When the Progressive Organisation of Women (POW) and the

AIFTU (both affiliated to the CPI (Marxist-Leninist) Jan Shakti faction, and active in Andhra Pradesh) began their attempt to organise these women in the mid-1980s, government statistics showed only a few hundred workers in the city; but when the Labour Department was pressurised to investigate in 1986, they found there were approximately 10,000. The union contacted the women by going from house to house, and held meetings at the only time the women came together: when they were delivering the completed beedis and collecting fresh raw materials. Initially women were scared to join the union, because they could easily be victimised and quite often were. Nonetheless, the union was registered in 1987, and by 1994 the membership had grown to around 5,000.

When the union was started, the rate of pay was far below the minimum wage, and one aim of the union was to obtain minimum wages for its members. There were strikes, but even more effective, perhaps, were demonstrations and other agitations which obtained city-wide publicity for the plight of the workers. They were successful in getting the rate increased, but it still constantly lagged behind the minimum wage, which kept increasing as inflation eroded its value. The struggle to regularise the employment of the workers was less successful; although employers were required to issue identity cards and appointment letters to the workers as proof of employment, hardly any of them did so. However, the workers did succeed in getting welfare cards from the government, giving them access to maternity benefit of Rs 250 for each of two births, and scholarships for their children. Paid holidays, leave and weekly off-days were not given anywhere. In most places, benefits were non-existent. Homework enabled employers to evade the obligation to provide exhaust fans, comfortable seating, and other facilities which would have reduced health and safety risks, and also meant that children, especially girls, got involved in it at an early age, so that the occupation tended to become almost hereditary.

There were also domestic problems. Many women were beaten by their husbands, and encountered as much opposition to involvement in union activities from home as from employers – indeed, employers initially instigated husbands against the union, saying, 'How can you let your wives walk the streets like this?' Some women were intimidated into dropping out, but others said, 'We want our families, but we also want to be part of this movement.' Fellow-workers and the POW intervened to put pressure on their husbands to allow them to participate actively in the union.

All the women who succeeded in getting involved in the union found it an extremely positive experience. The main advantages, in their eyes, were that they achieved (1) increased knowledge, of the world and of the 'system'; (2) increased power, not only *vis-à-vis* employers but also *vis-à-vis* husbands; and (3) enjoyment of the companionship of other women. In Hyderabad, a city which has seen horrific communal riots, this was a case of Hindus and Muslims organising jointly. Muslim women, who formed a sizeable minority of the membership, said they had not encountered communal prejudice in the union. However they did complain that all the leaflets and speeches were in Telegu, whereas they were Urdu-speaking, and it appeared that there were no Urdu-speaking activists in the union or POW. Moreover, union leaders sometimes berated Muslim women for not attending meetings, whereas, as one women pointed out, many of the Muslim women like herself did not wear a burqa (veil), and therefore were not recognised as being Muslim. This was probably not a case of conscious discrimination, but of insensitivity to a religious and linguistic minority.

One factor which seems to have been crucial to the success of this union is the existence of legislation which applies to beedi workers; this provided both a legal resource which could be used against recalcitrant employers, and a psychological source of strength to the women. As a result, they were able to improve their employment conditions and develop a sense of collective strength – but only up to a point. Their pay and conditions still remained very poor, and they could not go beyond that point because most of the labour laws effective in the formal sector did not apply to them. The cooperation of the POW was helpful in tackling domestic opposition to participation in union activities, although, unfortunately, since the POW too lacked Urdu-speaking activists, they were unable to help Muslim women, who therefore continued to be a disadvantaged minority even among women as a whole.

Sarba Shanti Ayog (SSA) and the Self-Employed Women's Association (SEWA)

A major problem for women, given a context of high unemployment with discrimination on top of it, is finding employment at all. SSA attempts to solve this problem by creating employment in cooperatives. It is unusual in experimenting with modern technology as well as making positive efforts to integrate women from minority communities. SEWA, already functioning as a union in the informal sector, started many of its cooperatives because its women members either needed employment, or had lost their jobs when they tried to organise and fight for improvements. It is a unique case of a union and cooperatives combined in the same organisation.

SSA was started in 1978 as a development organisation to promote artisan/craft producer groups. Subsequently the Sasha Association of Craft Producers separated out as a specifically marketing organisation. The Sasha shop was set up in 1981 in Calcutta, and sales in other parts of the country were handled through regular exhibitions and a wholesale unit supplying craft shops in different cities. An export market was also built up through Alternative Trade Organisations like Oxfam and Traidcraft. Marketing is carried out on a professional basis, and this has been crucial to the survival of the project in an extremely competitive market.

By 1995, SSA consisted of a network comprising approximately fifty craft groups and fifteen communities. The majority of craft groups consisted of women, but some were formed by men, and a few were mixed. They ranged from four or five to a hundred people, and were involved in a wide variety of activities. Groups come to SSA wanting help in setting up production units. Once an activity has been identified, SSA carries out a skills training programme, usually provided by people from other groups. Guidance on financial and production management and group functioning is also provided by SSA; in some cases this involves training not only in accountancy but even in basic literacy. The network provides the new group with an advance of up to 75 per cent – in exceptional cases 100 per cent – to stock raw materials if they are cheaper in bulk.

Once the groups are set up, SSA continues to provide assistance with product design and development, and, most crucially, with marketing. Other community activities sometimes branch out from the producer groups: health, education, childcare and environment programmes, for example. Groups of women touring other cities to exhibit and promote their products provides an occasion to break down communal barriers and combat prejudices against women from minority communities.

This example of employment creation for a large number of women owes much to the existence of a support network, including a sophisticated and complex marketing strategy. The women clearly have much greater control over their own working conditions and remuneration than most women in the informal sector, such as the beedi workers. The women said they enjoyed working in the friendly atmosphere: 'I like it here because we're all women'; 'It's like a family – sometimes we fight, sometimes we laugh together!' 'I like working here, and will stay on if I stay alive! I'm not yet on the Executive Board, but would like to be.' The main problem, they felt, was that earnings were too low. One reason for this is the low productivity of the work done in the groups, which could only be remedied by using more sophisticated technology and mass production methods. An experiment of this sort was in progress, namely the manufacture of herbal cosmetics using modern machinery. If this is successful in generating higher incomes, it could set the pattern for other producer groups.

SEWA was formed in 1971–2 when its founder, Ela Bhatt, left the Textile Labour Association to form a women's union. SEWA cooperatives are registered under the Cooperatives Act, while SEWA itself is registered as a trade union under the Trade Union Act, 1926. All members of cooperatives are also members of SEWA. SEWA provides the cooperatives with training in skills and business management, initial working capital and help with tackling policy issues; it also helps them with design and marketing. Apart from handicraft cooperatives, SEWA also has service cooperatives performing services like cleaning, cooking and childcare.

The existence of SEWA as an umbrella organisation provides the cooperatives with a medium through which they can interact with one another. Thus artisan cooperatives can share skills and designs with each other, while service cooperatives can provide one another with services. More interestingly, the link has proved very useful to the trade union constituents of SEWA. Since the women in these belong to the informal sector, attempts to organise themselves and demand even minimum wages are often met by victimisation and loss of employment. After a number of such experiences, 'The workers realised that unless alternative sources of work were provided their bargaining power would always remain low' (SEWA 1988: 49). Thus cooperatives were seen as complementing the union function and strengthening the bargaining power of the workers; when an agricultural cooperative was set up, the wages of local agricultural workers also went up.

Women in the cooperatives felt they had gained knowledge and self-confidence by joining SEWA: 'I've gained in education, experience, and economically. I've even been to Africa as a SEWA representative – something I would never have been able to do otherwise!' They also appreciated the chance to be with and talk to other women: 'I enjoy working with other women'; 'My mind gets spoiled when I'm alone!' Many suffered from problems at home, including domestic violence, and while SEWA did not help them with these, they did get emotional support and solidarity from the other women.

The combination of union and cooperatives thus seems to be a potent one for workers in the informal sector, strengthening the bargaining power of the union by providing a fall-back source of income for victimised workers. The formation of service cooperatives is also a novel and potentially powerful idea; performing the functions usually done by housewives and mothers, it offers them a low-cost service which helps to reduce their double burden. However, the very low level of earnings – one-tenth to one-fifth of what a woman worker in the formal sector with comparable seniority would be earning – continues to be a problem, and has sometimes resulted in SEWA members joining other unions in order to bargain with their own organisation for better pay.[4] The fundamental inequality of legal rights of all workers in the informal sector is a problem for these women too.

Conclusions

It is clear that autonomous organising of women workers in India has taken place not because of encouragement from the trade union movement, but due to the exclusion of women, either from the leadership (in the formal sector), or from the movement itself (in the informal sector). A common theme running through these very diverse situations is the satisfaction and self-confidence gained by women from participation in autonomous organisations.

The reasons for the abject failure of the trade union movement to take up the issue of equality – exemplified once again in a statement of the Joint Action Committee, comprising all the major unions, in Bombay on 23 September 2000 – are complex. The exclusion of underprivileged sections from the trade union leadership, both because discrimination excludes them from the unionised formal sector, and also, in the case of women, because it is virtually impossible to combine long hours of union work with domestic commitments, means that they are simply not in a position to pursue equality issues. In their absence, the predominantly male, caste Hindu leadership tends to reflect the deeply stratified nature of Indian society, many aspects of which have uncritically been absorbed into the trade union movement.

Starvation wages, appalling conditions, child labour and easy victimisation are the hallmarks of the informal sector, where the overwhelming majority of women workers are found. Blatant legal discrimination against this entire sector means that the proportion of women workers in it who have succeeded in organising is extremely small. Far more typical than the women workers in these case studies are millions of garment workers, largely confined to the informal sector, who are too terrified to attempt to organise because they know only too well – sometimes from bitter experience – that it is likely to result in the loss of their jobs. For them, having the same legal rights as workers in large-scale industry is a key demand.[5]

Organisations like SEWA and SSA have boosted the bargaining power of informal workers by setting up cooperatives, together with the necessary infrastructure, to provide a livelihood for victimised workers and mop up the pool of unemployed women. Yet income from these cooperatives remains at the extremely low level characteristic of the informal sector, even if working conditions are better. Such a strategy can supplement but not substitute for fighting for equal rights for the casual, temporary, small-scale and contract workers who comprise the informal sector. An organisation like the NCL could play a key role if they took up this demand and pressed other unions to join them in campaigning for it.

Overlapping with this source of inequality are others based on gender, caste and religious community. Once again, while proposals for equal opportunities policy and legislation have been put forward (Bajpai 1996), no major trade union has launched a struggle for this demand. This failure has not only deepened the divide between formal and informal sectors, but also resulted in job segregation and disunity within each.

Finally, lack of a systematic challenge to the gender division of labour in the home has had adverse effects on women workers. In the formal sector, where unions have fought for and obtained maternity benefits and creche facilities, it has resulted in exclusion of women. In the informal sector, women have to choose between an inordinately long working day without any help with childcare, and no paid employment at all. The domestic division of labour is also an obstacle to women's full participation in unions, especially in the case of those who are married and have young children. Traditional power relations in the home – the Indian version of patriarchy, where a woman generally goes to live with her husband's family and is controlled by them to a large extent – exacerbate this problem. Husbands and in-laws may object to a woman going out to work, or, even if she works outside, forbid her to participate in union activities. Such prohibitions, sometimes backed up by violence, prevent many women from playing an active role.

These sources of inequality affect all workers, not just women. Millions of male workers in the informal sector are equally deprived of legal rights, while the existence of this sector undermines job security in the formal sector. Discrimination hurts male dalits, Muslims and other underprivileged workers as well as women. Lack of recognition for the importance of caring work and the domestic responsibilities of male workers can cause problems for them as individuals; moreover, a statutory working week of 48 hours combined with rapid technological modernisation is leading to structural unemployment even within the informal sector. The assertion that all workers, men and women, have responsibilities outside their waged work could be an important component in struggles for a shorter working week, more parental leave, and part-time work with pro rata benefits, all of which would help to create employment (Hensman 1996b). And the exclusion of women and other sections from trade unionism weakens the movement as a whole.

In the short run, however, male workers from the dominant community benefit from the monopoly of the small number of formal sector jobs, and male unionists have a stake in a gender division of labour which allows them to evade all domestic commitments. This suggests that nothing will happen so long as the initiative is left to them. Women activists have shown much greater awareness of the importance of these issues. SEWA played a key role in pushing through the ILO Home Work Convention, 1996, which confers stronger legal rights on homeworkers, although it did not succeed in getting the Indian government to ratify or implement it. They also proposed a levy on *all* employers, which could be used to fund maternity leave and childcare, making these benefits more accessible to women in the informal sector and removing the incentive for employers to stop recruiting women in the formal sector. SSA and the Women's Wing of AIBEA consciously took up the issue of communal prejudice and discrimination. Domestic violence was seen as an important issue in the MMM, and the beedi workers' union tackled it directly. Women in all the organisations were unhappy about the gender division of labour in the home, MMM discussed it extensively, and the Women's Wing of AIBEA took demands for greater equality back into the mixed union. The fact that women expressed appreciation of being members of a women workers' organisation or group suggests some potential for mobilising as women workers around equality-related issues (Hensman 1996a), and the success of the anti-marriage-clause agitation shows how powerful such mobilisation can be.

However, it would be foolish to underestimate the difficulties. Neither the feminist movement nor women politicians have taken much interest in issues of equity in employment, and women in the trade union movement have been so marginalised that the solidly male leadership finds it easy to ignore them. Moreover, women workers themselves, extremely vulnerable to victimisation and without any social security to fall back on, would be unwilling to risk their jobs unless they were able to see some prospect of victory. Hence the importance of support from outside. The ILO Core Conventions, which uphold the rights to freedom of association and collective bargaining as well as equal remuneration and equality of opportunity among others, have so far lacked any mechanism by which they can be enforced, but the current context of globalisation provides resources and opens up possibilities previously non-existent. International Trade Secretariats and other union organisations assist organisations of women workers like SEWA, while NGOs like Traidcraft help to market the products of SSA. Codes of Conduct, forced on European and North American retailers by consumer campaigns, and claiming to guarantee basic rights to workers in companies supplying their products, may not work in India, with its long and shifting subcontracting chains in the informal sector; but solidarity action by consumer campaigners in particular cases can help women workers in the formal sector to win their rights. Another possibility is to work for a labour rights clause in World Trade Organisation (WTO) agreements which can be used by women workers and activists to put pressure on the government to enact and implement legislation based on the ILO Core Conventions. The current proposal for a social clause by the ICFTU has drawbacks, but women activists can participate in the debate around it, and help to draw up a proposal which can be used to fight for women workers' rights in the informal as well as the formal sector. Women Working Worldwide, based in the UK and linked with women workers' groups in several Asian and Central American countries, is one organisation exploring these possibilities, as well as attempting to link women workers in different countries working for the same multinationals. Such strategies offer opportunities to build solidarity with women workers, trade unions and labour rights groups in other parts of the world in a common struggle.

Notes

1 I would like to thank all the women who participated in these interviews and discussions, and especially those who helped me to set them up and carry them out: Sujata Gothoskar, Vasuda, Ilina Sen, Subhashini Kohli, Mirai Chatterjee, Asha Mokashi and Chanda Korgaokar.
2 Interview with Kamala Karkal, January, 1994.
3 Interview in February 1994.
4 Communication from trade union organiser of HMKP. See also Westwood 1991 for labour–management problems in SEWA.
5 Group discussions with women garment workers conducted by Chanda Korgaokar and myself between 1998 and 2000, as part of an education and consultation exercise on Codes of Conduct by Women Working Worldwide (WWW). Over this period, participants from one sweatshop were first locked out and then dismissed for joining a union.

References

Bajpai, A. (ed.) (1996) *Women's Rights at the Workplace: Emerging Challenges and Legal Interventions*, Bombay: Tata Institute of Social Sciences.

Banaji, J. and Hensman, R. (1990) *Beyond Multinationalism: Management Policy and Bargaining Relationships in International Companies*, Delhi, Newbury Park and London: Sage Publications.

Banerjee, N. (1981) 'Is small beautiful?', in Bagchi, A.K., and Banerjee, N. (eds), *Change and Choice in Indian Industry*, Calcutta: K.P. Bagchi, pp. 177–295.

—— (1985) 'Women and industrialisation in developing countries', Occasional Paper no. 71, Calcutta: Centre for Studies in Social Sciences.

Bhattacharjee, D. (1999) *Organised Labour and Economic Liberalisation. India: Past, Present and Future*, Geneva: International Institute for Labour Studies.

Government of India (1998) *Economic Survey 1997–98*, New Delhi: Government of India.

Hensman, R. (1988) 'The gender divisions of labour in manufacturing industry: A case study in India', *South Asia Research* 8, 2, November: 133–53.

—— (1996a) 'Urban working-class women: The need for autonomy', in Chhachhi, A. and Pittin, R. (eds) *Confronting State, Capital and Patriarchy. Women Organizing in the Process of Industrialization*, UK: Macmillan Press and USA: St. Martin's Press, Inc., pp. 183–204.

—— (1996b) 'Impact of technological change on industrial women workers', in Rao, N., Rurup, L. and Sudarshan, R. (eds) *Sites of Change*, India: FES and UNDP, pp.186–202 *

—— (1996c) 'The impact of industrial restructuring on women, men and trade unions', in Sathyamurthy, T.V. (ed.) *Class Formation and Political Transformation in Post-Colonial India*, India: OUP, pp. 80–104.

Holmstrom, M. (1984) *Industry and Inequality – the Social Anthropology of Indian Labour*, Cambridge: CUP.

Liddle, J. (1988) 'Occupational sex segregation and women's work in India', in Liddle, J. (ed.) *Women's Employment in India, Equal Opportunities International* 7, 4/5: 7–25.

Mani, M. (1995) 'New attempt at workers' resistance: National Centre for Labour', *Economic and Political Weekly* 7 October: 2, 485–6.

Mukul Sharma (1995) 'To organise the unorganised', *Economic and Political Weekly* 17 June: 1, 422–3.

Rees, T. (1992) *Women and the Labour Market*, London and New York: Routledge.

Self Employed Women's Association (1988) *SEWA in 1988*, Ahmedabad: SEWA.

Sen, I. (1995) 'A case study from the mining sector in India', paper prepared for United Nations University Institute for New Technologies.

Standing, H. (1992) 'Employment', in Ostergaard, L. (ed.) *Gender and Development: A Practical Guide*, London and New York, Routledge.

Westwood, S. (1991) 'Gender and the politics of production in India', in Afshar, H. (ed.) *Women, Development and Survival in the Third World*, London and New York: Longman Group.

6   From unintended to undecided feminism?

Italian labour's changing and singular ambiguities

Bianca Beccalli and Guglielmo Meardi

Introduction

This chapter will analyse the relationship between women and trade unions in Italy. That relationship is seen as particularly ambiguous, even more so than in other countries. On the one hand, the distinctive egalitarian policy of the Italian unions and the unique alliance they formed with the feminist movement served women's interests for a time and to an extent. On the other hand, the unions as organisations have remained rooted in basically male social, cultural and organisational models and they find it increasingly difficult to cope with the emerging issues of diversity (an example being the enduring diffidence towards potentially women-friendly atypical and part-time jobs).

The chapter will first give some background information on the gendered nature of the Italian labour market and on legislation concerning women's work. Subsequently, it will describe women's presence in the unions over time and their representation in the unions' organisational structure. Then, more detailed case-study research in progress will be presented on union gender policies. Finally, some observations will be made on other issues of 'diversity' the Italian unions are facing. Conclusions will then be drawn concerning the current change of paradigm in women's activity in the trade unions: will the particular Italian path affect the answers to the new challenges – challenges which are largely similar to those of other countries?

The national background: coexisting tradition and innovation

Labour market and gender segregation in Italy

The Italian labour market is deeply structured along gender lines. The overall unemployment rate in Italy is not much higher than the EU average: 11.3 compared to 9.2 per cent in 1999 (Eurostat figures). However, this is actually a statistical artefact hiding the gap between the lowest unemployment rate for adult, male 'heads of family' in Europe (around 2 per cent) and the sky-high unemployment rate for women (15.6 per cent) and youth. Moreover, Italy has the lowest female activity rate in Europe (45.7 per cent – EU average 59.6). The incapacity of Italian governments to tackle the gender gap has been one of the most important complaints from the European Commission in its recommendations on the Italian National Action Plan on employment (Council of the European Union 1999). Gender segmentation goes along with an ancient but deepening geographical segmentation: unemployment in the South is now more than three times higher than in the Central and Northern regions.

It is evident then that the Italian labour market is rooted not only in an economic model but also in a gender arrangement (Yeandle 1999). So-called 'heads-of-family' enjoy high employment security, while the unemployment of women and youth is, though socially dramatic, treated as a secondary phenomenon. Private, kinship-based solidarity networks interact and integrate with the welfare state provisions. This is confirmed by the fact that the Italian welfare state (currently undergoing a process of difficult reform) provides no income support for the unemployed – a case almost unique in Europe. By contrast, since the 1970s it has maintained an income guarantee (*Cassa Integrazione Guadagni* – Wage Fund Guarantee) exclusively for workers (almost always Northern men) made redundant by large enterprises. Culturalist explanations are unable to account for the Southern European specificity (Jurado and Naldini 1996); a shift is necessary towards an approach joining industrial relations, gender relations, and welfare studies in an interpretative framework (O'Reilly and Spee 1998).

Although the Italian gender arrangement endures, an important move towards feminisation has occurred. Women's share in the total employment, after having declined during the whole twentieth century, increased from 27 per cent in 1972 up to 36.4 per cent in 1998. Structural factors are usually cited to explain the change (Reyneri 1996): on the 'supply' side, the demographic drop (Italy, traditionally prolific, now has one of the lowest birth rates in the world) and the growing levels of female educational attainment; on the 'demand' side, the growth of the service sector and the increasing request for traditionally female skills and attitudes. However, feminisation can also be interpreted as reflecting cultural or subjective choices among women workers and within workplace settings.

Within the workforce, gender inequality is apparently less dramatic if one looks at wage gaps and occupational segregation. Gender gaps in wages were for a long time lower than in most countries, thanks in part to egalitarian union policies. Between 1969 and 1981 women's wages rose from 70 per cent to 85 per cent of men's. However, the partial repudiation of egalitarian policies in the 1980s and 1990s (especially the abolition of automatic wage indexing and the diffusion of productivity bonuses) immediately rewidened all wage differentials, including the gender one. Decentralisation of collective bargaining since 1993 has also increased wage differentials by sex, since women are over-represented in industries and companies where unions have limited bargaining power. At the end of the 1990s the differential has thus increased to 29 per cent, above the EU average (27 per cent).

Segregation is apparently limited, but in fact this applies only to horizontal segregation (Charles 1992), which hides strong vertical segregation (Bianco 1993). A sort of 'glass ceiling' prevents women from arriving at the very top of organisations, and most careers are still designed on male models.

Both low horizontal and high vertical segregation are probably linked to a distinctive feature of female employment in Italy: the scarce diffusion of part-time working. In 1998, only 14.1 per cent of Italian women worked part-time, the second-lowest percentage in Europe after Greece and well below the EU average (31.8). Moreover, uniquely in Europe Italy has no significant difference in part-time employment between women with children and without (European Foundation 1997), which confirms that women's careers are less and less discontinuous in the period of motherhood.

In the last two decades, ethnicity has emerged as a further form of diversity within the workforce. Italy, traditionally a country of massive emigration, in the 1980s turned into a destination for immigrants from poorer countries. In the late 1990s, there are 800,000 registered immigrants from developing countries, with an additional 200–300,000 undocumented immigrants (ISTAT 2000).

Legislative framework

The birth of the new Italian Republic after World War II involved the legal recognition, before most other countries and international organisations, of the principle of equality at work (art. 37 of the Constitution, passed in 1948). Due to a convergence on these issues between the Left and Catholic culture, the principle of equality was not opposed to, but rather continuously joined with, protective attitudes towards women workers, as exemplified by the same art. 37. It was against this background that a generous legislative protection for working mothers and the principle of equal pay went hand in hand in the 1950s.

The presence of strong protection and generically egalitarian policies had, however, the paradoxical effect of precluding the space for more explicit and targeted equal opportunities policies. The most important laws on female employment (the law on equal opportunities passed in 1977 and the law on positive actions of 1991) were passed without particular mobilisation and debate, and had only limited efficacy. Collective bargaining, rather than legislation, has in practice been more important for women's work. Not only did the trade unions play a leading role but the actual implementation of legislative measures also depended to a large extent on industrial relations developments – as we shall argue in the next section.

Another important issue, which indirectly touches women's positions in the trade unions, is the problem of 'quotas' (Beccalli 1999). In 1995 the Constitutional Court established that quota systems contravened the constitutional principle of political equality and it suppressed the electoral norms foreseeing gender quotas. Positive discrimination remained legal in non-electoral matters, like employment rights, or the internal organisation of associations and political parties. But the Court's decision had a strong impact not only on parliamentary representation (where women's presence fell in the 1996 elections partly because gender quotas had been cancelled), but also, indirectly, on political and trade union organisations: quotas altogether were de-legitimated in the Italian political culture by the authoritative Constitutional Court.

Women in the trade unions: an ambiguous relation

Italian political trade unionism

Historically, the Italian labour movement has been characterised by late development, and by its strongly political and mainly class-based nature. Today's three largest trade unions were created in the postwar (and post-Fascism) period, along mainly political lines: left-wing (mostly communist) CGIL; moderate (mostly Christian-democrat) CISL; and social-democratic UIL (Table 6.1). Union density based on only CGIL-CISL-UIL is 35.4 per cent, but an estimated 5–7 per cent should be added to include autonomous trade unions, whose influence has been increasing since the 1980s. The union confederations are organised along both horizontal (regional) and vertical (industry federations) lines.

Italian trade unions, previously weak and deeply divided, imposed their influence during the exceptional season of labour unrest starting with the 'hot autumn' of 1969. In the 1970s the Italian trade unions greatly increased their power both in the workplaces and at the political level. A 'unity of action' between CGIL, CISL and UIL was achieved, and unionisation grew from around 30 per cent in the 1950s to a peak of 49 per cent in 1977. In the second half of the 1970s, however, the worsening economic situation, together with political changes, led to a gradual retreat of labour; though less spectacular than that in many other countries, this continued into the 1980s.

In the 1990s, Italian unions managed to avoid the corruption scandals and the fall in participation rates that hit political parties. Workplace representation was reformed with the introduction of the RSU (Unitary Union Representatives), elected by all employees. Decentralisation of collective bargaining went along with centralised 'concertation', engaging trade unions in tripartite agreements with employers and governments.

Women's presence in the trade unions

If there is a shortage of gender analyses in Italian industrial relations, even more striking in many regards is the lack of gender analyses by the trade unions. The most evident proof of union 'indifference' is the enduring lack of data on unions' gender composition. Union feminisation in Italy is usually estimated at 40 per cent,

Table 6.1 Italy's main union confederations, 1998 (thousands)

Trade union confederation (ideological roots)	Active members	Pensioners	Total membership (active + pensioners + others)	Union density (active members/ total employees) %
CGIL (left wing)	2,301	2,891	5,249	15.9
CISL (Christian)	1,739	1,960	3,910	12.0
UIL (moderate)	1,082	430	1,604	7.5

Sources: Trade unions.

that is slightly more than the percentage of the workforce (36.4 per cent) but less than the 49 per cent CGIL claims (for example CGIL estimates include pensioners, where women are over-represented for demographic reasons). The fragmentary data available in 2001 from local or industry organisations reveals that the assumptions used in those estimates are over-optimistic (see in particular the Milan case below). Average women's membership in unions seems roughly proportional to their participation in the workforce, though there are variations in some sectors (Table 6.2).

Despite the high unionisation rate of women, their representation in union hierarchies goes down as one goes up the bureaucratic ladder. In 1991, among the 13,518 delegates at the local congresses for the XII General CGIL Congress, only 24.4 per cent were women. Moreover, these women occupied lower positions in their organisations than men: 26.5 of male delegates were members of the workplace executive committees, while only 18.4 of their female counterparts were (Ricci and Tagliavia 1993). The situation worsens at the top level: in 1999 only eight out of the 160 *Camere del Lavoro* general secretaries were women.

CGIL introduced a 'soft' quota system in 1991. In all bodies a 'gradual' objective of at least 40 per cent was established for each sex, starting from a baseline of 30 per cent 'except in proven cases of inapplicability, and guaranteeing in those cases the removal of causes and the implementation of positive actions'. In 1996 the rule was strengthened, setting a 40 per cent threshold everywhere. No local organisation has implemented this rule to date.

CISL, which has always been organisationally more 'fluid' and is politically more conservative, has been more sceptical about a rigid instrument like quotas. In 1989 (when only 15 out of 253 members of the General Confederation Council were women) a slim 20 per cent quota was introduced. The system was never implemented and was eventually abandoned in 1995 following the Constitutional Court's verdict. In 1997, women's presence in the various CISL confederal boards ranged from 7.7 to 19 per cent.

Table 6.2 Proportion of women in senior positions in three largest Italian unions, 1991–2000

	CGIL	CISL	UIL
Total membership	2,301,424	1,739,130	1,082,442
Women as percentage of members, 1999–2000	49 (declared)	36 (estimate)	36 (estimate)
Women as percentage of National Board members	n.d.	12	n.d.
Women as percentage of Congress delegates	24.4	15.8	n.d.
Women as percentage of national full-time paid officers	n.d.	15.8	n.d.
Women as percentage of regional full-time paid officers	n.d.	15.2	n.d.

Sources: Trade unions.

The historical evolution of women's presence in the labour movement

The fundamental developments of women's presence in the Italian labour movements can be sketched following Beccalli (1984, 1996).

1890–1922: the roots

Since their beginnings, Italian trade unions have been committed to equality. The labour movement used to compensate for the lack of any 'strong' craft core (due to the heterogeneity of the Italian working class) with political and ideological resources – first of all class solidarity. This was most true for the horizontal, class-based *Camere del Lavoro* (CdL). Already around 1900, the CdLs were formally in favour of equal pay for men and women; they established several women's commissions, and often involved not only workers, but the community at large, including non-wage-earning women.

In addition, a distinctive characteristic of Italian trade unions at that time was an openness to outside intellectuals. Their involvement accentuated the 'moral', political character of the Italian labour movement, well noted by Robert Michels (1908). The recruitment of leaders from outside intellectuals and politicians was also a frequent channel for women leaders' recruitment, and it guaranteed openness to feminism, at the turn of the century as well as in recent decades.

1945–65: joining equality and protection

After the Fascist period and World War II, union attention to women's issues increased, especially in the class-oriented, left-wing CGIL. In the postwar period, in spite of their weakness, the unions tried with a certain degree of success to espouse 'protection' and 'equality'. Emblematic of this double commitment was Teresa Noce, national secretary of the clothing and textile union and a promoter of both the law protecting working mothers (passed in 1950) and the principle of wage equality (achieved through national collective bargaining in 1960, before most other industrialised countries).

Trade union practices, however, also showed a number of contradictions. For instance, in the immediate postwar period (as in most other countries, especially the US) the unions ratified the expulsion of women from employment, in order to defend the [male] 'heads of family'. In collective bargaining, unions' active defence of lowest-paid workers indirectly benefited women and narrowed wage differentials by sex from 50 to 30 per cent. Yet, for years the unions maintained separate (worse) job classifications for women.

1965–85: the hot autumn and union feminism

At the end of the 1960s, an exceptional season of labour unrest (the 'hot autumn') dramatically changed – and strengthened – the trade unions. While the students' movement made an important specific contribution to trade unions' policies and organisation in the upsurge of militancy around 1970, that was not the case for women. Although very active, women in this period were marginal to union renewal; in the wave of collective enthusiasm, their specific needs were hardly perceived, and even the best sociological accounts of that period remained absolutely unaware of the fact that workers had a gender (e.g. Pizzorno *et al.* 1978; Crouch and Pizzorno 1978). Nonetheless, by shaking former hierarchies in the companies and in the unions, creating extensive networks of activists, and producing cultural and political changes, the workers' mobilisation did prepare a situation in which trade union feminism could develop. One wave of mobilisation – in a form theoretically described by Tarrow (1994) – prepared the resources for a second, different one.

Around 1975 the first 'collectives' of women trade unionists were formed, originally at the local level (Frogett 1981; Ingrao and Piva 1984; Bianchi and Mormino 1984). The first collectives developed in the areas of greatest working-class militancy, that is the manufacturing unions (especially the metalworkers'), and not in the sectors of highest feminisation (like textile and clothing). The roots of the collectives were in *political* activism, not in *employment* transformations. Without any doubt, female participation developed autonomously, not as an effect of instrumental recruitment concerns by unionists: being focused on militancy, the unions were not particularly concerned with recruitment (which was in any case rapidly increasing) and the structural changes associated with labour market feminisation were at that time only slowly beginning.

Much of the language and many of the techniques used by these groups were borrowed from the new feminism. The style of discussion was similar to that of consciousness-raising sessions. The basic rule was separatism – a real break with the tradition of working-class organisations. Women criticised the hierarchy and unequal division of labour, which they faced as union activists. In a feminist perspective, the prevalent style of union militancy was condemned as 'masculine'. Militant women started to proclaim their difference and their own orientation, defined as practical, affective and emotional. Their new approach dismissed 'equal opportunities' as a goal, and aimed rather at changing the rules of the game for both men and women. The strategy was self-organisation, not proportionality: feminists wanted to change the unions, rather than find a place in them.

Union feminists won their basic demand for an autonomous network of women inside the unions, although they initially met with considerable resistance especially among CGIL communists, staunch believers in working-class unity. The women's network spread rapidly and coordinating committees were formed at the local and national levels. The movement became generally visible when women workers by the thousands marched in separate sections of national union demonstrations. Feminist ideas were officially accepted into trade unions discourse, which would still have been unthinkable in other countries (Cockburn 1984).

During the 1980s women's presence in the unions was consolidated with several initiatives (especially education programmes[1]), but in a context of general decline in activism. Many feminist unionists quit the trade unions for political or cultural work, or left the public arena altogether. Divisions emerged among women unionists themselves, notably on issues in which the goals of equality and of difference were conflicting, like night shifts, part-time and non-traditional jobs.

1985–2000: equal opportunities and flexibility

In the 1990s, the militant nature of Italian trade unions is largely a memory of the past. Unions have grown as bureaucratic organisations and are involved in macro- and micro-corporatist arrangements. In the meanwhile, female presence in the workforce and in the unions has incessantly increased.

Exchanges with feminism have continued, but mostly with the more reformist components. Though women's autonomy is by now officially recognised even in the national union charters,[2] the 'separate' women's collectives and committees suffered a crisis. Symbolically enough, the highest women's union body, CGIL women's coordinating committee, was replaced with a lighter (but intentionally more visible and autonomous) Women's Forum. The national Forum is composed of representatives from all the various forms and levels of women's self-organisation in the union, which autonomously choose their own organisational form (groups, collectives, coordinating committees, Forums . . .). The creation of the Forum, as full recognition of women's self-organisation, arrived somewhat late, after the decline of militancy. Many leftist women even opposed the idea of a Forum, fearing that moderate unionists would dominate it. Officially planned in 1996, the Forum was eventually installed only in 1999, revealing the loss of dynamism of women's self-organisation in the unions (CGIL 1999).

Since the late 1980s, equal opportunities, which had been previously neglected, became the main field of activism for women unionists (see discussion below). Another important issue in the new unions' gender policies is working time. In the 1980s, trade union feminism pragmatically abandoned the a priori opposition to part-time work and, if reluctantly, accepted night shifts for women. Union feminists did not abandon, by contrast, either the claim of difference or the opposition to sexual division of labour in the family and in society: both were united in the debate about 'time to care' and the organisation of time. These themes have gradually entered into mainstream union elaboration (like the new CGIL Charter of 1996). Concretely, in collective bargaining more emphasis has been placed on part-time, 'hours' banks', and working time organisation (FIOM 1998). Italian trade unions in the 1990s have also strengthened their action for fighting sexual harassment in the workplace and for improving maternity benefits, which have been achieved in several national agreements. A unions-promoted law on parental leave, introducing some form of worker-centred flexibility and some fatherhood responsibility, was passed in 2000.

Recapitulating, the historic pattern of Italian unions displays a number of paradoxes and ambiguities, which endure in today's situation. It may be said that, thanks to their egalitarian orientation, until the mid-1970s the unions were feminist without knowing it: the reduction of the gender gap in pay was the best example of many unintended women-friendly practices. Later on, women's presence in the unions became much more visible, but the impact on policies and on organisation largely failed to meet the expectations: the unions now claim to be feminist, without being so.

In order to understand the nature of these contradictions and of these changes, it is necessary to look in more depth at the grassroots.

A leading case: Milan trade unions

Rationale and methodology

Milan is a particularly suitable observatory to analyse the latest developments in the relationship between unions and women. The area is economically the most advanced in Italy; after having been the largest industrial city, Milan is today the capital of services: finance, telecommunications, design. Moreover, Milan was central to the development of both unions' renewal and new feminism in the 1970s. Although union feminism has been more radical in Turin, Milan is usually where all new political trends are more visible.

This section will present some results from research in progress on the two largest trade unions, the CGIL (in particular its territorial organisation, the *Camera del Lavoro*) and the CISL (Milan *Unione Sindacale Territoriale*, Labour Territorial Union, and Lombardy regional federation). The local UIL is left aside because it is much weaker than the other two confederations.[3] In the CGIL case two industrial federations have been analysed more directly: metalworkers (FIOM) and banking (FISAC). The investigation, following a case-study methodology, is based on a collection of union documents in the period 1990–2000 and on in-depth interviews with officers and activists (all women).

Milan CGIL

Milan CGIL has been historically one of the most advanced Italian unions in the dialogue with feminism and in the struggles for women's rights. Milan *Camera del Lavoro* (CdL) as early as 1891 had claimed equal pay for men and women. In the late 1970s the original trade union feminism found much space there, especially in the metalworkers' federation.

In 1997, 39.7 per cent of CGIL members in Milan and its hinterland are women. This is, however, the average between 49 per cent among retired members and 33 per cent among active members. Feminisation remains lower in the unions than in the labour market (39 per cent in the Milan area). Women's presence declines at the higher levels of the organisation: in 1999 22.2 per cent of the secretariat's members and 35 per cent of the executive committee's members are women, which is less than the 40 per cent 'programmatically' required by the CGIL Charter. However, rather unusually in Italy, some women have gained visibility at the very top of union leadership, breaking the 'glass ceiling'. Two industrial federations have women as general secretaries in Milan, and two others at the regional (Lombardy) level. In general, from unionists' accounts there emerges a situation of 'partial awareness' by the organisation of gender difference:

> When electing a secretariat, men feel somehow ashamed of presenting electoral lists without women. On the other hand, as soon as there are one or two women they are happy and they feel some 'nuisance' if there are further female intrusions.
>
> (CdL officer)

Perhaps more important than the pure data, however, is the experience of women's self-organisation in Milan CGIL. Milan Women's Coordinating Committee was for a long time one of the most active in Italy. Recently, in line with the national decision, it transformed itself into a 'Women's Forum'. While this transformation went along with harsh conflicts between leftist and reformist factions at the national level and in other local organisations, in Milan the different areas of union feminism easily found an agreement. Women unionists do not restrict themselves to their different, specific identities (political and/or feminist streams), but tend to find a compromise around a wide pragmatic, reformist (women activists themselves prefer the word 'transformative') union feminism.

The Women's Coordinating Committee (now Forum) had struggled over its two decades of existence to obtain legitimacy and a voice within the CdL, finally gaining full recognition in 1996. Now, Women's Forum has the right to propose its own candidates to the Secretariat (although these candidates must be approved later by the congress, in a sort of 'double validation' which is not required of 'mainstream' candidates). Interestingly enough, this originally 'exceptional' prerogative was later extended to other minority groups (first of all immigrants), confirming that openness to gender differences can eventually open the way to openness to diversity broadly. Women-only structures (in whatever form women themselves choose) are recognised as official trade union structures, and not simply as additional bodies. The consequences are important both symbolically and practically. First, resources are allocated to women's autonomous organisation (above all, the opportunity for women activists to use union permits for activities of women's self-organisation). Symbolically, a 'class' organisation has agreed to allow, and even encourage to an extent, 'working-class' representatives to act as representatives of a specific group.

The Women's Coordinating Committee has managed, by transforming itself, to endure and possibly to increase its impact on the union altogether, but women's self-organisation nonetheless appears at a time of bewilderment. Outside the small circle of CdL women officers, female unionists are unable to explain in what ways the Forum differs from the former Coordinating Committee, apart from its more limited activity. Moreover, the other multiple forms of women's self-organisation in the Milan area have visibly declined over the last two decades. The industry-level women's coordinating committees have mostly disappeared, including that in the metalworkers'. Of the local women's ward committees, which were particularly innovative during the late 1970s in the new radical feminism elaboration, only one has survived, and it has progressively moved from trade union into more cultural activity. A different case is the banking sector, where the increasing feminisation of the workforce and the involvement in equal opportunities programmes allow the women's coordinating committee to keep an active role. The FISAC union has a female coordinating committee very active in both recruitment (feminisation is at

45 per cent) and workplace activity (for instance, in a programme of monitoring and career design to avoid disadvantages for part-time workers).

The decline in self-organisation is also a symptom of a crisis, after the exchanges in the 1970s and 1980s, in the relationship between unionism and radical feminism. The latter, while sometimes coming to terms with moderate unionists, is increasingly at odds with its former allies in the unions, i.e. left-wing groups. The struggle is no longer between feminism and unions, but within each – with each being composite and pluralist fields. On the one hand, feminists from the historic Milan group's Women's Bookstore (among whom some are former union activists) underline the positive potential of flexibility for women (Cigarini and Marangelli 1998) and advocate a change of paradigm for unionism: from general protection, to daily micro-conflicts at work for the affirmation of female difference; from representation, to self-defence and self-expression. The fact that extreme-left feminists turn out implicitly to converge with neo-classic economic arguments is apparently surprising, but actually similar to developments at the theoretical level outside Italy, where some authors use women's preferences and rational choice theory as de facto ex-post rationalisations of the status quo and its existing power relations (e.g. Hakim 2000). On the other hand, feminists more linked to a class paradigm contest any concession to flexibility, considering the rhetoric of female expectations as subordination and 'dimming of the perception of being exploited' (Rossanda 1997).

Milan CISL

CISL is, as a confederation, politically more moderate than CGIL. However, in the activist wave of the 1970s, it proved to be more open than CGIL and it recruited, especially among metalworkers, large numbers of radical activists. Among the activists were feminists: CISL was perceived as less based on a male-dominated class model and more 'heterodox'. CGIL culture, by contrast, appeared to many union feminists as purely 'emancipatory', focusing on the archetypally male, permanent, full-time, employment in manufacturing. A proof of CISL openness was the greater tolerance within the CISL for women's separate self-organisation and innovative practices (Bianchi and Mormino 1984; Nappi and Regalia 1978). The left-wing minority in the CISL, influential throughout the 1980s, was later progressively marginalised.

Today, the female presence in Milanese CISL seems in a worse situation than in the CGIL (Rosa CISL 1999), although no precise data on membership are available. Among officers, women are concentrated in the so-called 'technical' apparatus (mainly secretarial work), while the 'political' one remains dominated by men. Women are 30.4 per cent of all union officers and 8.3 per cent in the territorial secretariats. Female activists now wonder whether it was a mistake not to introduce quotas ten years ago: 'we opted for a political pact with the leadership instead of that for quotas; but leaders did not respect the pact' (Regional CISL officer).

In the 1990s, Milan CISL has been particularly involved in equal opportunities projects (see below). Equal opportunities has been an important occasion for launching extensive training of female activists. This has, however, touched 'mainstream' unionism only very weakly:

> It is as if instead of rehabilitating lame people, we spent time in making them aware of the fact that they are lame. All this emphasis on equal opportunities reinforces a culture of women as handicapped.
>
> (ex-UST officer)

> We tried to introduce equal opportunities into the training for union executives, now there is a module on it and some other gender stuff. It's me who runs these courses [for executives], and I see that during the module on equal opportunities the attendance rate among male participants suddenly drops.
>
> (Regional CISL officer)

The organisation model, in the CISL as well as in the CGIL, remains deeply male, pyramidal and 'militant' in the most 'military' sense. Here, however, in the absence of any quota system, women have developed a more general criticism. Some women officers (others being reluctant on this point) propose as an alternative a collegial model, avoiding the over-centralisation of responsibilities, which, in turn, reinforces the stereotype of the tough and unlimitedly available leader. In the job of union officer, or union delegate, time is an organisational problem for women. Female activists do not simply contest the model: they complain that unionists' unlimited time is largely a male self-perpetuating myth. Not only is this time often filled by easily avoidable rituals (e.g. never-ending meetings and overnight negotiations), but even rituals are disappearing: union offices after five o'clock or on Saturday are empty, but nonetheless women are still scared by (unnecessary) demands for extensive availability. The same applies to mobility: women are expected to be available anywhere, any time, but union officers actually travel very little. A CISL investigation of top union leaders shows that female leaders actually managed quite well to reconcile life and career, and this exposes the self-justificatory functions of the myths of unlimited availability and mobility.

Eventually, however, equal opportunities have sharpened the awareness of discrimination among women within the unions themselves. An increasing number of equal opportunities projects are carried on within the union. One of the most important was launched in Lombardy CISL. The first step has been an organisational analysis aiming at discovering the reasons for discrimination and for the lack of career opportunities for women employed in the 'technical' apparatus. A positive action plan is expected to follow.

Gender aspects of union practice in Milan

Women-backed issues are becoming more visible in 'mainstream' unions' bargaining activity. These issues include equal opportunities, motherhood and childcare, working time, and sexual harassment. In most arenas the three confederations

(CGIL, CISL and UIL) usually cooperate, although some differences persist: CISL appears more convinced about the 'participative' sides of equal opportunities projects, CGIL is more resolute about more classic demands.

Equal opportunities and positive action initiatives started in the second half of the 1980s, prompted by both unions and government on the basis of confidence in participatory industrial relations. The success of the first experiences led in 1991 to legislation and to the multiplying of such projects, although the law is not generously funded. In the last years, however, the programme is visibly slowing down. New projects are rarely presented, and several old projects have not been renewed because employers think that the bureaucratic requirements exceed the benefits. The projects are mostly concentrated in the northern part of the country, the Milan area leading with around one hundred projects in force.

In some company agreements on equal opportunities women are included as a third party, alongside the two traditional partners of industrial relations, although theirs is more a role of investigation and promotion than of negotiation. In some situations these 'third' bodies undoubtedly owe their origins to the trade unions (women's trade union committees), while in others the protagonists are formal or informal groups that have nothing to do with trade unions. This range of situations seems to be responsible for the incomplete and fragmentary results (Bergamaschi 1997).

In areas where the female presence is strong and skilled, as in the banking sector, equal opportunities projects have produced important knowledge and awareness about work organisation, which has been translated into incisive positive actions. In other cases, however, there have even been 'unholy' alliances between male unionists and management against women's action. In some cases positive action projects initially planned by joint equal opportunities committees (constituted by female unionists and second-level managers) were later dropped or 'watered down' during the real bargaining round, in which the sides were represented by male union leaders and male top managers.

There are other gender issues besides equal opportunities. Maternity leave is bargained mostly at the national level, recently with considerable success. Local and company-level bargaining often improves the situation on childcare leave. These issues have been put on the bargaining table seriously only in the 1990s: previously, they used to vanish from union proposals after the first negotiation round.

On part-time and working schedules, the attitudes of unions and women activists have deeply changed. In the 1970s, there was constant pressure to obtain for part-time workers not only protection proportional to that enjoyed by full-time employees, but even disproportionate benefits (some collective agreements at that time established as much as 60 per cent salary for 50 per cent part-time). This policy has certainly prevented a discriminatory and segregating use of part-time employment (as happened in other countries), but probably at the cost of precluding also 'voluntary' part-time. The union attitude originated in men's fear of being 'undercut', but this was shared by women activists as well. It is in the 1990s that a pragmatic-feminist attitude has prevailed, making the part-time option into a women's demand. Increase of part-time working has been obtained in most collective agreements and implemented (although still at a small scale) in company agreements, always with anti-discrimination measures.

Apart from part-time working, there is widespread negotiation of 'conciliation policies' introducing atypical working arrangements, which in the majority of cases affect women. Unions are trying to develop an alternative vision of flexibility, putting human life (not simply family life, which would reintroduce traditional gender roles) at the centre. Its implementation is still limited, but women's thematising of working time is, however, starting to have an impact on 'mainstream unionism' (e.g. on Milan CdL Congress's last document on 'city and times').

As for sexual harassment, workplace unions do not usually deal with it, but simply refer problems to specific offices like the 'Women's Centre' created within the CdL by the CGIL. As a matter of fact, women victims of harassment rarely turn to the unions for support.

'Mainstream' bargaining, however, remains largely in male hands, women's issues being treated outside the most important moments of negotiations. In this regard women officers charge that the unions still tend to favour male employees in the agreements on restructuring and redundancies. A fundamental problem remains in fact at the organisational level, still largely male-dominated in spite of some cracks in the 'glass ceiling'. The most alarming recent development is the very low (even in comparison with union headquarters) female presence in the newly elected workplace representatives (RSU): only 17 per cent in the 1997 electoral round in the private sector (CGIL source). The situation in the RSU, the most grassroots among union boards, immediately raises the issue of the patterns of female activism.

Self-organisation and beyond

Separate self-organisation has been a fundamental experience for women in the Italian trade unions, and represented a clear rupture with previous activism patterns (Lunadei *et al.* 1999). In the 1990s, however, the experience of self-organisation has visibly slowed. Participants started to define women's coordinating committees as unwieldy and centralised (Lunadei *et al.* 1998; Donati 1993). Some of the separate bodies disappeared (starting with the previously avant-garde metalworkers'), while others took a lower profile. Women activists mention various reasons for this slowing down:

- Originally, women's committees refused to be 'organisations' in a structural sense, being rather anti-hierarchical bodies fitting the definition of 'water in the cage' (Bocchio and Torchi 1979); once trade unions moved from a social movement to an institutional model, a dilemma about their identity arose.
- In a structured organisation, women's committees turned out to be costly 'duplicates' on many issues.
- Rivalries among women, and in particular strains between women's self-organisation and the 'mainstream' progressively emerged. Plural loyalties and

different political orientations among women grew in importance, undermining women's unitary self-organisation.
- A basic ambiguity between gender- and general representation was never resolved, leading to the incapacity to challenge the essence of unions' bargaining practice; the gap between theoretical elaboration and bargaining practice increased disorientation.
- The committees, originally a space of freedom and self-determination, turned out to be often perceived as a filter for the individual freedom of single women (especially the youngest).

All these reasons contain a part of the truth. The in-depth investigation carried out in Milan suggests, however, that there has been a change in attitudes among female activists as well. First of all – and this is a change experienced by male activists too – activists are much less willing to spend time in meetings and tend to see them as tiresome, time-consuming rituals: 'today's frenetic rhythms do not allow of wasting time in meetings as before' (FIOM officer). Women unionists are aware of this change and report their efforts to find new forms of involvement, more individualised and outside traditional union meetings.

Moreover, a generational break raises new dividing lines. Younger activists are often critical of their older comrades. Young women too stress their difference from the previous generation, with some scepticism about the activity of their older female colleagues. Fundamental rights that had been secured through long struggles are now seen as 'natural'. Gender difference itself is seen as obvious, as if it no longer needs to be asserted against male-based generic representations of the norm. Moreover, women's committees themselves are sometimes seen as a legacy of the past, and other, more individualised, forms of activism are preferred. The interviews collected in Milan, as well as previous research carried out in the early 1990s (Donati 1991) and other research on trade union activists (Meardi 2000) show that young women activists prefer general- to gender representation, though keeping a sharp awareness of gender difference. Having seen the current limits of women's policy in the union, young women fear that gender representation ('dealing only with women's matter') would eventually marginalise them.

This does not imply that self-organisation belongs to the past. Fieldwork research (Meardi 2000) shows that on specific matters women's and youth groups can be very effective not only for the minority concerned, but also for transforming the unions into more 'discursive' organisations. The new 'equal opportunity committees' may also be seen as a form of self-organisation (although not explicitly separate). Moreover, separate organisation has become a model for other groups such as immigrants and younger people, which suggests that the decline in women's self-organisation is contingent and generational. Given the endurance of gender inequality it is not unlikely that in the near future another generation of young women will rediscover self-organisation, or reinvent it in new forms.

Widening equal opportunities to minority groups

Other important issues of 'diversity' are currently emerging within labour. Ethnic minorities have become an issue in Italian society only since the 1980s. Trade unions have had a positive, supportive attitude, promoting for instance, since 1986, various laws for undocumented immigrants' legalisation. This point deserves some consideration because it could not have been taken for granted at the outset (notably in a situation of high unemployment) and it contrasts with unions' reticence in many other countries.

Immigrant workers' presence in the trade unions has rapidly increased. In 1999 93,410 immigrants were CISL members, three times more than at the beginning of the decade. The other trade unions have a much smaller presence of immigrants: 43,108 in the CGIL (1998) and about 30,000 in the UIL. Altogether, this suggests a respectable unionisation rate among legal immigrants, close to 30 per cent and hence not much lower than among Italian nationals. Italian trade unions are also open to undocumented immigrants: 16–17 per cent of immigrants frequenting CGIL structures do not have a valid stay permit.

Immigrants' attitudes towards the unions is often instrumental: many joined the unions to receive assistance in the legalisation process or for welfare-related needs (as is the case of most domestic servants). Their backgrounds as to association and union behaviour are very varied. However, there is today (thanks also to a significant effort in training) a significant number of foreign officers and representatives (165 elected officers in the CISL in 1999, 82 in the CGIL in 1998). Immigrants' presence seems not yet 'normalised' in mainstream unionism but, after some initial mistakes, collective bargaining is beginning to understand and consider minorities' demands (Allievi 1996; Mottura and Pinto 1996). Direct competition with the local workforce has emerged only rarely, mostly in agriculture.

Another important area of diversity is disability. Unions' policy in this regard has been widely criticised for insufficient attention, prompting a tendency among the disabled to organise outside trade unions (either in radical, militant forms like the League for Disabled People's Rights or in institutional, welfare-oriented forms like the Civil Mutilated and Disabled National Association). The first national agreement heralding disabled people's employment programmes was that of the metalworkers of 1976; but only a few years later the unions failed to resist the massive expulsion of disabled workers during the restructuring processes, which made disabled people the first victims of the tripartite agreement of 1983. In the 1980s the unions created specific offices to deal with disabled workers (e.g. CGIL *Ufficio H*). At the political level the unions were among the promoters of the new law on disabled people's employment, passed in 1999. At the company and industry levels (where employers' resistance is strong) the engagement is less evident. Research on the specific case of the mentally disabled (Meardi 1993) did not reveal any appreciable role of the unions.

Other issues of diversity (sexual orientation, past detention, drug addiction . . .) are dealt with by the unions through specific offices such as the Social Policy Offices in the CGIL. And there are some innovative practices, for example the creation of centres for transsexuals' rights in Bologna and Turin by the CGIL in cooperation with the Italian Transsexuals' Movement. Altogether, these various out-groups (from women to stigmatised groups) present new, diversified demands on the unions, starting with the need for specialist legal protection.

Conclusions

Politically, Italian unions have been strongly egalitarian. Examples are numerous: unions have supported equal pay for men and women, obtaining it before most other industrialised countries; they have advocated investment and active employment policies in the South, even at the cost of wage restraint in the North; more recently, they have organised the largest demonstrations in favour of immigrants' rights. The egalitarianism of Italian unions has, however, been indifferent to gender. In a country where the gender arrangement is strongly unequal, such indifference had largely perverse effects: whatever the intentions, in reality Italian unions have not arrested or reversed women's segregation and the discrimination practised against them.

But women are not only 'objects' of union policies; they are also – and above all – subjects of union renewal. Although women's self-organisation, after very positive experience, is going through a period of crisis, Italian women activists are contributing with their difference to the transformation of the unions into more 'discursive' organisations. This may in turn allow developing forms of solidarity with people outside the borders of the 'working class' as traditionally defined (Hyman 1999). In a way, it can be said that sex difference, as an archetypal difference, is teaching the unions how to deal with diversity within the national workforce and maybe even beyond the national borders. By connecting work experience with life experience, women are also in a position to develop new forms of union politics, different from former party loyalty and reconsidering the established 'protective boxes' of work regulation. Women are already much more likely to raise issues of environment protection and encompassing social policy than men.

On the other hand, the behaviour of men in the Italian trade unions illustrates a discrepancy between official and 'underground' levels of action – a familiar pattern in Italian politics and industrial relations (Regini 1995): while they have accepted (even more willingly than elsewhere) women's self-organisation, pay equality and, in the CGIL case, gender quotas, their resistance, if passive, is nonetheless weighty. This is evident, for example, in the failure to implement the official quotas in CGIL and in the small number of women elected to the company-level union bodies.

However, the current situation reveals a break with the past. For a long time women's presence in Italian trade unionism was prompted by political activism, in a way 'external' to the workplace. It emerged in the most politically militant sections of the workforce (the metalworkers, paradoxically the most male-dominated) and it was organised often outside the workplaces, in the form of coordinating, inclusive committees. While this form of presence is declining, new forms of female activism, more individualised and more focused on 'mainstream' workplace policies, are now developing around the issues of equal opportunities and working time. Women are now strongest in the groups (e.g. banking) where they are numerous and have produced knowledge based on their own work experience. This change of perspective, from politics to work, opens up new possibilities for women in unions, where they used to be autonomously present in the organisation but too weak in shop-floor bargaining as delegates or experts.

The unions' very future may depend on the success of this new strategy. The next decade will show whether the peculiar Italian labour tradition (strong preference for equality, but little 'targeted' attention to diversity) will become a resource or a hindrance in face of the new challenges of flexibility and inequality that Italy largely shares with other countries.

Notes

1   Very important was the experience, started in the late 1970s, of the '150 hours' autonomous workers' education courses, fully paid and in working time (Caldwell 1983).
2   The new CGIL Charter adopted in 1996 affirms 'a trade union of women and men, and the accomplished representation of CGIL complexity, made of pluralism and diversities' (art. 6).
3   UIL, although generally supportive of women because of its 'laic' roots, has not exhibited particular initiatives in this field over the last years.

References

Allievi, S. (1996) 'Immigrazione e sindacato: un rapporto incompiuto', *Sociologia del Lavoro* 64: 153–69.
Beccalli, B. (1984) 'Italy', in Cook, A, Lorwin, V. and Daniels, A. (eds) *Women and Trade Unions in Eleven Industrialized Countries*, Philadelphia: Temple University Press.
—— (1996) 'The modern women's movement in Italy', in Threlfall, M. (ed.) *Mapping the Women's Movement: Family Politics and Social Transformation in the North*, London: Verso.
—— (ed.) (1999) *Donne in quota*, Milan: Feltrinelli.
Bergamaschi, M. (1997) *Equal Opportunities and Collective Bargaining in the European Union. Selected Agreements from Italy, Phase II*, Dublin: European Foundation.
Bianchi, M. and Mormino, M. (1984) 'Militanti di se stesse. Il movimento delle donne a Milano', in Melucci, A. (ed.) *Altri codici. Aree di movimento nella metropoli*, Bologna: Il Mulino.
Bianco, M.L. (1993) 'Percorsi della segregazione femminile, meccanismi sociali e ragioni degli attori', *Polis* 7, 2: 277–300.
Bocchio, F. and Torchi, A. (1979) *L'acqua in gabbia. Voci di donne dentro il Sindacato*, Milan: La Salamandra.
Caldwell, L. (1993) 'Courses for women: The example of the 150 hours in Italy', *Feminist Review* 14: 71–83.
CGIL (1999) *Donne per lo sviluppo. Forum delle donne della CGIL, 22–3 febbraio 1999*, Rome: Ediesse.
Charles, M. (1992) 'Cross-national variation in occupational sex segregation', *American Sociological Review* 4, 57: 483–502.
Cigarini, L. and Marangelli, M. (1998) 'Pratiche politiche per creare libertà', *Via Dogana* 37: 3–4.

Cockburn, C. (1984) 'Introduction: Trade unions and the radicalizing of socialist feminism', *Feminist Review* 16: 43–6.

Crouch, C. and Pizzorno, A. (eds) (1978) *The Resurgence of Class Conflict in Western Europe since 1968*, London: Macmillan.

Donati, E. (ed.) (1991) *Il sindacato delle ragazze*. Milan: Ediesse.

Council of the European Union (1999) *Joint Employment Report*. Brussels: EC 13607/99.

European Foundation (1997) *Gender and Working Conditions in the European Union*, Luxembourg: Office for Official Publications of the European Communities.

FIOM (1998) *Previsioni del tempo. Metalmeccaniche a confronto su orario e orari*, Rome: Meta.

Frogett, L. (1981) 'L'acqua in gabbia: A summary and discussion', *Feminist Review* 8: 35–43.

Hakim, C. (2000) *Work-Lifestyle Choices in the 21st Century: Preference Theory*, Oxford: Oxford University Press.

Hyman, R. (1999) 'Imagined solidarities: Can trade unions resist globalization?', in Leisink, B. (ed.), *Globalization and Labour Relations*, Cheltenham: Elgar.

Ingrao, C. and Piva, P. (1984) 'Union power and the problem of work', *Feminist Review* 16: 51–5.

Jurado, T. and Naldini, M. (1996) 'Is the South so different? Italian and Spanish families in comparative perspective', *South European Society & Politics* 1, 3: 42–66.

Lunadei, S., Motti, L. and Righi, M.L. (eds) (1998) *Le donne nel sindacato italiano: gli anni del femminismo. Atti del seminario, Roma, 31 ottobre 1998*, Rome: Istituto Gramsci, mimeo.

—— (eds) (1999) *E' brava, ma . . . Donne nella Cgil 1944–62*, Rome: Ediesse.

Meardi, G. (1993) 'L'inserimento lavorativo dei disabili psichici. Due progetti mirati nelle municipalizzate milanesi', Tesi di laurea, Università di Milano.

—— (2000) *Trade Union Activists, East and West: Comparisons in Multinational Companies*, Aldershot: Ashgate.

Michels, R. (1908) *Il proletariato e la borghesia nel movimento socialista italiano*, Turin: Frat. Bocca.

Mottura, G. and Pinto, P. (1996) *Immigrazione e cambiamento sociale. Strategie sindacali e lavoro straniero in Italia*, Rome: Ediesse.

Nappi, A. and Regalia, I. (eds) (1978) *La pratica politica delle donne*, Milan: Mazzotta.

O'Reilly, J. and Spee, C. (1998) 'The future of regulation of work and welfare: Time for a revised social and gender contract?', *European Journal of Industrial Relations* 4, 3: 259–81.

Pizzorno, A., Regalia, I., Regini, M. and Reyneri, E. (1978) *Lotte operaie e sindacato in Italia: 1968–1972*, Bologna: Il Mulino.

Regini, M. (1995) *Uncertain Boundaries: The Social and Political Construction of European Economies*, Cambridge: Cambridge University Press.

Reyneri, M. (1996) *Sociologia del mercato del lavoro*, Bologna: Il Mulino.

Ricci, C. and Tagliavia, C. (eds) (1993) 'Foto di gruppo', *IRES Materiali* 4.

Roberts, E. (1984) *A Woman's Place: An Oral History of Working-Class Women 1890–1940*, Oxford: Blackwell.

Rosa CISL (1999), *La presenza delle donne all'interno dell'organizzazione*, Milan: mimeo.

Rossanda, R. (1997) 'Intervento', in FIOM-Le Nove-IRES Torino, *Esplorare il lavoro. Sfide e provocazioni delle metalmeccaniche*, Rome: Meta.

Tarrow, S. (1994) *Power in Movement: Social Movements, Collective Action and Politics*, Cambridge: Cambridge University Press.

Yeandle, S. (1999) 'Women, men, and non-standard employment: Breadwinning and caregiving in Germany, Italy, and the UK', in Crompton, R. (ed.) *Restructuring Gender Relations and Employment: The Decline of the Male Breadwinner*, Oxford: Oxford University Press.

7 Changing gender relations in German trade unions

From 'Workers' Patriarchy' to gender democracy?

Sigrid Koch-Baumgarten

Introduction

When in 1999 the German federal union, DGB, celebrated its fiftieth anniversary, the political scientist and trade union researcher Ulrich von Alemann (1999: 728) pointed to 'a relatively homogeneous membership' as one of the most significant features of the German trade union model. Does Germany therefore represent a deviant case of homogeneity in a book dealing with diversity and unions in an international context? On the contrary, women unionists, including the DGB's female vice-president Ursula Engelen-Kefer, made the voices of women and migrants heard in a broad political initiative of female politicians, demanding a 'new societal contract' intended to realise a modern democracy, based on equal rights and opportunities for all citizens – women, men, and migrants – and designed towards 'partnership, equal opportunities, justice and tolerance' (Aktionsbuch 1998). Has the German trade union model[1] thus changed from homogeneity to heterogeneity? Actually, the German union membership has never been as homogeneous as claimed in trade union research. Women always accounted for about one sixth of the entire union membership. German scholarly literature, however, heavily influenced by the idea of (class or interest group) homogeneity, ignored the division of labour and of its organisation by gender – and likewise by ideology, generation, qualification, status, and nation (Kerchner and Koch-Baumgarten 1998), although early women's studies drew attention to the female outposts within the union landscape and to the special interests and identities of female employees and union members (e.g. Pinl 1977; Lippe 1983). Only in recent years has trade union research identified an increasing fragmentation of the German labour force as well as the pluralisation of employees' interests, views and values. This fragmentation is owing to the socio-economic shift from the industrial to the post-industrial society and to German unification (Hoffmann *et al.* 1990). Obviously, the East–West division is a significant and peculiar feature of the German case. Nevertheless, empirical research on diversity and gender within German unions is still scarce. In particular systematic and detailed investigations of gender relations within *individual* unions are nearly non-existent. Even recent studies, which note the transformation of centralist union organisations into rudimentary network-unions and which thereby acknowledge diversity within the union membership, have so far only mentioned gender issues in passing (Alemann and Schmidt 1998; Klatt 1997; Martens 2000). Therefore my investigations are based on the evaluation of published and unpublished documents, placed at my disposal by women's departments of the German trade unions.

In this chapter I want to analyse changing gender relations in German trade unions as part of a comprehensive process of negotiated institutional change, since the unions have to respond to the challenge of political and economic changes in their organisational environment, and to recognise the increasing diversification of interests within the workforce and union membership. Do the unions provide women with equal access to power and decision-making positions, allowing them to influence policy-formulation and implementation? I regard corresponding organisational reforms as the result of political negotiations, internal conflicts and power struggles among competing crucial membership groups, including the unions' women's movement, and the union leadership and administration. Thus it is necessary to focus on the actors' strategies in gender politics and to the power resources commanded by them as well. Since the adaptation of organisations to structural change is one of the most difficult and complex demands made of social actors – involving innovation and continuity, reform and the maintenance of the status quo – a variety of future scenarios is conceivable. The establishment of gender democracy and equality within the unions is one possible outcome. On the other hand, path dependencies and the strength of inertial forces could lead to the adoption of 'symbolic solutions' which merely cover up existing problems, thus relieving the pressure on political actors and eventually leading to the obstruction of reforms and finally to the 'successful failure' (Seibel 1991) of the organisation.

The tradition of the German worker's patriarchy

In the postwar years the German unions were founded as a unitary movement based on 17 autonomous industrial unions ('one firm one union'), affiliated with the umbrella organisation DGB.[2] The DGB claimed to include and represent the interests of both blue- and white-collar workers, skilled and unskilled employees, men and women, Christians, communists and social democrats. In fact, however, the union membership, the union elites and the union culture and interest policies were dominated by one group, which was generally identified with the prototypical German class and union member: the male blue-collar worker with formal training, a distinctive occupational identity, high wages, stable and secure full-time employment across the lifespan, and socialist orientation. Blue-collar workers had a membership share of 82.6 per cent in 1950, and of 61.9 per cent even in 1998 (Ebbinghaus and Visser 2000: 336, 322, 329–30).

White-collar workers and unskilled and migrant workers remained a minority among union members. The same was true for women, accounting for only one-third of the paid employed in Germany. The number of women unionists only slowly increased from 1.0 million (16.4 per cent of the total union membership of 5.5 million) in 1950 to 2.4 million (24.6 per cent of 7.9 million) in 1989. The degree of unionisation among (often female) white-collar workers and women workers remained low: in 1970 only 17.2 per cent of the female employees were affiliated to a union (compared to 44.9 per cent of male workers). By 1990 in West Germany this number had risen to 21.7 per cent for women workers and 45.3 per cent of male workers (Müller-Jentsch 1997: 127). Orientated towards the prototypical male worker the German unions regarded women with distinctive working and living conditions as outsiders or inferior labour – with discontinuous career paths, often lacking formal training, low-paid, working part-time as a result of their family commitments and with both a familial and an occupational identity. Women unionists were excluded from the unions' power elites; their representation in decision-making bodies remained marginal for decades. Thus, previous feminist findings considered the German unions a 'workers' patriarchy' (Pinl 1977). Women's political participation was restricted to segregated female spaces and to special women's structures which commanded neither power nor status within the hierarchical organisations. In 1980 these structures were in place in some (eight out of 17, Lippe 1983: 63) unions in the form of target group departments (*Personengruppenabteilungen*), which existed as well for youth, white-collar workers and sometimes for migrants. However, they aimed to integrate groups of the membership and to produce 'consensus and compliance' (Hassel 1999: 89), rather than to represent a constituency, to voice particular group interests and secure their influence on policy-formulation. In some instances, male members of the executive were responsible for the work of the women's departments well into the 1980s (Bilden *et al.* 1994: 63).

With the exception of maternity protection and the special (in fact, discriminatory) protection from heavy manual labour and night work, little attention had previously been paid to the particular interests of women workers. There were even objections in principle to the paid employment of women within the unions, in keeping with the conservative model of the male as the breadwinner with the female as a complement of the reproductive worker or source of supplementary income (cf. DGB 1993; Kurz-Scherf 1994). It is likely that such views prevailed in German society as a whole and heavily influenced institutional gender policies in Germany. They also affected the centralised and moderately corporatistic 'German model' of industrial relations, characterised by sectoral collective bargaining coverage and comprehensive collective agreements. They formerly included special gender pay grades, even for equal work, with average lower differences of 20–5 per cent for the women's grades. These lower rates were abolished not as a result of union initiatives, but by a Federal Constitutional Court ruling in 1955. Afterwards the social parties introduced so-called 'light-work' pay grades in the collective agreements which had the same effect on female labour and which partially survived until the 1980s (Pinl 1977: 31–55; Lippe 1983: 79–82). Although comparable forms of direct discrimination disappeared with the equal rights legislation there remained severe obstacles to equal opportunities for women: the systems of skills classification and demands and stresses in the workplace privilege the male and full-time worker through the unequal evaluation of physical strength and social competencies, through seniority rules and through the disregard of special demands and strains at

Table 7.1 Gross monthly income by gender, Germany, 1999 (DM)

		Old states	*New states*
Blue-collar workers	men	4783	3584
	women	3507	2841
White-collar workers	men	6609	4981
	women	4617	3832

Source: Statistisches Bundesamt 2000.

women's workplaces (Winter 1998). Up to now a considerable gender income gap in Germany has survived (partly as a result of female part-time work and the occupational and hierarchical gender segregation in the labour market – see Table 7.1). In 1999 in the Old states female employees on average earned between one-quarter (blue-collar workers) and one-third (white-collar workers) less than men for similar work; in the New states one-fifth to one-quarter.

Challenges to union homogeneity

Women in the labour market

The hegemony of the male qualified blue-collar worker and the 'workers' patriarchy' have been put under intense pressure with the erosion of the comprehensive conservative societal gender regime since the 1980s. Its mainstays were the gender-specific division of the public and the private, the model of the male as the breadwinner, and the limited inclusion of women in a labour market characterised by the predominance of the (male) industrial sector and by a rigid horizontal and vertical gender segregation. Owing to tertiarisation processes and to German unification the employment of white-collar workers and of women has been increasing considerably, while at the same time the employment of men in industry has been declining. In 1999 women accounted for 43.2 per cent of the total labour force (in 1970 for only 34), and the female activity rate rose to 63.8 per cent in the same period. In East Germany an 'equality advantage' of women on the labour market and a high level of female employment have survived: the female activity rate in the German Democratic Republic stood at 82.3 per cent in 1989 compared to 39.9 per cent in the Federal Republic. The East–West divide is apparent, first of all, in a higher activity rate of Eastern women (73.9 per cent compared to 59.9 per cent), especially of women with children (95.3 per cent and 57.2 per cent in 1996), and second in a stronger orientation towards full-time work in the East, where the gender income gap is lower, too. In general, the unequal division of domestic labour still means that approximately one-third of women (37.3 per cent in West and 20.1 in East Germany in 1996) work part-time; in 1999, women accounted for 88.2 per cent of part-timers and 78.3 of marginal part-timers (Statistisches Bundesamt 1998, 1999, 2000; Bundesministerium für Familie, Senioren, Frauen und Jugend 1998: 61). The labour market is still horizontally and vertically segmented along gender lines (Table 7.2). A majority of the female workforce is concentrated in a few

Table 7.2 Employment by sector and gender, Germany, 1998

Sector	Male	Female	Male	Female
	Percentage of male/female labour force		*Percentage of sectoral employment*	
Agriculture, Forestry	3.1	2.5	62	38
Industry, Mining	30.4	15.7	72	28
Building	1.2	2.7	87	13
Energy, Water Supply	13.5	0.4	79	21
Commerce, Hotels, Restaurants	14.2	21.9	43	57
Transport, Communication	6.7	3.5	71	29
Banking, Insurance	3.1	4.1	47	53
Real estates, Services for enterprises	6.6	8	46	54
Public administration	9.2	8.6	59	41
Public and Private Services	11.9	32.5	31	69

Source: Statistisches Bundesamt 1999.

professions, in part time work, and in low hierarchical positions. In East Germany female employees are slightly better represented in low management positions and skilled labour (Bundesministerium für Familie, Senioren, Frauen und Jugend 1998: 61). Most women work in the almost feminised service sector, in commerce, education, health services and in public service. In industry female employees – only a minority of the workforce – are working either in special 'feminised' branches (for instance in the cleaning sector in the construction industry), in office jobs or in low-paid occupations with little possibility of promotion and a high level of stress.

However, women's positions in the labour market cannot be characterised as homogeneous any more. There are differences among East- and West-German women, among blue- and white-collar workers, full-timers and part-timers or even marginal part-timers – in unprotected jobs, and until recently without social insurance. Additionally, 7 per cent of the entire female workforce are migrants, with a contrasting social and professional profile: the rate of married women among migrants is significantly higher, as is the rate of manufacturing professions and of industrial workers (Statistisches Bundesamt 1998: 78–9). Of great – if not decisive – importance for the positioning of women in the labour market, for their career opportunities and for women's interests and identities is the distinction between women with and without children. By 1998, the latter already formed the greater part (53.3 per cent) of the female workforce (Statistisches Bundesamt 1999: 108). The spectrum of women's paid employment now ranges from the full-time, low-paid and low-skilled (often foreign) industrial worker to the part-time semi-skilled white-collar worker or marginal part-timer in the service sector, to the high-skilled, high-paid senior executive in a globally operating finance company (Young 1998). Thus, women unionists and their strategies also have to respond to diversity within the group of women itself.

German unification and the establishment of multi-sector unions

Female union membership rates only slowly increased before 1990. Feminised employment areas like the private service sector, where only 6.5 per cent of the workforce is unionised (Hassel 1999: 38), still remains a wasteland of non-unionism. In the beginning the unions hardly responded to the growing diversity in the labour force. They did not concentrate on addressing and recruiting new occupational groups, for instance freelancers, women and white-collar workers in the service sector or in (union-free) enterprises of the New Economy. Thus, even now, the union membership social structure fails to keep up with the post-industrial employment structure (Hassel 1999: 41), given the remaining predominance of blue-collar (more than 60 per cent) and male workers (nearly 70 per cent) in the total union membership (Ebbinghaus and Visser 2000).

However, a boost in female membership followed German unification. In 1990, after the Free German Trade Union Federation (FDGB), the communist led organisation in the GDR, had dissolved and its industrial member unions had adapted to the West German union landscape and model, their members finally affiliated with the West German individual unions (Table 7.3). This meant a major, but short-lived increase in the overall union membership in 1991, which rose from 7.9 million in 1990 to 11.8 million in 1991, dropping back to 8.0 million in 1999. Given the higher traditional employment rate of women in the GDR and a considerably higher proportion of women members in the East German (48.6 per cent in 1991) than West German states (24.5 per cent), the proportion of women in the entire DGB membership rose from 25 per cent (absolutely 2.4 million) in 1989 to 33.2 per cent (4.6 million) in 1991. Afterwards the rate levelled off to 30.4 per cent (2.4 million) in 1999, since nearly half of the East German women, initially accounting for 52 per cent (resp. 37.6 per cent in 1995) of the entire female

Table 7.3 Female membership of German unions (DGB), 1999

Union	Total membership ('000)	Percentage of DGB membership	Female members ('000)	Female share (percentage)
IG BAU	585.4	7.28	70.8	12.1
IG BCE	922.8	11.48	174.7	18.9
GdED	338.1	4.21	68.3	20.2
GEW	273.8	3.41	185.4	67.7
HBV	457.7	5.70	303.7	66.4
GHK	132.9	1.60	21.4	16.1
IG Medien	179.1	2.23	57.6	32.2
IG M	2702.0	33.62	520.0	19.2
NGG	270.0	3.36	107.0	39.6
ÖTV	1526.9	19.00	703.1	46.0
GdP	190.6	2.37	33.8	17.7
DPG	457.5	5.69	198.8	43.5
DGB	8036.7	–	2444.6	30.4

Source: DGB 2000.

membership, left the unions during the post-unification decade. The overall degree of women's unionisation (21 per cent) still remains lower than that of men (36.7 per cent in 1997) (cf. DGB 1999; Ebbinghaus and Visser 2000). In line with the labour market segregation, the proportion of women in the traditional industrial unions is low, whereas the unions of the service sector have become feminised; unions, whose membership is spread evenly over the secondary and tertiary sector (IG Medien[3] and the Food, Drink and Tobacco and Catering Union, NGG), occupy an intermediate position.

In addition, German unification in general led to a significant East–West division within the German unions (Alemann 1999: 730). The affiliation of East German unionists to the DGB unions in 1990, brought a great number of 'newcomers' into the Western organisations, who had been politically socialised in an authoritarian state, in a socialist society and economy. Inexperienced with the West German labour market and industrial relations and accustomed to a completely different model of a socialist union organisation, they have represented contrasting organisational and professional cultures and identities within the predominantly West German membership from the beginning. Mergers of individual industrial unions,[4] following shortly after reunification – owing to the severe membership decline and the establishment of multi-sectoral unions – likewise brought together union members of various organisational structures and cultures (Klatt 1997). Thus, diversity in the German unions has increased considerably.

Responding to diversity

Steps towards the network-union

Diversity within the unions has challenged the traditional organisational German model of centralised unions. However, research on organisational union reform emphasises restrictions on reform, the strength of opposition to innovations, continuities and 'soft compromises' (Alemann and Schmid 1998: 48–9, 54, 426). On the other hand, a future union structure is emerging in the multi-sector and network union (Martens 2000), where oligarchic and hierarchical organisational structures have broken down and have been replaced by decentralised systems of 'loosely linked anarchy' (Alemann and Schmidt 1998: 30). Besides the traditional formal decision-making bodies and special departments for professional groups, white-collar, young and women workers, a variety of informal working groups have come into being (cf. also Klatt 1997), providing minorities and newcomers with opportunities for participation and policy formulation.

Migrants, for decades a small neglected minority of union members – representing between 1.2 per cent (DPG) and 7.8 per cent of union membership (IG CPK, Kühne *et al.* 1994: 312) – now establish informal working groups alongside formal target group structures, which have existed in some individual unions like the IG M since the 1970s. Special departments were established in the union executives (IG M, IG BCE, DGB) in order to deal with the particular problems and interests of migrants. Unions demand equal opportunities for migrant workers and they oppose racist attitudes and behaviours in union membership and in the workplace through educational work and publications. Additionally, special works agreements were concluded in important enterprises like VW and Thyssen by works councils and the management, to support equal treatment for migrants and Germans in the workplace and to prevent discrimination by sex, nation, religion, ethnicity and origin (DGB and IG BCE 1998).

Even sexual diversity has sometimes become recognised. Gay and lesbian unionists were able to overcome initial union resistance and to establish stable albeit small and decentral working groups within the DGB and a few service sector unions (GEW, ÖTV, HBV). Their objectives are to sensitise the unions for lesbian and gay concerns, to convince them to engage in opposition to workplace discrimination based on sexual orientation and to seek to identify the unions with the broader struggle for the acceptance of sexual diversity in society and the provision for equal rights in law (Holzhacker 1999).

In this context of increasing pluralism and decentralisation the formal women's departments have also been extended and complemented by various informal female working groups and bodies (see below). Diversity within the group of female union members itself has risen. This heterogeneity is not only constituted by the labour market – by profession, status and qualification – but likewise in private life: by personal living conditions and familiar commitments. A recent feminist study points to the differences in interests and identities among women unionists with and without children, married and unmarried, young and old (Bilden *et al.* 1994: 19). Additionally, there are substantial differences in orientations, beliefs and behaviour among women unionists from different individual albeit amalgamated unions (IG BAU 1996: 31–2; 1997: 19, 22–7) and from West or East Germany (cf. GEW 1998; IG BSE 1994). Due to their equality advantage on the labour market and as a consequence of their experience in the GDR, where no autonomous and feminist women's movement existed, East German women do not focus on equality issues or particular women's issues arising from the private sphere and from reproduction work. They often reject special women's departments and policies, since they derive their collective identity mainly from their professional and occupational status without considering gender a decisive source of inequality. This diversity, of course, makes it more difficult to define women's collective aims and politics and it thus affects strategic options of women unionists, too.

Union strategies on gender issues

Three major union strategies on gender issues can be identified among German unions:

1 Traditional 'proletarian' anti-feminism This approach traditionally focused on the biological differences between the sexes, and used these differences to legitimise a rigid separation of the 'female' private sphere and the 'male' public sphere. Its proponents objected to women performing any type of paid work or becoming involved in the trade unions or political institutions. A 'patriarchal blindness to women's issues' (Kurz-Scherf 1994) and a fundamental view of women as inferior has been preserved in its modernised form. Traditional anti-feminism rigidly obstructs innovations in gender policy, the autonomous voicing of women's interests, women's entitlement to political participation, and any form of affirmative action (Bilden *et al.* 1994: 57, 619).

Anti-feminists are to be found among the union membership and in the lower ranks of the hierarchy rather than the power elites; and in the traditional male-dominated industrial unions rather than the service-sector unions. Indeed, unions with a 'proletarian' culture maintain a male identity based on the model of the male breadwinner, manual labour and the associated occupational pride. However, there are also general reports of misogyny, exclusion and gender aggression (GEW 1997: 51; 1998: 435–6; Naumann 1992: 247). At the firm, local and district levels a lack of acceptance for women's policy and a lack of interest or activism with respect to women's issues are to be found in many unions (ÖTV 1996; GEW 1998: 428; IG M 1999c, 20; NGG 1997: Appendix, 3).

2 The paternalistic 'advancement of women'   This approach is based on the triad of equal opportunities, partnership and the advancement of women (Stiegler 1998: 20), and is another traditional aspect of the German trade unions. There have always been officials in the firms and organisations who have advocated including women in the unions, improving women's opportunities to participate, and supporting women's interests. Examination of female unionists' career paths also reveals that many women officials were 'discovered' and 'sponsored' by men (Bilden *et al.* 1994: 124–5). The motives for this can be political – a declaration of support for 'women's liberation' – or tactical, i.e., recruiting and integrating larger numbers of women unionists with the aim of ensuring that the union as a whole remains representative and maintains the power to act. In this model, too, women are regarded as an inferior 'special group' needing particular support (in the form of training) in order to achieve parity with the 'normal' worker/official as defined by men. Women's issues are seen as 'special interests' of secondary relevance, and are advocated on condition that they do not pose a threat to either the asymmetric power relations between men and women within the union or to the 'permanent employment privilege' of men (Hausen 1993: 7), i.e., men's preferential entitlement to socially recognised, high-grade employment, to higher pay, political representation and power. Or, as H.M. Pfarr put it for the ÖTV:

> Union policy for affirmative action is not near the top of the agenda for most male unionists. The widespread attitude is rather that women's interests can only be represented as supplementary interests, that is, as long as they do not call into question traditional principles and are of no cost to men. Above all, they should not interfere with structures which have been tailored to men and further male patterns of life.
>
> (ÖTV 1996: 13)

This approach is prevalent in the power elites as well as in the intermediate ranks of the hierarchy and in important membership groupings such as the works councils. It emerged in the 1980s, when women became the target of union recruitment drives (Kathmann 1998: 285) and a first phase of moderate affirmative action was initiated. While the unions became more receptive to the 'special needs' of women, these were still felt to be less important than many other issues. In a 1985 survey of DGB officials, 'equal pay rights for men and women' took only sixth place on the list of union priorities, after the safeguarding of jobs, protection against rationalisation, employment policy, the maintenance of the social security system, and co-determination rights (Niedenhoff and Pege 1987: 345). A survey of the officials and members of the IG BAU, a classical male-dominated industrial trade union, revealed that even in the mid-1990s, little had changed: equality issues were the sixth most important concern for officials and the seventh most important for members. Only just over 40 per cent of officials and 30 per cent of members felt this area of policy to be at all relevant, figures more or less corresponding to the proportion of women respondents (IG BSE, GGLF and SALSS 1995: 10, 35–7).

3 Pragmatic-innovative women's / equal opportunities policy   Male power elites and groupings within the membership may become receptive to the innovations of women's policy and equal opportunities policy as a result of the demands of organisational policy and the need to consolidate their own power base. When processes of modernisation and reform in the trade unions take the form of power struggles (Alemann and Schmid 1998: 407), thus developing into processes of political negotiation in which traditionalists and other interest groups can put up stiff resistance to reform, women unionists and women's committees may become relevant as allies to the modernisers on all levels of the organisation. Whether political concessions can be reached would then be dependent on the organisational weight and power resources which women introduce to the debate. In decentralised, heterogeneous and highly complex modern multi-sectoral and network unions, a new type of union official is emerging: the 'collegial communication manager', a mediator between various interest groups and power blocs (Prott 1998). He arranges pragmatic deals based on stable, informal networks of connections (ibid.: 337), which could stretch to include women unionists. Likewise, other newcomers with previously marginalised interests (e.g., freelancers, male part-timers, migrants), could enter into alliances in areas of common interest (time management, reform of the pay rates structure, improvement of committee representation, equal opportunities). In women's studies, too, a new 'dynamic' type of official has been identified: he is receptive to gender policy and uses women's and equal opportunities policy to further his own career (Bilden *et al.* 1994). But even where pragmatic deals with mutual benefits are concerned, it has proved to be counterproductive for union power elites and membership groupings to make equal rights concessions if these then have to be forced through in the face of fierce resistance from core groups of members. Such arrangements would thus appear to be a viable alternative mainly for unions with a majority or significant minority of women members and a network of influential women's committees, such as the service sector unions and the IG M.

Women's strategies

The women unionists, too, changed their strategy in the 1980s. Proclaiming the 'end of modesty', they renounced the fundamentally defensive policy and the attitude of 'active self-limitation' (DGB 1993: 110, 127) or 'self-denial' (Lippe 1983: 82–3) that had been characteristic of the postwar generation of women union activists, who often accepted the traditional gender roles and hierarchy themselves (cf. DGB 1993). A new generation of qualified women – socialised at a time of growing plurality in societal orientations and disintegration of the traditional gender relations, and increasingly influenced by the independent women's movement – now made more aggressive demands for enhanced participation rights within the unions. Four different strategies for women unionists can be distinguished (cf. a slightly different typology in Bilden *et al.* 1994).

1 The career-oriented, gender-transcending approach   These women derive their sense of identity primarily from their professional and occupational status. They concentrate on general union policy, in which women's interests – particularly those relating to non-work life – and equal opportunities policy play a subordinate role, if any. They view their trade union activism as furthering the interests of both women and men. Women unionists with no active interest in women's policy are to be found in all DGB unions, and many women officials consider involvement in the domain of women's policy to be detrimental to their career (IG M 1995b: 26). Women from the former East are among the most determined opponents of the feminist/women's policy approach in all of the individual unions. Many of them reject the quota system, the establishment of women's structures as a 'union within a union' (IG BAU 1997: 39), and the voicing of women-specific and particularly 'private' demands (GEW 1998: 172–3, 430, 191; IG BSE 1994: 39f).

2 The traditional women's policy approach   This is based on the classical triad of equal opportunities, partnership and the advancement of women (Stiegler 1998: 20). It operates within separate women's structures and advocates the 'special needs' of women – particularly with regard to women's career paths and the balancing of work and family commitments – but without calling into question the gender hierarchies of the trade unions and society as a whole. Proponents of this approach favour cooperative strategies as a means of gaining the support of male power elites and membership groupings, accept 'soft' instruments for affirmative action pro-grammes, and are prepared to put aside group-specific goals which threaten the social cohesion of the membership (DPG 1997: 3). The policy and strategy options available to women activists are determined by the specific environment and organisational culture of each of the unions. Particularly in male-dominated industrial unions, which belong to the conservative wing of the DGB, women emphasise the need for a strategy of gender cooperation (IG BAU 1997: 37,173). This approach also prevails in some of in the more feminised unions, however (DPG 1997: 3).

3 The feminist-socialism approach   In the IG M, on the other hand, where the general position is more adversarial and critical of society, a socialist-feminist approach critical of both capitalism and the patriarchal structure has emerged (IG M 1995a:

6). Its proponents see the female identity as defined by the double exploitation of the woman worker; and collective action is directed towards the transformation of both the economic structures (in cooperation with male workers) and the gender-specific division of labour and power in the unions and society as a whole (in opposition to men). This dual objective can lead to tension in the setting of political priorities and in the selection of cooperative or adversarial strategies. Feminist socialists otherwise share the concerns raised in the equal-opportunities approach described below.

4 The innovative, equal opportunities/feminist approach Since the mid-1990s, women unionists influenced by the new women's movement, women academics and the EU have adopted the concept of *equal opportunities policy* and *gender mainstreaming*. This breaks with central premises of traditional 'women's policy' such as the organisational and content-related segregation of women's 'special interests' and the concept of women as inferior labour. The approach is based on the four pillars of *quota regulations, standardisation, mainstreaming* and *autonomous practice* (cf. Stiegler 1998: 14–27). Equal opportunities policy is given priority in union activism, the objective being to identify and dismantle gender discrimination within the organisations and their policies, as well as in legislation, economic life and society as a whole. Proponents of this approach aim to establish gender democracy and egalitarian gender relations in the trade unions, in political institutions, on the labour market and in the workplace, and to formulate union policy, which will ensure equal opportunities in all domains, from social policy to wages (IG M 1999c; ÖTV 1999; Synopse 1998; GEW 1997; DGB 1997).

> Women increasingly feel irritated by the idea of the advancement of women. They don't want to be considered a minority in need of special support. They require equal opportunities. Particular personal and occupational biographies, different qualifications have to be recognised as equal. Whereas the concept of women's promotion explicitly addressed women only, new approaches also address men and a cooperative distribution of work. . . . Gender mainstreaming means integrating the idea of equal opportunity for women and men into union programmes and policies. Already in planning, the particular experiences, needs and interests of women and men have to be taken into account.
>
> (IG M 1999c: 3)

Special women's structures for the autonomous voicing of women's interests are to be maintained, but at the same time equipped with their own human and financial resources and with powers of delegation, publication and decision-making, and embedded in intra- and inter-union networks. Equal representation of the sexes is to be secured by quota regulations stipulating that women must be represented on all levels of the organisation in proportion to their numbers in the broader membership (Synopse 1999). This includes the egalitarian representation of women in external negotiating teams – for example in tripartite consultations, such as the national 'Alliance for Jobs', and in a corporate system structurally closed to women's interests.

In the modern service-sector unions GEW, ÖTV, and HBV, as well as in the DGB and IG M, this equal-opportunities approach has made a particular impact on the policy formulation of the women's committees since the mid-1990s and, with increasing networking between the women's structures, this impact is now extending to other unions, too (Synopse 1999).

Representation of women in decision-making bodies

Since in the 1980s the 'advancement of women approach' and its female counterpart, the traditional women's policy approach, became influential in most of the German unions. The consolidation of institutionalised women's policies and internal 'affirmative action programmes' made it onto the union agenda, the aim being to increase the marginal representation of women in decision-making bodies and to pave the way for 'equal opportunities' by providing special training schemes for women. Initially however, the proportion of women among the union officials hardly changed. Resistance against obligatory quotas, demanded by union feminists, remained strong. They could only be pushed through after a number of failed attempts in the 1990s (Kathmann 1998: 291), and then only in the unions with a high proportion of women members and feminist strategies, such as the ÖTV, DPG, IG Medien, HBV and, in 1999, in the IG M. A special regulation exists in the GEW, a tandem model, which stipulates gender parity within its chairs and their deputies. In the IG Medien, HBV and DAG, additional women can be appointed if quota regulations for wage councils are not fulfilled. And in the HBV, women are to be given priority in the filling of political secretary positions until the quota has been met (Synopse 1998, 1999).

Overall, the proportion of women in decision-making bodies in most cases has now been brought into line with their representation in the broader membership on the federal level: in the unions' congresses and in their general executives. The most serious deficits in the implementation of quota regulations are concentrated in the lower territorial levels (IG M 1995a, 1999a; ÖTV 1996: 30), where the traditional anti-feminism is strong. Irrespective of union quota regulations women are still under-represented in the top-level positions, on the regional level, and particularly on the district level and in the full-time administrative machinery, i.e., in what might be called the ministerial bureaucracy of the unions. Female trade union presidents are a rare breed at all territorial levels; the GEW and HBV – with a 'feminine' membership, female president and vice-president – are exceptions to the rule (Kathmann 1998: 292). Gender parity and the fulfilment of quota regulations have been achieved neither in the union bargaining committees, nor in the influential works councils, which are formally independent in the dual system of interest representation, but remain closely linked to the unions. On average, women accounted for 11.4 per cent of works council members in 1968 (Lippe 1983: 126) and 23.4 per cent in 1994. And the proportion of women on the union bargaining committees ranges from approximately 5.8 per cent in the IG BAU, to 14.5 per cent in the IG M and 25 per cent in the ÖTV. It ranges between 0 per cent and 66.5 per cent in the IG Medien, depending on the occupational group.

Consolidation and reform of women's committees

Today all of the DGB member unions have established women's committees, aiming at the independent policy formulation of women unionists, with representation in the union executives and with their own conferences. There is comprehensive coverage at the federal and regional level, less so at the local and branch level. In general, the women committees and conferences are entitled to file applications to the general conferences and executive committees, but only in exceptional cases to the union bargaining committees (HBV, DAG, ÖTV). They are entitled to elect or propose women's representatives for the executive committees, or delegates for union congresses and external committees. However, in most cases the women's structures have no autonomous decision-making powers; and their representatives in the union executives may even be restricted to an advisory status (Synopse 1999; NGG 1993, 1997). Often, they still lack prestige. In this case, women's departments have been barely able to overcome the structural deficiencies of target group work which, beyond a female sub-population, offers *symbolic* rather than *concrete* opportunities for participation.

However, women's departments particularly in the DGB, IG Medien, ÖTV, HBV, and IG M have actually managed to expand their power base. They are represented at all organisational levels, they sometimes manage their own budgets and are entitled to make public statements, to independently voice demands beyond the union structures and fill positions in external committees (Kathmann 1998: 294). In the ÖTV the regional women's secretaries are *ex officio* voting members of the union bargaining committees. If decisions, policies or demands made by the general union organs contravene the principles of equality, these women's committees have the right to object (as in the HBV and DAG) or the suspensory right of veto (IG Medien). In the IG M, the women's committee has the right to object to decisions which primarily apply to women; in the ÖTV, they enjoy the right to appeal if quota regulations are not fulfilled (IG M 1999c: 63; Synopse 1998, 1999; Stolz-Willig and Klenner 1996: 390).

Innovative forms of organisation have been established in many of the individual unions. A network of informal, decentralised, theme-based working groups, projects, workshops and – in the HBV – collective bargaining policy panels – have been set up to complement or replace formal, centralised and hierarchical women's departments. This has made the organisational substructure of institutionalised women's policy considerably broader and more flexible. New forms of participation have been opened to women unionists, in response to diversity, to serious declines in women's membership, and to a crisis of participation (IG M 1999c: 45, 53; GEW 1997: 27, 31; ÖTV 1997: 2; Synopse 1999). The decentralised, informal structures partially extend into the workplace; in 1997, for example, the IG M set up an 'equal opportunities in the workplace' network for interested works councils, groups of migrants, equal opportunities officers and both unionised and non-unionised women (IG M 1999b: 8–9; 1999c: 25–7). The informal women's groups have no institutional rights within the trade unions, however (Kathmann 1998: 294).

Links have been forged between the women's policy networks of the various unions, and connections established with non-union organisations, from the political parties and the ministries to academia and the autonomous women's movement, from which women unionists had still distanced themselves in the 1980s. Both the internal and institutional networking of the union women's committees is well developed in comparison to other women's group in Germany (Schreiber *et al.* 1996: 73–4). Thus, in recent years a 'party and union feminism' (Kontos 1994: 19) has developed and is making itself felt in various political arenas, pressing for equal right policies.

Approaches in union policies

Union policies remain ambiguous. On the one hand declarations of support for affirmative action and, since the mid-1990s, for equal opportunities have been incorporated into most of the union constitutions and programmes (Kathmann 1998: 287). Even sexual harassment has become a target of union policy in the enterprise. In particular, women's committees in the service sector unions and the IG M have commenced to systematically inspect the male-centred models, as well as the programmes, constitutions, demands and policies of the unions with respect to discrimination against women. It is their aim to integrate women's interests into all of the unions' policy areas. Shifts in consciousness are no longer demanded exclusively of women, but of both sexes. Those in managerial positions are to be sensitised to gender roles by means of 'gender training' (ÖTV 1996: 16, 1999; DGB 1997: 35). Audits identifying indirect discrimination in collective bargaining agreements and models for the non-discriminatory reevaluation of occupations have been drawn up (HBV 1990; IG M 1998; Degen and ÖTV 1998; ÖTV 1999; Winter 1997). Women unionists have initiated a variety of programmes reevaluating task requirements for women's jobs and the regrading of undervalued occupations (Winter 1994; IG M 1995b: 55–7). For example, cleaners belonging to the ÖTV in the state of Hesse have begun autonomously to determine the task requirements of their jobs. In the ÖTV, an equal opportunities officer for wages policy has been appointed to the general executive.

On the other hand the unions' daily work and policies are changing only very slowly. The mainstreaming of gender questions or equal opportunities targets in union policies is proving to be difficult. The unions often still privilege traditional politics, the 'advancement of women'-approach. There are no signs that they plan to prioritise the closing of the gender pay gap in union wages policy or collective bargaining by reforming the pay rates structures of collective agreements (Nauditt 1999). However, they are prepared to push through over-proportional pay rises for the (mostly female) employees in the lower-income grades, as did the IG BSE for women of the commercial cleaning sector (Jindra-Süß and Kleemann 1992: 7, 37–9). In 1997, the DGB organised an 'employment summit' without reference to equal opportunities issues or female participation, prompting women unionists to hold their own employment policy meeting in 1998. The corporatist Alliance for Jobs – including the unions' delegation – initially closed its doors to women, making no provision for equal opportunities policy (IG M 1999c). Some unions have hesitated to sponsor the long overdue introduction of equal opportunity legislation in the private sector, which has been seen as an infringement on free collective bargaining (Kodré 1997: 14). At the same time the DGB and other member unions and women unionists have campaigned for an equal opportunity act in the private economy, committing all enterprises to affirmative actions for women and to the reduction of occupational segregation. In Germany, only in the public sector do equal opportunity laws require the implementation of (weak) affirmative action (Schiek *et al.* 1996; Degener 1997). When health and safety laws which discriminated against women (bans on night work and on work in areas such as construction sites) were repealed in 1994, individual unions – including their women's committees – even opposed these equal rights amendments (IG BAU 1996: 41, 43; IG BSE 1990: 147–8; NGG 1997: 23).

Equal opportunities policy, however, has recently become a target of collective bargaining in the private sector, after the first union programmes for 'affirmative action in the workplace' had already been adopted in the mid-1980s (Weiler 1998). Numerous special agreements were concluded in the 1990s, which often place priority on facilitating the combination of career and family commitments, rather than on achieving an equal integration of women into the labour market. In contrast to the centralised German collective bargaining system, which normally stipulates binding regulations in sectoral agreements, covering the entire industry, the collective equal opportunity regulations in most cases are 'soft law' and limited to plant level. They draw up guidelines at industry level and leave concrete planning and implementation to ensuing plant agreements (see for instance the chemical industry, BAVC and IG BCE 1999). As such, private sector agreements on equal opportunities and affirmative action are still limited to a few industries – 150 firms and half of the employees in the chemical industry are affected – and a few prosperous large-scale enterprises.

Affirmative action measures in the workplace focus on arrangements such as parental leave, support for returners, family-friendly working hours, and offers of part-time work. An HBV initiative for the establishment of a 'career and family' fund to compensate for the loss of income incurred by parents and carers performing part-time work could not be pushed through (Stolz-Willig and Klenner 1996: 387). Only in exceptional cases have issues of recruitment and qualification been touched upon in an effort to dismantle gender-specific hierarchies and sectors of employment. Prioritising women's applications when candidates have the same qualifications (e.g., the rail company), deliberately employing more women in managerial positions and male-dominated domains (VW; chemical industry),[5] and institutionalising equal opportunities policy by means of women's officers, working groups and agreements protecting against sexual harassment in the workplace, have remained exceptions to the rule (Weiler 1998; Stolz-Willig and Klenner 1996; IG M 1999b). Most of them are based on the principle of 'soft' voluntary self-commitment, and renounce 'hard' instruments (such as the quota system), controls and sanctions.

Conclusion

The realignment of gender relations in the German trade unions is proving to be a complex and contradictory process. The unions have responded to the diversity of interests and the pluralism of orientations within their membership and workforce. Women's influence on policy-formulation has increased considerably, and their demands have been partially integrated into individual policy areas. However, political traditionalism coexists with innovations towards gender equality and democracy. Even today, unions often privilege traditional gender politics, which focus primarily on facilitating the combination of family and career commitments. Their objectives are organisational rather than egalitarian; to recruit members and maintain loyalties. They do not threaten the status quo or block the preferential access to power and representation of core groups within the male membership. Allowing women equal access to the labour market, to income and power would in fact be tantamount to a 'large-scale project of welfarist redistribution' (Hausen 1993: 10) between the sexes. Legitimised by their 'existential crisis', the unions show little interest in the 'secondary area of confrontation' of gender policy (ÖTV 1996: 13–14) or the 'luxury' of 'special interests' in equal opportunities policy (IG BAU 1997: 19).

While 57 per cent of the women unionists claimed to be satisfied with the results of their involvement within the union, a significant minority of 43 per cent felt that too little had been achieved (Schreiber *et al.* 1996: 63). Further steps towards expanding women's access to power and policy formulation and towards the mainstreaming of gender questions in union policies might prove to be hard to realise. Future success will also depend on external developments, on the gender politics of the institutions of the German welfare state, which in the past have proved to be significantly resistant to equal rights reforms (Kodré 1997). Concerning gender equality Germany in general is still a remarkably conservative and 'old-fashioned' country.

Notes

1   When the following illustrations refer to 'Germany', the 'German model' or 'German unions' *before* 1989 it is referring exclusively to the Federal Republic of Germany (and the DGB unions). With unification in 1990 the West German institutions and practices of industrial relations and the existing West German organisations of labour and capital were extended to East Germany, while the institutions of the former German Democratic Republic were abolished. If the chapter refers to the latter it is explicitly noted. *After* 1989 the description applies to unified Germany. When specific features of East (the New States) or West Germany (the Old States) are mentioned this is explicitly indicated.

2   I do not take into account some smaller rival unions of white-collar (DAG), Christian workers (CGB), and tenured civil servants (*Beamte*, DBB); see also note 1.

3   The IG Medien resulted from a merger involving the traditional industrial Printing and Paper Union amongst others, and thus has a very heterogeneous structure. More than a third of the members are blue-collar workers, but freelancers and students, who are recorded in the membership statistics under the same category as pensioners, the unemployed and trainees, also constitute a good third of the membership (DGB 1999).

4   The Union in the Textile and Clothing Industry and the Union in Wood and Plastic Manufacturing became part of IG M; the Industrial Union in Mining and Energy (IG BE), the Union in Chemicals, Paper and Ceramics (IG CPK) and the Leather Industry Union merged to form the Union in Mining, Chemical and Energy (IG BCE); and the construction union (IG BSE) amalgamated with the agriculture union to form the

Industrial Union in Construction, Agrarian and Environmental Sectors (IG BAU). In July 2001, as expected, a unified service sector trade union, Ver.di was created from the HBV, ÖTV, DPG, IG Medien and the DAG – a white-collar workers' union not previously affiliated to the DGB. With a combined membership of three million, Ver.di is now the largest DGB union.

5   The proportion of women in management committees rose from 3.5 per cent in 1989 to 7.7 per cent in 1998 in the chemicals industry (BAVC and IG BCE 1999; footnotes o.J.).

German trade unions cited in the text

DGB	Deutscher Gewerkschaftsbund (German Trade Unions' Federation)
DBB	Deutscher Beamtenbund (German Federation of Civil Servants)
CGB	Christlicher Gewerkschaftsbund Deutschlands (Christian Trade Unions' Federation)
DAG*	Deutsche Angestellten-Gewerkschaft (German Union of Salaried Employees)
DPG*	Deutsche Postgewerkschaft (Postal Employees' Union)
GEW	Gewerkschaft Erziehung und Wissenschaft (Union in Education and Science)
GGLF	Gewerkschaft Gartenbau, Land- und Forstwirtschaft (Union in Horticulture, Agriculture and Forestry)
GHK	Gewerkschaft Holz und Kunststoff (Union in Wood and Plastic Manufacturing)
GK	Gewerkschaft Kunst (Union of Artists)
GL	Gewerkschaft Leder (Leather Industry Union)
GTB	Gewerkschaft Textil, Bekleidung (Union in Textile and Clothing Industry)
GdED	Gewerkschaft der Eisenbahner Deutschlands (German Railway Union)
GdP	Gewerkschaft der Polizei (Union of Policemen)
HBV*	Gewerkschaft Handel, Banken und Versicherungen (Commerce, Banking and Insurance Union)
IG BAU	Industriegewerkschaft Bauen-Agrar-Umwelt (Industrial Union in Construction, Agrarian and Environmental Sectors)
IG BCE	Industriegewerkschaft Bergbau, Chemie, Energie (Industrial Union in Mining, Chemical, Energy)
IG Medien*	Industriegewerkschaft Medien (Industrial Union in Media)
IG M	Industriegewerkschaft Metall (Industrial Union in Metal and Allied Trades)
IG BE	Industriegewerkschaft Bergbau und Energie (Industrial Union in Mining and Energy)
IG BSE	Industriegewerkschaft Bau, Steine, Erden (Industrial Union in Building and Allied Trades)
IG CPK	Industriegewerkschaft Chemie, Papier, Keramik (Industrial Union in Chemicals, Paper and Ceramics)

NGG   Gewerkschaften Nahrung, Genuß, Gaststätten (Food, Hotel and Restaurant Union)
ÖTV*   Gewerkschaft Öffentliche Dienste, Transport und Verkehr (Public Services, Public and Private Transport Union)

* now: Ver.di

References

Aktionsbuch (1998) *Frauen wollen eine andere Politik. Selbstverpflichtungserklärung für einen neuen Gesellschaftsvertrag*, Düsseldorf.

Alemann, U. von (1999) 'Das deutsche Gewerkschaftsmodell auf dem Prüfstand', *Gewerkschaftliche Monatshefte*, 50, 12: 727–31.

Alemann, U. von and Schmid, J. (eds) (1998) *Die Gewerkschaft ÖTV. Reformen im Dickicht gewerkschaftlicher Organisationspolitik*, Baden-Baden: Nomos.

BAVC and IG BCE (1999) *10 Jahre Sozialpartner-Vereinbarung Chancengleichheit in der chemischen Industrie*, Hannover.

Bilden, H., Marquardt, R. and Poppe, N. (1994) *Frau geht voraus. Frauen – ein unterschätztes Innovationspotential in den Gewerkschaften*, München and Wien: Profil.

Bundesministerium für Familie, Senioren, Frauen und Jugend (ed.) (1998) *Frauen in der Bundesrepublik Deutschland*, Bonn.

Degen, B. and ÖTV (1998) *Ein- und Höhergruppierungsrecht für Frauen am Beispiel des BAT/BAT-O. Rechtliche Wege gegen Lohndiskriminierung*, Stuttgart: ÖTV.

Degener, T. (1997) 'Der Streit um Gleichheit und Differenz in der Bundesrepublik Deutschland seit 1945', in Gerhard, U. (ed.) *Frauen in der Geschichte des Rechts. Von der Frühen Neuzeit bis zur Gegenwart*, München: Beck, pp. 871–99.

DGB (ed.) (1993) 'Da haben wir uns alle schrecklich geirrt . . .'. *Die Geschichte der gewerkschaftlichen Frauenarbeit im Deutschen Gewerkschaftsbund von 1945 bis 1960*, Pfaffenweiler: Centaurus.

DGB (1997) *Geschäftsbericht der Abteilung Frauen im DGB-Bundesvorstand*. Berichtszeitraum 1993–96, Vorgelegt auf der 14. DGB-Bundesfrauenkonferenz vom 6 – 8.11.1997 in Magdeburg, Düsseldorf: DGB.

DGB (1999) *Mitgliederstatistik*, in: http: //WWW.dgb/wir/statistik/1999.index.htm accessed 15.9.2000.

DGB and IG BCE (1998) *Migrationspolitische Handreichungen. Diskriminierung am Arbeitsplatz – aktiv werden für Gleichbehandlung*, Düsseldorf: DGB.

DPG (1997) *Richtlinie für Frauenarbeit*, hekt.

Ebbinghaus, B. and Visser, J. (2000) *Trade Unions in Western Europe since 1945*, Basingstoke and Oxford: Macmillan.

GEW (1997) *GEW-Frauen. Statistische Angaben zur GEW Frauenarbeit*, o.O.: GEW.

GEW (1998) *Geschäftsbericht 1993–1997*, Frankfurt a.M.: GEW.

Hassel, A. (1999) *Gewerkschaften und sozialer Wandel. Mitgliederrekrutierung und Arbeitsbeziehungen in Deutschland und Großbritannien*, Baden-Baden: Nomos.

Hausen, K. (ed.) (1993) *Geschlechterhierarchie und Arbeitsteilung. Zur Geschichte ungleicher Erwerbschancen von Frauen und Männern*, Göttingen: Vandenhoek & Ruprecht.

HBV (1990) *Unmittelbarer und mittelbare Diskriminierung von Frauen wegen des Geschlechts in Betriebs- und Gesamtbetriebsvereinbarungen*. Untersuchung: Rose Engel, Düsseldorf: HBV.

Hoffmann, J., Hoffmann, R., Mückenberger, U. and Lange, D. (eds) (1990) *Jenseits der Beschlußlage. Gewerkschaften als Zukunftswerkstatt*, Köln: Bund-Verlag.

Holzhacker, R. (1999) 'Labour Unions and Sexual Diversity in Germany', in Hunt, G. (ed.)

Unions and Sexual Diversity Across Nations, Philadelphia: Temple University Press, pp. 238–52.

IG BAU (1996) *Wir können! Wir wollen! Wir wagen! Tätigkeitsbericht 4.* Bundesfrauenkonferenz der IG BAU 16., 17.11.1996, Frankfurt a.M. o.J.: IG BAU.

IG BAU (1997) *Wir können! Wir wollen! Wir wagen! Protokoll 4.* Bundesfrauenkonferenz der IG BAU, 16 – 17.11.1996, Frankfurt a.M.: IG BAU.

IG BAU (1998) *Satzung*, Frankfurt a. M. o.J.: IG BAU.

IG BSE (1990) *Ohne uns läuft nichts. Protokoll 2.* Bundesfrauenkonferenz der IG BSE, 27 – 28.10.1990, Frankfurt a.M. o.J.: IG BSE.

IG BSE (1994) *Wer – wenn nicht wir? Protokoll 3.* Bundesfrauenkonferenz der IG BSE am 20 – 21.11.1993 in Weimar, Frankfurt a.m.

IG BSE, GGLF and SALSS (1995) *BAU Gewerkschaft 2000. Meinungsbilder im Vergleich*, Frankfurt a.M., Kassel and Bonn.

IG M (1995a) *Frauenpolitisches Programm der IG Metall*, Frankfurt a.M.: IG M.

IG M (1995b) *Geschäftsbericht zur 15.* Frauenkonferenz der IG Metall in Sprockhövel vom 27 – 29.4.1995, Frankfurt a.M.: IG M.

IG M (1997) *Chancengleichheit durch Euro-Betriebsräte. Projektbericht*, Frankfurt a.M.: IG M.

IG M (1998) *Uns geht's ums Ganze. Frauen in der IG Metall.* Problemskizze zur mittelbaren Diskriminierung in Metalltarifverträgen. Rechtliche Problemskizze (Barbara Degen); Arbeitswissenschaftliche Problemskizze (Karin Tondorf), o.O.: IG M.

IG M (1999a) *Frauen in der IG Metall: Zahlen. Daten. Fakten 1999*, Frankfurt: IG M.

IG M (1999b) *Chancengleichheit im Betrieb*, Frankfurt a.M.: IG M.

IG M (1999c) *Geschäftsbericht zur 16.* Frauenkonferenz der IG Metall: Frauen schaffen neue Perspektiven, Frankfurt a.M.: IG M.

Jindra-Süß, D. and Kleemann, U.*(1992) *Frauenarbeit in der Gebäudereinigung*, ed. by the IG BSE, Frankfurt: IG BSE.

Kathmann, M. (1998) 'Von der Rand- zur Zielgruppe? Frauen in den Gewerkschaften', in Alemann and Schmid, pp. 285–94.

Kerchner, B. and Koch-Baumgarten, S. (1998) 'Geschlechterbilder in der politischen Auseinandersetzung', in Kerchner, B. and Koch-Baumgarten, S. (eds) *Geschlechterbilder in den Gewerkschaften. Internationale Wissenschaftliche Korrespondenz zur Geschichte der Arbeiterbewegung*, 34, Schwerpunktheft 3–4, Berlin, pp. 316–42.

Klatt, R. (1997) *Auf dem Wege zur Multibrachengewerkschaft. Die Entstehung der Industriegewerkschaft Bergbau-Chemie-Energie aus kultur- und organisationssoziologischer Perspektive*, Münster: Westfälisches Dampfboot.

Kodré, P. (1997) *Gleichbehandlungspolitik zwischen europäischer und nationalstaatlicher Regelung: Verflechtungen im Europäischen Mehrebenensystem* (= ZeS-Arbeitspapier Nr. 16), Zentrum für Sozialpolitik, Universität Bremen.

Kontos, S. (1994) 'Jenseits patriarchaler Alternativen: Grenzen der Gleichstellungspolitik', in Biester, E., Holland-Kunz, B. and Maleck-Levy, E. (eds) *Gleichstellungspolitik. Totems und Tabus: eine feministische Revision*, Frankfurt a.M. and New York: Campus.

Kühne, P., Öztürk, N. and West, K.-W. (eds) (1994) *Gewerkschaften und Einwanderung. Eine kritische Zwischenbilanz*, Köln: Bund.

Kurz-Scherf, I. (1994) 'Brauchen die Gewerkschaften ein neues Leitbild der Erwerbsarbeit? Oder: Brauchen die Frauen eine neue Gewerkschaft', *Gewerkschaftliche Monatshefte* 45, 7: 436–49.

Lippe, A. (1983) *Gewerkschaftliche Frauenarbeit. Parallelität ihrer Probleme in Frankreich und in der Bundesrepublik Deutschland 1949–1979*, Frankfurt a.M. and New York.: Campus.

Martens, H. (2000) 'Die Netzwerkgewerkschaft – eine Zukunftsoption?', *Gewerkschaftliche Monatshefte* 51, 5: 306–15.

Müller-Jentsch, W. (1997) *Soziologie der industriellen Beziehungen. Eine Einführung*, 2. erw. Aufl., Frankfurt a.m. and New York: Campus.

Nauditt, B. (1999) 'Entgelttarifverträge gegen Diskriminierung – Experiment mit verzögertem Start', *WSI-Mitteilungen* 52, 2: 99–108.

Naumann, B. (1992) 'Frauen in DGB-Strukturen – die unzureichende Einbindung von Fraueninteressen', *WSI-Mitteilungen* 45, 4: 241–9.

NGG (1993) *Tätigkeitsbericht 6*. Bundesfrauenkonferenz 22 – 23.10.1993, Mannheim, Hamburg: NGG.

NGG (1997) 7. Bundesfrauenkonferenz 21 – 22.11.1997 in Erfurt. Tätigkeitsbericht, Hamburg: NGG.

Niedenhoff, H.U. and Pege, W. (eds) (1987) *Gewerkschaftshandbuch. Daten, Fakten, Strukturen*, Köln: Deutscher Institutsverlag.

ÖTV (1996) 2. Ordentliche Bundesfrauenkonferenz. 31.1.-2.2.1996 in Magdeburg. Reden, Beschlüsse, Foren, Stuttgart: ÖTV.

ÖTV (1998) *Sechste Berichterstattung zur Umsetzung des Frauenförderplanes (hauptamtlicher Bereich)*. Stand 31.12.1997, Stuttgart: ÖTV.

ÖTV (1999) *Aufwertung von Frauentätigkeiten. Dokumentation und Materialsammlung*, Stuttgart: ÖTV

Pinl, C. (1977) *Das Arbeitnehmer-Patriarchat*, Köln: Kiepenheuer and Witsch.

Prott, J. (1998) 'Der Gewerkschaftssekretär. Eine konfliktreiche berufliche Rolle', in Alemann and Schmid (1998), pp. 329–40.

Schiek, D., Buhr, K., Dieball, H., Fritzsche, U., Klein-Schonnefeld, S. and Malzahn, M. (1996) Frauengleichstellungsgesetze des Bundes und der Länder. Kommentar für die Praxis zum Frauenfördergesetz für den Bundesdienst und zu den Frauenfördergesetzen, Gleichstellungsgesetzen und Gleichberechtigungsgesetzen der Länder, mit dem Beschäftigtenschutzgesetz, Köln: Bund.

Schreiber, R., Grunwald, M. and Hagemann-White, C. (1996) *Frauenverbände und Frauenvereinigungen in der Bundesrepublik Deutschland*, Stuttgart, Berlin, Köln: Kohlhammer.

Seibel, W. (1991) 'Erfolgreich scheiternde Organisationen', *Politische Vierteljahresschrift* 32, 4: 479–96.

Statistisches Bundesamt (1998) Im Blickpunkt: Frauen in Deutschland, Wiesbaden: Metzler-Poeschel.

Statistisches Bundesamt (1999) Statistisches Jahrbuch für die Bundesrepublik Deutschland, Wiesbaden: Metzler-Poeschel.

Statistisches Bundesamt (2000) Statistisches Jahrbuch für die Bundesrepublik Deutschland, Wiesbaden: Metzler-Poeschel.

Stiegler, B. (1998) *Frauen im Mainstreaming. Politische Strategien und Theorien zur Geschlechterfrage*, Bonn: FES.

Stolz-Willig, B. and Klenner, C. (1996) 'Chancengleichheit als Aufgabe der Tarifpolitik', *WSI-Mitteilungen* 49: 379–90.

Synopse (1998) Frauenpolitik in den Satzungen und Richtlinien der Gewerkschaften DAG, DPG, GEW, HBV, IG Medien und ÖTV (Fassung vom 27.7.1998), hekt. Mscr.

Synopse (1999) Von den außerordentlichen Kongressen bzw. Gewerkschaftstagen [DAG, DPG, HBV, IG Medien, ÖTV] beschlossene Anträge [zur Gleichstellungspolitik und Frauenorganisation], hekt. Mscr.

Weiler, A. (1998) *Gleichstellung in Tarifverträgen und Betriebsvereinbarungen. Analyse und Dokumentation*, ed. DGB and WSI, Düsseldorf: DGB.

Winter, R. (ed.) (1994) *Frauen verdienen mehr. Zur Neubewertung von Frauenarbeit im Tarifsystem*, Berlin: Sigma.

—— (1997) *Aufwertung von Frauentätigkeiten. Ein Gutachten im Auftrag der ÖTV.* Unter Mitarbeit von G. Krell, Stuttgart: ÖTV.

—— (1998) *Gleiches Entgelt für gleichwertige Arbeit: ein Prinzip ohne Praxis*, Baden-Baden: Nomos.

Young, B. (1998) 'Editorial', in Globalisierung und Gender. *PROKLA. Zeitschrift für kritische Sozialwissenschaft* 28, 111: Westfälisches Dampfboot.

8 Gender, diversity and mobilisation in UK trade unions

Fiona Colgan and Sue Ledwith

Introduction

Women, black, disabled and lesbian and gay members have been pressing for change in UK union structures, cultures and agendas. Over the last twenty years they have increasingly been recognised as significant stakeholders as UK unions have had to address their criticisms that unions are 'male, pale and stale' (TUC 1998a). The challenge is how to reformulate notions and practices of trade union democracy; to recognise that union membership is increasingly diverse, and diversely politicised, and that new structures and new cultures need to be developed to deliver union democracy and equality. This is crucial to collective organisation, renewal and mobilisation within UK trade unions.

This chapter first focuses on the changes taking place within the British labour movement in order to meet this challenge. Among UK unions, progress has been uneven, piecemeal and incremental. We argue that three factors have been important in forging a context for change. One key factor in the development of this new trade union agenda on equality, solidarity and collective action has been the activism of women, black, lesbian and gay, disabled and young trade unionists to establish themselves as legitimate constituencies within trade unions whose needs and concerns must also be addressed (Colgan 1999a; Colgan and Ledwith 2002). A second key factor is the presence of vanguard equality activists and officers with the commitment and expertise to develop broader equality coalitions and alliances to push for change. Here, the presence of feminist lay activists and union officers has been identified as a key driving force for change in UK unions (Colgan and Ledwith 2000; Kirton and Healy 1999) The third factor has been a context wherein union hierarchies have been perceived as unstable thus allowing previously marginalised groups to conceive an alternative to the status quo. For twenty years, the changing political and social environment, membership decline and union mergers have provided the fluid conditions in which groups of women, black, lesbian and gay, disabled and young workers have mobilised to take collective action and push for change in UK trade union culture, structure and the allocation of resources (Colgan and Ledwith 2002; Colgan 1999a; Heery 1998; Humphrey 1998; Healy and Kirton 2000).

The second part of the chapter examines this process following merger within UK trade unions. The GPMU, the industrial print union, was the product of a merger between SOGAT and the NGA in 1991. In the GPMU, women are in the minority, with 17 per cent of the membership and few members of other minority groups. The other case study is the public service union UNISON which was formed from a merger amongst COHSE, NALGO and NUPE in 1993. UNISON has a diverse membership of whom 72 per cent are women. Structural changes have been made in both of these merged unions to introduce forms of self-organisation and admit women to elected bodies in proportion to their membership. UNISON has taken the lead among UK unions in making these changes, whereas the GPMU has introduced them more slowly.

Gender, diversity and UK trade unions

Trade unions are ostensibly democratic organisations which are an important source of individual social identity for their members, and in particular of a collective identity of solidarity and unity among workers (Hyman 1975,1994; Kelly 1998). Yet as recent studies have shown there are also significant differences amongst different membership constituencies, for example in situations around workplace trade union democracy, local bargaining and industrial action (Colling and Dickens 1989, 2001; Colgan 1999a; TUC 2000a). As Hyman (1994) acknowledges in his discussion of changing trade union identities and strategies, trade unions are organisations for the representation of interests which act 'on behalf of specific constituencies, with criteria of inclusion which are at the same time principles of exclusion'. As a consequence, officials and activists in most UK unions are drawn from 'high-status, male, native-born, full-time employees' (Hyman 1994; LRD, 2000a, 2001d). A key challenge for UK unions during the 1980s was that they 'were charged whatever their governing structures, with being fundamentally undemocratic on the grounds that they failed properly to represent the interests of a large and growing proportion of their members' (Terry 1996).

As feminist critiques have emphasised, trade unions are gendered organisations and as a consequence, there has often been a divergence of interests between a union's structures, culture and negotiating priorities traditionally geared towards a white, male membership and their women (and other minority) members. The subsequent problems faced by UK unions in improving women's representation and participation as lay members (Colgan and Ledwith 1996; Kirton 1999) and officers (Dickens 2000) and their presence in collective bargaining (Colling and Dickens 2001) and at wider policy making forums (Cockburn 1995) is now well documented. The resulting 'democratic deficit' for women (and other minority groups) is clearly problematic as Dickens (1997) has observed given that 'issues of *internal* equality' are connected to 'issues of *external* equality'. Studies have shown that even where covered by collective bargaining, women and minority groups have rarely been involved in the process of negotiating, and collective bargaining agreements have often formalised and perpetuated tacit discrimination rather than challenged it (Campbell and Oliver 1996; Colling and Dickens 2001; Hunt 1999; TUC 2000a).

UK context

The economic, political and legal context for unions in the UK following the election of a neo-liberal Conservative government in 1979 was extremely difficult. Successive acts of Parliament restricted the activities of trade unions at all levels and numerous controls and sanctions were placed on trade union organisation and industrial action. Union areas of strength in the primary and manufacturing sectors were undermined by international competition and the drive to restructure. Despite a number of mergers to counteract this decline, influence within the trade union movement shifted towards predominantly public sector unions with larger female memberships (Dickens 2000), and in turn their areas of strength were undermined by privatisation, compulsory competitive tendering and contracting out (Millward *et al.* 2000). Trade union density dropped from 54 per cent of all workers in 1979 to 29.4 per cent in 2000 (Labour Force Survey (LFS), quoted in Labour Research Department (2001d)). Between 1987 and 2000 for example, the GPMU saw a 40 per cent drop in its membership and UNISON a drop of 22 per cent. The new organising imperative became union renewal by recruiting from previously marginalised groups such as women, black, young, lesbian and gay and part-time workers (Heery and Abbott 2000).

Following the election of a Labour government in 1997, most of the Conservative anti-union laws have been left in place and the policies of privatisation, albeit in different forms, are likely to be continued. However, the climate for unions is a more optimistic one given that the prospects for a recovery of union membership and influence are better now than for the last twenty years (Kelly 2000). Unemployment has been falling steadily for the past six years. The new government has been more positive about implementing European Union employment directives. It has extended some individual employment rights and has begun to focus on policies with an equality dimension concerning for example 'family friendly' and 'work-life' balance. It has strengthened the provisions of anti-discriminatory disability and race relations legislation, and – significant for unions – it has reintroduced the legal right to trade union recognition.

Although less constructive than hoped for by the unions, this new employment relations climate has had some positive effects. Trade union membership rose in 1998 for the first time in twenty years (LRD 2000b) and unions in 2000 were winning record numbers of new recognition deals (LRD 2001a). Table 8.1 summarises the variation in trade union density by gender, sector and employment, and shows the significance of female membership. In 1997, 28 per cent of black workers were in unions or staff associations compared with 30 per cent of all workers. However, there were wide variations between ethnic groups. For example, 36 per cent of Afro-Carribean workers were trade union members, compared with only 16 per cent of Pakistani and Bangladeshi workers. Black women (29 per cent) were more likely to be members of unions than black men (27 per cent) and women workers generally (28 per cent) (TUC 1998b).

Table 8.1 UK union density, 1989–2000 (%)

Category	1989	1998	1999	2000
All employees (excluding self-employed)	39.0	29.6	29.5	29.4
Men	44	31	31	31
Women	33	28	28	29
Full-time work	44	33	33	32
Part-time work	22	20	20	21
Manual workers	44	30	29	29
Non-manual workers	35	30	30	30
Production	45	31	29	29
Services	38	30	31	31
Less than 25 employees	19	15	15	16
25 or more employees	49	37	37	36
Public sector	n/a	61	60	60
Private Sector	n/a	19	19	19

Source: Labour Force Survey, Autumn 2000; LRD (2001d)

Trade union response

The key issue is whether trade unions have developed the capacity to adapt to this new and changing environment. Kelly (2000) is optimistic; in his view trade unions have shown a 'remarkable transformation in the composition of the trade union movement'. He suggests that there is now little difference at all in the unionisation rates of men and women and that the gap between part-timers and full-timers is shrinking. Surveys by Whitston and Waddington (1994) suggest that people join unions principally for collective or solidaristic reasons. The two major reasons cited were support in the event of a problem at work and improved pay and conditions.

However, research does indicate that unions still have some way to go in reaching out to their targeted and previously neglected groups. A TUC survey of non-union employees who wished to be union members found that they were more likely to be young, female, work in the private sector and work in small companies than trade unionists (TUC 1998b). A government commissioned report (1999) found that the low level of unionisation among workers posed a long-term threat to the future of trade unions (LRD 2001b). The need for trade unions to be aware also of the needs of black and ethnic minority workers was highlighted by the 1996 Labour Force Survey which showed that although union density among black workers was traditionally high, it was declining more rapidly among black and ethnic minority workers than white workers. In 1995/1996 it fell by 5 per cent for black employees compared to only 1 per cent for white employees (LRD 1998).

Membership representation and retention as well as recruitment is a key issue for unions. Waddington and Kerr (1999a) found that the public service union UNISON could reduce its membership turnover by at least a quarter by improving aspects of workplace organisation. They found that satisfaction about contact with predominantly male branch officers, stewards and full-time officers was much lower among women than among men, and that this was having an impact on the retention of women members. A TUC survey on challenging institutional racism at work, found that black representatives were vital in tackling racism (2000a). Another TUC survey (2000b) found that having a clear policy on lesbian and gay representation had been important as a foundation for attracting and retaining lesbian and gay members. However, it also found that although 44 per cent of lesbians and gay men said they had experienced discrimination at work related to their sexuality, two thirds had not looked to their union for help because of a reluctance to be 'out' and because of low levels of confidence in their union.

Trade unions and organising

This chapter focuses on the slow changes taking place within UK unions in order to address gender and diversity. As set out earlier, three factors have been key to the changes taking place. The first is the activism of women, black, lesbian and gay, disabled and young trade unionists as they have established themselves as legitimate constituencies through autonomous, or self-organisation, within trade unions (Colgan and Ledwith forthcoming; Virdee and Grint, 1994; Colgan 1999a; Humphrey 1998; LRD 2001b). Second has been the presence of vanguard equality activists (Colgan and Ledwith 1996); these are often women in whom political and feminist consciousness is strong (Kirton and Healy 1999). These trade unionists may work with or also be members of black, disabled and lesbian social movement organisations so enabling the development of broader equality coalitions and alliances to agree agendas, campaigns and strategies which can then be progressed through trade unions (Colgan and Ledwith 2000a; Gooding 2000). The third factor contributing to a challenge to the status quo has been the cumulative perception that there is a democratic deficit within trade unions; previously marginalised groups have drawn attention to this and conceived and proposed solutions for this problem. The changing political and social environment, membership decline and union mergers over the last twenty years have provided the fluid conditions for such campaigns for change (Colgan and Ledwith 2002; Heery 1998).

A linked element in this changing context has been the shift between different models of trade union organisation and government. UK unions are following the example of North American and Australian unions in supplanting the servicing model with the organising model (Heery *et al.* 1999). The organising model with its emphasis on recruitment and organising of new members and its recognition of the 'like recruiting like' principle in successful organising campaigns has assisted those who argue that trade unions must reflect equality and diversity within their own organisational structures and practices if trade unions are to achieve renewal. Those arguing for these equality changes may do so using 'social justice' and/or 'business case' type arguments. Equality seeking activists may emphasise the former but are often required to use the latter in order to win the union leadership and broader membership over to change.

Within UK unions, two types of change in government systems have emerged. First is the development of representative structures for target groups. Second is a move by the union leadership to centralise decision-making within unions to allow the redistribution of resources from the core to previously marginalised groups (Heery and Abbott 2000). It has been suggested that in the UK there may be some evidence that the organising and equality agendas are developing in tandem in the trade union movement and that this may be because diverse groups such as women or black members promote organising or because unions have recognised that they need to bolster their equality agendas to attract 'non-traditional' members (Heery and Abbott 2000) or both. Nevertheless, the process is not uncontested. Although greater investment in organising (and equality initiatives) may be a condition for the revival of unions, there are 'groups whose interests may not be immediately served by such a policy' (Heery and Abbott 2000). However, union mergers provide a fluid set of circumstances whereby union structures, resources and cultures are open to debate, negotiation and change.

Reflecting diverse constituencies: self-organisation

It is in this changing context that women's self-organisation, and in some unions self-organisation among black, disabled and lesbian and gay members has been gaining recognition and acceptance (Briskin 1993; Colgan and Ledwith 2002). Separate organising is in effect a form of institutionalised faction, which union executives have felt constrained to accept (Healy and Kirton 2000). Dickens (2000) has argued that progress in terms of internal equality has been slow and the picture across UK unions is 'uneven and not always linear'.

Development of self-organisation

In the late nineteenth and early twentieth centuries, the establishment of separate unions for women was principally a response to exclusion from mainstream 'male' trade unionism (Boston 1987). Women only unions can be characterised as one form of separate, or autonomous organising (Briskin 1993). A second form of self-organisation has developed within British trade unions in the last twenty years. Described as semi-autonomous organising (Briskin 1999) or interim separatism (Colgan and Ledwith 1996) this takes many forms.

Slowly unions have been moving from a range of liberal measures designed to remove barriers to women's (and other group's) participation while leaving existing union democratic structures in place, towards more radical measures with a direct impact on union government (Colgan and Ledwith 1996). Liberal action on equal opportunities has led to the introduction of measures such as courses for women, black, lesbian and gay members, etc., main streaming equal opportunities into all courses, child care support, changing times and locations of meetings and the development of publicity materials for all of the target groups. More radical measures have also been campaigned for. These seek to intervene directly in organisational practices to achieve fair representation and a fair distribution of rewards among groups and include committees for women, black, lesbian and gay and disabled groups, conferences and officer support and reserved seats on the union's primary decision-making body (Colgan and Ledwith 1996; SERTUC 2000).

Table 8.2 summarises the progress made in implementing equality structures and measures within thirteen UK unions. By 2000, a number of unions had introduced gender proportionality and/or reserved seats and thus the representation of women at National Executive Committee (NEC) level within UK unions has improved during the 1990s. Progress in improving women's representation has been slower at lower levels within the union as reflected by the lower representation of women at union conferences in Table 8.2. Progress then followed with respect to the establishment of formal structures and resources for black members. Structures and resources for disabled and lesbian and gay members are also now being developed within unions. So far however, as Table 8.2 shows, only the public service union UNISON in addition to introducing gender proportionality and fair representation has gone down the radical road of formally constituted self-organised groups, each with their own structures, officers, and support systems, for women, black members, disabled members and lesbian and gay members (Terry 1996; Colgan and Ledwith 2002).

Unions which have introduced self-organised structures have called on the Trades Union Congress (TUC) to move in this direction too (e.g. UNISON, MSF, NATFHE, CWU, Equity and NAPO). In 1999, the TUC began a consultation on its structure and constitution (TUC 2000b) and at the TUC Conference in 2000 it established a motion-based TUC Disabled Workers conference in addition to those already in place for Women (established in 1925), Black Workers (since 1993) and Lesbian and Gay Workers (since 1998). It also introduced seats for the representation of lesbian and gay and disabled members on the TUC General Council in addition to the reserved seats for women and black members (TUC 2000b). The extent to which these radical equality developments within the TUC and individual unions may stimulate the further development of self-organisation in other constituent unions (such as the GPMU) remains to be seen.

Self-organisation: the integration/autonomy dilemma

Self-organisation has been developed as an important mechanism to encourage the representation of and participation among diverse constituencies within trade unions. However, it can only work where trade unions are prepared to ensure adequate resources and linkages with 'mainstream' union structures at all levels. Unions also need to be prepared to hear, engage with and respond to the issues raised by the previously marginalised constituencies. Across unions there is still evidence of uncertainty, opposition and qualified support as well as support among the membership concerning some of the new forms of union democracy, particularly for more radical equality measures including self-organisation (Colgan and Ledwith forthcoming).

Self-organisation can enable women (and the other designated groups) to be legitimately represented as an out-group or an 'oppressed social group' (Cockburn 1995: 92). So, for example, women elected or appointed via this route can explicitly

Table 8.2 Equality structures in thirteen selected UK trade unions, 2000/2001

	AEEU	CWU	FBU	GMB	GPMU	NATFHE	NUT	MSF	PCS	TGWU	UNIFI	UNISON	USDAW
Women as members (%)	10	60	3	38	17	44	75	33	58	20	68	72	60
Women on NEC (%)	10	53	4	40	17	46	41	33	44	32	31	62	53
Women at conference (%)	10	n/d	4	25	14	34	55	n/d	28	18	39	58	44
Women													
Reserved seats*	Y	N	Y	Y	Y	Y	N	Y	N	Y	N	Y	N
National committee**	E	Y	Y	E	Y	Y	Y	Y	E	Y	E	Y	Y
National conference***	Y	Y	Y	E	Y	Y	E	Y	Y	Y	N	Y	Y
National officer****	E	E	N	E	E	E	E	E	Y	E	E	Y	E
Race/Ethnicity													
Reserved seats*	Y	N	Y	N	N	Y	N	Y	Y	Y	N	Y	N
National committee**	E	Y	Y	Y	E	Y	Y	Y	E	Y	E	Y	N
National conference***	N	Y	E	Y	N	Y	Y	Y	Y	N	N	Y	Y
National officer****	E	E	N	E	E	E	E	Y	Y	E	E	Y	E
Lesbian/Gay													
Reserved seats*	N	N	Y	N	N	Y	N	Y	N	N	N	Y	N
National committee**	E	Y	Y	E	E	Y	Y	Y	E	Y	E	Y	N
National conference***	N	N	E	E	N	Y	Y	Y	Y	N	N	Y	N
National officer****	E	E	N	E	E	E	E	Y	Y	E	E	Y	E
Disabled Workers													
Reserved seats*	N	N	Y	N	N	Y	N	Y	N	N	N	Y	N
National committee**	E	Y	Y	E	E	Y	N	Y	E	Y	E	Y	N
National conference***	N	Y	E	E	N	Y	E	Y	Y	N	N	Y	N
National officer****	E	E	N	E	E	E	N	Y	Y	E	E	Y	E

Sources: SERTUC 1998, 2000; Labour Research 2000; LRD *Union Action for Race Equality*, 1998.

Notes

Y = Yes; N = No; E = Generic Equality rather than group specific

* one or more seats on the national executive council

** centralised, formal committee or group dealing with this constituency's issues

*** at least one conference or special meeting has been held specifically for or about this constituency

**** a national officer with specific responsibility for the issues raised by this constituency (may have responbility for other groups as well).

speak for these members. Women elected in reserved seats or via mechanisms such as proportionality are elected as members of a sex category representing a mixed regional or occupational constituency (men and women) which can stop women from raising 'women's issues' as they feel they are bound to represent their mixed gender membership (Healy and Kirton 2000). Self-organisation and linked seats on 'mainstream' committees can provide previously marginalised groups with the opportunity to debate that group's concerns, develop consciousness, confidence and skills, experience and acknowledge the diversity of priorities among the group, formulate policies and practices, and build strategies to get these on to the trade union agenda. Membership may cross over the women's, black, lesbian and gay and disabled self-organised structures so ensuring that issues of gender, race, sexuality and disability are represented within the union.

Briskin (1993) argues that the success of separate organising depends upon maintaining a balance between 'autonomy' from the structures and practices of the labour movement and 'integration' into those structures. Too little integration and the separate organising is marginalised; too much integration and the radical edge can be blunted. A relatively successful 'balancing act' between the two produces powerful representation of the constituency grouping plus the level of legitimacy key to ensuring adequate resources.

Self-organisation does not operate in a vacuum and in itself does not guarantee achievement of the oppressed social group's aims, existing in a state of almost permanent challenge from mainstream traditionalists and institutionalised norms (Mann *et al.* 1997; Colgan and Ledwith 2000b). Inevitably, a number of barriers may operate such that self-organised constituency issues may not make it on to the 'mainstream' agenda (McBride 2001; Colgan and Ledwith 2000b; Healy and Kirton 2000). As Dickens (2000) points out notwithstanding the gains made in terms of internal equality through self-organisation, women (and other minority groups) are still largely under-represented in 'mainstream' structures and crucially when it comes to collective bargaining and trade union officer posts.

Kelly (2000) has argued that UK trade unions have developed the capacity to adapt to their new and changing environment including an increasingly diverse trade union membership. Dickens (2000) agrees that they have identified the need to attract and retain groups such as women and have developed internal structures to do so but she is less convinced that the transformation this calls for within unions in terms of power structures, union culture, agendas and priorities is taking place. The question Colling and Dickens (2001) raise is how 'deep' is the commitment of UK unions to trade union renewal through tackling internal and external issues of equality. At one end of the spectrum, some 'male-focused' unions may remain viable in their 'niche' and see no need to make changes, those in the middle who need to increase their recruitment from an increasingly diverse workforce such as the GPMU are harder to call whereas at the other end of the spectrum, unions such as UNISON with a large diverse and female membership are likely to retain their momentum for 'transformational change' (Cockburn 1991).

Case studies: the GPMU and UNISON

The unions offer some interesting comparisons in their differences. Most obvious are size, sector and the male/female balance in membership. While almost three-quarters of UNISON's members are women, in the GPMU women make up only 17 per cent of the membership, thus offering limited scope for women to have a substantial impact on the union. As might be expected, it is evident that UNISON's approach to equality is radical, even offering a transformational agenda (Cockburn 1991), while the GPMU can be seen to have adopted a liberal or short agenda approach to developing equal opportunities within the union. Both unions are seeking change in order to close a democracy gap, primarily focusing on women as the engine for transformation – an aim of UNISON's constitution and of many of its women activists. The GPMU's aim is more modest; to change from a union dominated by white middle-aged men to one where women and young members are more central.

We found that the establishment of the principles of proportionality (for the GPMU and UNISON) and of fair representation (of members from the range of diverse groupings – black, lesbian and gay, disabled, part-time and full-time, and occupational and industry sectors) and self-organisation (for UNISON) have been important in changing the perception and delivery of equal opportunities in both unions. Nevertheless, in each union, equality activists were experiencing difficulties in maintaining the required balance between autonomy from the structures and practices of the labour movement, and integration into those structures. A lack of key structural linkages and political opposition within UNISON meant that autonomy constantly placed self-organisation and its issues in danger of margin-alisation by the mainstream at national level although the picture was more varied given the range of democratic structures and social processes at regional and branch level (Colgan and Ledwith 2000b). Within the GPMU, the opposite problem was observed as women activists sought to guard their autonomy over decision-making and resources in the face of co-option and incorporation by a powerful male union hierarchy (Colgan and Ledwith forthcoming).

The research

The research programme took place over the period 1994–8, following both union mergers. It was funded by the Economic and Social Research Council. Question-naire surveys were carried out in both unions at two main levels. The first questionnaire was for women active within self-organisation and/or the mainstream in each union and the second was sent to women and men who were active at workplace level in case study UNISON regions and GPMU branches. In addition semi-structured interviews were carried out with over 200 women and men activists and officers at national, regional and workplace levels within both unions. In each union we carried out more detailed case study work in three regions (UNISON) and two branches (GPMU). In addition we attended a range of conferences, committees and education courses and policy weekends. Documentation was collected from each union.

GPMU: Equality structures

When the GPMU was formed from the amalgamation of SOGAT '82 and the NGA in 1991, both unions had already established equality measures, and these were carried forward and consolidated in the new union. These were an elected national women's committee, a national women's conference (now biennial) and women-only courses. Prior to the merger, SOGAT was led by a woman general secretary with a commitment to a liberal equality agenda. In each partner union, equality measures had been campaigned for by women activists working with male allies and ultimately supported by the union leadership. In this work, an influential argument was the need of the union to increase its appeal to women workers if it wished to increase recruitment in the sector (Cockburn 1983; Ledwith *et al.* 1985, 1990).

The GPMU established a National Women's Committee in 1991. The women's biennial conference (BWC) has been workshop based in order to encourage women's development and participation. Recommendations emerged from the workshops which were taken forward by the women's committee to the national executive. Responsibility for equal opportunities was held by the male Deputy General Secretary; he was assisted by a female Equality Policy Adviser, an administrative rather than an elected position.

Despite the progress made through the establishment of women's structures, the representation of women on elected bodies other than the national executive remained poor. Following campaigning by women activists, who pointed to the initiatives being taken in other unions, the leadership agreed that this issue had to be addressed. In 1996 women's proportionality was introduced to the union for the first time under a new rule of Guaranteed Proportional Representation (GPR). This applied to all elected structures. At national level, the introduction of GPR has improved the representation of women within lay positions although progress at full time officer level has been less marked (Table 8.3). Also in 1996 a national Young Members Committee was set up with a reserved seat on the national executive. The first seat was held by a woman. It was estimated that 40 per cent of the union's young members (those aged under 26) were women. Women and young members have become key target groups for GPMU recruitment.

Along with the decline in the union's traditional membership it has also been experiencing difficulties in gaining and retaining trade union recognition in the printing and publishing industry sector. The union leadership has increasingly recognised that its culture of the white middle-aged male is no longer appropriate. A young members' conference has been established. In 2000 the union launched a new policy to 'eradicate discrimination in the workplace' accompanied by a model equal opportunities agreement, guidelines and training, in an attempt to explicitly include black members, disabled members and lesbian and gay members and carry out further work on women's inequality (GPMU 2000b). It also established an elected Equality Committee and informal network groups to attempt to improve the representation of its black, lesbian and gay and disabled members (SERTUC, 2000).

Table 8.3 Proportion of women in the GPMU and UNISON, 1991–2000

Women as a percentage of:	GMPU				UNISON			
	1991	*1993*	*1998*	*2000*	*1991*	*1993*	*1998*	*2000*
Members	17	17	17	17	70*	68	78	72
NEC	5	5	22	17	49	42	65	62
Conference	10+	11	15	17	n.a	48#	54	58
Union's TUC delegation	6	4	15	17	40	54	61	58
National Officers	0	0	13	13	30	20	38	21
Regional Officers	n.a	n.a	5	4	20	31	24	30

Sources: Colgan and Ledwith 1996; SERTUC 1992, 2000; LRD 1994, 2000.
* UNISON's figures for 1991 are arrived at by averaging those for COHSE, NALGO and NUPE.
# UNISON 1995 conference figure.
+ GPMU figure arrived at by averaging the latest SOGAT and NGA figures.

UNISON: Equality structures

The delivery of gender equality was central to UNISON's aims both during the pre-merger discussions between the three partner unions COHSE, NALGO and NUPE, and when the new union was set up in 1993 (Terry 1996; Colgan and Ledwith 2002). All three unions already had equality structures and policies and NALGO had established self-organised groups (SOGs) during the 1980s (Mann *et al.* 1997; Colgan 1999b).

Recognising that women would be in the majority in the new union's membership, the three unions agreed a new approach building on the elements of women's self-organisation which each already had in place. The mechanism for achieving gender equality was three-fold: proportionality; fair representation; and self-organisation.

First, women's proportional representation – *Proportionality* – in all the elected structures was to be achieved by the year 2000. Built into proportionality was the provision for a number of places to be allocated to low-paid women, to ensure the inclusion of manual women workers. As Table 8.3 illustrates, although an improvement in women's representation on the NEC and on TUC delegations has been made, the union still has some way to go before proportionality is achieved at its national conference and especially within officer positions. Staff restructuring following the merger has actually led to a decline in the number of women officers (Colgan and Ledwith forthcoming).

The second mechanism was *Fair representation* whereby representation should aim to reflect the spread of members throughout the union; manual, non-manual, part-time, black, lesbian and gay, disabled and so on (UNISON 1997a: 10). The principles of fair representation apply to all elections and the composition of conference delegations within the union. The difficulty with the definition is that it is by nature broad and without a fairly sophisticated form of monitoring is proving harder than proportionality to implement and monitor (UNISON 1995, 1997a).

Proportionality and fair representation were not to be just a 'numbers game'. They were also about getting women and the other identified groups involved in the union's structures and in setting the collective bargaining agenda (Mills 1994). *Self-organisation* was to exist at national, regional and branch levels and was to be supported by dedicated women's officers at national and regional levels. The black, lesbian and gay and disabled members self-organised groups were also established with national officers and – for women only – dedicated regional support. Self-organisation in UNISON offers an important political and personal space for its particular members as well as a place for developing skills, identity, consciousness and action (Colgan and Ledwith 2000a)

Support for equality measures

The following sections will draw on the case study research to illustrate the range of views held by activists on union equality measures following the formation of the two new unions.

As might be expected, in each union more women than men were in favour of their union introducing equality measures for women, black, disabled and lesbian and gay members (Colgan and Ledwith 2000b). During the interviews within each union, we found three broad schools of thought on their union's equality measures and approach at all levels. These can be summarised as opposition, support and qualified support.[1] Those articulating the first position tended to be more comfortable with liberal equality arguments, the second with radical, social justice and transformational arguments and the third group were prepared to shift from a liberal to a quasi-radical position so long as this was underpinned by a business case for equal opportunities. Examples of the three schools of thought will be presented for each union below.

GPMU

Opposition

A substantial minority of men had vocalised their opposition to GPR and the development of women's committees and conferences in the union on the grounds that women were getting 'special treatment' with reports of men complaining about 'all this attention paid to women' during the amalgamation process. One male branch secretary described the ongoing grumbling from men at branch meetings; they frequently asked:

> 'When are we going to have a men's meeting in the branch', or 'When are we going to have a national men's conference?', and to that the response is generally from x [woman on branch] or the like, 'You have that thing every two years; it's called the BDC'.[2]

(Male Branch Secretary 1996)

A small number of women in addition to men, expressed reservations on the grounds that a 'member is a member, whether they are male or female', and while wishing to see women represented in the union they thought women 'should get on in their own right'.

One woman tried to explain the opposition from 'traditionalists' on both left and right of the union:

> Sometimes those people are very close adherents and advocates of the existing democratic process of the union and sometimes that appears to be not quite democratic as they see it, i.e. taking special measures to encourage a particular section of the membership.
>
> (Woman activist 1994)

Support

Support for measures to improve the representation for women had come from men as well as women, it had cut across 'political views' gaining support from the left and 'some notable right-wing men'. Support for the measures was linked to the view that if the union was going to successfully recruit and organise a diverse workforce these changes were required to assist the union to do this. Some impatience was expressed that progress was too slow and that the national union needed to put its own house in order and set an example.

> We haven't got a national women's officer. They talk about all these things regarding equality and making recommendations to branches on branch committee representation, BDC delegation and representation and all the rest; they haven't even bloody done it themselves.
>
> (Male Branch Secretary 1996)

There was a desire particularly from feminist activists campaigning for change to see the new union establish more democratic structures,

> Democracy to me is something alive and is changing and is reflecting the needs of people, not something that is written in tablets of stone that never changes because then the process ceases to become democratic and in fact becomes totally undemocratic – the system of representation for instance, that has worked terribly well to ensure that all sections of the membership in trade terms are represented but which actually prevents space being created for sections of the membership that those people regard as new, i.e. women, young people, black people and so on, ceases to be democratic because it's no longer representative of the needs of workers, or society generally or progress of the trade unions.
>
> (Woman activist 1994)

Qualified support

Although there was support for improving representation of women in the union through GPR, a national women's committee and branch women's/equality committees, it was not agreed by this group that self-organised women's structures was the way forward.

> It's an industrial problem, it's not a woman's problem . . . We shouldn't isolate men, we should put them right in the forefront and say 'It's the committee that's dealing with industrial problems, okay, aimed at women but there's nothing wrong in putting a man in charge of that.'
>
> (Woman activist 1996)

Although these activists recognised the union needed to present a more diverse face in order to recruit women, young and ethnic minority workers, they were more comfortable with a liberal rather than a radical equal opportunities approach. They had shifted to a quasi-radical position. Although they did accept that GPR was a necessary albeit short-term measure to ensure women's representation, they were less comfortable with establishing forms of self-organisation.

UNISON

UNISON's equality approach included proportionality, fair representation and self-organisation; each of these will be considered under the three headings below.

Opposition

Given the high proportion of women members, there was little articulated opposition to proportionality at national level although some members claimed that it was 'very hard to know that some extremely good men have had to go in order to make way for women' whom they perceived as less experienced (UNISON activist 1997). At regional and workplace level, opposition was mainly focused on ignoring the proportionality rule. If women didn't come forward for election, men would often be elected instead. Also common was the practice of insisting on a definition of parity (50:50) rather than strict numerical proportionality (Colgan and Ledwith forthcoming).

The stated opposition to fair representation tended to be on the grounds that it was impractical:

> Structurally it's impossible to achieve, I mean you can attain proportionality but fair representation was really some kind of stalemate really. I don't know how you guarantee you can get it.
>
> (Male activist 1997)

A vocal minority of activists were opposed to self-organisation on the grounds that they saw it as divisive and undemocratic.

The dictionary states that 'union' is a 'joining together; the state of being united'. In my opinion, having SOGs is a contradiction of these terms. I am a member of a 'union' and wish to stay that way, not be fragmented by small groups.

(UNISON women's survey 1995)

Discriminatory attitudes from a small minority of activists interviewed did underpin some of the hostility to fair representation and self-organisation. However as with the GPMU, opposition predominantly came from trade union 'traditionalists' who saw self-organisation as divisive, as giving special treatment, and as using up union resources (Mann *et al.* 1997).

Support

Women in particular cited the importance of proportionality in making UNISON more women friendly and encouraging them to come forward and take up positions:

I think UNISON is the best thing that has happened, particularly for women. I also feel that being alongside women manual workers has given me a wider view and I enjoy being in the company of other women. I believe that the commitment to proportionality will also mean that the sexism in the trade union movement is now being addressed and more important, at last recognised.

(Women activists' survey 1995)

Those supporting fair representation also considered some of the problems to be politically based rather than rooted in the difficulty of the definition or mechanisms for delivery. One woman thought fair representation would be the hardest thing of all for UNISON to achieve and would be met with 'great opposition' because it would mean ousting people (both women and men) who had been in positions for years and years. 'If people follow the principles then it will mean that someone will have to go and power bases will shift, and things like that.' However, this was a necessary part of transforming the culture of the union:

It's essential if UNISON is going to achieve and become a union with vision; there are going to have to be changes. Otherwise it's going to be the run of the mill union that every other union is. UNISON was meant to be different, and if it doesn't achieve those aims then it will just be the same, and it will be a tragedy.

(Woman activist 1997)

Support for self-organisation ran in a similar vein:

There is still a lot of doubt about self-organisation and a lot of people who still do not accept there is a need for it. But it's part of the union and it has to work

> ... I don't think they are fully aware of the whole problem of discrimination;
> that people can't actually get elected because of the discrimination that exists.
>
> (Woman activist 1997)

Qualified support

Those giving qualified support to proportionality tended to see it as a necessary element in the short term but one that should be rendered unnecessary in the medium to long term. Views on the necessity of women's self-organisation varied in this group from those who opposed it saying, 'If you have proportionality, why do you need women's self-organisation?' Others however, acknowledged that in order to achieve proportionality and fair representation women's self-organisation was needed to act as a catalyst to encourage women's participation and involvement in the union.

This grouping accepted that there was a need to have fair representation and self-organisation in order to ensure the diversity of the membership was reflected in the structures:

> I see self-organisation as a way of giving people the opportunity to progress in the union without the union itself putting barriers in the way ... you allow these groups to organise themselves and you allow them a say, that's self-organisation. Where many colleagues differ is what happens when that becomes almost a separate part of the organisation; we are not a federal trade union, we are a collection of parts and that's where the arguments come.
>
> (Male activist 1997)

However, this group was not completely comfortable with the existence of self-organised groups (SOGs) and their location within the structure of the union. While valuing the role of the SOGs in encouraging new members to join, be active and raise their issues within union structures, elements of this grouping sought to limit the power and influence of the SOGs within the union. Their view was that the role of the SOGs was primarily to 'put themselves out of a job'. Until proportionality and fair representation was achieved there was an acceptance that SOGs were necessary but that surveillance was required to ensure they complied with UNISON rules and did not 'get out of control'.

Do women think the formation of the new union has provided them with opportunities to introduce equality measures?

Given the new structures and policies aimed at improving representation in both unions and the conflicting positions outlined above, male and female activists were asked about the impact of the merger and equality measures. These results are considered in greater depth elsewhere (Colgan and Ledwith forthcoming). The remaining space will allow a brief overview of the issues raised in the interviews by women activists.

GPMU *women*

Within the GPMU, slightly more women activists than men took the view that amalgamation had been good for women:

> because the existing provisions that both unions had separately for women like the NGA had a Women's Committee and SOGAT didn't. SOGAT had a Women's conference – just. The NGA didn't and happily both of those have been preserved despite predictions to the contrary and since we have amalgamated, we in theory haven't gone back, we haven't actually lost in terms of the theoretical democratic process and in terms of policy we haven't lost either. . . . I've still got mixed feelings about it, I mean I still very much adhere to the view that it [the merger] has not in theory been a setback for women . . . women members have made progress. Not least of which is the decision – the historic decision to approve the policy of proportional women's representation (GPR) on the EC.
>
> (Woman activist 1994)

The policy of the union on GPR was first that women were guaranteed representation of women on the EC and second on national delegations in proportion to national membership. The third element was to encourage branches to coopt women on to committees although this was not obligatory. In the view of some women activists, this had been won as a consequence of:

> the building up of a major head of steam over successive women's conferences and supportive activity by women and men equally and as well and in particular the activities of the General Secretary who . . . made the call supporting that.
>
> (Woman activist 1994)

For others, it was recognised that in the male dominated politics of the GPMU, although pressure from women may have won the union leadership round, it was the General Secretary who had 'delivered it [GPR] for us, we didn't deliver it for ourselves, he got it for us' (Woman activist 1994).

It was agreed that the period before, during and after merger had provided opportunities for women to push for change:

> The new union is very different because you've got different cultures clashing together. I mean I think the union's going through a period of trying to come to terms with the fact that it's neither one thing or the other. . . . so I think one of the problems that everybody's got . . . is that there isn't any longer any set pattern or familiar route to do the biz. Now in some ways that can be a benefit for women because a) we can bring freshness, b) we can catch everybody napping while they're all worrying about their lost territory we can steam straight through the middle.
>
> (Woman activist 1994)

Representation

The yes vote for women's GPR at the union's 1995 national delegate conference (where women made up only 11 per cent of the delegates) was seen by women as a major achievement. It was also the culmination of a long period of preparation; the principle of women's representation on the EC had been agreed at the union's previous national conference two years earlier.

However, women activists reported in interviews that after the successful election of women on to the EC, male colleagues were already querying the need for the additional women rule which had been put into place to ensure gender proportional representation (GPR); that if women were being elected in their own right the new rule was unnecessary. Yet it was precisely having the new GPR mechanism which had encouraged women to stand for election, knowing that they were not automatically in danger of 'knocking off the EC' a male colleague who had in some way a seat 'as of right' either through being senior in the union or the seniority custom which gave priority to long serving members.

As one woman pointed out, in a union where women are in the minority, this kind of threat will always be around. Also that the women elected on to the EC by a mixed constituency will be elected on the grounds that are perceived as 'acceptable' to the predominantly male membership and union leadership (Woman activist 1996). She also recognised that the women could lose GPR at the next conference in the male-dominated union,

> If somebody decides to mobilise the troops against the women, it could be taken away but it won't be taken away as long as they are comfortable with the women they've got. Now the problem with being comfortable you have to then draw a line between being comfortable with them and being complacent about the issues and that's where the next test is going to be, really, because we've got all the structures now and the girls actually want to put them into practice. It's whether the boys will allow that to happen.
>
> (Woman activist 1996)

To lose GPR would also be to lose the foothold gained in collective bargaining since, as a consequence of EC membership, women were now participating for the first time on the union's national sub-committees including the main national industry negotiating panel. This was described as a 'major achievement; the Women's Committee weren't even allowed to talk about it three years ago' (Woman activist 1996).

Self-organisation

Women were very positive about the potential of the new structures established within the GPMU:

> There is now a women's committee, there's a women's conference, it's written into the constitution and rule book of the union, all of these are positive steps.
>
> (Woman activist 1996)

The Women's Committee provided a useful strategic forum for women as well as a training ground for the women who were elected onto the EC:

> The Women's Committee sit and look at the position of women ongoing in the industry, and look at things that affect women; i.e. where we are establishing changes including things like claims that we're making on behalf of women . . .
>
> (Woman activist 1997)

However, it was agreed that it had been difficult to maintain the autonomy of the Committee within the union. In part, this was because women were in the minority within the union. It was also because the committee was attended by the male Deputy General Secretary responsible for equal opportunities. Although the male union leadership was seen as enthusiastic, it was also seen as interventionist, 'vetting the Women's Committee Agenda' and 'always trying to block things put forward by the Women's Committee (Woman activist 1996). As a consequence, women thought the appointment of a National Women's Officer to assist with the work of the Committee was a priority. Part of the leadership vigilance was thought to stem from their fear of the development of 'a new power block' (of women) within the union.

As women activists were often isolated from each other, the BWC was a very important means of support and opportunity for women to meet, network and develop an agenda:

> The [women's] conference is planned by the women's committee, it is run by the women's committee and we encourage new women to put forward recommendations which are then taken on board. . . . Educating and training and assisting them and encouraging them in the industry. . . . And then following actually to the conference so that they use that knowledge to bring policies forward that they want to see adopted by the national union for the future.
>
> (Woman activist 1997)

Otherwise, women maintained their networks with women 'on the phone because we're all so scattered . . . that's why the women's conference was so wonderful' (Woman activist 1994).

At branch level, GPMU recommended practice was GPR on the branch committee, plus a seat for young members plus a woman liaison officer and a women's committee. Although always in a minority on branch committees, women did use the branch amalgamation process to push to implement union equality policy. Women sought to establish a joint forum to allow former NGA and SOGAT women to meet together. They then worked to establish women's/equality committees. Although this was in line with union policy, women in some branches reported the need to move forward with caution so as not to alienate their male allies at local level:

> I'd like to see a women's committee. Not meeting too regularly because that would upset them [men] for a start, but if we said every six months.
>
> (Woman activist 1996)

In some of the branches where a women's committee had already been agreed, women were concerned at the lack of autonomy and resources it was permitted. So although national union policy was having an impact, opposition or qualified support at lower levels of the union in some branches was stopping further progress taking place. In more supportive branches, women's/equality committees were proving to be catalysts in providing information, support and education to members and branch committee members. This ensured that members knew their rights and that officers were adequately informed to represent them on a range of equality issues. Women's liaison officers were also established on branch committees. Their main role was to deal with sexual harassment cases of members. In the union's clerical branch, links were being made with the union's unfolding organising agenda of recruitment of young and diverse members.

Moving forward

Women in the GPMU recognised that in comparison to other unions, the GPMU still had some catching up to do:

> It's always bitter-sweet when I talk to women in other unions . . . because although they have problems, they always seem to be in a much better position than we are . . . Unions that have started to actually do something to create the conditions whereby women can come forward have found that more women have come forward and that's what we want to do ourselves.
>
> (Woman activist 1994)

Young women, particularly those working in clerical areas, were critical of the union for being 'old style'; for example, one described finding her branch conference 'quite sexist . . . not in a threatening way, just the whole culture of it and the type of humour' (Woman activist 1996). A black woman who attended the same conference agreed:

> The branch conference was male-dominated . . . there was only one other chap who was black and we conversed on that and we were quite shocked. And we looked around and there were about 60 delegates all told and only two of us – and I don't know what the reason for that is but it's noticeable.
>
> (Woman activist 1996)

Women activists were clear that the GPMU needed to improve the representation and involvement of black, lesbian and gay and disabled members. 'Let's have some representation from people who are not white, male and straight. It's vital' (Woman activist 1996). Bargaining and organising were identified as key with women agreeing that a national women's agenda did exist.

UNISON

During the UNISON merger talks, each union negotiating team brought a range of specific democratic issues to the negotiating table with NALGO for example raising the question of lay-control and self-organisation and NUPE seeking to safeguard the representation of manual workers and COHSE the representation of health workers. The working party on equal opportunities was the only forum where women were in the majority during the merger discussions (Terry 1996; Fryer 2000). One aim was to ensure that women were 'part of the mainstream rather than a marginal group within UNISON'.

> I think one of the good things about the merger was that you had women who had come through the trade unions in the mid-80s who were in key positions within their three unions to push that agenda . . . they were not pushing that agenda as the sole objective of UNISON, I mean it was part and parcel of their responsibility to ensure that the women's perspective was built in at every opportunity . . . I think what happened is that as the negotiations ensued you had a critical mass of women in key positions to push that.
>
> (Woman activist 1996)

In addition, the equality activists linked up with their counterparts in the other partner unions and campaigned hard using social justice and business case arguments to ensure that self-organisation would exist in the new union. As one lesbian SOG activist said 'we had been sold the new union on the basis that we wouldn't lose anything we already had' (Colgan 1999b). The intention was to ensure that an appropriate 'balance' between autonomy and integration was established. However, some elements of the equality agenda were blocked:

> It's always irritated me that when UNISON was set up . . . there was a rule when all of the schemes were being drawn up to have self-organised group representatives on every negotiating committee in each service at every level and this was blocked by . . . surprise, surprise, the Service Groups.[3] They said that it would be perfectly impossible . . . that all would be fine and that it wasn't necessary . . . and then people said 'we've got women among our negotiators anyway', and all the usual sort of watering down things happened. Although some inroads have been made in some areas like representation at service group conferences and the right to put motions there and speak (which was refused in the early days), that representation has not been possible.
>
> (Woman activist 1997)

Nevertheless, the formation of UNISON and its commitments to proportionality and fair representation had been important factors in encouraging women to become more active according to a number of women in our interviews.

> I think that the UNISON constitution has actually worked in giving women opportunities they would not have had in the past.
>
> (Woman activist 1996)

Women from previous partner unions said that they especially valued aspects of UNISON which supported women particularly the union structure, its membership-led policies and culture, women's education courses, self-organisation and the support provided by the women's officers and SOG officers at national and regional level. The existence of SOGs for black, disabled and lesbian and gay members also provided important routes into activism for lesbians and disabled women.

> I was a NUPE member for a couple of years, and then 6 months after vesting day which was 1993, I was actually given a booklet on the aims and objectives of UNISON, and it actually says in there that I can exist, that lesbians and gays actually exist within the union, and that I was allowed to be lesbian and gay and that the support would be there for me . . . I wasn't out as a lesbian at work and this union i.e. UNISON was actually saying that not only could I exist but that they would support me, that I could actually belong to a group of lesbian and gay people.
>
> (Lesbian activist 1997)

Thus, a key gain from UNISON's commitment to proportionality, fair representation and self-organisation was that it raised expectations among women and other minority groups that the union's democratic deficit would be addressed.

Representation

UNISON's structure is far more complex than that of the GPMU so this section will summarise some of the views expressed in the interviews by women activists concerning representation. The flexibility which exists in terms of delivering proportionality and fair representation within lay member structures was seen to have led to a wide variation in women's representation at branch, regional and national levels. In national structures, progress was being made towards proportionality. However, many branches and regional groups aimed for 'parity' (50 per cent women) at best rather than proportionality (72 per cent women). Women reported fighting constant battles to try and ensure rulebook commitments on proportionality and fair representation were implemented.

The lack of clarity in the rulebook about self-organised representation on mainstream committees left the SOG constituencies, their issues and agendas marginalised from mainstream bargaining and campaigning priorities:

> The barriers I have are mainstream trade unionists who marginalise what we bring out . . . I think the problem of the National Women's Committee is that we can't make decisions, we are not a policy-making committee, we have to go elsewhere. Everything we want to do has to be ratified elsewhere and it is very frustrating.
>
> (Woman activist 1997)

Although UNISON was making progress, albeit unequal, in improving the numerical representation of women within the union, the union was making slower progress in its implementation of the principle of fair representation. Manual workers complained of being marginalised within the new union (Haunch 2000). Black women were challenging the lack of fair representation in the union on the grounds that the improvements in women's representation in the union 'did not include black women' (Woman activist 1997). Where progress was being made it was due to a combination of electoral change, monitoring, education, strategy working groups, revised methods of working, women and SOG members moving into regional positions and a number of the other positive initiatives. However, where the union's goals were not understood or commitment was 'lukewarm', the ongoing struggle, lack of resources and antagonistic social processes at branch, regional and national levels were blocking efforts to implement proportionality and fair representation and becoming a 'women (and member) friendly' union (Colgan and Ledwith 2000b).

In fact, the hostility some women reported experiencing was actively discouraging them from becoming active in the union. Ex-NALGO women were particularly disappointed at some of the political barriers encountered in moving the equality agenda forwards.

> In NALGO, we had reached quite a good level of involvement in the union. UNISON came along and we got the ex-NUPE and COHSE people who hadn't heard of self-organisation, they certainly hadn't any lesbian and gay self-organisation, and it seemed to give those people in ex-NALGO who had bigoted and homophobic ideas a lift rather than the opposite.
>
> (UNISON women's survey 1995)

> I felt UNISON would be a positive move towards promoting women in the union, but it has been the opposite. Equality issues are constantly forced off the agenda. Paid officials are nearly all male, especially at most senior levels. I feel really let down by UNISON, which I did not feel in NALGO.
>
> (Women activist's survey 1995)

For others, the legitimacy awarded to equality through the union's constitution was an important lever for use in the fight for proportionality, fair representation and self-organisation. 'I could just point to the rule book and say "come on, we've got rules"' (Woman activist 1997).

> I got into some quite nasty rows about that because I would say, 'No we're not doing our job if we allow men to go in those places that should be filled by women. We should be looking at why it is that we haven't got women coming forward'.
>
> (Woman activist 1997)

Self-organisation

A major trigger encouraging women to become active in UNISON was self-organisation. Elsewhere we have discussed the importance of self-organisation in developing a sense of self and representation for previously neglected constituencies (Colgan 1999b; Colgan and Ledwith 2000a). For many women in UNISON, self-organisation was seen as a place where they could participate actively in the union, it was a place to feel safe, empowered and where group consciousness could develop,

> I think being part of any women's self-organisation is helpful, because you feel like you belong somewhere, and there are people who share similar ideas and outlooks . . . not necessarily that we all feel the same, but there are some basic things you do agree on, which makes your world view similar. . . . You're not always battling about everything . . . there's somewhere you can go and gain support.
>
> (Regional activist 1997)

Black, disabled and lesbian women interviewed had been encouraged to join and become active in UNISON because of self-organisation:

> In terms of the union, I've got to say that it is very white and I didn't really want to subscribe to some white organisation that I wasn't going to get anything out of or that wasn't actually going to do anything for me or support me . . . it would just be a waste of time giving money to that organisation . . . once I knew about the Black Members Group it was different because at least there were people there that you could relate to and talk to . . . you would have a say, you would get a support for whatever endeavour and so that really encouraged me to pay my subscriptions.
>
> (Black woman activist 1996)

For disabled members, a crucial element in their becoming active was the establishment of the Disabled Members SOG plus the efforts UNISON was making to hold meetings and conferences in accessible venues, provide papers in accessible formats, fund facilitators and other appropriate measures: 'If it wasn't for self-organisation, I wouldn't be a UNISON activist' (Disabled activist 1997).

The formation of UNISON had been a spur to activism among many of the women we interviewed. Proportionality and fair representation in the branch presented one trigger to becoming active. Education and development opportunities offered by self-organisation provided another. For this woman manual worker, becoming involved in women's self-organisation had helped her understanding of gender politics and was instrumental in her becoming active in mainstream structures: 'It's been so encouraging, the women's group, and supportive . . . I first went on this women's weekend and I started to think about the balance of power between men and women and it was a real eye opener' (Woman activist 1997).

Self-organisation gave the women the opportunity to develop their skills as activists, through the formal means of education courses, mailing lists, rotation of chairing at meetings, job-sharing of positions, less bureaucratic-style meetings and attendance at regional and national workshops and conferences as well as the informal opportunities provided for networking, mentoring, assistance with writing motions, speeches and so on. The self-organised group conferences in addition to allowing debate and the development of policy, enabled women to learn how unions worked:

> I think one of the reasons the national women's conference was set up was to be a training ground for women, so that when they went to a national delegate conference they weren't completely overwhelmed. You know, I think knowing what a motion is is pretty good and standing orders and points of order, and how things work, how things are moved around on agendas. No one would teach you that.
>
> (Woman activist 1997)

Moving forward

One of the positive features of UNISON was the encouragement of networking, coalition forming and transversal working across the SOGs at workplace, regional and national level.

> The union has been very complacent and . . . it has to change. One thing self-organised groups have realised there's no way we can work in isolation from one another, we have to be working together.
>
> (Woman activist 1994)

Although some SOG activists expressed frustration at what could appear at times to be 'deep-seated opposition' in the union to undermine self-organisation, others were proud to see their issues being taking up as part of UNISON's campaigning and bargaining agenda:

> I know that UNISON can be very bad at some things but it can be very good on others and even now we are miles out in front of the majority of other unions and I have to say that at the TUC and at the Labour party this year . . . our union stuck to its policy commitment for disabled people which is more than you can say for other unions.
>
> (Disabled woman activist 1997)

One of the dangers for the SOGs however, was to avoid marginalisation by mainstream activists given levels of opposition in some areas, a lack of adequate structural links and SOG representation on mainstream committees.

One solution to this was the establishment of the right for SOGs to send motions to mainstream conferences. For the most part this had been achieved. Another solution was to establish representation on mainstream committees at branch, regional and national level as SOGs were campaigning to do (Colgan and Ledwith 2000b). A third route to moving the equality agenda forward was for women to elect to leave the safety of self-organisation to engage with the mainstream and take on mainstream positions to progress that agenda. The importance of doing this to avoid the marginalisation of SOG issues was explained by a woman active in both the women's and disabled SOGs. She saw the increasing involvement of SOGs across all structures of the union as an important catalyst for change.

> When you become part of a self-organised group . . . you start exploring where the oppression is, where you want things changed within your union, within your world, within your workplace, within every arena. Having done that, to me, you start applying it within the union because that's your point of reference . . . You then need to work within that structure, you can change that structure but in doing so you need to work within it to start off with. Self-organisation can't exist on its own – you just can't self-organise and then not offshoot into the union. . . . I'm not saying change'll happen overnight 'cos I think so many women get into structures and then don't change them and start functioning within those structures as the structures were . . . you need to stay in touch with your roots in self-organisation . . . because you need to stay in touch with where you're coming from.
>
> (Woman activist 1996)

Despite often considerable differences within women's self-organisation about priorities, it was agreed that once an agenda was 'hammered out' there was caucusing across union structures to progress it. Further, within 'mainstream' structures at national, regional and workplace level, the SOGs tried to work towards a shared 'equality agenda' taking a common view on motions and making a conscious effort to support each other's initiatives (Colgan 1999b). Given the high number of women members and UNISON's diverse membership, a critical mass did exist to push for change. There was evidence of the successful implementation of proportionality, fair representation and self-organisation resulting in a shift in union structure, culture and agenda particularly in supportive workplaces and regions (Colgan and Ledwith 2000b).

Conclusion

In this chapter it has been possible to see that there are a number of key conditions for changing trade union attitudes and practices in relation to equality. Of prime importance is the context whereby membership loss can be stemmed or even reversed and union renewal can take place through the recruitment and organisation of the increasingly diverse workforce. From the evidence in the UK, there does seem to be room for some optimism about the regeneration of the labour movement through new forms of more inclusive trade unionism. The material conditions at the time of writing are reasonably promising; the economy is buoyant, the political and legal climate reasonably more favourable and trade union membership is beginning to increase once more.

What is key is the new and diverse composition of the new membership and the extent to which it is able to set the agenda for change. Unions have been increasingly realising that if they are to both recruit *and* retain these members they need to seriously address the equality and diversity agenda. Almost all have now reached the position of pursuing liberal equality measures, with the leading unions moving to a more transformative agenda. The data in the chapter show that among the largest UK unions most have some form of equality system for increasing women's elected participation in union structures. Progress is being made but has been slower for the other, minority groups.

However, it is a *combination* of mainstream trade union mobilisation for equality together with the work of vanguard activists, representing the interests of the new constituents whom unions seek to recruit, which is central to the dynamic of renewal. These vanguard change agents are able to make particularly effective use of self-organised structures following merger as sites from which to prepare the ground, develop the arguments, counter opposition, empower and mobilise equality-seeking activists to work towards a transformational agenda. The two examples in this study illustrate some of the key differences in the development of equality and diversity agendas in UK unions.

The GPMU organises in an industry where occupational skill is strongly gendered and women's subordinate positions at work are reflected in the union. Women members form a minority in a strongly masculinised and patriarchal traditional industrial union, where even moving to a liberal equality agenda has taken twenty years. It is only in the last few years that the union has acknowledged its black members, and that lesbian and gay members actually exist. It is more comfortable with building organising among women and young members. The numbers of female activists are small, and they are scattered geographically making networking and alliance building difficult. In these circumstances, the opportunity for women to organise semi-autonomously has been extremely important and their action as change agents has been significant for the union. Their lead is starting to be being built on by other equity seeking groups. However, it can also be seen from their testimony that in the GPMU the equality agenda is always contested, and women's self-organisation is in constant danger of co-option.

In UNISON, where women form nearly three-quarters of the membership, radical, and even transformational policies and practices have been developed. UNISON has been seen by other unions in the UK and abroad as a leader in its innovative, tri-partite equality constitution. However, policies and structures although essential, are not sufficient. Equal rights have to be delivered in practice. In UNISON this has been acknowledged by committed activists working both within self-organisation and the 'mainstream'. In UNISON the resistance that strong self-organisation sets up from those who oppose it or offer only qualified support means marginalisation is a continuous threat. As in the GPMU, the balance between autonomy and integration for self-organisation is a fine one, hard to establish and harder to maintain.

Notes

1   A fourth grouping included those who were undecided or claimed not to know. See Colgan and Ledwith (forthcoming) for further discussion.

2 BDC stands for the GPMU's Biennial Delegate Conference.
3 The Service Groups in UNISON coordinate bargaining on pay and service conditions in the public services where UNISON organises, i.e. energy, health, higher education, local government, transport, water.

UK trade unions cited in the text

COHSE	Confederation of Health Service Employees (merged to form UNISON in 1993)
CWU	Communication Workers Union
FBU	Fire Brigades Union
GMB	General Municipal & Boilermakers Union.
GPMU	Graphical, Paper and Media Union
MSF	Manufacturing Science Finance (merged with AEEU in 2002 to form AMICUS)
NALGO	National & Local Government Officers Association (merged to form UNISON in 1993)
NATFHE	National Association of Teachers in Further and Higher Education
NGA	National Graphical Association (merged to form GPMU in 1991)
NUPE	National Union of Public Service Employees (merged to form UNISON in 1993)
NUT	National Union of Teachers
PCS	Public and Commercial Services Union
SOGAT	Society of Graphical and Allied Trades (merged to form GPMU in 1991)
TGWU	Transport and General Workers Union
USDAW	Union of Shop, Distributive and Allied Workers

References

Boston, S. (1987) *Women Workers and Their Trade Unions*, London: Laurence and Wishart.

Briskin, L. (1993) 'Union women and separate organizing', in Briskin, L. and McDermott, P. (eds) *Women Challenging Unions*, Toronto: University of Toronto Press, pp. 89–108.

—— (1999) 'Autonomy, diversity and integration: union women's separate organizing in the context of restructuring and globalization', *Women's Studies International Forum* 22, 5: 543–54.

Campbell, J. and Oliver, M. (1996) *Disability Politics: Understanding Our Past, Changing our Future*, London: Routledge.

Cobble, D.S. (1993) 'Introduction: Remaking unions for the new majority', in *Women and Unions: Forging a Partnership*, Cobble, Dorothy Sue (ed.) Ithaca, NY: ILR Press, pp. 3–23.

Cockburn, C. (1983) *Brothers: Male Dominance and Technological Change*, London: Pluto.

—— (1991) *In the Way of women: Men's Resistance to Sex Equality in Organizations*, London: Macmillan.

—— (1995) *Women and the European Social Dialogue: Strategies for Gender Democracy*, Equal Opportunities Unit, European Commission, V/5465/95-EN.

COHSE, NALGO, NUPE (1991) *A Framework for a New Union*. Report of the COHSE, NALGO and NUPE National Executives to the 1991 Annual Conferences, London.

Colgan, F. (1999a) 'Recognising the lesbian and gay constituency in UK trade unions: moving forward in UNISON?', *Industrial Relations Journal* 30, 5: 444–63.

—— (1999b) 'Moving forward in UNISON: lesbian and gay self-organisation in action' in Hunt, G. (ed.) *Laboring for Rights: Unions and Sexual Diversity Across Nations*, Philadelphia: Temple University Press.

Colgan, F. and Ledwith, S. (forthcoming) *Negotiating Gender Democracy: New Trade Union Agendas*, Basingstoke: Palgrave.

—— (2002) *Employee Relations*, 24, 2.

—— (2000a) 'Diversity, identities and strategies of women trade union activists', *Gender, Work and Organization* 7, 4: 242–57.

—— (2000b) *Women in UNISON: Report to the Union*, London: UNISON.

—— (1996) 'Sisters organising – women and their trade unions', in Ledwith, S. and Colgan, F. (eds) *Women in Organisations: Challenging Gender Politics*, Basingstoke: Macmillan.

Colling, T. and Dickens, L. (1989) *Equality Bargaining – Why Not?*, Warwick: Warwick University/EOC.

—— (2001) 'Gender equality and the trade unions: a new basis for mobilisation?', in Noon, M. and Ogbonna, E. (eds) *Equality, Diversity and Disadvantage in Employment*, Basingstoke, Palgrave.

Collinson, M. and Hearn, J. (1994) 'Naming men as men: implications for work, organization and management', *Gender, Work and Organization*, 1, 1.

Cully, M., Woodland, S., O'Reilly, A. and Dix, G. (1999) *Britain at Work*, London: Routledge.

Dickens, L. (1997) 'Gender, race and employment equality in Britain: inadequate strategies and the role of industrial relations actors', *Industrial Relations Journal* 28, 4: 282–91.

—— (2000) 'Promoting gender equality at work – a potential role for trade union action', *Journal of Interdisciplinary Gender Studies*, 5, 2: 27–45.

Davis, M. (1993) *Comrade or Brother?* London: Pluto.

Drake, B. (1984) *Women in Trade Unions*, London; Virago (reprint from 1920 edition; Labour Research Department).

Fosh, P. and Heery, H. (1990) *Trade Unions and their Members, Studies in Union Democracy and Organization*, London: Macmillan.

Franzway, S. (1998) *Sexual Politics in Labour Movements*. Paper to 14th World Congress of Sociology, Montreal, 26 July–1 August.

Fryer, B. (2000) 'The making of UNISON: a framework to review key events, processes and issues', in Terry, M. (ed.) *Redefining Public Sector Unionism: UNISON and the Future of Trade Unions*, London: UNISON, pp. 23–48.

Gooding, C. (2000) *Report of the Third TUC Conference on Disability Issues*, London: TUC.

GPMU (2000a) 'Opportunity Knocks'. *GPMU Direct*, journal of the Graphical, Paper and Media Union, March.

—— (2000b) 'Equality Street', *GPMU Direct*, journal of the GPMU, July.

Haunch, P. (2000) 'Understanding conflict in UNISON', paper presented to the ESRC Centre for Business Research, University of Cambridge, 23rd May.

Healy, G. and Kirton, G. (2000) 'Women, power and trade union government in the UK', *British Journal of Industrial Relations* 38, 3: 343–60.

Heery, E. (1998) 'Campaigning for part-time workers', *Work, Employment and Society* 12, 2: 351–66.

Heery, E. and Abbot, B. (2000) 'Trade unions and the insecure workforce', in Heery, E. and Salmon, J. (eds) *The Insecure Workforce*, London: Routledge.

Heery, E. and Kelly, J. (1988) 'Do female representatives make a difference? – women full-time officials and trade union work', *Work, Employment and Society* 2, 4: 487–505.

Heery, E., Simms, M., Delbridge, R. and Salmon, J. (1999) 'Organising unionism comes to the UK', *Employee Relations* 22, 1: 58–75.

Humphrey, J. (1998) 'Self organise and survive: Disabled people in the British Trade Union movement', *Disability and Society* 13, 4.

Hunt, G. (1999) *Labouring for Rights: Unions and Sexual Diversity Across Nations*, Philadelphia: Temple University Press.

Hyman, R. (1975) *Marxism and the Sociology of Trade Unionism*, London: Macmillan.

—— (1994) 'Changing trade union identities and strategies', in Hyman, R. and Ferner, A. (eds) *New Frontiers in European Industrial Relations*, Oxford: Blackwell

Kelly, J. (1998) *Rethinking Industrial Relations; Mobilization, Collectivism and Long Waves*, London: Routledge.

—— (2000) 'Unions in the new millennium', *Labour Research* 89, 1 (January): 11–13.

Kirton, G. (1999) 'Sustaining and developing women's trade union activism: a gendered project?', *Gender, Work and Organisation* 6: 213–23.

Kirton, G. and Healy, G. (1999) 'Transforming union women: the role of women trade union officials in union renewal', *Industrial Relations Journal* 30, 1: 31–45.

Labour Research Department (LRD) (1994) 'Still a long road to equality', *Labour Research* 83, 3: 5–7.

—— (1997) 'Are unions out and proud?', *Labour Research* 86, 7 (July): 16–19.

—— (1998) *Union Action for Race Equality*, London: LRD.

—— (2000a) 'Women everywhere but at the top', *Labour Research* 89, 3 (March): 17–19.

—— (2000b) 'TUC welcomes upturn in union membership', *Labour Research* 89, 7 (July): 3.

—— (2001a) 'Recognition deals raised', *Labour Research* 90, 2 (February): 7.

—— (2001b) 'Unions search for ageing cure', *Labour Research* 90, 1 (January): 10–11.

—— (2001c) 'Union density steady again', *Labour Research* 90, 8 (August): 7.

—— (2001d) 'Where are all the black officials?', *Labour Research* 90, 8 (August): 14–15.

Ledwith, S., Colgan, F., Joyce, P. and Hayes, M. (1990) 'The making of women trade union leaders', *Industrial Relations Journal* 21, 2: 112–25.

Ledwith, S., Hayes, M., Joyce, P. and Gulati, A. (1985) *Women in SOGAT '82: Report of a Research Project into the Role of Women in the Union*, Hadleigh: SOGAT '82.

McBride, A. (2001) *Gender Democracy in Trade Unions*, Aldershot: Ashgate.

Mann, M., Ledwith, S., Colgan, F. (1997) 'Women's self organising and democracy in the UK: Proportionality and fair representation in UNISON', in Pocock, P. (ed.) *Strife: Sex and Politics in Labour Unions*, NSW: Allen & Unwin, pp.194–221.

Mills, G (1994) 'Proportionality – not just a numbers game', *PSI Focus* 4, December.

Millward, N. Bryson, A. and Forth, J. (2000) *All Change at Work?* London, Routledge.

Rainbird, H. and Munro, A. (1998) *UNISON's Return to Learn Programme*, London: UNISON.

Southern & Eastern Region TUC (SERTUC) Women's Rights Committee (1987) *Moving Towards Equality*, London: SERTUC.

—— (1992) *A Step Closer to Equality*, London: SERTUC.

—— (1997) *Inching Towards Equality – extremely slowly*, London: SERTUC.

—— (1998) *Inching Towards Equality*, London: SERTUC.

—— (2000) *New Moves Towards Equality: New Challenges*, London: SERTUC.

Terry, M. (1996) 'Negotiating the government of UNISON: Union democracy in theory and practice', *British Journal of Industrial Relations*, March: 87–110.

Trades Union Congress (TUC) (1996) *New Unionism – Organising for Growth*, Campaigns and Communications Department, September.

—— (1998a) *New Unionism: Meet the Organising Challenge*, TUC Conference, 14 November.

—— (1998b) *Black Trade Unionists Today*, London: TUC.

—— (2000a) *Resisting Racism at Work*, London: TUC.

—— (2000b) *Annual Report*, London: TUC.

UNISON (1995) *Integration and Participation in UNISON: From Vision to Practice*, Report of Joint Working Group, London: UNISON.

—— (1997a) *Playing Fair: UNISON Guidelines on Fair Representation*, London: UNISON.

—— (1997b) *UNISON Rules*, London: UNISON.

Virdee, S. and Grint, K. (1994) 'Black self-organisation in trade unions', *Sociological Review* 42, 2: 202–26.

Waddington, J. and Kerr, A. (1999a) 'Membership retention in the public sector', *Industrial Relations Journal* 30, 2: 151–65.

—— (1999b) 'Trying to stem the flow: union membership turnover in the public sector', *Industrial Relations Journal* 30, 3: 85–96.

Whitston, C. and Waddington, J. (1994) 'Why join a union', *New Statesman and Society* November: 36–8.

9 Professional and highly qualified women in two contrasting trade unions

Geraldine Healy and Gill Kirton

Introduction

This chapter provides insights into the gendered practices and orientations of women activists in two UK, TUC affiliated trade unions that explicitly aim to recruit professional workers. One union, Manufacturing, Science and Finance (MSF), is numerically dominated by men, and the other, National Union of Teachers (NUT), by women. This focus allows a comparison of unions which recruit professional and highly qualified workers, one organising a heterogeneous group predominantly employed in the private sector, and the second organising a more homogeneous and almost exclusively public sector workforce. The paper explores two key issues: women's structures in the union and the gendered nature of trade union orientation of women union activists who are also professional and highly qualified workers.

By concentrating on professional and highly qualified workers, the chapter enables a consideration of occupations that are numerically expanding and reflect the changing composition of labour in the UK and internationally. The link between high union density of teachers and the more mixed picture of white-collar professionals is also of importance, a pattern evident in the UK and internationally (e.g. Ferner and Hyman 1998; Lawn 1985). Walby (1997) has shown how young women are increasingly entering traditionally male dominated professions, e.g. law and medicine providing some optimism for women's future employment opportunities. Nevertheless patterns of horizontal and vertical segregation are persistent. Significantly for unions, women represent 40 per cent of professionals overall in the UK (EOR 1998) and dominate in other white-collar and service occupations, where most job growth is predicted. Teachers are a relatively homogeneous group, the intra-sector differences notwithstanding, and can therefore be said to constitute an occupational community with common interests and concerns not necessarily shared by the wider professional community. Whereas, professional workers as a whole are a heterogeneous group, with salient variations in sector, status, pay and conditions. The sense of an 'occupational community' is thought to be important to union participation, but only if the collectivity values such participation (Klandermans 1992). These factors indicate the value of examining the nature of women's experience in unions that explicitly aim to recruit professional and highly qualified workers.

Union density among women in general is variable, with industry and sector being the most significant factors (Hartley 1992). Whilst the union movement as a whole has lost members in the period 1979–96, individual unions have increased their membership over this period. It is noteworthy that of the 14 TUC unions that have increased membership during the period, 11 organise workers who may be characterised as occupational unions recruiting professional or highly qualified workers (Kelly 1998).

Female managers and professionals are shown to be more likely than are their male peers to be union members in Britain (Cully *et al.* 1999: 196). Further analysis using the Labour Force Survey (2000), which disaggregates professional and managerial occupational groups into three demonstrates that managers and administrators are made up of 65 per cent male and 35 per cent female; professional occupations are 53 per cent female and associate professional and technical workers are 64 per cent female. A comparison of the proportions with trade union members demonstrates that in each of these occupational groups women are more likely to be union members than men, suggesting at this level of occupational attainment, women have a relatively strong union orientation. In the case of the case study unions, it is evident from Table 9.1 that women dominate the NUT and men dominate the MSF. It is further the case that after some years of decline, the NUT has seen a growth in membership since 1993 and a corresponding increase in women's membership. The MSF membership has declined since 1990 but the proportion of women has increased. In both cases women constitute a critical proportion of membership both in terms of density and in terms of future growth prospects.

From the above discussion and from Table 9.1, it is evident that sex differences in unionisation may be mediated by sectoral and occupational differences which will influence union strategies in relation to their women members and the strategies that activists themselves adopt. This chapter therefore explores union and activist gender equality strategies within contrasting internal union contexts and the inter-relationship between professional commitment and union orientation.

Table 9.1 Proportion of women's membership of the MSF and NUT, 1990–1999

Year	MSF women's membership	Percentage of total membership	NUT women's membership	Percentage of total membership
1990	141,443	22	123,826	73
1991	130,844	22	120,924	73
1992	143,520	26	120,508	74
1993	135,449	26	125,631	74
1994	140,903	29	131,878	75
1995	137,082	31	132,098	75
1996	133,227	31	140,877	75
1997	131,096	31	143,602	75
1998	135,582	33	145,810	75
1999	133,141	32	152,380	76

Sources: Equal Opportunities Review (EOR) Nos. 42 (1992), 48 (1993), 65 (1996), 76 (1997), 94 (2000).

Professional commitment and union orientation

The relationship between professional commitment and union orientation is under-explored. The literature on professions, including that on gender and professions, rarely mentions trade unionism (e.g. Macdonald 1995; Witz 1992). The omission may be partly the result of neglect or based on assumptions around the perceived incompatibility of being a professional worker with trade union membership. (This latter point is best illustrated by the perception that a key trade union strategy, industrial action, is deemed 'unprofessional'.) Yet to neglect this crucial relationship denies the value of a significant aspect of the employment experience of many workers characterised as 'professional'.

The term professional is of course contested. The literature ranges from the attributes approach (see Macdonald 1995) to more gendered and political analyses focusing on closure and power (see for example, Johnson 1972; Witz 1992). Johnson's (1972) work is seminal since he focused on profession as an institutionalised means of controlling occupational activities. The state was important in his analysis and he pointed to state mediative control as operating to support or oppose the views of an occupational group. These insights are important in demonstrating the interrelationship between strategies of professional groups and trade unions. Witz importantly pointed to the gendered nature of closure practices in professionalising occupations (1992: 5) an insight of relevance to gendered practices in trade unions.

It has been suggested that an occupation such as teaching (alongside nursing and social work) is a 'semi-profession' or 'quasi-profession' one that is dominated by women and the state (Etzioni 1969). Following arguments made in earlier papers, this chapter asserts that the gendered nature of the teaching profession and its state employment are, for example, crucial structural influences on employment and unionisation. However, to suggest that these characteristics are defining of teachers' status among professions is not only pejorative to women's status, but also analytically unhelpful (Healy 1997). Witz reveals the implications of these terms by drawing on Simpson and Simpson (1969), who emphasised the subordinate position and compliant nature of women in semi-professions, who are ideally suited to the role of the 'handmaidens of a male occupation that has authority over them'. Witz summarises this sterile debate by stating that because 'women are not men, semi-professions are not professions' (Witz 1992: 60). It is time that the concept of semi-profession was generally acknowledged for what it is, a gendered socially constructed project complicit in the subordination of women's occupational groups.

'Professional' work cannot be characterised in a uni-dimensional way and needs to be understood in all its complexity (Freidson 1994). Crompton (1999: 181) argues that attempts to identify a universal definition of 'profession' have been abandoned and there has been a shift towards the analysis of the processes of professional emergence and restructuring, in which many different routes (and thus professional types) can be identified (Crompton 1999). To avoid the dangers of classification, the subjects of this chapter are highly qualified workers with high human capital who perceive themselves as professional workers. To some extent this would include managers, administrators and paid trade union officials[1] as part of the study. However, there is a mindfulness of Crompton's (1999: 123) distinction between professional and managerial occupations, by arguing that the professional knowledge and expertise are regulated by an external standard, whereas managerial expertise is directly evaluated by the employing organisation. These insights are important to our discussion on professions and trade unions, although it is the case that much restructuring of professions has led to a blurring of these distinctions. Professional work is important in identity formation, which may relate to the expectations of high material rewards, access to power resources or be driven by altruistic motives. Many state employed professional workers demonstrate commitment to their occupation, what has been characterised as a form of moral or vocational commitment and which may conflict with commitment to the organisation (Healy 1999a). Inherent then in the professionalisation of work is the potential for conflict with the employer about control over that work.

Nevertheless, the conventional wisdom is that the professionalisation process might mitigate against a collective orientation. For example, much of the work carried out by professionals in the public sector, especially by women, involves people rather than products. There is often an ethos of 'putting the people first', whether the people are patients (as in the case of nurses and health visitors), pupils (teachers) or other client groups. Conflicts in professional values are also evident in private sector professional work where 'client' or 'customer' is part of the managerial control system. In other words, this shift shapes and perhaps enhances the tensions of work commitment. The customer culture alongside marketisation and managerialism have led to a blurring of distinctions in the nature of professional and managerial work between the private and the public sectors and impacts on the agenda and practices of trade union activism.

Whilst this might suggest a tension between professional and union commitment, it is likely that professional workers, including women, may object to managerial interventions, which undermine the quality of care or service. In this sense, the union has a role to play in upholding professional standards. For example, the NUT has used the media to voice its members' concerns about standards in schools, in relation to various educational reforms. Thus, grievances may be collectively channelled through a trade union, thereby opening up possibilities for dual professional and union commitment. It is also possible that professional commitment strengthens union commitment if the union is perceived to effectively challenge management initiatives, which are likely to prove deleterious for workers and 'clients' alike. Further examples of unions' ability to reconcile or manage the tension between professional and union commitment can be found within the MSF context. The union's health sector-based newsletter 'NHS News' regularly contains articles on professional topics ('clinical governance', for instance), alongside traditional union topics (Working Time Regulations, for instance), indicating that what is deemed a matter for the professions cannot be entirely separated from issues of concern to union members as 'workers'. Similarly, the Guild of Healthcare Pharmacists – an industrial grouping within MSF – awards various annual prizes for individual members' contributions to pharmacy. The Guild also put a motion to its Group Delegates Meeting in 1997: 'This meeting requests Guild Council to become actively involved in expediting national negotiations towards compulsory continuing professional development for all practising pharmacists' (MSF 1998).

To explore whether or not professional work is fertile ground for the construction of a union orientation, it is also necessary to consider the nature of the day-to-day work carried out by professionals. The degree of autonomy or control over work is important. Cully *et al.* (1999: 41) report that professionals and highly qualified workers have a relatively high degree of discretion over how work is done. Linked to this, Lawrence (1994) finds that such job autonomy is positively associated with union activism, in that it facilitates the negotiation of the balancing of work and union activities. Nevertheless, issues of control and autonomy are central issues in professional work; the state for example seeks to wrestle control from professional workers who may turn to unions (or professional associations) as means of resistance. Further, long working hours are common among managerial and professional workers: Cully *et al.* (1999) find that 10 per cent of women managers and professionals, including those employed in education, worked in excess of 48 hours per week, possibly leaving little time for trade union activism. It is also likely that greater numbers work between 35 and 48 hours per week. Time constraints are especially salient in the case of women professionals and trade unionists who are mothers. It is axiomatic that women typically assume the burden of the majority of domestic labour and if trade union activism is added to an already busy work and family life, to voluntarily take on another role would seem to be counterintuitive.

An important factor relevant to union orientation among professional and highly qualified workers is the stronger likelihood of their having experience of participating in meetings, of speaking in public domains and generally of having the confidence to articulate ideas and opinions in front of others. Generally, the absence of these kinds of skills and experiences is said to deter women from getting involved in their unions (Lawrence 1994; Rees 1992). Professional and highly qualified women are also likely to work with and to socialise with other similar women and since this group is over-represented among union representatives, they are also likely to encounter union representatives on a peer group basis. Thus, the general concerns about women having less facility with union procedures and jargon (Cockburn 1991) because of their lesser exposure to union representatives and discourse, is less likely to apply to professional and highly qualified women. The chapter now outlines the research approach used in exploring women's activism in the two case studies, which whilst not directly comparable provide complementary insights.

Research approach

Most UK trade unions now have structures and strategies aimed at increasing women's representation in union decision-making and increasing women's participation in union affairs. MSF has developed a radical, interventionist strategy, whilst the NUT strategy is somewhat more liberal. Whilst both unions have national women's committees, the NUT's has advisory status, whilst that of MSF is a sub-committee of the National Executive Committee (NEC), giving it greater status and power. MSF also has four seats reserved for women on its NEC (drawn from the women's committee), thus creating a structural link between the women's committee and the NEC (Healy and Kirton 2000). These structural conditions set the context of a consideration of the gendered orientation to unionism. Klandermans' gender neutral approach assesses union orientation in a number of ways, union joining, participation and quitting (Klandermans 1986). In the MSF we focus particularly on participation and with the NUT on union joining. In addition in both unions, we also explored gendered bargaining issues.

The case study of MSF draws on union documentation and qualitative data from an interview programme carried out in the autumn of 1996 (16 interviews) and summer of 1998 (two interviews). Thus, 18 senior union women; 10 NEC (National Executive Committee), lay women in regional, industrial, reserved women's seats and one reserved race committee seat; and eight women regional and national paid union officials. The 10 lay officials in the sample were mostly managerial or professional women, the exception being one shop floor, manual worker. This group comprised a health visitor, a national charity director, an IT manager, two laboratory scientists, a financial services manager, a computer analyst, an insurance underwriter and a personal assistant to a member of parliament. The eight paid officials can be classified as professional trade unionists, in that seven of this group had a lengthy history in their roles (of at least six years), whilst one newer woman (with one year's service with the union) was highly qualified. This group had previous professional and managerial experience in, for example, journalism, engineering and the finance industry.

In the case of the NEC interviewees, these are women who have built their union 'careers' (demanding attendance and participation in the evenings and often at weekends) at the same time as their time-greedy paid work careers. In this context, it is noteworthy that seven of the women in the sample were mothers, three of whom had children under 16. Thus, the sample represents a group of women who, by sustained participation in union affairs, demonstrate commitment to the union and therefore a strong union orientation. The in-depth interviews allow a thorough and detailed examination of senior union women's views and the micro social processes shaping their perceptions, experiences, motivations and attitudes within their union, thus contributing to an understanding of women's trade union orientations and activism at the micro level. Further work on this study may be found in Kirton (1999), Kirton and Healy (1999) and Healy and Kirton (2000).

In the case study of NUT, we draw on recent union documentary evidence to provide insight into gendered practices and quantitative and qualitative data drawn from a survey of NUT members to examine the orientation of women members and their expectations of their union, enabling a consideration of broad patterns of women's instrumental and solidaristic collectivism. A sample of 3,600 teachers was surveyed by postal questionnaire in 1994 and a number of women activists informed the design of the study. The sample was structured to ensure broadly representative proportions of primary and secondary and women and men teachers in England and Wales: 1,855 questionnaires were returned, representing a response rate of 52 per cent, 34 per cent from men and 66 per cent from women (43 per cent in the primary and 53 per cent in the secondary sector[2]). Sixteen per cent (303 respondents) were trade union representatives (21 per cent men and 14 per cent female). The part of the study that this chapter draws on relates particularly to why women respondents joined the NUT and the expectations of the NUT in relation to their individual career development. These questions enable an exploration of the dual relationship between union and profession (a more detailed consideration of these issues may be found in Healy (1997, 1999b).

Manufacturing, Science and Finance (MSF)

Union structures

MSF is the UK's fifth largest union, with about 420,000 members (Labour Research 2000). The union was formed in 1988 as a result of a merger between the unions TASS (Technical, Administrative and Supervisory Staff) and ASTMS (Association of Scientific, Technical and Managerial Staff).[3] In 1990 the Health Visitors Association (HVA) merged with MSF introducing an overwhelmingly professional, female membership drawn from the public sector. Thus, MSF has a heterogeneous membership predominantly consisting of skilled and professional people in private services and industry, and with a smaller public sector constituency. In structural terms, MSF has much in common with other UK trade unions, including a domination of men in decision-making positions. Among a minority of UK unions MSF has achieved women's proportionality (around 30 per cent) on its national decision-making body, the National Executive Committee (NEC). However, proportionality has not been achieved in the ranks of paid officials.

This is the context within which we explore senior MSF women's roles and activities in the union. In terms of barriers to women's trade union participation, one of the salient factors is male domination of union decision-making. It is thought that this has created a perception among many women that union business is men's business (see for example, Bradley 1999, Cockburn 1991, Cunnison and Stageman 1995), as well as creating an environment in which women feel uncomfortable and unwelcome. However, what is interesting about professional women in MSF is that many work in non-traditional occupations or at levels of organisations where there are few women. To work among men as peers is not as unfamiliar to many professional women as it is within more gender segregated occupations, and it could be postulated that because of this professional women may be better equipped to cope in male-dominated environments. For example, one interviewee worked as a senior computer analyst in the aerospace industry representing about 1,000 members, the vast majority of whom were male. When asked why it was important to her as a woman to be a union activist, she stated, 'There's lots of sexism in the workplace. Management and union are very macho in the engineering industry. It's hard as a woman to survive in a male dominated environment. You need to be hard especially in the private sector.' Similarly, for paid officials, it is paradoxical that a hostile masculine environment may also create a challenging learning experience:

I come from a very strong trade union work environment and [another official] from a cut throat industry, so perhaps we are better equipped to deal with this than younger inexperienced colleagues. We have been active trade unionists, girl and woman, and I think all of that hardens the veneer.

In terms of internal gender equality, most senior MSF women were generally in favour of radical, interventionist strategies aimed at achieving the full representation of women in all union decision-making bodies. For example, an overwhelming majority of the sample (17) was in favour of retaining reserved women's seats on the NEC, even though proportionality had been achieved. However, this support was not unequivocal. Some women were concerned that special treatment for women was tantamount to tokenism, or that identifying a separate women's agenda could undermine unity and solidarity within the union movement. These reservations notwithstanding, they were united in seeing women's structures as essential to maintaining a critical mass of women to advance a feminised union agenda. Thus, it can be argued that women's trade union orientation is underpinned by a feminist paradigm, in that it is feminist politics that have posed a challenge to the marginalisation of women in unions (Bradley 1999; Colgan and Ledwith 1996). Cockburn (1991) posits that the ideology of feminism has had an important influence on women's trade union activism and at the same time on union agendas, structures and to a lesser extent union culture. Not all women within our MSF sample were self-identified feminists (although 13 were) (see Kirton 1999), but they all used a feminist lexicon to describe their attitudes to and perceptions of the union and the strategies needed to effect gender equality.

In the context of the discussion about professional union women, it is important to note that the group of women on the NEC is not entirely representative of the occupational diversity of the union. In the case of MSF, an activist commented: 'Union meetings can become a social elite where university educated women are more likely to feel comfortable', but then went on to argue that the Women's Committee provided a less formal and elitist environment to absorb and critique the masculine union culture. That said, professional and highly qualified women do dominate senior positions within the union. Their routes to these positions are varied and do not always mirror the traditional male path from union activist to paid official. One paid official alluded to this: 'Most of our male colleagues were MSF reps before becoming paid officials, whereas the women often come via higher education or some professional background. So to some extent we are a different breed.'

Gendered orientations to unionism

Looking to external equality strategies, the perceived need for unions to develop a feminised, 'pro-women' bargaining agenda (Cockburn 1991), arises from the belief that women workers have different bargaining priorities to men. We emphasise the word 'priorities' and use it in preference to 'needs' or 'concerns', because men and women workers also share many bargaining concerns, for example pay, health and safety. Dickens points out that there is a tendency to think of equality in terms of 'women's measures' rather than equality measures (which concern men also) (Dickens 2000: 6). This is important but the tendency is understandable as within modern gender relations women still have a separate (as well as joint) bargaining agenda, which stems from their domestic and familial roles and the intersection of these with workplace issues. Related to this, one MSF interviewee reported,

> Their [women's] life experience is broader than men's simply because of the role they're cast in as women. There's a very positive side to women's life experiences – it gives them a different perspective on tackling problems, in dealing with people.

However, it may be difficult to incorporate these different perspectives into a bargaining agenda where a numerically dominant group exists, since their interests are likely to prevail. The importance for gendered bargaining of having a critical accumulation of women in union decision-making is that it is largely women who raise 'women's issues':

> It's very difficult in a male-dominated environment to get some men, not all, to understand women's way of looking at things. It's not just about negotiating a pay rise. I mean there are other issues such as childcare, flexitime, sexual harassment. You need to get these issues across to employers – it's not all about pay.
>
> (NEC member)

Within MSF there is a critical mass of senior women who believe that women's presence makes a difference, echoing previous research (e.g. Cockburn 1991; Colling and Dickens 1989; Heery and Kelly (1988; Kirton and Healy 1999). Thus there is a circular relationship between internal and external gender equality strategies. The women in the study adopt various strategies to ensure that women continue to have proportional representation within decision-making structures and that the wider female membership has 'voice' within the union. One of these strategies was women's networking, which took a variety of forms: internal and external, formal and informal. It rests upon the premise that women's separate organisation represents a strategy for improving the participation of women and for empowering women (Briskin and McDermott 1993). Thus, at the heart of the strategy of women's separate organisation is the belief that women need to organise *collectively* to overcome the barriers they *collectively* encounter within male-dominated environments.

In MSF, as in many unions, the formal vehicle for internal lay women's networking is the National Women's Sub Committee (NWSC), whilst the formal vehicle for external lay women's networking is the TUC Women's Committee. Most of the women interviewed attended NWSC meetings, even if infrequently. Women who were delegates to the TUC Women's Committee were asked to provide reports of that committee's activities and decisions to the NWSC. The NWSC was described as a supportive environment where women could safely express feelings of isolation and lack of confidence and could find support and help from other women. This was contrasted with the more hostile environment of the NEC, where women often felt discomfited by male behaviour and alienated by the lack of friendliness and mutual support: 'A lot of the men are hecklers, especially when women are talking. They also use obnoxious body language to undermine women when they're talking', a comment made by an experienced trade unionist. The overwhelming majority of the sample was in favour of the separate women's committee. Even if they had doubts about its efficacy in fundamentally transforming union structures, strategies and culture, or about its separatist ideology, there was general agreement that it was at least necessary as an interim strategy to help in overcoming the historical gender inequalities within the union movement.

On the one hand separate women's structures function as safe retreats from male-dominated structures where women often feel unwelcome or out of place, but on the other hand such structures are not simply 'talking shops' or 'comfort zones'. They also represent sites in which gendered strategies can be developed (Healy and Kirton 2000). This dimension is evidenced by the practical work of women's committees. In MSF this includes organising a national women members' conference, regular women-only courses, publishing literature on 'women's issues' and mounting campaigns around issues such as the 'glass ceiling', domestic violence, women's health. The Glass Ceiling Campaign, for instance, featured prominently in the work of the female National Secretary for Equality and the NWSC in 1996/7. The union teamed up with the national pressure group 'AWISE' (a group for women in science, engineering and technology) to campaign for a new attitude from government and employers to women in these sectors. The campaign pivoted around a survey of MSF members and involved media publicity and political lobbying, in order to raise awareness of the blockages to women's career advancement. More recently the female equalities researcher has worked with the NWSC in campaigning around 'family friendly' issues, on which the NWSC organised a women's weekend school in 1999. All of these activities inject women's equality issues into the life of the union, ensuring that women are visible both internally (within the union) and externally (by for example media coverage).

Whilst formal networking enhances women's visibility in the male-dominated union context, *informal* networking was also important to the MSF women both on an intra- and inter-union basis as a gendered response to the male dominated environment. Internally this ranged from women developing friendships with other women, which they described as providing essential support: 'There's a mutual understanding of what it's like to be a woman doing trade union work – it's something men just can't relate to.' Women also networked with female trade unionists from other unions: 'I do think it's important to get to know other women for support. I notice I always try to talk to other women at the TUC conference, for example.' As these quotations illustrate, women's informal networking serves a different, more personalised function, but it is nevertheless deemed essential by many union women to the maintenance of women's activism.

What emerges from the discussion of MSF women's orientations, their activities and roles within women's structures and their separatist networking strategies, is that the group was working towards the goal of gender equality. In a highly qualified and professional union, this involves addressing the traditional women's trade union agenda (low pay, childcare and sexual harassment as well as issues relating to vertical segregation). That is, professional and highly qualified women share some of the concerns of less qualified women but they also have some gender priorities specific to their status and occupations. The women interviewed had a strong union orientation in that they saw the union as having a vital role to play in achieving gender equality goals for all women as well as being focused on highly qualified and professional women.

National Union of Teachers (NUT)

NUT is the UK's largest teaching union (in the context of competitive multi-unionism) with approximately 228,000 members (Labour Research 2000) and considered the most militant. It is also the oldest teacher union; its origins go back to 1870 and from its inception women have been activists with early commentators suggesting that 'women are no longer the apathetic group of teachers' (Thompson 1927: 114).[4] This background is important since it shows first the long-standing relationship between professional concerns and trade unionism. Second, women as active agents have been strong in the union since its inception, and their early contribution needs to be acknowledged alongside second wave feminists.

Women now make up over 75 per cent of NUT membership. About 75 per cent of their membership is in primary schools, whose teachers are 80 per cent female. In the secondary sector women and men teachers are fairly evenly represented. Not only is the gendered pay gap in teaching resilient (*The Teacher* 2000) but so is the gendered distribution of organisational power in the union; despite the numerical domination of women in the NUT, men dominate the decision-making bodies of the union.

Union structures

The evidence presented in the most recent SERTUC Report (2000) demonstrates that women have not succeeded in achieving proportionality in the main decision-making bodies in the NUT and also that the NUT has not taken on board the range of separate organising initiatives that the MSF has. Given the early influence of feminism in teaching and women as the numerically dominant group in the union, this position demands some explanation.

Part of the explanation may lie in the history and the commitment of the NUT to education and in particular to the education of working-class children (Thompson 1927) and to the importance of socialism and feminism in the union (Ironside and Seifert 1995). The well known factional differences in the NUT (Calveley and Healy 2000; Seifert 1984) do not obscure the fact that women's structural progress is mediated by an enduring gendered oligarchy and an associated struggle to access power resources (Healy and Kirton 2000: 343). Central to the debates about education is that the intersection of gender and class is more than the lived experience of workers, but also part of the ideological resources used to make sense of the world and to influence action. Thus in many cases, the professional aspects of the work, i.e. the interests of children, may be given more weight than equality issues. Those interests which are common are likely to be the ones pressed. This is illustrated in the recent NUT policy statement on Gender and Education, which whilst acknowledging the hierarchical gender imbalance, focuses on the educational impact of the interaction of class, gender and ethnicity (NUT 2001).

Despite the domination of men in the hierarchies and decision-making bodies, women are active in the NUT. They make up 43 per cent of the executive and 55 per cent of conference attendees (SERTUC 2000: 31). Notwithstanding the lack of proportionality, the NUT has an equal opportunities advisory committee for gender. The issues dealt with by the gender committee demonstrate the complexity of gender issues in education, in particular how they are integrally involved with education itself and therefore issues of professional concern as well as of career concern. Issues of career concern included age diversity in employment and part-time working. But the more extensive list of issues of professional concern included personal, social and health education as in the revised National Curriculum, social exclusion and teenage pregnancy (SERTUC 2000: 31). Again this tension is illustrated by the lack of a women's conference in the NUT but the existence of an annual equal opportunities conference where the key issues again centre around professional concerns: gender equality, renewing anti-racism in education, equality and school improvement. There are also black teachers' and lesbian and gay equality conferences. Parents' involvement in conferences is facilitated by the provision of a crèche or the payment of childcare expenses. The NUT has full-time officers whose remit is women members, black and ethnic minority members and gender equality and to ensure that local informal structures exist for women. In addition, there is an annual national women's education course which deals with career issues such as personal development, job sharing and promotion.

Gendered orientation to unionism

Teachers' orientation to unionism is considered in relation to union joining and career development as this gives some insight into the attitudes of highly qualified professional workers to trade unionism. NUT members demonstrate a higher level of collectivism than is evident in the Waddington and Whitston's (1994) study of white-collar workers and Healy (1997) found teachers joined the NUT for both instrumental and solidaristic reasons. The support for the union's instrumental collectivist role is in line with other studies (Deery and Walsh 1999; Guest and Dewe 1988; Kerr 1992; Waddington and Whitston 1994).

Instrumental motives reflect the belief that individuals on their own cannot protect and improve their own conditions of work without the strength of a collectivity (Healy 1997: 130). Thus, the union's support and negotiating functions were important for both women and men; acknowledging that whilst women and men may have different priorities, many of their material concerns will be similar.

Whilst women and men NUT union members demonstrate higher levels of instrumentalism and solidarity than in unions generally (see Waddington and

Whitston 1997), this is intensified in the case of activists (see Table 9.2). Both women and men activists, defined in this chapter by those identifying themselves as union representatives, were more solidaristic than the NUT members in the sample. However male representatives were still more unionate[5] when they joined the NUT than women representatives. This has some resonance with Ledwith *et al.*'s (1990) study which showed that whilst some trade union activists had a prior orientation to trade unionism, for others this emerged from the experience of work. What is interesting about the activist respondents is that they not only demonstrate higher solidaristic collectivism in relation to their union, but they also demonstrate greater instrumentalism and individualism than their less active colleagues. Thus, on joining, women and men union representatives demonstrate a higher degree of union commitment to the comprehensive meanings associated with trade unionism (Healy 1997).

From a gendered analysis, it is clear NUT women members, and to a greater extent, women activists, have a much higher commitment to unionism than do union members generally. However, there is still a persistent gendered gap in the 'belief' in trade unions as identified by Sinclair (1995, 1996); this would appear to be as much about perhaps critical and cynical perceptions of unions as organisations, illustrated in the MSF case. Nevertheless, there was little significant difference between women and men in their joining the NUT 'because it appeared more active than other teacher unions'; importantly in the context of current debates about youth and trade unionism, an active union was more important for younger women than for older women.

With regard to equality bargaining, the NUT data are drawn from responses to a question asking what 'your union can do to facilitate your career development' (see Table 9.3 and Healy 1999b for a full account). This was an open question and responses were subsequently coded.

Table 9.3 demonstrates important similarities between women and men. However from a gendered perspective there were crucial differences. Both women and men wanted the trade union to have a collectivist (whether instrumental or solidaristic) role in their career development. Whilst a highly differentiated set of needs emerged, there was a desire for an integrated response. Again the structures of constraints faced by teachers emerging from the effects of educational reform help explain the collective response of teachers to an inquiry into the union role in career development (Healy 1999b: 225), and more specifically professional development.[6] Note the collective nature of the following response and its emphasis on professional values:

> The union defends and voices the opinion of many teachers, which, without them, would not be heard. It is right to criticise and if necessary obstruct certain government decisions, which are detrimental to the education of our children. . . . Without such strong action, the opinion of teachers would be ignored.

Women, however, attached greater importance to equality issues than did men. This should not be surprising since various studies have shown how, in different

Table 9.2 The four most frequently cited reasons for joining the NUT (columns (a), (b)) analysed by sex and trade union representative as compared to a national survey on union joining, analysed by sex (column (c))

Cited reason	N	%	National survey on union joining* (%)
	(a)	*(b)*	*(c)*
To support me if I had a problem at work			
Sex:			
Men	490	79	68
Women	986	80	76
Total	1,476	80	
TU Representative:			
Men	96	74	
Women	134	78	
Total	230	76	
To improve my pay and conditions			
Sex:			
Men	337	54	42
Women	577	47	31
Total	914	49	
TU Representative:			
Men	75	52	
Women	90	55	
Total	165	55	
I believe in trade unionism and wished to take part			
Sex:			
Men	369	59	20
Women	511	42	13
Total	880	49	
TU Representative:			
Men	97	75	
Women	88	51	
Total	185	61	
The NUT appeared to be more active than other teacher unions			
Sex:			
Men	265	43	Not
Women	482	39	applicable
Total	747	40	
TU Representative:			
Men	73	56	
Women	71	41	
Total	144	48	

Source: Adapted from Healy 1997: 149, 151.
Notes
1 Percentages are rounded up or down.
2 Figures exclude respondents who did not identify sex.
* Figures drawn from large survey of new members conducted by Waddington and Whitston (1997), which influenced the design of the NUT survey.

Table 9.3 The proportion of respondents stating instrumental and solidaristic issues in response to the question on what the NUT union should do to facilitate respondents' career development, by sex

Instrumental issues	%	Men %	Women %
Pay and conditions	19.7	18.1	20.7
Training issues	12.6	12.8	12.6
Equality issues	7.9	2.4	11.4
Heads and deputies needs	0.7	0.7	0.7
Total	40.9	34	45.6
Solidaristic issues			
Policy issues	11.8	13.6	10.6
Better funding for education	10.1	11.0	9.5
Trade union structure and organisation	6.6	9.5	4.7
Political action	5.1	7.0	3.9
Improve public image	4.4	4.6	4.2
Total	38.0	45.7	32.9
N	1,151	453	698

Source: Adapted from Healy 1999b: 219, 222.

ways, women are disadvantaged in their teaching careers (e.g. Acker 1989; De Lyon and Migniulo 1989; Healy and Kraithman 1996; NUT/EOC 1980). Women were more likely to be on atypical contracts (e.g. fixed term, part-time, temporary, supply) than were men. Women wanted their union to tackle the contractual inequity they faced, one woman wanted the NUT to 'do something about the number of fixed term contracts. I won't know until the end of July if I have a contract for September. This is generally too late to find anything else.' The structural disadvantages faced by teachers on their return following a career break were clear areas for union action.

Notwithstanding the demand for equality to be put on the bargaining agenda, what was also clear from the study was the way union involvement also facilitated career development. One activist woman (a trade union representative, a mother of three, and head of a sixth form) pointed to the significance of her trade union participation: 'my involvement in the NUT has given me experience of high level meetings and opportunities to develop confidence and skills I lacked' (cited in Healy and Kraithman 1996: 202). Whilst there exist good examples of where union involvement mutually benefits the member and the union, it should not be forgotten that there are other cases in teaching where active union participation has had serious negative consequences for the activist (Calveley and Healy 2000) and may lead to the curtailment of professional careers.

Conclusions

A comparison between the two unions provides valuable insights into not only gendered structural differences between the unions but also the impact of the occupational context on union orientation. Within MSF there is a clear women's (feminist) agenda, with the union consciously pursuing gender equality strategies in the context of the enduring male dominated structures and culture. The fact that MSF has a smaller proportion of women means women's recruitment is high on the agenda. The reality of proportionality will be less threatening to the male dominated hierarchy than would be the case in the NUT where women are numerically dominant and where proportionality would lead to a direct threat to the male domination of the union. The chapter has provided insight into a range of equality initiatives and structures in both unions; this suggests, perhaps controversially, that there is a danger in simplistically relating proportionality to success in gender equality. The heterogeneity of the MSF also creates a differentiated membership base that is less likely to mobilise on single occupational issues, thus paradoxically leaving the gendered nature of unionisation more focused. For example, MSF women are putting considerable effort into achieving and sustaining *internal* gender equality.

The more homogeneous nature of teaching and its associated professional ideologies leads to a more complex analysis of gendered unionisation. The gendered tension that emerges in teaching is not between union and profession as might be expected, but between career and profession. The findings suggest that under certain conditions, women professional workers will campaign for conditions relevant to their profession alongside their male colleagues. The education of children and the health of 'clients', for example, may be perceived as of more urgent priority than the gendered nature of occupational segregation in the profession or in the union. Whilst people may join unions for protection at work, in the case of the NUT the solidaristic dimension in relation to their profession is also central and, the evidence suggests, may at particular moments in time take priority over individual gendered career and union development. In contrast, within MSF issues of career development, including vertical segregation, are prioritised as evidenced by the union's high profile Glass Ceiling Campaign.

Tensions emerged in the balance and nature of equality bargaining issues in both unions. The differences between the unions are manifested in their different natures. One reflects a more cohesive occupational community and the other a more disparate occupational grouping. In the case of MSF, the occupational base is more diffuse and therefore the chapter has indicated that the prioritising of equality employment issues is complicated not just by a gendered oligarchy but also by the potentially conflicting demands of professional issues. This is not to suggest that trade unionism is at odds with professional membership; on the contrary it draws out sharply the tensions and importantly the complementarity of this joint commitment. Professional women's identity then is shaped by the gendered experience of professional work and its intersection with trade unionism. As an MSF woman activist reported: 'We are professionals and are committed to doing our jobs properly, but we can still be trade unionists.'

Notes

1   Like managers, trade union paid officials' professional status is ambiguous. The recent development of the role has been characterised by increasing professional emergence indicated by training, appraisal systems and a dominant body of knowledge, a high proportion of which is laid down by statute. In this study, the trade union official shares many of the professional processes associated with professional types (Crompton 1999). Contrary to the Watson (1988: 179) view that this work is not professional but characterised by a political commitment, we would view officials' work as not only constrained by regulation (as are other professionals) but also sharing an ethical commitment to their work which is an important characteristic of 'professional work'.

2   In the UK, the primary sector educates children from the ages of five to 11 and the secondary sector from 11 to 18.

3   MSF merged with the Amalgamated Engineering and Electrical Union in 2002 to form AMICUS.

4   Indeed women teachers were active in the women's movement at the turn of the century and were involved in campaigns around demands for universal adult suffrage and equal pay (Webb 1915), improved terms and conditions and increased women's representation in the union (Ironside and Seifert 1995: 91). Gender has historically been a key issue in teachers' union organisation. The second largest teachers' union, NAS (National Association of Schoolmasters), split from the NUT over equal pay in 1922 and even in the 1950s asserted that the NUT surrendered to feminism and became an adjunct of the feminist movement (Ironside and Seifert 1995: 95). The NUT has traditionally adopted professional and career aims and explicitly aimed to benefit the working-class child 'who was to be given as broad a literary and scientific culture as was thought to be necessary for the child of the middle class' (Webb 1915: 19).

5   The term 'unionate' is normally used, following (Blackburn 1967), to describe an organisation as more or less unionate according to the extent to which it is a whole-hearted trade union, identifying with the labour movement and willing to use all the powers of the movement and is linked to measures of unionateness (Blackburn 1967: 18). Here the term unionate is adapted to describe members' commitment to the unionateness of their trade union.

6   It is noteworthy that the NUT places a very high priority on professional development issues.

References

Acker, S. (ed.) (1989) *Teachers, Gender and Careers*, Lewes: The Falmer Press.

Blackburn, R.M. (1967) *Union Character Social Class: a Study of White-Collar Unionism*, London: B.T. Batsford Ltd.

Bradley, H. (1999) *Gender and Power in the Workplace*, Basingstoke: Macmillan.

Briskin, L. and McDermott, P. (eds) (1993) *Women Challenging Unions*, Toronto: University of Toronto Press.

Calveley, M. and Healy, G. (2000) 'The Politics of Workplace Relations: Collectivism in "Failing School"'. Paper presented at the The Association of Industrial Relations Academics of Australia and New Zealand (AIRAANZ) 14th Annual Conference, Newcastle, New South Wales, Australia.

Cockburn, C. (1991) *In the Way of Women*, Basingstoke: Macmillan.

Colgan, R. and Ledwith, S. (1996) 'Sisters organising: Women and their trade unions', in Colgan, F. and Ledwith, S. (eds) *Women in Organisations – Challenging Gender and Politics* Basingstoke: Macmillan.

Colling, T. and Dickens, L. (1989) *Equality Bargaining – Why Not?* Equal Opportunities Research Series, London: HMSO.

Crompton, R. (ed.) (1999) *Restructuring Gender Relations and Employment – Decline of the Male Breadwinner*, Oxford: Oxford University Press.

Cully, M., Woodland, S., O'Reilly, A. and Dix, G. (1999) *Britain at Work*, London: Routledge.

Cunnison, S. and Stageman, J. (1995) *Feminising the Unions*, Aldershot: Avebury.

De Lyon, H. and Migniulo, F.W. (1989) *Women Teachers*, Milton Keynes: Open University Press.

Deery, S. and Walsh, J. (1999) 'The decline of collectivism? A comparative study of white collar employees in Britain and Australia, *British Journal of Industrial Relations* 37(2): 245–70.

Dickens, L. (2000) 'Collective Bargaining and Gender Equality: The Need for Trade Union Action and Its Likelihood'. Paper presented at the The Association of Industrial Relations Academics of Australia and New Zealand (AIRAANZ), 14th Annual Conference, Newcastle, NSW, Australia.

EOR (1998) 'Women in the labour market', *Equal Opportunities Review* 79 (May/June): 30–1.

Etzioni, A. (ed.) (1969) *The Semi-professions and their Organisations*, New York: The Free Press.

Ferner, A. and Hyman, R. (eds) (1998) *Changing Industrial Relations in Europe*, Oxford: Blackwell.

Freidson, E. (1994) *Professionalism Reborn – Theory, Prophecy and Policy*, Cambridge: Polity Press.

Guest, D. and Dewe, P. (1988) 'Why do workers belong to trade unions? A social psychological study in the UK Electronics Industry', *British Journal of Industrial Relations* 26(2): 178–94.

Hartley, J.F. (1992) 'Joining a trade union', in Hartley, J.F. and Stephenson, G.M. (eds) *Employment Relations – The Psychology of Influence and Control at Work*, Oxford: Blackwell.

Healy, G. (1997) 'Gender and unionisation of professional women workers', in Fitzpatrick, B. (ed.) *Bargaining in Diversity: Colour Gender and Ethnicity*, Dublin: Oak Tree Press, pp. 123–44.

—— (1999a) 'Structuring commitments in interrupted careers: The case of teachers', *Gender Work and Organisation* 6(4): 185–281.

—— (1999b) 'The trade union role in career development – a membership perspective', *Industrial Relations Journal* 30(3): 212–28.

Healy, G. and Kirton, G. (2000) 'Gender, power and trade union government in the UK', *British Journal of Industrial Relations* 38(3): 343–60.

Healy, G and Kraithman, D. (1996) 'Different careers – equal professionals: Women in teaching', in Ledwith, S and Colgan, F. (eds) *Women in Organisations*, Basingstoke: Macmillan.

Heery, E. and Kelly, J. (1998) 'Do female trade union representatives make a difference?: Women full-time officials and trade union work', *Work Employment and Society* 2(4): 487–505.

Ironside, M. and Seifert, R. (1995) *Industrial Relations in Schools*, London: Routledge.

Johnson, T. (1972) *Professions and Power*, London: Macmillan.

Kelly, J. (1998) *Rethinking Industrial Relations: Mobilization, Collectivism and Long Waves*, London: Routledge.

Kerr, A. (1992) 'Why public sector workers join unions: An attitude survey of workers in the Health Service and local government', *Employee Relations* 14(2): 39–45.

Kirton, G. (1999) 'Sustaining and developing women's trade union activism: A gendered project', *Gender, Work and Organization* 6(4): 213–23.

Kirton, G. and Healy, G. (1999) 'Transforming union women: The role of women trade union officials in union renewal', *Industrial Relations Journal* 30(2): 31–45.

Klandermans, B. (1986) 'Psychology and trade union participation: Joining acting, quitting', *Journal of Occupational Psychology* 59: 189–204.

Klandermans, G. (1992) 'Trade union participation', in Hartley, J. and Stephenson, G. (eds) *Employment Relations*, London: Blackwell.

Labour Research (2000) 'Women everywhere but at the top', *Labour Research* (March): 17–19.

Lawn, M. (ed.) (1985) *The Politics of Teacher Unionism – International Perspectives*, Beckenham: Croom Helm.

Lawrence, E. (1994) *Gender and Trade Unions*, London: Taylor and Francis.

Ledwith, S., Colgan, F., Joyce, P. and Hayes, M. (1990) 'The making of trade union leaders', *Industrial Relations Journal* 21(2): 112–25.

Macdonald, K. (1995) *The Sociology of the Professions*, London: Sage Publications.

MSF (1998) *Guild News – Newsletter of the Guild of Healthcare Pharmacists*, no. 36, April.

NUT (2001) *Gender and Education: NUT Policy Statement*, London: NUT.

NUT/EOC (1980) *Promotion and the Woman Teacher*, Manchester: NUT/EOC.

Rees, T. (1992) *Women and the Labour Market*, London: Routledge.

Seifert, R. (1984) 'Some aspects of factional opposition: rank and file and the National Union of Teachers 1967–1982, *British Journal of Industrial Relations*, 22(3): 372–90.

SERTUC (2000) *New Moves Towards Equality – New Challenges*, Southern and Eastern Region TUC.

Simpson, R.L. and Simpson, I.H. (1969) 'Women and bureaucracy in the semi-professions', in Etzioni, A. (ed.) *The Semi-Professions and their Organizations*, New York: Free Press.

Sinclair, D. (1995) 'The importance of sex for the propensity to unionise', *British Journal of Industrial Relations* 33(2): 173–90.

—— (1996) 'The importance of gender for participation in and attitudes to trade unionism', *Industrial Relations Journal* 33(2 September): 239–52.

The Teacher (2000) 'Whatever happened to equal opportunities?', *National Union of Teachers*, March: 12.

Thompson, D. (1927) *Professional Solidarity Among the Teachers of England*, New York: Columbia University Press.

Waddington, J. and Whitston, C. (1994) 'Why do managerial and professional, and technical staff join unions? – Some evidence on individualisation and trade union activity'. Paper presented at the IREC Conference Trade Unions: Designers or Dedicated Followers of Fashion?, Brussels.

—— (1997) 'Why do people join trade unions in a period of membership decline?', *British Journal of Industrial Relations* 35(4): 515–46.

Walby, S. (1997) *Gender Transformations*, London: Routledge.

Watson, D. (1988) *Managers of Discontent*, London: Routledge.

Webb, B. (1915) Special Supplement on English Teachers and their Professional Organisation, *The New Statesman*.

Witz, A. (1992) *Professions and Patriarchy*, London: Routledge.

10 Women in the labour movement

Perceptions of gender democracy in South African trade unions[1]

Malehoko Tshoaedi

Introduction

Thousands of women joined the unions during the 1970s and early 1980s in the struggle against apartheid and exploitation in the workplace. However, while the struggle produced immense results for the political rights of workers, gender issues are far from being successfully addressed. Women's presence in the unions is not reflected in their levels of union participation or in union leadership structures, nor are their interests reflected through collective bargaining in their terms and conditions at work.

Women's rights to equality in all sectors of society, social, political and economically have been enshrined in the constitution. New legislation to address gender and racial imbalances in the labour market and the broader society has been introduced. However, 'the struggle is not yet over since in practice, the situation for women has not changed despite changes in the law' (Madlala, Member of Parliament in 1994, quoted in Meer 1999: 142).

This chapter examines the situation of women in South African trade unions in the first five years after the new constitution was introduced. Comparisons are made with the high level of women's union seniority and activism under the apartheid regime, and explanations sought for the disappointing outcomes, so far, of gender in the newly free trade unions of the new South Africa.

The chapter will commence by looking at the South African context, where democratic elections have led to the introduction of progressive legislation to address gender and racial imbalances in the workplace and the labour market. In spite of the legislation, women continue to be disadvantaged in terms of occupational mobility and accessing the labour market. The same experiences can also be observed with the labour movement generally in South Africa. The Congress of South African Trade Unions (COSATU) has, since inception, adopted the principle of equality and non-racialism. While race has not been a central issue within its affiliate unions, debates on gender equality have haunted the organisation since the early 1980s. The chapter will conclude with a focus on the strategies employed by women unionists to change the status quo of women in unions and the response of COSATU and its affiliates to these challenges.

Methodology

COSATU is acclaimed for its role in the fight against discrimination in society and the workplace as it spearheaded the struggle against apartheid. The influential role that COSATU and its affiliates have played in advancing workers' rights and those of women in the workplace makes it important to examine the forms of inequalities that have developed within these organisations.

This chapter is based on a research report that was conducted amongst the affiliates of the COSATU in August 1998 in the Gauteng region. The aim of the study was to develop an understanding of gender inequality in trade union employment.[2] The unions where interviews were held included Paper, Printing, Wood and Allied Workers Union (PPWAWU); Chemical Workers Industrial Union (CWIU); National Union of Metal Workers of South Africa (NUMSA); South African Municipal Workers Union (SAMWU); South African Commercial, Catering and Allied Workers Union (SACCAWU); National Union of Mineworkers (NUM); Construction and Allied Workers Union (CAWU); South African Railways and Habour Workers Union (SARHWU) and COSATU as a federation.[3]

Interviews with thirty-three women from different unions and varying occupations were conducted. Six of the women interviewed had been in the trade unions since the early 1970s, and five of them had left the unions for other avenues. Among this six, four had held positions of general secretary in their unions (although three of them ended up becoming administrators in the late 1980s), whilst the other two had served as education officer and media and information officer respectively. In addition, six senior male officials were included in the study (Table 10.1).

South African context

It was a joyous celebration for the majority of South Africans when the African National Congress (ANC) won the first democratic government elections in 1994. Since the ANC has been one of those liberation organisations that has always maintained the principle of equity and non-discrimination, the same was expected

Table 10.1 Union officials included in the South African study

Position	Number interviewed	Sex
Administrator	16	Woman
Gender coordinator	4	Woman
Education officer	3	Women (2) and man (1)
Organiser	5	Woman
Publications officer	1	Woman
President	1	Man
General secretary	4	Man
Former unionist	5	Woman

Note
To update information on some sections, additional telephonic interviews were conducted (on 10 April 2001) with two full-time officials from COSATU and SATAWU.

from its government. The victory of the ANC brought hope to those who have had their human rights violated and been denied equal access to the labour market and the economy.

After two years in government, the ANC passed the South African Constitution, which comprised a Bill of Rights. The Bill of Rights guarantees all groups in society rights to be treated equally. According to section 9.2 of the constitution, equality is defined to include 'the full and equal enjoyment of all rights and freedoms such as political rights, social and economic rights'. The new constitution guarantees protection and outlaws unfair discrimination by the state or individuals on 13 grounds, including race, gender, sex and marital status. Also included after considerable lobbying and pressure, were lesbians and gay rights (Jara *et al.* 1999).

The South African Constitution makes provision for the establishment of a Human Rights Commission that will see that an environment free of human rights abuses is created. The responsibilities of the commission are, among others, to promote respect and a culture for human rights as well as to promote the protection, development and attainment of human rights. In addition, the ANC brought forward other pieces of legislation designed to protect and enhance workers' rights and develop a climate of equality. A new Labour Relations Act (LRA) was enacted in 1995, a Basic Conditions of Employment Act (BCEA) and an Employment Equity Act (EEA) were enacted in 1998.

Within the government's programme of transformation, gender has also been central. Although race and class were the dominant issues in the struggle, the oppression of women, particularly black women, in society, the workplace and the political sphere has always been a concern in the struggle for liberation. During the negotiation process in the early 1990s women's groups and activists called for the introduction of mechanisms to ensure the promotion and protection of gender equality (Meer 1999). Gender was seen as an integral part of the political and social transformation process.

The Commission for Gender Equality, which was established through section 187 of the constitution in 1996, is an institution that is aimed at ensuring the realisation of gender equality in society. According to the Constitution, the objective of the CGE is to:

> Promote gender inequality and to advise and make recommendations to Parliament or any other legislature with regard to any laws or proposed legislation which affects gender equality and the status of women.

The commission monitors and evaluates the policies and practices of government, the private sector and other organisations to ensure that they promote and protect gender equality. In a nutshell, the Commission acts as a watchdog against any practices that may be deemed discriminatory against women.

The introduction of such progressive legislation in South Africa is significant in the sense that it guarantees all groups in society, blacks, women, lesbians and gay men, disabled workers and those with HIV/AIDS a right to be full participants in the social, economic and political spheres. This is extremely significant as it comes after a long period of struggle to end apartheid and positions South Africa to move forward as a democratic state based on equality, dignity and respect for human rights for all.

Although South Africa has some of the most progressive equality legislation in the world, implementation is still a challenge. In order to promote constitutional rights, minority groups in society and women in particular, need to have access to the labour markets. Without access to jobs, social and economic resources, it will be difficult to assert these rights.

Labour markets in South Africa

Colonialism and apartheid have produced a racially segmented labour market (Standing 1996). This has resulted in skewed income and occupational distribution favouring whites (Torres 2000: 391). Gender discrimination is another aspect of the South African labour market. Over the years white men have been given preference in terms of job opportunities and occupational mobility. However, white women were in a better position to their counterparts. Black women, on the other hand, were discriminated against on the basis of their race and gender. Being from the privileged racial group, white women have had access to educational and economic resources. Many are skilled and occupy skilled positions with higher salaries than black women (or even black men).[4]

It has been six years since the new democratic government was elected into power. As we have seen, labour relations and equality policies have been implemented to redress the inequalities of the past. However, unequal distribution of resources is still a defining feature of the South African labour market as large numbers of blacks and women still have limited access to economic resources and employment. As Table 10.2 illustrates, compared to other racial groups, Africans and Coloureds form the majority of the unemployed.

Women form a large proportion of the unemployed. Table 10.2 shows the differences amongst women in accessing the labour markets. High proportions of African women remain outside the labour market, while only a few white women remain unemployed.

Table 10.2 Economically active population (EAP) by race and sex (percentage), 1999

	Africans	*Coloureds*	*Indians*	*Whites*	*All population groups*
Unemployed					
Women	51.9	28.4	23.8	7.3	43.2
Men	36.7	19.3	17.8	6.3	30.0
Total	44.0	23.6	20.2	6.8	36.2
Employed					
Women	48.1	71.6	76.2	92.7	56.8
Men	63.3	80.7	82.1	93.6	70.0
Total	56.0	76.4	80.0	93.2	63.8

Source: October Household Survey, 1999, Pretoria: Government Printer.

As indicated above, occupational segmentation is one of the commonest characteristics of the South African labour market. Because of lack of educational opportunities, most women (mainly black) occupy the unskilled and low paying jobs in the market. Statistics show that 49 per cent of public servants are women, but they are less represented in management and senior management levels of the public sector (Budlender 1996). Similar findings have been made in the private sector, where it is shown that most of the women occupy unskilled, clerical, semi-professional or technical occupations. Table 10.3 illustrates employment by occupation and sex, and shows that the representation of women in the occupational groups is largely distributed in junior and unskilled jobs. There is also a high representation of women in clerical and domestic occupations. Research conducted by Tothill (1998) shows that women professionals in South African universities occupy low positions. Women constitute only 9 per cent of full professorship positions, while 50 per cent of lectureship positions and 48 per cent of junior lecturers are women.

Table 10.3 Employment by occupation and sex, South Africa, 1999

Category	Male Number employed	Proportion of total (%)	Female Number employed	Proportion of total (%)	Total
Legislators, senior officials and managers	511,000	75	171,000	25	684,000
Professionals	300,000	54	253,000	46	554,000
Technicians and associate professionals	488,000	47	553,000	53	1,042,000
Clerks	371,000	35	699,000	65	1,071,000
Service workers, shop and market sales workers	684,000	56	541,000	44	1,225,000
Skilled agricultural and fishery workers	349,000	74	120,000	26	469,000
Craft and related trades workers	1,153,000	85	202,000	15	1,355,000
Plant and machine operators and assemblers	933,000	85	158,000	15	1,092,000
Elementary occupations	1,066,000	56	835,000	44	1,901,000
Domestic workers	36,000	4.5	763,000	96	799,000
Occupation not adequately defined	96,000	69	43,000	31	138,000
Occupation unspecified	22,000	57.8	16,000	42	39,000
Total	6,009,000	57	4,353,000	42	10,369,000

Source: October Household Survey, 1999.
Note
There is some rounding of figures.

Inequalities in the labour market can also be observed in wages or salaries between women and men. For every male earning less than R60,000 a year, there are eight women. The census findings indicate that educational levels between women and men do not account for differences in earnings. Amongst university graduates, 71 per cent of male employees were earning R4,000 or more a month, in contrast to less than 47 per cent of women employees with the same level of education (Budlender 1996). Wage discrimination is across all levels. According to the study conducted amongst workers in elementary positions in the textile sector, women earn R50 less per week than their male counterparts (Jarvis 1997).

Industrial relations and legislation in South Africa

During the apartheid period, labour relations in South Africa were characterised by conflict and adversarialism. The Labour Relations Act (LRA) that came into effect in 1996 is aimed at making the shift from adversarial relations to cooperation between employers and trade unions. The Act is a result of negotiations between employers, trade unions and government. The LRA provides the legal framework for industrial relations in the workplace (Torres 2000; Baskin and Satgar 1996). The principal features of the Act comprise the following:

- It offers workers the *right to belong to a trade union* and to *organise*.
- The Act gives *organisational rights* to a representative registered trade union.
- The Act also institutionalises *collective bargaining* through the collective bargaining council system.
- The Act also tries to strike a balance by offering workers the *right to strike* and employers the *right to lockout*. Unlike the previous LRA, the new Act gives a definition of a legal strike. Procedures for a strike have been simplified. The Act protects workers from dismissal or victimisation by the employer in legal strikes.
- To bring workers and management to the same table, the Act has established the formation of a National Economic Development and Labour Chamber (NEDLAC), which is a *tripartite institution* involving government, employers and trade unions. The function of this institution is to negotiate and reach agreements on policy issues concerning economic and labour matters.
- The Commission for Conciliation, Mediation and Arbitration (CCMA) is the primary conflict-resolution mechanism introduced by the new LRA.

The emphasis in the 1996 LRA is indeed cooperation and consultation between workers and employers in the workplace. The new democratic dispensation has created opportunities for the labour movement to be involved at a broader level, influencing the transformation process in South Africa. Baskin and Satgar perceive the LRA as an attempt to 'reform' and 'modernise' industrial relations:

This modernisation agenda is co-determinist in vision and tripartite in structure, and regards unions as an integral part of economic decision-making.

This recognition of the role of labour is a major step forward for the unions and the working class.

(Baskin and Satgar 1996: 104)

Other legislation that has been introduced includes the BCEA, which accords workers the right to work in a 'humane' and safe working environment with maternity leave, annual and sick leave, minimum wages and aims to eliminate child labour. The EEA has been introduced to promote equity and non-discrimination in the workplace. The EEA outlaws discrimination in the workplace on 17 grounds including race, gender, sex, sexual orientation, marital status and HIV/AIDS status (Jara *et al.* 1999). The Act aims to correct the demographic imbalance in the nation's workforce by compelling employers to remove barriers to advancement of Africans, Coloureds, Indians, women and the disabled, and actively advance them in all categories of employment by affirmative action (Grogan 1999: 207). Both the BCEA and the EEA include a clause acknowledging the 'life partner' of any employee for the purposes of family responsibility, so recognising all types of families inside and outside traditional marriage including same-sex couples (Jara *et al.* 1999).

Trade unions in South Africa

For a long time, race has been a dividing factor in South African industrial relations (Buhlungu 2000). The industrial relations in the country were classified as dual, where one group of workers was legally recognised and protected in the workplace, while the other group was not. Until the 1970s, only white workers had rights to organise and form trade unions while their black counterparts did not.

The early 1970s thus signify the emergence of a strong black trade union movement. Due to increasing pressure in the early 1970s, the government realised the need to incorporate black workers into the legal system. This came after 1973 when workers in Durban engaged in a series of strikes over wages. After its investigation of the strikes the Wiehahn Commission, appointed by government, recommended the recognition of black trade unions. This was based on the fact that if black workers continued to be outside the industrial relations system, the government would have no control over their activities. To have control over and be able to monitor the activities and organisations of black workers, the government gave recognition to black trade unions, thus extending organising rights to this group of workers (Baskin 1991). Currently, there are three major federations in South Africa. These include COSATU, the Federation of Unions of South Africa (FEDUSA) and the National Council of Trade Unions (NACTU).

COSATU was formed in 1985, largely composed of those unions established in the early 1970s. The formation of COSATU brought together 33 unions that were organised under the Federation of South African Trade Unions (FOSATU), representing a total of 462,359 paid-up members (Buhlungu 2000). There are three main principles that may be attributed to COSATU's ability to strengthen itself on the shop floor. These principles are non-racism, one union one industry, and a strong emphasis on worker control (Baskin 1991).

COSATU unions started off as blue-collar, black workers' union, but the characteristics of its membership have changed over the years. As COSATU unions expanded, increasing their power and influence in the workplace, their membership categories also expanded. More skilled and professional workers were recruited into the unions. Unions such as SARHWU, NUMSA, NUM and CWIU[5] recruited skilled workers with educational qualifications. New unions, which recruited professional workers (South African Democratic Teachers' Union (SADTU), National, Education, Health and Allied Workers Union (NEHAWU), emerged in the late 1980s. With the democratic changes in government, the racial composition of COSATU membership has also changed as white workers are joining unions. Unions that have largely represented white skilled workers (such as SASBO, The Financial Union) have also joined COSATU, increasing the diversity amongst its membership.

COSATU membership is estimated at 1.75 million in 17 affiliates. In the period between 1985 and 1993, COSATU and its unions experienced a sharp growth in membership levels. An earlier study by Macun and Frost (1994) shows membership growth in COSATU unions between 1985 and 1991 to have increased from 462,359 to 1,258 853. A survey by Filita (1997) indicates that between 1991 and 1996, COSATU membership grew by an additional 680,000 members, representing an increase of more than 50 per cent over the five years. Naidoo's research (1999) shows that COSATU membership has grown from 1.3 million in 1994 to over 1.7 million, this represents an increase of 30 per cent since 1994 and 330 per cent since it was launched in 1985 with 400,000 workers.

Naidoo, however, cautions that since 1996 membership growth has slowed, as a consequence of massive retrenchment and job losses in industries. Public service unions are COSATU's fastest growing unions whereas there has been a downward slide in the mining and manufacturing unions. The rapid growth of the public service unions has counterbalanced the decline of some of the other unions so allowing this sectoral shift to occur without undermining COSATU's growth pattern (Naidoo 1999). COSATU's membership size, campaigns and activities, the public profile of its leadership and the influence it has in relation to employers and the state makes it more visible than its counter federations (Buhlungu 2000: 10). COSATU and its affiliates are perceived as more central on labour issues as well as economic and political issues in the country. This has resulted in poor focus on the two other federations. As a result, there is limited information available on the activities of NACTU and FEDUSA. Not much has been documented on gender representation or gender relations within these two federations.

The Federation of South African Labour (FEDSAL) was formed in 1992, and later renamed FEDUSA in 1997. Most of the unions affiliated to this federation are the old white craft unions. Although there has been a drive by the federation to change its image and recruit more black and blue-collar workers, the membership still remains largely white skilled workers (Buhlungu 2000; Torres 2000). The paid-up membership currently stands at about 515,000 workers organised in 27 affiliates (Torres 2000).

NACTU is also a product of those unions that emerged during the strikes in the 1970s. It was formed in 1986 with a total paid-up membership of 200,000 and in

1998 it had 450,000 paid-up members (Buhlungu 2000). Like COSATU, it had a predominantly black, blue-collar membership. The point of difference however is the strong influence of the black consciousness movement. NACTU has always emphasised black leadership and rejected the involvement of white intellectuals in the black labour movement (Torres 2000).

Since 1992, organised labour has been in a much more stable period and after a long history of oppression and struggle South Africa has a growing and vibrant union movement. The ILO estimate for 1995 showed South Africa had a union density of 41 per cent which puts it amongst the most unionised countries in the world. Naidoo's (1999) estimate for 1998 puts South Africa's union density as high as 50 per cent. These strong unions are well positioned to have a powerful bargaining role and play an important part as change agents in a rapidly changing society like South Africa.

Gender, diversity and union membership in South Africa

Recent analysis of South Africa's 1995 October Household Survey by the National Labour and Economic Development Institute (NALEDI) provides a profile of union membership in South Africa (Naidoo 1999). The analysis shows that men make up 71 per cent of union members and women 29 per cent. According to Naidoo (1999), this was primarily because men held most of the formal sector jobs whereas women were in most of the un-unionised, informal sector jobs. Where the results were examined for men and women in the formal sector, 32 per cent of women were union members compared to 37 per cent of men. This led the researchers to conclude that 'the chances of a woman joining a trade union are much the same as a man' (Naidoo 1999).

Table 10.4 shows the breakdown of union membership by race. African workers made up 70 per cent of all union members, white workers were second with 16 per cent of union membership. However, when the data were examined according to the size of the different population groups, the researchers concluded that African workers were more likely to join unions with 40 per cent of all African workers in unions whereas whites were least likely to join.

The NALEDI research also concluded that unions were not attracting young workers, which was a particular problem in South Africa that has a relatively young population. It drew a profile of workers inside and outside South African trade unions. This is summarised in Table 10.5.

Table 10.4 Trade union membership and race, 1999 (%)

	African	*Indian*	*Coloured*	*White*
Share of union membership	70	3	11	16
Proportion of racial category in unions	40	33	31	25

Source: Naidoo (1999) *Unions in Transition*, NALEDI.

Table 10.5 Characteristics of unionised and non-unionised workers, 1999

Common characteristics of unionised workers	Common characteristics of workers who are not unionised
• 37% of male workers are in unions • 40% of African workers are in unions • 39% of workers aged between 35 and 44 years are in unions • 48% of plant and machine operators are in unions • Mining, manufacturing and the public sectors have the highest proportion of workers in unions.	• 68% of women workers not in unions • 75% of white workers are not in unions • 78% of workers aged between 15 and 24 are not in unions • Over 65% of service workers, clerks and professionals are not in unions and 73% of lower grade workers are un-unionised. • The service, agriculture and construction sectors have the lowest union densities.

Source: Naidoo (1999) *Unions in Transition*, NALEDI.

Trade union strategies for membership growth in South Africa are focusing on recruiting and organising women, young workers, casual workers, workers in small employers and targeting specific non-unionised jobs, sectors and provinces within South Africa (Naidoo 1999). However, one of the problems currently facing unions in recruiting and organising women is the under-representation of women in leadership positions in South African unions. This raises some key questions for South African unions given the early role played by women in their formation.

Although COSATU and its affiliates have been up-front about their position on women and gender inequality within their organisations, the same has not been observed on the issue of lesbian and gay equality. Although the constitution and principles of COSATU are based on non-discrimination and equality of all members, including lesbians and gay men, it has not adopted a formal position on lesbians and gay men within the unions. According to one informant from the COSATU, 'The organisation has been silent on the issue, we do not have a well thought out resolution on gays and lesbians' (Interview, 09/04/2001). However, the official noted that the organisation is aware that it needs to focus on the issues of the lesbian and gay membership within COSATU and its affiliates. Although there have been significant legal and constitutional changes in relation to lesbians and gay men, many South African individuals, organisations and institutions including trade unions have been slow to alter their practices towards sexual minorities (Jara *et al.* 1999: 191).

South Africa is a democratic country with one of the most progressive constitutions when it comes to guaranteeing the rights of individuals. It is a multi-cultural society, with people from different backgrounds, and trade unions need to show themselves willing to respond to the opportunities and challenges the New South Africa presents. We now turn to a consideration of the progress being made to recruit and encourage the representation of women in South African unions.

Role of women in the formation of unions

When trade unions for black workers emerged in the early 1970s, their main concern was to build strong worker organisations to challenge inequalities in the workplace. The structural position that both sexes occupied in the workplace and in society, being black and oppressed by white management and the state, influenced the development of a common identity, resulting in intense solidarity between women and men.

Unlike women in most developed countries who joined unions after their formation, South African women became involved at the initial stages of trade union formation in the 1970s. Emma Mashinini, founder of SACCAWU, Maggie Magubane, founder of the Sweet Food and Allied Workers Union (FAWU), and Lydia Kompe, national organiser of Metal and Allied Workers Union (MAWU, now known as NUMSA), and many other women played significant roles in the formation of trade unions in South Africa. It is their meaningful activism in trade unions that promoted the participation of other women in trade union activities.

Whereas the participation of women in trade unions was opposed by men in most of the developed countries (Beale 1982), men in the South African context accepted the involvement of women in these organisations. As unions were small organisations in their early formation years, everyone had a meaningful contribution to make in advancing the struggle of the workers. During this period, the priority of the unions was on building powerful organisations to challenge discriminatory practices in the workplace.

It is in such an environment where occupational positions were not linked to power or any influence in the organisation, that women occupied positions such as general secretary and president. Thembi Nabe, who has been in the unions since the early 1970s, related her experience as follows:

> I was a shop steward in the company that I was working at, within a month I was elected into the branch executive committee. In that committee I was elected to sit in the central committee. Within that period I was elected as vice president of the union (MAAWU). After being in the committees for some time, in 1982 I became an organiser in the union.
>
> (NUMSA administrator, August 1998)

Both black and white women played a role in the struggle for trade union formation. However, their involvement in trade union activities has always been at different levels. Race still plays a role in the segmentation of women within the unions. As a group that was privileged, white women had access to educational resources that allowed them to acquire skills that black women lacked. For most white women who were in the unions, participation in the unions has largely been at an occupational level. Unlike their black counterparts, they have always been regarded as knowledgeable and treated with more respect in the unions.

The legalisation on trade unions and the subsequent growth of these organisations raised new challenges for women. The legalisation changed the scope within which these organisations operated. Unlike in the early 1970s where the struggle was on gaining recognition, unions had the opportunity to enter into collective bargaining with employers, negotiating with management on various issues concerning workers. The increasing power and influence of unions in the workplace and society led to the redefinition of union officials' roles premised on societal gender role expectations.

As the scope and activities of trade unions went beyond the factory floor to include broader political and societal issues, a gendered division of labour occurred with a separation between the domestic and the public sphere emerged. Office based work like administration became routinised and was assigned to women, while positions like organising and general secretary, which involve interacting more with the public occupied the public sphere, and men were given these positions. According to Bonner, the growth of unions went along with the development of a 'traditional occupational structure, with men in organising positions and women in administration'.

According to Grice, who had been one of the women unionists in the early 1970s, in the early days of trade union organising, a general secretary position was still considered as administrative; it did not have political status and power as it came to have in the late 1980s. She further argued that:

> With the transition, it moved from women as general secretaries to men as general secretaries because their role had changed. They were now involved in politics, negotiations with government and all those sorts of things. When it became an important position, suddenly women started moving out.

The changing roles of unions and the redefinition of union positions led to many women being pushed to the margin. Women like Maggie Magubane (FAWU), Thembi Nabe (MAWU) and Refiloe Ndzuta (PPWAWU), who were general secretaries during the first phase of trade union development, were removed from these position to more administrative posts (Tshoaedi 1999). According to Nabe, 'it was felt that male comrades should occupy organising positions and women had to occupy administrative positions'.

Increasingly, women's contribution in the unions was being devalued as their work was being criticised by men officials. With increasing dominance of patri-archal attitudes, men challenged women's capabilities for being in leading positions of the unions. Maggie Magubane, who is one of the women who went through this experience, explained that 'they were always pushing you down so that you can become disillusioned and think of leaving your position'. Another woman who had a similar experience, Thembi Nabe, explained factors that pushed her off the general secretary's position as follows:

> You know how these people are, they will start criticising you, when you talk they will regard you as a woman. I realised that there was too much pressure and I decided to resign from that position. My colleagues had a problem with me being a general secretary.

Although there might be various factors that contributed to the relegation of women, results of this research indicate that women were 'pushed off'.

> We found that as unions got bigger, we were sidelined, the male leadership became very dominant, pushed you aside. As a result, unless you were prepared to fight and push, you became sidelined. I ended up adopting that attitude of ignoring the struggles that were going on and started focusing more on my work in the office. So you became increasingly sidelined as a woman as unions got bigger.
>
> (Bonner, former CWIU General Secretary, August, 1998)

As unions developed an exclusive male culture that kept women outside influential positions of the unions, a 'boys' club' also developed. It is in this club where men hold union caucuses in bars and make decisions in the absence of women. The role of women was slowly fading away as men had found ways of excluding them. To illustrate this point, Bonner argued that:

> You would go to a meeting, but really nothing would be decided in the meeting. Women ended up not wanting to go to those meeting anymore because everything was really decided by the 'big boys' caucuses. You wanted to raise your voice and you were not listened to. So I just kind of opted out. I did not want to carry on and I focused more on my work.

The decline of women in leadership has largely been associated with the strength and power that unions were gaining in the early 1980s. According to Forrest who was also a woman unionist during this period 'the fact that unions were gaining more power meant that it was no longer a place for women to be in, it was a place for men. Men are the leaders and power is associated with them'.

Participation and representation of women in unions

Leadership positions

Although the representation of women in leadership structures of unions began to decrease around the mid-1980s, their membership remained significant. In a 1992 survey, women's membership in COSATU unions was 36 per cent (Pityana and Orkin 1992). In spite of the fact that they had been pushed to the margins of the unions, denied leadership opportunities and participation on decision-making structures, women remained in the organisations and fought for their right to belong to these organisations.

Women's membership in COSATU in 1998 was estimated at 29 per cent, indicating a decline from 36 per cent in 1992 (Naidoo 1999). This may be explained in part by a decline in employment particularly in those sectors where women are dominant. This may have an effect on the unionisation rate of women. Nevertheless, there is still a significant number of women members in unions, particularly when women's membership in the unions is grouped into three categories. The first group is in unions where women make up more than 60 per cent of membership in the unions. The unions include SACCAWU, NEHAWU, South African Clothing and Textile Workers Union (SACTWU) and SADTU. The second group is those unions where women comprise more than 20 per cent of membership and these unions are SAMWU, The Finance Union (SASBO), TGWU, Police and Prisons Civil Rights Union (POPCRU), Communication Workers Union (CWU), and PPWAWU. And in the third group, women comprise a small (about 15 per cent) but significant component of union membership, and these unions are NUM, NUMSA, CAWU, CWIU and SARHWU.[6]

However, although women form a significant part of the unions, this is not reflected in leadership structures of the organisations. In all the leadership levels (this includes local, regional and national) there is no clear representation of women, even in those unions where women comprise more than 60 per cent of membership. Pityana and Orkin's 1992 survey indicates that only 14 per cent of shopstewards in COSATU affiliates are women. Shop floor leadership is often regarded as an entry point into union politics, it is regarded as 'the most important step in leadership development and an important recruiting ground for other leadership positions in the unions' (Orr 1999: 10).

Not having access to shop stewards positions disadvantages women in terms of accessing regional and national leadership. Because of their longer previous experience on the shopfloor as shop stewards, men seem to be elected more often for union positions. Gender stereotypes also play a major role in the election of leadership positions. Since leadership qualities are often associated with masculinity and strength, women are often regarded as weak candidates. Similar to men in the unions, women still have the stereotypical view of men as leaders, and therefore offer no support or show no confidence for women who stand for election in leadership positions. As a result, very few women have the courage to challenge male dominance and stand for elections, allowing only men to be elected.

The proportion of women who are in regional leadership is low. A survey by Naidoo (1999) shows that only 18 per cent of women in COSATU affiliates are Regional Office Bearers (ROBs). In spite of having representation at this level, women ROBs tend to occupy less influential positions such as treasurers. 'This means that women regional office bearers do not sit on national structures since it is Regional Secretary and Chairperson who automatically form part of the national structure' (Orr 1999: 4). Only 8 per cent of women are secretaries (these include branch, regional and national). At the national level, there is only 16 per cent of women who are National Executive Committee members and 10 per cent who are National Office Bearers.

Although Table 10.6 shows that in some unions there is a high percentage of women in the president and chairperson positions, this is not the actual fact as this category includes national and regional office bearers. It should also be noted that most of the women in the president and chairperson positions occupy vice and deputy positions. The table further shows that SASBO, which is a financial union sector largely dominated by women, has a high (71 per cent) representation of women at

Table 10.6 National and regional women's leadership in COSATU, 1999 (%)

Union	*NEC delegates*	*NOB*	*ROB*	*Secretary*	*President/Chair*	*Treasurer*
CAWU	8	0	13	0	0	43
CWIU	14	17	15	0	0	50
CWU	33	0	3	0	8	0
FAWU	11	0	24	0	40	0
NEHAWU	16	33	34	0	10	80
NUM	0	0	2.5	8	0	9
NUMSA	0	0	6	0	0	20
POPCRU	0	0	0	0	0	0
PPWAWU	13	0	13	0	0	43
SAPPAWU	17	17	28	0	50	57
SACCAWU	11	33	16	0	16	44
SACTWU	38	33	30	0	31	66
SADTU	3	0	7	0	5	20
SAMWU	4	17	14	0	24	10
SARHWU	33	0	12	20	0	22
SASBO	50	14	71	84	50	66
TGWU	22	0	22	20	22	11
Average	16	10	18	8	15	32

Source: Naidoo 1999.

regional level. However, this figure represents women in branch committees, which is not at the same level as ROB positions. Powerful and influential positions are still dominated by men.

Occupational positions

The occupational structure of trade unions does not present a different picture from the one observed above. About 41 per cent of women are employed in COSATU and its union affiliates as full-time union officials in different occupational positions (Buhlungu 1997). However, similar to the findings reported earlier on the public and the private sector, women in trade unions are found at the bottom of occupational positions. Table 10.7 gives the representation of women and men in the occupational structure of COSATU and its affiliates.

The picture that is reflected in Table 10.7 is not much different from the one observed in the South African labour market as a whole, where gender is one of the defining features for occupational segmentation. There is a traditional occupational structure in trade union employment, where women occupy the bottom positions with limited participation or influence on decision-making structures. For instance in the positions of organisers which are crucial for recruiting new membership and negotiating and putting forward the interests of the workers in the workplace, at all levels women are under-represented. This has major implications for the unions in terms of increasing women's membership, as well as recruiting women in the largely

Table 10.7 Occupational positions by gender, 1997

Current position	Sex Men	Women	Total	Women as percentage of total
Local administrator	2	32	34	94
Branch administrator	1	24	25	96
Regional administrator	3	48	51	94
H\O administrator	5	53	58	91
Local organiser	79	7	86	8
Branch organiser	33	8	41	20
Regional organiser	46	6	52	12
National organiser	24	3	27	11
Branch secretary	17	4	21	19
Regional secretary	23	1	24	4
General secretary	10	0	10	0
Research officer	6	3	9	33
Legal officer (regional)	14	3	17	18
Legal officer (national.)	2	3	5	60
Education officer (branch)	4	0	4	0
Education officer (regional)	12	0	12	0
Education officer (national)	11	3	14	21
Media officer	5	0	5	0
Other	43	40	83	48
Total	340	238	578	41

Source: Union officials survey (Buhlungu 1997).

un-unionised sectors. As shown earlier, women form the majority of the un-unionised and are most vulnerable to exploitation and abuse of their rights as workers.

Low education levels have been used to justify the invisibility of women in leading positions of the unions (Baskin 1991). However, results from the study conducted by Buhlungu (1997) show that women's educational levels in trade union employment are improving. In fact, his findings show that 15.9 per cent of women officials in COSATU unions have tertiary education, compared to 18.2 per cent for men. This contradicts the conclusion that women in unions have low educational levels, making it difficult for them to occupy key positions in the organisation.

Barriers to women's participation and representation in the unions

Although some notable achievements on tackling discrimination have been made, struggles to incorporate issues related to gender and sexuality within the unions have been fraught with difficulty. Results of this study indicate that domestic and childcare responsibilities affect women's chances of advancing within the unions. Full participation in trade union activities, combining domestic responsibilities with trade union work is a difficult task for many women.

Sometimes it may be that women have too many responsibilities. Working in a union and having domestic duties is too much for women. For instance if a woman is a general secretary of the union, it may be impossible for her to participate in union activities like her male counterparts because of family responsibilities.

(CAWU, Regional Administrator)

However, organisational factors also have an impact on women's occupational mobility. The findings suggest that the dominance of a male-dominated, heterosexual organisational culture, that often regards women as inferior and less capable, is used to block women from occupying senior leading positions in the unions. It would seem that despite the promise of the new constitution and labour relations and equality legislation the development of trade union policies on gender equality has been slow and haphazard (Jara *et al.* 1999).

Organisational culture in trade union employment

With the entrenchment of a male organisational culture in unions, a sexual division of labour is evident in the occupational structures. Men dominate decision-making structures and therefore the appointment of union officials is largely influenced by gender stereotypes dominant in society. Administrative positions are largely reserved for women unionists. Acknowledging the fact that women are often discriminated against during the recruitment process, PPWAWU male general secretary indicated that:

It is true to the extent that if the post for an organiser is advertised, as the union leadership we do not expect that a female can also apply. For instance if there is a position for a local organiser post and there is a woman who has applied for that post, normally it is true that people will look at the CV and then say, 'look it's a woman'. Already your judgement will be biased because you will think that because she is a woman she will not do the job well. This happens across trade unions. We always anticipate that if a post for local organiser comes, it is for men. So we are still trapped in that mentality, that certain jobs are suitable for particular sexes.

(PPWAWU general secretary, September 1998)

With men dominant in leadership positions, the selection process is mostly influenced by men's perceptions of 'good' candidates. The criteria that are mostly used in selecting candidates for union positions largely depend on men's cultural influences, which may sometimes be biased against women. According to SACCAWU's gender coordinator:[7]

The recruitment committee will look at you as a woman, who has family responsibilities, and therefore won't be able to perform. For example, if you are an organiser, the job requirements are that you must be flexible, must be able

to work after hours, able to travel around. Then obviously when women apply
for organising positions that is taken into consideration.

(SACCAWU gender coordinator, September 1998)

Cultural stereotypes seem to play a major role in creating barriers for women.
Women have internalised the gender stereotypes common in society. Similar to
women union members, full-time women officials have poor confidence amongst
women themselves, as they underestimate their capacities. Many do not have
confidence in applying for senior positions in the union. This is partly related to
not being taken seriously by the unions, with the result that women are often not
motivated to apply for other positions. One woman administrator interviewed in
this study was discouraged from applying for an organising position after male
officials told her that 'none of the workers would listen to her, most of the workers
are men. No men will listen to a woman'.

In some cases women fear rejection since only men are often called for the job
interviews. According to PPWAWU's gender coordinator, when applications from
aspiring organisers come, the first thing that is considered is the sex of the person.
'Immediately they see that it is a female, then they'll put it aside.'

For those women who have been successful in breaking through the glass ceiling,
the struggle still lies ahead of them. They have to continuously challenge the gender
stereotypes held by men about women's inferiority. Evidence shows that women
who are in senior positions, which are usually accorded respect, are often treated
as women, rather than unionists (Franzway 1997). Being in positions that are mostly
reserved for men and thus associated with masculinity, women are often not
regarded as real unionists. Men officials who have developed an exclusive closed
male culture that keeps women at the margins of the union often challenge their
presence in these positions. According to Patricial Appolis, who is a gender
coordinator at SACCAWU:

> When I go to these meetings that are dominated by men, sometimes I start
> doubting myself, wondering if the things I am saying make any sense, are they
> taking me seriously. Going to these meetings that are dominated by men is a
> struggle, one has to work very hard, you have to be assertive and aggressive.
>
> (SACCAWU gender coordinator, September 1998)

Women's attempts to break through into this closed male culture have been
observed in their participation in union structures that are dominantly male.
Women often find themselves having to prove that they are at the same level as the
'boys'. Referring to her experience in these structures, SACCAWU's gender
coordinator contended that:

> You feel that because you are in that position you have to perform like them,
> you have to be at the same level. But you have to assert yourself if you wanted
> to become one of the guys. If you are not able to assert yourself and show that
> you know the issues and so on, you are regarded as a bad official.
>
> (SACCAWU gender coordinator, September 1998)

Women who are in senior positions are often put under pressure to show their competency to the unions and to their male colleagues. Talking about her participation in union structures, Appolis further argued that it is the pressure that made her want 'to do my best. I need to prove myself and that meant working extra hard to prove that I am as good as they are'.

Discrimination against women in unions also occurs in very subtle and indirect ways. Women gave an example of exclusion from important activities by either not being notified, or being notified at the last minute. One woman pointed out: 'That is done to discredit you as an individual, people would look at you as disorganised and not capable of doing your job' (NUMSA administrator).

Another official pointed out that the reason for this behaviour was because men often feel threatened by women who are more informed of trade union issues. As a result they will always try to bring women down and undermine them by not giving them adequate information on trade union activities.

Strategies employed by women for challenging gender inqualities

The growth of trade unions and the broadening focus of political debates within South Africa opened space for other debates within the unions. The period of the 1980s is generally known as a period of organisational renewal throughout society, as community, students and women's organisations were established. It was during this period that the women's rights movement was gaining ground. This partly had to do with the influence of intellectual white women who had been following the feminists' debates since around the 1970s.

As unions began challenging racism and inequality at a societal level, gender inequality within the unions also became an issue for debate within the union movement. The growing dominance of 'male organisational culture' was developing in the unions, and being pushed to the margins of the organisations awakened women to the realisation of gender issues within the unions. Debates concerning issues of gender and equality within the trade unions emerged around this period.

By 1984 women unionists began pressurising their organisations to start taking women's issues in the unions and in the workplace seriously. They called for more attention to be given to women's issues; women's forums were established to push their unions towards improved harassment and violence policies, maternity leave provisions, occupational and pay equality and union representation (Baskin 1991). The retail sector union SACCAWU, which is mainly dominated by women, took the leading position in demanding that women's rights in the workplace be addressed. Other unions that followed suit include SACTWU and NUMSA (Baskin 1991).

Women won their first round of the struggle in 1985 when the COSATU congress committed itself to fight all forms of unequal and discriminatory treatment of women at work, in society and in the federation. Admitting that inequalities existed between women and men in the federation and in unions, the congress signalled its approval for the establishment of women's committees in affiliate unions.

The call in 1987 for the introduction of women's committees in COSATU unions was another initiative by women unionists in challenging male domination in unions as well as to ensure that women's interests in bargaining structures are taken seriously like other union issues. The argument by women was that 'women's issues are union issues'. However, even in COSATU, the more progressive federation, the development of policies and gender practices has been slow

According to Baskin (1991), men officials, who argued that women's committees were going to create divisions and separate power structures within the unions heavily opposed the establishment of such structures. Some men raised the fear that women and women's issues would be further marginalised. However, women emphasised that without these structures, women's issues were already marginalised to the extent that they were not even put on any union agenda (Shefer 1991). According to Baskin:

> Separate women's structures are seen as a place where union issues can be brought to women, and women's issues are brought to the union. They give women an opportunity to raise issues affecting them directly and ensure that these are attended to within the union's formal structures.
>
> (Baskin 1991: 381)

By calling for the introduction of women's committees, women made the first initiative to change the mindset of trade unions and those of men unionist concerning their perceptions of women in the organisation. Although it was a slow process implementing these structures, largely because of male resistance in the unions, women have used these committees to alert unions to the problems of women in society and in the workplace in general. COSATU first sponsored a women's conference in 1988.

As men have become exposed to the issues affecting women in their surroundings, the realisation that women's issues are union issues has increased. The debate about women's issues widened, and unions realised the importance of such issues being addressed by both women and men. There was a move from women's issues to gender issues that affected both sexes in the unions. For instance Shefer (1991) notes that unions used the concept of parental rights in the struggle for maternity and paternity benefits.

However, in 1991 at the COSATU General Congress, women had to fight to maintain the gender forums as women only spaces for encouraging and developing women. Jara *et al.* (1999) suggest that this struggle ended with the 'explicit provision that men could be part of these gatherings'. Debate over these forums continues and a 1995 report indicated that 'women were still taking responsibility for organising them but that men tended to dominate the discussions in these forums when they attended' (COSATU website 'No Women, No Cry, Zabalaza, quoted in Jara *et al.* 1999).

Women's committees are now referred to as gender committees to signal their inclusiveness. Full-time gender coordinators in some unions have been appointed to give more attention to gender education in unions. The appointment of gender coordinators in the union movement has been useful in broadening the scope of gender committees and issues to be addressed. Some of the issues that gender committees have pushed forward include the issue of sexual harassment in the unions and the federation, and as a result a code of conduct on sexual harassment was adopted in March 1995. A growing number of unions have negotiated collective agreements with good provisions for maternity leave, childcare facilities and allowances and have made commitments to fight for pay equity and tackle sex discrimination (Jara *et al.* 1999).

Events within the South African labour movement also point towards this shift from women's issues to gender issues. At the 6th national congress in 1997,[8] COSATU made the most progressive resolution, which looks at gender education as not only relevant for women unionist, but for men unionists as well. According to the congress, 'the barriers that exist between women and men workers need joint efforts to be broken down' (COSATU 1997). COSATU resolved to target groups of men to be trained on gender issues so as to assist in women's development and step up the education of both women and men on gender issues (COSATU 1997).

However, although gender committees have gained acceptance and recognition within the unions, there are still some challenges. Gender structures are not at the core of the work in the unions. As a result, gender coordinators are often administrators, who are often not given space to do gender work and generally do not have status and influence in unions (COSATU Political Education Booklet 2000). Very few unions have full-time gender coordinators.

COSATU has identified a key problem with the gender structures in its affiliates: unions have not developed adequate aims, objectives and roles of the gender structures (COSATU Political Education Booklet 2000). Failure to align the goals and objectives of the gender structures with those of the union is a large problem as unions fail to see the link between these structures and the unions in general. In most cases, gender structures fail to get the support required from the unions. This has been illustrated by inadequate budget allocations to these structures, as they are not regarded as important.

Over the years, resolutions that have been taken at COSATU's national congresses have been progressive in terms of addressing gender inequalities. In spite of COSATU's outspoken commitment to fighting gender inequality in unions and the federation, resolutions that have been taken thus far have not translated into visibility of women in unions and the federation. Although the resolutions have created space for women to become part of unions and to participate in these organisations, this is still at the lower margins, women remain under-represented in positions of power (Naidoo 1999).

Some unions have adopted the quota system to address the under-representation of women in their organisations (Table 10.8). The unions include National Education, Health and Allied Workers Union (NEHAWU) with a 50 per cent quota; the South African Transport and Allied Workers Union (SATAWU) with 20 per cent quota; the Chemical, Energy, Paper, Printing, Wood and Allied Workers Union (CEPPWAWU) 25 per cent quota; and SAMWU 30 per cent quota

Table 10. 8 Strategies to address under-representation
of women, 1999

Unions	Quota percentage
CCEPPWAWU	25
NEHAWU	50
SAMWU	30
SATAWU	20

(COSATU 2000). The percentage for the quota has largely been based on the union representation of each union.

It is however surprising that SACCAWU, which represents more than 60 per cent of women in the retail and service sector, and SACTWU, which has between 70 and 80 per cent women membership in the textile industries, are opposed to the quota system. In fact 60 per cent of SACWTU leadership is men. According to a senior male official of SACCAWU, implementation of the quota system in the trade unions would seem like saying that 'women are disabled, therefore 50 per cent should be women in terms of leadership, and run away from the actual democratic process of electing people chosen by the floor'.

Other unions that have not supported the call for quota system in the unions include SADTU, CAWU and NUM. Unlike CAWU and NUM, which are male dominated, SADTU has at least adopted measures aimed at improving women leadership within its organisation. For instance the union has portfolio positions on their national, provincial, regional and local executive structures, and it has also reserved seats for deputy secretaries at regional level for women. Both these measures are aimed at developing women leadership as well as creating space for women leaders within the organisation (Naidoo 1999). As part of its commitment to building women leadership, SADTU is one of the few unions that has collected statistical data on women representation within its organisation and is keeping track of progress being made.

The 1997 COSATU national congress rejected the proposal for a 50 per cent quota. The proposal for a quota system was another of the bold initiatives that women have made through gender committees. Delegates from opposing unions argued that women need to be groomed before their placement in senior positions and the criteria should be based on skills and capability. A senior male official from CAWU argued that 'we are not going to accept that we must put women in leadership positions for the sake of the quota, not being sure of their capability'.

According to Connie September, the former first vice-president of the federation, 'people have reacted strongly to the proposal for a 50 per cent quota system because it is targeted at the top levels of power in the unions' (cited in Orr *et al.* 1997: 13). The PPWAWU general secretary viewed the rejection of the quota system as based on fear of change. The quota system is a challenge to most men officials in the unions since it means restructuring the occupational structure of these organisations. He explained that:

This was one of the attempts aimed at advancing women in the unions and other people felt threatened by that, because it meant that unions had to undergo a restructuring process. For something like proportionality or a 50 per cent quota for women in the leadership, it meant that COSATU in that Congress was supposed to elect two women. That would have meant that all affiliates must follow suit, and ensure that women are represented. It has that potential of threatening people in their positions.

(PPWAWU general secretary, August 1998)

The quota system threatens established male dominance in the unions and it has been resisted. SARHWU gender coordinator argued that the rejection of the proposal for a quota system in the union movement 'is a way of preventing women from getting into top positions. Men are taken straight from the shopfloor and receive on-the-job training'. Other women unionists see the unions as having 'double standards against women' as there are men officials who are in leadership positions who still need to be groomed. According to Mandy Moussouris, education officer of CWIU:

As an educator that whole grooming rubbish has never existed in the unions before. We practise the policy of each one teaches one, we grow within the organisation. We learn by being involved in debates, being shopstewards and so on. That whole emphasis on education goes against all the principles of the organisation. When you see organisations turning against principles that built them just because people are women, it drives me round the bend.

The rejection of the quota system by the COSATU congress shows the contradiction between principles and practice in the unions. On the one hand, unions want implementation of such policies in workplaces for their members to address the inequalities produced by the systematic exclusion of black people from the economic structures by whites. On the other, they reject the implementation of such policies in their organisations to address inequalities that have been created by the systematic exclusion of women.

While many observers viewed the rejection of the quota system as a 'step back' for the trade union movement, the debate signified progress for COSATU leadership. Vavi, the then COSATU deputy general secretary, argues that for people who understood the patriarchal nature of society, the quota debate in the COSATU Congress was a step forward, rather than a setback. According to him:

It's a slow movement. In 1989 a woman general secretary from TGWU made a suggestion for a quota and she was not taken seriously, she was laughed at. In 1991 that same union made the same suggestion and it was not even discussed, it was a major joke. People used to laugh when you mentioned gender issues, and it becomes the liveliest thing, with everyone in the congress whistling. In 1997 we spent four hours debating a quota. The percentage of delegates supporting the quota system has been steadily increasing.

(Vavi, COSATU August 1998)

After the congress failed to reach an agreement on the quota system, it was resolved that affiliates should at least consider implementing measures to address women's representation within unions. Not much progress has been recorded since. The 2000 congress did not debate the quota system but proposed that affiliates set targets for increasing women's leadership based on women's employment in each sector.

Clearly, COSATU's resolutions reflect the organisation's commitment to addressing gender inequality. But then the question that one asks is, why is it taking so long to address gender imbalances when progressive resolutions are made at each congress? To answer this question, one has to ask by which officials and at what level these resolutions are supposed to be implemented. Obviously, men dominate the leadership structures, where implementation is supposed to take place. The decisions and actions belong to them. Although there has been some progress in women's struggles in the union movement, gaining access to leadership positions has been a 'highly contested process'.

Conclusion

South African women unionists have played a crucial role in the building of unions in the country. They have put in as much effort as their male counterparts in the struggle for trade union recognition and rights for black workers. Women form a major part of unions despite their under-representation in trade union structures. However, under-representation of women in senior positions of the unions is not only a problem about achieving representation, but also about equality. It is not a problem simply for women but for the whole union movement in South Africa. Men unionists need to realise that women are part of the unions and gender equality is a crucial aspect that needs to be taken seriously.

Not having women well represented in the leadership structures brings challenges for organising or recruiting women and representation of women's interests in the collective bargaining and policy making structures (Tshoaedi 1999). Representation of women's needs is especially important given the changes in the labour market where there is an increase in service sector employment dominated by women. Unions need women for their survival and it is important that they commit themselves to full representation of women's needs and interests. Unions have to look at strategies of achieving good representation of women in senior positions. The quota system is one such strategy that has been successfully employed in other organisations.

With the democratisation of the country and the granting of rights to all groups in society, equality in all sectors of society has become crucial. South African trade unions have played a crucial role in the drafting of equity legislation such as the Employment Equity Act. As trade unions are regarded as workers' representatives, there is a need for more women in leadership structures to fully represent the interests of all their constituencies. Unions need to recognise the diversity within their membership and create space for both women and men to develop and exercise their capabilities to benefit the unions and workers in general. This means that unions need to start looking at women not in terms of their female attributes, but their capabilities and the meaningful contribution they can bring to the organisations. Therefore, unions need to engage actively in removing the barriers that women experience in fully participating in trade unions and to promote strategies aimed at increasing women's leadership.

Notes

1 Thanks are due to several people who have supported me in writing this chapter. Sakhela Buhlungu, who has been my supervisor even after finishing my Masters' thesis, has always shown confidence in my writing skills. The Fafo office, Liv Torres and Line Eldring, who have not only given me space and time to write but have given invaluable comments. Sabata Nakanyane, always a comrade who volunteers to help, thanks. I would also like to thank Sue Ledwith and Fiona Colgan who have been of great help in the shaping and structuring of this chapter by raising important questions about the chapter; thank you for your patience.

2 However, the chapter looks at women in both elected and appointed positions in the unions.

3 Please note that CWIU and PPWAWU merged in February 1999 and are now called Chemical, Energy, Paper, Printing, Wood and Allied Workers' Union (CEPPWAWU). SARWHU and TGWU also merged in May 2000 to form the South African Transport and Allied Workers Union (SATAWU). The report has maintained the old names since the research was conducted before these changes.

4 In the South African context, African refers to a black person, Coloured refers to a person of mixed origin and Indian refers to a person of Asian origin. However, all three racial categories are also classified as black.

5 See below for full union names cited in the text.

6 Because of limited surveys on trade unions and poor record keeping by trade unions, there is lack of statistical analysis on gender or racial representation of each COSATU affiliate.

7 Since 1985, COSATU unions introduced gender structures to look at issues of gender equality in the unions. Gender coordinators (mainly women) are appointed to play a central role in the implementation and plan of action on gender equality within the unions.

8 COSATU national congress takes place every three years. This is a congress where the federation assesses its achievements, challenges and strategies to be adopted. Delegates from different affiliates attend, unions with the highest membership have the most delegates. The participation of women in these congresses has been questioned as very few women are delegated by their unions.

The main South African trade unions and institutions cited in the text

CAWU	Construction and Allied Workers Union
CCMA	Commission for Conciliation, Mediation and Arbitration
CEPPWAWU	Chemical, Energy, Paper, Printing, Wood and Allied Workers Union
CWIU	Chemical Workers Industrial Union
CWU	Communication Workers Union
NACTU	National Council of Trade Unions
NEDLAC	National Economic Development and Labour Council
NEHAWU	National Education, Health and Allied Workers Union

NUM   National Union of Mine Workers
NUMSA   National Union of Metal Workers of South Africa
POPCRU   Police and Prisons Civil Rights Union
PPWAWU   Paper, Printing, Wood and Allied Workers Union
SACCAWU   South African Catering, Commercial and Allied Workers Union
SADTU   South African Democratic Teachers' Union
SACTWU   South African Clothing and Textile Workers' Union
SAMWU   South African Municipal Workers Union
SARWHU   South African Railways and Harbour Workers Union
SASBO   The Finance Union
SATAWU   South African Transport and Allied Workers Union
TGWU   Transport and General Workers Union

References

Baskin, J. (1991) *Striking Back: A History of COSATU*, Johannesburg: Ravan.

Baskin, J. and Satgar, V. (1996) 'Assessing the new LRA: A framework for regulated fexibility', in Baskin, J. (ed.) *Against the Current. Labour and Economic Policy in South Africa*, Johannesburg: Ravan Press.

Beale, J. (1982) *Getting It Together: Women as Trade Unionists*, London: Pluto.

Budlender, I. (1996) *Women and Men in South Africa*, Pretoria: South Africa Statistics.

Buhlungu, S. (1997) Working for the Union: A profile of union officials in COSATU. Labour Studies Research Report 8, SWOP, University of the Witwatersrand, Johannesburg.

—— (1999) 'Generational transition in union employment: The organisational implications of staff turnover in COSATU unions', *Transformation* 38.

—— (2000) Labour's dilemmas under democracy and globalisation in South Africa. Unpublished paper.

Cockburn, C. (1991) *In The Way of Women: Men's Resistance to Sex Equality in Organizations*, London: Macmillan.

COSATU (1995) National Congress Resolutions.

COSATU (1995) 'No Woman, No Cry', Zabalaza: report on COSATU, Gender Winter School, 1995.

COSATU (1997) 'COSATU sets the pace for social transformation', *The Shopsteward* 6: 5.

COSATU (2000) Understanding gender. A struggle within the struggle. COSATU Political Education Booklet.

Franzway, S. (1997) 'Sexual politics in trade unions', in Pocock, B. (ed.) *Strife: Sex and Politics in Trade Unions*, Australia: Allen and Unwin.

Filita, T. (1997) 'COSATU marching forward', *South African Labour Bulletin*, 21, 1.

Grogan, J. (1999) *Workplace Law*, Kenwyn: Juta and Co Ltd.

Jara, M., Webster, N. and Hunt, G. (1999) 'At a turning point: organized labour, sexual diversity and the new South Africa', in Hunt, G. (ed.) *Labouring for Rights: Unions and Sexual Diversity across Nations*, Philadelphia: Temple University Press.

Jarvis, D. (1997) 'Textile, clothing and footwear workers poorly paid and on short-time', *Agenda* 35.

Macun, I. and Frost, A. (1994) 'Living like there's no tomorrow: Trade union growth in South Africa 1979–1991', *Social Dynamics* 20, 2.

Mills, J. (1988) 'Organization, gender and culture', *Organization Studies* 9, 3.

Meer, S. (1999) *Women Speak. Reflections on our own struggles*, Cape Town: Kwela Books.

Naidoo, R. (ed.) (1999) *Unions in Transition: COSATU into the New Millennium*, Johannesburg, National Labour and Economic Development Institute (NALEDI).

Needleman, R. and Tanner, L.D. (1987) 'Women in unions, current issues', in Koziara, K.S., Moskow, M.H. and Tanner, L.D. (eds) *Working Women: Past, Present, Future*, United States: The Bureau of National Affairs.

Orr, L. (1997) 'Quota systems as a strategy for strengthening women's leadership in trade unions'. Unpublished paper.

—— (1999) *Women Leadership in COSATU*, Johannesburg: National Labour and Economic Development Institute.

Orr, L. *et al.* (1997) Quota systems as a strategy for strengthening women's leadership in trade unions: The international and South African experience, Johannesburg: NALEDI Publications.

Pityana, S. and Orkin, M. (1992) *Beyond the Factory Floor*, Johannesburg: Ravan Press.

Shefer, T. (1991) 'COSATU Women's Forums: Separate to get strong', *Agenda* 9.

Standing, I. (1996) *Restructuring the Labour Market: The South African Challenge*, an ILO Review, Geneva: ILO.

Statistics South Africa (2000) October Household Survey, 1999.

Torres, L. (2000) *Amandla. Ngawethu? The Trade Union Movement in South Africa and Political Change*, Norway: Fafo Institute for Applied Social Science.

Tothill, A. (1998) 'Women in research: Women academics in the humanities and social sciences at South African universities', *Women's Studies*, 10, 1.

Tshoaedi, M. (1999) Functional differentiation in trade union employment: A case study of gender inequality with specific reference to women union officials, MA Thesis, University of the Witwatersrand.

11 On the edge of equality?

Working women and the US labour movement

Dorothy Sue Cobble and Monica Bielski Michal

Introduction

The power of US unions – measured either by membership numbers or by economic and political clout – has sometimes seemed to be in virtual free fall in the last decades of the twentieth century. Yet the breathtaking decline of labour may have finally bottomed out and may even be beginning to reverse itself. In 1999, union density (the percentage of the labour force that is unionised)[1] reached its lowest point since the 1930s with only 14 per cent of workers (10 per cent of the private sector and 37 per cent of the public sector) belonging to unions (USDL 2000). But under the relentless drum beat of 'organise, organise' emanating from the AFL-CIO's[2] new leadership under President John J. Sweeney, the haemorrhaging of membership has slowed. For the first time in 20 years, union density remained the same in 1999, and the absolute number of union members actually *increased* by some quarter of a million, boosting union membership to sixteen and a half million members. Of equal significance, the Sweeney administration's aggressive leadership in politics since 1996 and its willingness to rethink 'business as usual' has earned it grudging respect from politicians, business leaders, and the public at large (Meyerson 2000).

Yet the US labour movement will have a long road back to the power and prestige it once enjoyed. Despite polls showing that a majority of US workers desire collective representation at work, actually organising a union and securing a contract is not easy (Freeman and Rogers 1999; Hart 1998). US labour law erects formidable hurdles to collective representation. Some one-third of the labour force fall outside the protections of the law, and many others face legal delays and loopholes that render freedom of choice and the right to association farcical (Cobble 1994a). US employers also oppose collective representation more vehemently than employers in other industrialised nations. The number of workers fired in organising campaigns continues to rise in the US, and many employers refuse to negotiate first contracts even *after* a majority of workers votes for union representation. Moreover, unionised employers persist in adversarial attitudes, bypassing contract mechanisms for problem solving and seeking out management consultants who specialise in de-unionisation strategies (Bronfenbrenner 1994).

Labour's revitalisation in the US depends in large part on the degree to which this hostile legal and social environment can be modified. Yet labour's fate also depends on whether it can transform itself to meet the needs and aspirations of a changing workforce. Although opinion polls show consistent support for the *idea* of collective representation, attitudes towards what are perceived as the common *practices* of US unions are considerably less enthusiastic (Freeman and Rogers 1999; Hart 1998). The labour movement as we know it today emerged in the World War II era, some 50 years ago, and was created primarily to meet the needs of a male factory workforce. Yet the *majority* of workers are now in service and white-collar jobs and close to half are female. In part it is the ability of organised labour to recognise these discontinuities and remake itself to attract this new workforce that will determine whether workers opt for paternalistic, individualistic or collective solutions to their workplace dilemmas.

Labour women have been pushing for cultural and institutional change within the US labour movement for decades, and, as this chapter will argue, the impact of their efforts is now being increasingly felt. In the 1970s, a new labour feminism emerged, largely in conjunction with the rise of the larger middle-class women's movement – a movement that reverberated throughout the society in the 1960s and 1970s, remaking law and sexual mores, and breaking apart many of the economic and social barriers that constrained women. In 1974, over three thousand women from 58 AFL-CIO unions descended on Chicago to found CLUW, a national organisation dedicated to improving the status of women, both as workers and as unionists (Milkman 1985: 311). Clerical workers, flight attendants, household employees, and others also formed organisations *independent* of the AFL-CIO unions in the 1970s, and in many cases they improved their wages and working conditions by relying on picketing, publicity, and lawsuits as well as traditional collective bargaining (Cobble 1999). The momentum continued into the 1980s with women in the large public sector unions leading successful pay equity strikes across the country (Hallock 1993). Although the middle-class women's movement peaked by the end of the 1970s, the new assertiveness on the part of *labour* women has continued to force changes in the leadership and agenda of trade unions. Indeed, although the labour movement still retains vestiges of its industrial, male-identified past, as the twentieth-first century dawns, labour is repositioning itself as a leading institutional force for women's economic advancement.

Organised labour has much to gain by this new partnership. Women could once be ignored – few were in unions and the paid labour force was predominantly male. But today, the power of labour rests as much on the loyalty and activism of its women members as its men, and labour's future may well hinge on its ability to win the allegiance of the millions of women – some 88 per cent of all women workers – who are outside its ranks. Fortunately for labour, women are more favourably inclined to union membership and hence are more likely to respond to union organising appeals. This gender gap in union attitudes has held steady since the late 1970s. The latest Hart poll, conducted in 1997, found that 49 per cent of unorganised women would vote for union representation compared to 40 per cent of men (Hart 1998). And, when given the opportunity, women act on their pro-union beliefs, casting 'yes' votes in union elections more frequently than do men (Bronfenbrenner 1998).

Labour would do well to listen to its women members. For it is the issues women are articulating and the new institutional practices they are pioneering that are salient for the twenty-first century workforce, male and female. The feminisation of work and the transformation of the family have meant that the experiences of many men are coming to resemble those once associated solely with women. In the new competitive, restructured economy, men increasingly face low wages, lack of benefits, and economic insecurity. A greater proportion of men also hold service and white-collar jobs, work long dominated by women. And, with the rise of two-income families, more men now face what once was thought to be a peculiarly 'woman's problem': how to balance the dual demands of paid work and family. Women are at the forefront of economic change, and they are at the forefront of devising new forms of unionism that will appeal to a new generation of workers.

Women of course need unions as much as unions need them. The large-scale economic and political upheavals of the late twentieth century have stratified wealth, and women have not been immune from this phenomenon. In the US, women's economic status has improved relative to men, but inequities *among* women by class and race have increased (Blau 1998). Unions can help lessen these new economic inequalities among women. Unions also remain crucial to increasing the power and voice of working women politically and to securing democracy, dignity, and fair treatment at work.

On 11 March, 2000, some 25 years after the founding of CLUW, thousands of union women once again gathered in Chicago under the auspices of the Working Women's Department (WWD) of the AFL-CIO, hoping to be the forerunners of a new surge of labour feminism. An ebullient Rosa L. DeLauro, Democratic Congresswoman from Connecticut told a cheering audience: 'We now stand on the edge of equality. This generation of working women will write a new chapter in our story. It will say that in this time, working women seized the country's agenda, shattered the glass ceiling and removed the last of the remaining barriers' (AFL-CIO 2000a). DeLauro's sweeping prediction may be premature, but certainly, as this essay will show, there are grounds for optimism.

In the sections that follow, we identify the concerns articulated by working women and assess the degree to which unions are serving as a means to realise these aspirations. We conclude with an analysis of the barriers to further progress. Our conclusions are based primarily on data drawn from Cobble's earlier historical and case study research on women and unions (Cobble 1991, 1993, 1994a, 1994b, 1996, 1999). In addition, we rely on new data generated through telephone and face-to-face interviews with fifteen key union respondents and a written questionnaire we administered that solicited information from all national unions with over 100,000 women members. The response rate was 83 per cent and included a representative group of blue-collar as well as white-collar unions.

The feminisation of labour

Women's share of union membership grew steadily in the decades following World War II as the feminisation of the workforce picked up speed. Less than a tenth of union members (or 800,000) were female before 1940; by 1954 close to 3 million women belonged to unions, some 17 per cent of all union members. In the 1960s and 1970s an even more dramatic change in the gender balance of organised labour occurred as unionism spread to female-majority sectors of the economy such as education; federal, state and municipal government; and, to a more limited degree, health care. Many of the most powerful and vocal internationals within the labour movement – AFSCME, SEIU, and the teacher unions – now had large female constituencies (Cobble 1993: 10–11). Today, 40 per cent of the labour-movement is female, approaching parity with women's 46 per cent share of the labour force (USDL 2000). And, as Karen Nussbaum, head of the AFL-CIO's WWD, is fond of pointing out: 'With five and a half million women members, the AFL-CIO is the largest working women's organisation in the country' (Nussbaum 2000).

Union leadership has feminised as well, spurred in part by the growing numbers of women members. Yet some of the most recent gains in female leadership, particularly at the national level, are also a result of the emergence of a new commitment to inclusion and diversity at the highest levels of the US labour movement. In 1995, for example, with the election of new national officers at the AFL-CIO, an immediate and dramatic change occurred in the number of women in executive level leadership within the Federation. The 'New Voice' slate, which won the first contested election for top officers since the AFL-CIO's founding in 1955, consisted of John J. Sweeney (SEIU) for Federation President, Richard Trumka (UMWA) for Secretary-Treasurer, and Linda Chavez-Thompson (AFSCME) for the new position of Executive Vice-President. Chavez-Thompson, a Mexican-American born to Texas sharecropper parents, had spent years organising public sector workers as a local AFSCME vice-president after an initial stint as a secretary for a local union affiliated with the Laborer's International (Meyerson 1998; Gray 2000). With her election, a woman became a top officer of the AFL-CIO for the first time, and a new third executive officer position was added to the Federation structure. The new administrative team moved quickly to bring other women and minorities into leadership within the Federation. They expanded the AFL-CIO Executive Council, the top Federation governing board, from 35 to 54, thus making it possible to diversify leadership significantly. The council now has seven women members (making it 13 per cent female), a far cry from 1980 when Joyce Miller, then president of CLUW, became the first woman to infiltrate its all-male ranks. Four of the seven are women of colour (Gray 1993; Gilliam 2000; AFL-CIO 2000b).

Sweeney also established a new department devoted to the interests and needs of women, the WWD. Its mandate was 'to bring the concerns of working women into every nook and cranny of the labour movement and to turn the labour movement into an activist voice of all working women' (Nussbaum 1998: 57). Sweeney convinced Karen Nussbaum, a veteran clerical organiser, to leave her directorship at the US Women's Bureau and take over as the Department's head. Finally, Sweeney increased the number of women department heads at the Federation headquarters from 6 to 50 per cent, prompting one prominent female AFL-CIO staffer to declare that truly a 'qualitative change' had occurred within the Washington headquarters (Meyerson 1998; Nussbaum 1998; Mills 2000).

Women made noticeable inroads into the executive suites of a growing number of the largest and most powerful of the national unions in the 1990s as well, broadening a trend evident in the 1980s. As Table 11.1 reveals, the last two decades have witnessed a significant jump in the number of women on the executive boards of AFSCME, SEIU, and the garment unions (now merged as UNITE). Increases also occurred on the top governing boards of the CWA, UFCW, and HERE. In addition, the UAW, a union that had always reserved one executive board position for a woman, now has two women board members, one of whom was the first woman *elected* to a *non-reserved* slot (Gray 2000). A 'glass ceiling' still blocks the rise of women into top executive positions in some sectors of the labour movement. Yet as Table 11.1 shows, the heavily male-dominated executive boards of the IBT (with one woman) or the IBEW (with no women) are now the outliers rather than the norm among unions with large numbers of women members.

The movement of women into top leadership positions is likely to continue, given the number of talented women in the pipeline. The lower and middle levels of union leadership feminised earlier than did the top executive offices, and the change has been more extensive. A critical mass of secondary women leaders emerged in the decades following World War II in the large CIO industrial unions (Cobble 1994b). The wave of public sector organising in the 1960s and 1970s produced additional women leaders. By the 1980s, the number of women local officers as well as the number of women paid staff at the local and regional level in some unions was considerable (Needleman 1986; Gray 1993). According to our recent survey, these gains have been sustained and extended in the last decade. In 2000, for example, some 46 per cent of AFSCME's 3,641 locals and approximately 35 per cent of SEIU's 300 locals have female leaders. Other unions such as the CWA, NEA, and UNITE also report large numbers of women staff and local leaders.

Data on minority women and union leadership is virtually non-existent. Yet what data does exist suggests a little-noticed but significant phenomenon. Women of colour, like white women, continue to be severely under-represented in union leadership, especially at the higher levels, but the representation gap may actually be less for African-American women than for white or Latina women. In a national survey conducted in the late 1970s, the US Commission on Civil Rights (1982: 18), found, for example, that although a smaller *absolute* number of African-American women held local leadership positions than white, a greater *proportion* of African-American women were in leadership. More recently, the propensity of African-American women to move into formal and informal leadership has been noted by Diane Harriford (1993) in her study of the New York City chapter of CLUW. She attributes black women's activism to long-standing traditions of black female leadership in the church and the civil rights movement.

But to what degree has the rise in the number of women members and leaders been accompanied by a corresponding shift in the agenda and institutional practices of the US labour movement? We attempt to answer that question in the following sections by identifying the workplace issues being articulated by working women and assessing the degree to which they are finding an ally in organised labour.

Table 11.1 Female membership and leadership in selected labour organisations with large numbers of women members, 1978–2000

Labour organisation	Year	Women members (thousands)	Women as percentage of members	Women as percentage of officers and executive boardmembers
NEA	1978	1,240	75	55
	1985	1,000	60	33
	1990	1,600	72	45
	2000	1,500	61	33
AFSCME	1978	408	40	3
	1985	450	45	4
	1990	600	50	17
	2000	728	52	38
UFCW	1978	480	39	3
	1990	663	51	8
	2000	700	50	11
SEIU	1978	312	50	15
	1985	435	50	18
	1990	420	45	34
	2000	650	50	32
AFT	1978	300	60	25
	1985	366	60	32
	1990	455	65	32
	2000	600	60	39
IBT	1978	481	25	0
	1985	485	26	0
	1990	400	25	0
	2000	450	30	4
CWA	1978	259	51	0
	1985	338	52	6
	1990	338	52	6
	2000	320	51	12
HERE	1978	181	42	4
	1985	200	50	8
	1990	143	48	4
	2000	185	48	18
ACTWU	1978	331	66	15
	1985	228	65	9
	1990	160	61	20
Now UNITE	2000	165	66	30
ILGWU	1970	279	80	7
	1983	219	85	13
	1990	145	83	22
Now UNITE	2000	165	66	30

Sources: For 1978–1990 see Cobble (1993): 11. Data for 2000 are from a written survey of unions conducted by Cobble and Michal with the help of Mary Jean Soupis.

Women and wages

US unions consistently identify raising wages as a central demand of the movement. The last decade is no exception. The recent AFL-CIO slogan, 'America Needs a Raise', and President Sweeney's book of the same title are indicative of the Federation's priorities (Sweeney 1996). Indeed, some pundits claim that the US labour movement is doing more than any other institution to return questions of economic inequality to the forefront of liberal and progressive reform in the US (Meyerson 2000). The need is pressing since class and race income disparities have widened in the US since the early 1970s. Real wages inched forward in the late 1990s, after declining since 1973, but the rise in overall *wealth* of the top fifth of the population far outpaced the gains for the bottom two-fifths. In particular, African-Americans saw their income and wealth erode in relation to Euro-Americans (Levy 1998).

Realising that collective bargaining could only *partially* solve the wage problem given the small percentage of unionised workplaces and the weakened economic clout of US unions, the AFL-CIO intensified its efforts in the political arena. The AFL-CIO pressed Congress to raise the minimum wage, and, in partnership with community groups, churches, and civil rights organisations, led a nationwide movement to pass 'living wage ordinances'. Both campaigns have enjoyed a surprising degree of success. In 1996, legislation raised the federal minimum wage from \$4.25 to \$5.15, the first increase in five years. 'Living Wage Ordinances', which usually require the payment of a wage higher than the federal minimum along with health benefits and other entitlements, were enacted first in Baltimore in December 1994. They have now spread to dozens of municipalities across the country (Kusnet 1998; Uchitelle 1999).

Although not targeted specifically at women, these kinds of universal initiatives do benefit women disproportionately. Sixty per cent of minimum wage workers in the US are female, some seven million women. The majority of these women are white, but women of colour are over-represented: they represent 22 per cent of US women but one-third of all minimum wage workers (Malveaux 2000). Any action improving wages for the poorest workers thus affects women and minorities more than any other group.

But what about the persistent wage gap between men and women? Minimum wage and living wage legislation help this problem because such approaches raise women's wages disproportionately. Organising women into unions closes the gender wage gap as well. Research has shown, for example, that union women earn 38 per cent more than non-union, and that the gender wage gap is less among organised than unorganised workers (WWD 2000; Spalter-Roth *et al.* 1994). But many labour women are endeavouring to ensure that strategies specifically focusing on closing the gender wage gap are included in labour's wage campaigns. And it appears they have partially succeeded. Since 1998, much of the AFL-CIO activity directed towards raising wages has been conducted under the rubric of 'America's Working Families', and 'fair pay' for women has been a key element of the programme.

In 1997, the WWD launched a full-scale political campaign on behalf of 'fair pay' legislation. The labour movement had been the key player in the bitter and extensive comparable worth battles of the 1980s – battles that resulted in major wage gains for unionised women in the public sector. Indeed, significant pay equity wage hikes occurred *only* in states with strong public sector unions. But the movement stalled in the late 1980s, stymied by unfavourable court decisions and the resistance of private sector employers (Hallock 1993). Women workers, however, continued to identify equal pay as their number one priority, in part because after decades of steady but slow progress, the gender wage gap was still wide. In 2000, women earned 72 cents for every dollar earned by men, a slight decline from the 74 cents they received in 1996. White women faired best, earning 73 per cent of what all men make. African-American and Latina women made less relative to all men, earning 65 and 53 per cent respectively (NCPE 2000; Cummings 2000).

In 1998, the AFL-CIO supported the Paycheck Fairness Act, national legislation that would amend and improve the 1963 Equal Pay Act. As the Equal Pay Act currently stands, pay discrimination claims are limited to the few situations where women and men are doing 'substantially the same' work. The new legislation would allow a broader range of jobs to be evaluated for gender bias. It would also toughen the remedies allowed under the Equal Pay Act and funnel more resources into enforcement. Although the federal legislation sought by the AFL-CIO appears unlikely to pass in the near future, five 'fair pay' laws have passed at the state level and additional laws are being considered in 27 states, pushed primarily by the state federations of the AFL-CIO. Indeed, for the first time equal pay has made its way to the *top* of the list of the legislative priorities determined by the state federations (Nussbaum 2000; Cummings 2000).

In line with the AFL-CIO's emphasis on 'America's Working Families', fair pay has been presented more as a family issue than one of economic justice for individual women. The literature from the WWD calls attention to the loss of family income when women experience discrimination in pay. 'Unequal pay hurts men too,' the WWD points out, especially those in so-called 'women's jobs' (WWD 2000). The strategy is an inclusive one that downplays gender division and emphasises the benefits of fair pay for women, men, and children. Yet as the five thousand cheering Chicago attendees at the Working Women's Conference 2000 demonstrate, 'fair pay' is still an issue that is linked to women's empowerment and that resonates deeply with women's desire for recognition and respect.

Work and family: it's about time

Women workers desire time off for themselves and their families as well as income and benefits that allow for the best possible care for loved ones. Organising around 'the politics of time', to use Carmen Sirianni's phrase, has a long history in the US (Sirianni 1988). The demand for shorter hours was the principal concern of the US labour movement in the nineteenth century (Roediger and Foner 1989). In the early twentieth century, the labour movement continued to press for shorter work hours through collective bargaining clauses and legislative statutes such as the Fair Labor Standards Act, which established the forty-hour, five-day week as the norm in 1938. In the post World War II era, work time declined further as unionised workers achieved retirement benefits, vacations with pay, sick leave, and even, as in the case of the longshoremen, a guaranteed annual wage. Yet these advances did little for parents or other caregivers trying to balance the demands of household labour with those of wage labour. The free time came as 'lumps of leisure' – the weekend, the month of vacation – or as time at the end of one's life in the form of additional years of retirement. Those bearing and raising children needed more time off from employment in their child rearing years, a shorter work *day*, good part-time jobs, and more control over their time so that the unpredictable day-to-day demands of the household sphere could be met.

Only in the last decade has a movement emerged in which time for dependent care was central. With the entry of married women and mothers into the wage sphere, the dissolution of the traditional family, and the aging of the workforce, the problems of those juggling paid work and family life are pressing. In 1993, former President Clinton responded to a coalition of labour and women's groups voicing these concerns by signing the FMLA, a law that had been vetoed twice before by the first President Bush. The FMLA requires employers with over 50 employees to grant up to three months of unpaid leave for the birth or adoption of a child or for the care of a sick family member. It is shockingly inadequate when compared to the rights and benefits for caregivers legislatively-mandated in most other industrialised countries. Forty-one million workers (40 per cent of the private sector) are not covered; the leave is also short and *unpaid*. Yet it was the first federal law in the US that provided a universal right or entitlement to caregivers. US family policy before the 1990s consisted of income supplements for widows (so-called mothers' pensions), income support for poor female heads of household and their children (welfare), and universal but minimal tax deductions for dependants and for child care expenses. (Katz 2000; Gordon 1994).

Given this lacklustre governmental response and the continued lengthening of work hours – the US now has the longest working hours among the wealthy nations – it is not surprising that the candidates in the US 2000 Presidential race felt the need to offer some promises of relief. One problem for political reform, however, is the lack of consensus on exactly what public policies would make a difference to the majority of working parents. A second involves the small (but at times vocal) part of the US population that actively *opposes* both governmental *and* private sector initiatives benefiting families, arguing that 'family-friendly' policies discriminate against single and childless individuals. Just as troubling, a sizable percentage of the American public is simply indifferent to the problem or believes that family issues are private and best addressed *without* the help of government or employers. Even in surveys conduced by the AFL-CIO, many of the reforms necessary to resolve the work and family dilemma do not emerge as high priorities (Hart 1998: 79, 83). Yet as Gerstel and Clawson (2000) have noted, the low ranking of work and family concerns may reflect workers' reluctance to see family benefits as a legitimate social entitlement and may say more about the low expectations of workers than about the actual level of worker need.

Despite the many obstacles, the movement perseveres. Their approach has been appropriately multi-pronged, targeting business practices, legislative statutes and public attitudes. In the 1980s and 1990s, many businesses instituted so-called 'family-friendly' benefits such as childcare, flex-time, and paid leaves, largely to retain the talents of women professionals and managers. Few of these benefits were extended to the blue-collar, non-professional workforce (Holcomb 2000). A small but growing number of unions have tried to change that situation, at least for unionised workers, by bargaining for a range of family benefits. ACTWU, AFSCME, HUCTW, and other unions established child care centres and secured contract clauses providing paid leave, flex-time, limits on overtime, and wage and benefit parity for part-timers. The union approach to family policy historically also has included bargaining for health care coverage, higher wages, and economic security (York 1993; Landau 1999; Grundy and Firestein 1997; Firestein 2000; Cowell 1993).

In addition, since the 1970s, the labour movement has been an active partner in the coalitions pushing for increased public funds for child care centres. These initiatives drew fierce opposition from the business and conservative community. At the federal level, they met defeat first from a Republican Presidential veto and then from a Republican-dominated Congress. But in the 1990s, a union-initiated child care coalition in New York won substantial state monies for a child care fund; other union-led coalitions are at work in Washington, Massachusetts, and California. The labour movement has also been the leading advocate of improving the quality of child care by raising the pay and working conditions of child care providers. Nationally, child care workers are the lowest paid occupational group, earning less than parking lot attendants. In 1999, child care workers voted to unionise in Philadelphia and Seattle, and many joined with parents in 'worthy wage campaigns' aimed at increasing state subsidies for child care centres (Nussbaum 1998; Landau 2000; Lazarovich 2000).

Further, the labour movement has lobbied for improved family leave at the state and federal level. One goal is to amend the federal FMLA, extending the law to additional sectors of the economy and mandating that the leave be paid rather than unpaid. At the state level, the labour movement and its allies among women's organisations, religious groups, and low-wage community groups seek to pass state laws with more generous leave provisions and to include pregnancy and family care as a legitimate reason to claim disability or unemployment. In May of 1999, a labour-led coalition in Maine succeeded in passing a state law that extended the benefits of the FMLA to a broader range of workplaces (Nussbaum 2000).

Although progress on paid leave as well as 'family-friendly benefits' to date has been slight, work and family issues may be the next reform frontier. The AFL-CIO rhetoric emphasising America's working families is ubiquitous, and male union leaders such as Gerald McEntee, president of AFSCME, and Brian McLaughlin, head of the NYCLC, have been outspoken supporters. McLaughlin called child care 'a fundamental issue, like the 8-hour work day, minimum wage or occupational health and safety'. The NYCLC also adopted a 'Work and Family Bill of Rights' in September 1998. Developed by a group of New York women labour activists in conjunction with the Labor Project for Working Families in Berkeley (California), the 'Work and Family Bill of Rights' is now in the process of being endorsed by additional labour bodies. A far-sighted, inclusive document, it claims five 'funda-mental rights related to work and family': 1) the right to a living wage, including fair pay; 2) the right to paid family and medical leave; 3) the right to have control over work hours; 4) the right to quality child and elder care that provides living wages for the care provider; and 5) the right to adequate health care coverage (Grundy and Firestein 1997; Firestein 2000).

Labour women will need partners outside of organised labour if substantial progress is to occur in recognising and securing such rights. Yet if the passage of the FMLA is any indication, coalitions can be built when work and family concerns are conceptualised broadly. Despite the naysayers, the work/family dilemma affects everyone. It is about the reproduction of society and how children are nurtured. It is about how each and every citizen will spend their elderly years. And, it is about ensuring that the everyday pleasures of friendship, family, and community are not sacrificed to the seemingly insatiable demands of the global market for more time on the job.

Organising and representing women

Not only has the leadership and agenda of labour been feminised, but there are signs that institutional practices are starting to change as well. For years, a myth persisted that women workers were harder to organise, and that labour should invest its organising resources where the supposed likelihood of return was greater, that is, among labour's historic base of male manufacturing workers. Despite the persistent poll results contradicting these notions – some even showing that the hardest units to organise were factories with white male employees in the majority – labour continued to spend only a fraction of its organising resources in reaching the female-majority occupations and industries (Bronfenbrenner 1998).

But attitudes towards women as potential organising targets changed significantly in the 1990s. More women than men joined unions in the 1990s, and many of the organising breakthroughs occurred among women, particularly women of colour and immigrant women. HERE membership rebounded, for example, as the union organised thousands of women and non-white service workers in the giant hotels of Las Vegas and elsewhere in the 1980s and 1990s (Cobble and Merrill 1994). Similarly, SEIU experienced success in its campaigns among home health care workers, predominately African-American and Latina women (Cobble 1996). These victories bode well for the future of organising, especially given the current composition of the labour force. In 1999, 23 per cent of the labour force was minority (13 per cent African-American, 11 per cent Hispanic, and 4 per cent Asian), and the numbers are growing, particularly among Hispanics (Hunt and Rayside 2000: 401).

Yet the shift of resources towards sectors in which women and minority men predominate is but a first step in changing long ingrained institutional practices. Of equal importance is the need to rethink the very assumptions embedded in a unionism whose institutional structures arose in the context of mass production. The legal and institutional framework within which labour relations is currently conducted is a product of the New Deal era. Relying on the factory as the prototypic work place, policy and practice assumed a rigid and non-overlapping demarcation between employee and employer, an adversarial relation between worker and boss, and a homogeneous, semi-skilled workforce with little interest in career advancement or workplace governance (Cobble 1991, 1994a).

The dichotomous, adversarial model of labour relations, still dominant today, is not a good fit for today's workforce. In many work places the roles of employer and employee are blurred: employees work in teams, take responsibility for control over quality, work design, and work organisation, and may even take on such 'management' functions as hiring, firing, and co-worker discipline. Indeed, for many service and white-collar workers, the quality of the service they provide and the amount of control they exert over the service interaction or the provider–client exchange is as central to their financial security and job satisfaction as the employer–employee relationship. Many front-line service workers, for example, desire a new kind of unionism in which preserving the intrinsic rewards of the service encounter – seeing the patient's health improve, calming a distraught two-year old – is seen as a critical aspect of employee representation (Cobble 1996). Similarly, many professionals and knowledge workers want a unionism that devotes attention to professional development, training, and improving the status of their occupations. Indeed, the majority of workers (regardless of industry and occupation) indicate a desire for a less combative unionism. They want a union that helps secure the success of the enterprise, enables employees to advance individually and collectively, and responds to workers' psychological as well as their economic needs (Hart 1998; Freeman and Rogers 1999).

A number of unions have begun rethinking traditional models. Unions organising professionals and white-collar workers such as the teacher unions (NEA and AFT) and the new organisations emerging among doctors, psychologists, and computer programmers are now seriously engaged in reconceiving their representational practices to better meet the needs of these groups (Kerchner *et al.* 1997). Unions representing non-professional (or non-credentialled) pink and white-collar workers also are sending a different message to their constituencies.

SEIU, for example, broke with traditional models of both organising and representation in their efforts to unionise home care workers in the 1980s and 1990s. Home care workers typically assist the elderly and the disabled in their own homes, offering an alternative to institutionalised care. Rather than organise on a site-by-site basis, SEIU relied on community-based organising in which they targeted all home care aides within a particular locale and drew upon local institutions and community leaders for support. They emphasised the quality of the service relationship between client and aide and the ways in which the union would benefit both parties. By 1995, some 45,000 home care workers had signed up in California alone; flourishing union locals also existed in Chicago, New York, New Orleans, and other cities (Kilborn 1995; Walker 1994). In 1999, after a twelve-year campaign, an additional 75,000 home care workers in Los Angeles County voted for union representation. Their first contract, signed in August 1999, boosted home care worker salaries to $6.25, provided health benefits for the first time, and established a job registry. The job registry helped enhance the service relationship by making it easier for clients to find potential aides and for aides in problem situations to find new employers (Cobb 1999).

HUCTW, which secured its first contract with Harvard University in 1988 (after a *fourteen*-year battle), has also been consistently innovative in organising and representation. As epitomised in their slogan 'You don't have to be anti-Harvard to be pro-union', the HUCTW organisers rejected the anti-boss, anti-employer approach to organising (Hurd 1993). In the words of Kris Rondeau, one of the lead organisers, 'we didn't organise against the employer. Our goals were simply self-representation, power, and participation' (Green 1988: 5). And once HUCTW began collective bargaining negotiations with Harvard, the union insisted on a non-traditional approach. Collective bargaining sessions took place in the style of the Polish Solidarity negotiations, with large numbers of small teams grouped around tables, working out compromises on specific issues. Collective bargaining involved, according to Rondeau, 'many initial days where our people simply told their life stories. You see, management needed to know the realities of our lives and to know that our lives were as important as theirs' (Rondeau 1991).

The first round of negotiations produced significant wage gains for clericals, new child-care and family-leave policies, and a decidedly experimental form of workplace governance. Instead of the older industrial model of problem solving in which management takes responsibility for productivity, quality, and discipline, the HUCTW-Harvard agreement called for an elaborate system of joint committees. These committees would resolve disputes between workers and supervisors and recommend improvements in service delivery and working conditions (Hoerr 1993; Hurd 1993).

Some commentators view the involvement of unions in these kinds of partici-patory cooperative structures as a sign of declining militancy and union weakness. The Harvard model suggests otherwise. It demonstrates that militancy and employee solidarity need not be based on unwavering opposition to management. Their more flexible, open-ended, and 'cooperative' structures enhanced their power *vis-à-vis* management. By creating structures that encouraged involvement, the union forged a powerful organisation in which commitment and creativity flourished. In their last round of negotiations, HUCTW won a 30 per cent wage increase, improved benefits, and in one of their hardest-fought battles, finally achieved raises, enhanced job security and benefit parity for part-time employees (Cobble 1996; Landau 2000).

HUCTW has paid attention to negotiating *relationships* as well as negotiating *contracts*. For many clerical workers, the rules and norms governing their interactions with students, faculty, and other 'clients' are as important as their wages and benefits. An opportunity for the union to renegotiate the traditional service norms arose in the early 1990s when the Harvard administration offered 'skills training' for clerical workers in how to handle the stress of working with intemperate and demanding students, faculty (the worst), and other university personnel. At one infamous session, a management trainer counselled the attendees to 'think of yourself as a trash can' – a vessel that would simply fill up with everyone's ill humour throughout the day and then could be dumped after work. Needless to say, many of the clerical workers did not want to think of themselves as trash cans. At that point, the union pushed for its own training classes that would emphasise the necessity of ending the 'customer is always right' rule and developing more humane norms for clerical–customer relationships (Eaton 1996).

HUCTW is not alone in its attention to curtailing abusive employee–customer relationships. Flight attendant unions, for example, have pressed for more leeway in customer–client interaction and disputed management's continuing allegiance to the notion that the customer is always right, whether belligerent, sexually overbearing or abusive. In one showdown in the early 1990s, American Airline attendants struck successfully for higher wages, more control over their schedules, and an end to management practices such as sending attendants home who report to work with pimples and firing workers who return incivility in kind. A mandatory 'Commitment to Courtesy' class in which instructors divided flight attendants into small groups and assigned them to draw pictures showing 'attendants being nice' particularly galled the women. 'People got livid', one activist explained (Ciotta 1994; Kilborn 1993).

The unilateral attempt by employers to regulate customer interaction can backfire with disastrous consequences for the employees, in part because such regulation constricts women's own methods of controlling interpersonal interactions, especially with aggressive men. In 1999, the Oakland, California, Safeway grocery store chain instituted a new policy, requiring clerks to smile, make extended eye contact, and offer to carry groceries for able-bodied male customers. One employee, uncomfortable with the behaviour of two male customers, asked to be excused from carrying their groceries. The manager refused, insisting that she accompany the men into the parking lot, and she was assaulted. The UFCW local's complaint about the new rules failed to generate much of a response from Safeway, but the 'smile rule controversy' provoked an uproar in local print and electronic media. Radio call-in talk shows, editorial columns, and internet exchanges buzzed with opinions about whether 'smile rules' were a consequential and serious labour issue and who had the right to create the rules of social encounter (Ross 1999; Veverka 1999; McNichol 1998). In her 1983 book, *The Managed Heart*, Arlie Hochschild argued that many service jobs involve 'emotional labor' or forced emotional effort. She called for a new workplace movement that recognised a worker's right to control their emotions (their 'heart') in much the same way as nineteenth-century factory workers insisted that their bodies be protected from unwarranted abuse. Her call is being heard by an increasing number of unions.

Sexuality, sex discrimination, and the workplace

Unions have been and continue to be more effective in advancing the needs of women when those needs are seen as compatible and even complementary with those of men. Thus, raising women's wages, increasing union membership among women, and even establishing family-friendly benefits have all garnered male support in part because they have been framed as *class* demands that would benefit working women *and* men. Union leaders, male and female, have argued that fair pay for women would increase family income, organising women would strengthen the entire labour movement, and family-friendly benefits would help everyone. It has been more difficult, however, to construct a rationale for cross-gender coalitions dedicated to changing traditional sexual practices and deeply embedded gender norms at work. Issues of sexuality and gender ideology have divided working-class men and women in the past and continue to do so today.

Historically, the labour movement helped men achieve 'manhood' by winning for them a provider wage, by giving them more control, autonomy, and independence at work and by fighting to diminish expectations of deference and servility, especially in those service jobs held by minority men (Montgomery 1979; Chateauvert 1997). In contrast, if achieving manhood was a central animating concern of the labour movement for men, many women, especially since the late 1960s, sought to use their workplace organisations to *dismantle* notions of 'womanhood' and 'femininity' on the job. Women clerical workers in the 1970s, for example, formed separate advocacy organisations such as 9to5 because they felt male-dominated unions were not sensitive to their concerns. For them, wages were secondary to securing respect and dignity – goals that could be achieved only by *ending* gendered job expectations such as serving coffee, running personal errands for the boss, or having one's personal appearance be more important in hiring and promotions than any other criteria (Cobble 1999).

Similarly, flight attendants, organised by the Pilots, Transport Workers, and Teamsters in the post-World War II decades, broke away from the male-dominated unions en masse in the 1970s, forming their own unions and, in 1972, setting up a cross-class women's alliance called Stewardesses for Women's Rights. Their issues, like those of clerical workers, involved changing the gendered norms for their occupation – issues they rightfully perceived would be misunderstood or considered frivolous by many men. They were concerned about the new more sexualised uniforms they were required to wear, the indignities that followed from the company ads presenting flight attendants as 'sex objects in the sky', and the pressures to appear forever young, slim, and sexually alluring. Flight attendants knew that the airlines were making a profit by selling their personalities and sexuality. They wanted to end 'sexploitation' by desexualising their image and by having more say over how their personalities would be packaged and at what price they would be marketed. In short, they wanted control over and just compensation for their sexual *and* their emotional labour (Cobble 1999).

By the end of the 1970s, the separatist organising among women ebbed, and many women's labour organisations reaffiliated with mixed-gender national unions or, as in the case of 9to5, negotiated an affiliation agreement with SEIU that set up a new clerical division within the union, allowing for considerable autonomy. Yet the ideological divide between union men and women concerning sexuality and appropriate gender roles has not closed. Segregation by sex in working-class jobs is still firmly entrenched, despite ongoing efforts to end sex-typing and help women break into the higher-paid male-dominated trades (O'Farrell 1999). Indeed, the lack of progress in integrating blue-collar men's jobs is all the more glaring given the rapid movement of women into white-collar male bastions such as law, medicine, and management (Reskin and Padavic 1994). And, although many labour organisations now publicly endorse such policies as moving women into non-traditional jobs and ending sexual harassment, women often find their local union unable to help when problems implementing these policies arise.

The most glaring recent example of such local union failure occurred in the Mitsubishi Auto plant in Normal, Illinois. In this relatively new plant, women held one-fifth of the high-wage auto jobs, an unusually high proportion of women for an auto assembly plant. On 9 April, 1996, the EEOC filed one of the largest class action sex discrimination suits in US history, claiming that as many as 500 of the 893 women in the plant had suffered sexual harassment. In June of 1998, Mitsubishi settled the case, agreeing to pay $34 million dollars to the plaintiffs, the largest cash settlement of its kind. Unfortunately, many of the aggrieved women felt that their local union, UAW Local 2488, failed to take their repeated complaints of harassment seriously. The union local did file grievances on behalf of women whose jobs were threatened by harassing supervisors; they also backed a male union member whose job was jeopardised because of alleged harassment. But they did little to eliminate or contain the problem of male *union* members sexually harassing female co-workers (Grimsley and Swoboda 1996; Crain and Matheny 1999; UAW 2000).

Of course, the reactions of this one union local should not be taken as the pattern followed by the majority of local unions or as indicative of the behaviour or attitudes of national labour leadership. At other unionised auto plants, for example, the UAW had managed to set up joint labour–management committees empowered to deal with the problem. Mitsubishi, however, resisted the UAW's attempt to add such committees to their contract; they also refused the International Union's proposal in June of 1996 for a jointly sponsored sexual harassment awareness programme (Grimsley and Swoboda 1996; UAW 2000). Yet it is significant that in the last three decades, many (if not the majority) of sex discrimination and sexual harassment suits in unionised workplaces have been filed *without* the active support of the union. Women workers frequently are forced to turn for help to outside organisations such as the National Organisation of Women, or as in the Mitsubishi case, to the Chicago-based women's group, Women Employed (Crain and Matheny 1999).

Thus, a problem exists for many women union members that needs greater attention from the labour movement. The explosion of litigation and public debate over sexual harassment makes it clear that the forced expression of sexuality at work is objectionable to women and that many women experience negative employment consequences because of it. Women who refuse sexual advances are often fired and/or suffer considerable loss of income and promotional opportunities. In many non-traditional blue-collar settings, a hostile work environment can be physically dangerous as well as emotionally debilitating. In other words, sexual harassment is a union issue: it's about job security, wages, and health and safety as well as basic workplace dignity. Yet many unions have not yet found a way of communicating these ideas to their members. Until they do, they will be unable to respond to the audible and expressed needs of many of their women members without alienating other members.

Some scholars have argued that class-based structures such as unions are premised on a 'united front ideology' and are *inherently* incapable of addressing gender issues like sexual harassment. They have advocated 'separately-organised women's unions' and changes in the labour law that would allow employers to bargain with groups organised around identities other than class (Crain and Matheny 1999: 1,600). But in the US context of adversarial class relations, care must be taken to preserve the class power of women as well as their minority rights within male-majority unions. Strengthening the intra-union bargaining power of women through women's committees, women's departments, and set-asides that guarantee minority representation in leadership would best accomplish these dual goals.

Extensive educational initiatives are also in order. Many unions have excellent policy statements about sexuality, affirmative action, and gender discrimination, but these sentiments have yet to reach the shop floor level. Educational programmes must tackle the problem head-on by engaging the profound differences that shape men's and women's experience of gender and sexuality. A culture of unity can only be built and maintained when the real differences among members are acknowledged. For women, sexuality is about pleasure, but it is also about physical danger and violence in a way difficult for most men to understand. Yet there is reason to believe that the differences can be bridged and that a basis for unity is possible. The issue of sexual harassment, it is important to remember, did not enter the vocabulary until the late 1970s; it is only now being publicly debated. Union men joined with women to support pay equity and eventually came to embrace it as a matter of gender justice. Similarly, it is likely that they will come to view sexual harassment as an affront to women and as a violation of the union principles of fairness, equality, and dignity for all.

The recent emergence of a formal alliance between labour and the gay rights movement certainly indicates that unions can take the lead on issues of sexuality. In the last two decades, the workplace sexual norms of enforced heterosexuality and the practice of linking workplace privileges and benefits to heterosexuality and heterosexual marriage have come under increasing criticism. Sexual minorities, unlike other minorities, are not included as a 'protected class' in the 1964 Civil Rights Act, the federal statute prohibiting employment discrimination on the basis of race, religion, sex, national origin, age, and disability. In 39 of the 50 states, once their sexual identity is public, sexual minorities can be immediately fired. Since only marriages between men and women are legal in the vast majority of states, same-sex couples are denied access to health care, pension coverage, and other workplace-based benefits. Sexual minorities also suffer adverse employment consequences because they often can not participate comfortably in the workplace rituals and bonding that are premised on heterosexual identity. As a result, they are sometimes perceived as poor team players, loners, or social misfits (McCreery and Krupat 1999; Schneider 1988).

In August 1997, the AFL-CIO affiliated a new constituency group of lesbian, gay, and bisexual workers, called Pride at Work (PAW). The momentum for such an alliance had been building for decades. Gay and lesbian union members began mobilising for workplace rights in the 1970s, forming local caucuses at individual work sites and setting up gay rights committees within national unions. In October 1983, SEIU won passage of a resolution condemning discrimination on the basis of sexual orientation at the AFL-CIO convention, 'a small but significant first step towards formalising and nurturing a budding alliance between gay activists and union activists', wrote AFL-CIO President Sweeney. In 1987, when the AFL-CIO sponsored a reception at their Washington headquarters for gay and lesbian union activists, talk about forming a national organisation turned to action. The SEIU's 'lavender caucus' took the lead, and in 1994 PAW had its founding convention (Lander 2000; Sweeney 1999; Roberts 1993).

PAW, unlike other social identity groups affiliated with the AFL-CIO such as CLUW, is open to union and non-union workers. And, although PAW relies principally on labour organisations to help achieve its aims, it sees itself as raising issues of class and worker rights within other gay rights groups. Specifically, PAW calls for passage of ENDA, which would prohibit employment discrimination on the basis of sexual orientation, and the broadening of the FMLA to include domestic partners in the definition of family. They also encourage unions to bargain contract language protecting gay workers from discrimination and extend spousal benefits to domestic partners. The Senate narrowly defeated ENDA in 1996, after intense lobbying from the AFL-CIO and other civil rights allies, but a similar version of the bill is currently pending in Congress. And, since 1974, when Ann Arbor, Michigan, bus drivers negotiated the first collectively bargained ban on 'discrimination based on sexual preference', auto workers, janitors, grocery store clerks and countless others have pushed for and won such provisions. As of October 2000 some one-fifth of the largest employers have such policies, many having added them in the last year. The top three auto companies, for example, recently agreed in negotiations with the UAW to offer domestic partner benefits to some 400,000 employees nationwide. The strong gay and lesbian subgroup in the UAW is widely credited for the victory. The war against homophobia and employment discrimination is far from won, but the increasing commitment of the labour movement to gay rights as fundamental human rights is a notable advance (Sweeney 1999; Tillotson 2000; Brook and Silverstein 2000; Chernow 2000).

Racial/ethnic minorities and US labour

The particular situation of women of colour has been noted throughout this essay. The wage gap is greater for African-American and Latina women than for white, and they suffer more acutely from long-standing patterns of job segregation and discriminatory pay and promotion practices. Not surprisingly, as the US labour movement eliminated the remaining racial bars to membership in the post-World War II era, women of colour outpaced other workers in joining unions. African-American women, in particular, are more organised than other groups and, as mentioned earlier, are highly visible as leaders and activists in their unions (AFL-CIO 2000a)

Approximately one-fourth of the membership of the US labour movement is minority, making it one of the most integrated institutions in the US. Still, racial and ethnic minorities continue to organise separately *within* the labour movement to advance their interests inside the house of labour as well as in society at large. At the national level, women of colour belong to a number of AFL-CIO constituency groups organised on the basis of race and ethnicity. African-Americans founded the first of these, the APRI, in the late 1960s. An outgrowth of the civil rights movement, the APRI seeks 'racial equality and economic justice' by engaging in political and community education, legislative action, and voter registration, and by supporting union organising campaigns. The APRI was later joined by other constituency groups based on racial/ethnic identity: the Coalition of Black Trade Unionists (CBTU) in 1972, the Labor Council for Latin-American Advancement (LCLAA) in 1973, and the Asian Pacific American Labor Alliance (APALA) in 1992 (Hunt and Rayside 2000; AFL-CIO 2000a; APRI 2000).

In addition to these national constituency groups, women of colour have organised alongside minority men to form caucuses within national and international unions; they have also participated in organising separate conferences and leadership institutes specifically for women of colour. The national women's committee of CBTU, for example, has held an all-day women's conference every year since 1982 with over a thousand black women participants. In 1999, LCLAA and CLUW sponsored their first Leadership Conference for Latina Women (LCLAA 2000; Needleman 2000).

Conclusion

Progress in forging a strong and equal partnership between women workers and the US labour movement has been slow and at times barely visible. Yet as we enter a new century there is evidence that considerable change has now occurred in that relationship. Women make up two-fifths of union membership, they are approaching leadership parity in many unions, many of their concerns have been incorporated into labour's agenda at the highest levels, and attention to diversity is now more the norm than the exception within the labour movement.

Yet the inclusion of women and the adoption of an agenda that better meets their needs has occurred within a framework that is limited by its failure to acknowledge fully the gender differences that still exist between men and women. Women and men still work in very different kinds of jobs, and while they have common problems, they also have some starkly different experiences as well. The labour movement must acknowledge these differences by embracing a variety of organisational and representational practices and by inventing new approaches better suited to the service and white-collar sectors in which women predominate.

Moreover, the reframing of issues such as pay equity and dependency care as family issues has been important in gaining male support (a pragmatic necessity that cannot be overlooked). But the emphasis on 'family' rather than on 'women' must not obscure the still fundamental reality that these are issues that affect men and women *differently* and that women's needs are only *partially* met when they are defined as the same as men's. Many women's relationship to the family is different because they bear and nurse children and because the burdens of dependent care still fall on them. Gender norms and sexuality affect job expectations and social interactions for men and women in profoundly different ways. These differences need to be understood just as the differences *among* women must be acknowledged. It is not too much to expect that men (as well as women) build a movement in which solidarity is based on empathy as well as mutual identity and self-interest. The politics of diversity is not a zero sum game. The strongest bonds are those that grow out of recognising difference as well as commonality.

At bottom, gender progress for working women is dependent on forces outside the labour movement as well as forces within. The fate of organised labour (and the fate of its women members) will be determined in large part by political, economic, and social forces beyond its control. The labour movement needs to remake itself and reach out to new constituencies, but its resurgence is predicated on the degree to which those constituencies respond and whether the larger society sees labour and 'the labour question' as legitimate and worthy of support. The labour movement is transforming in light of the new realities of identity politics; so too must its natural allies – the so-called new social movements based on identity – change as well. They must reciprocate the favour and begin to incorporate and understand issues of class. Indeed, the very dichotomy of 'social identity movements' and 'class-based movements' must be dissolved. Class, the late E. P. Thompson insisted, is a social identity, one that is made out of the cultural and material fabric of our lives (Thompson 1963). The question is not whether class or gender or race should be given priority, but whether it will finally be understood that workers come in all sizes and shapes, and that there is no *one* class identity or consciousness because there is no *one* worker. A new and vibrant working-class politics can be built, but only when no one *particular* experience is taken as the *universal*.

Notes

1   In the US, union density is a measure restricted to dues-paying employees in workplaces where employers have signed collective bargaining contracts.
2   The US labour movement has one national federation, the AFL-CIO. It was created in 1955 from a merger of two older federations, the AFL and the CIO. Currently there are some 68 national or international unions (international is used for those unions with membership in Canada) affiliated with the AFL-CIO. These national/ international unions have close to 30,000 locals, many of which affiliate with the 51 AFL-CIO state federations and the 590 central labour councils that exist (Meyerson 2000; AFL-CIO 2000b). There are also national/international unions as well as local unions that are not affiliated with the AFL-CIO. These are commonly called independent unions.

Abbreviations

APRI   A. Philip Randolph Institute
AFL-CIO   American Federation of Labor-Congress of Industrial Organizations
ACTWU   Amalgamated Clothing and Textile Workers Union
AFSCME   American Federation of State, County and Municipal Employees
AFT   American Federation of Teachers

APALA	Asian Pacific American Labor Alliance
CBTU	Coalition of Black Trade Unionists
CLUW	Coalition of Labor Union Women
CWA	Communications Workers of America
EEOC	Equal Employment Opportunities Commission
ENDA	Employment Non-Discrimination Act
FMLA	Family and Medical Leave Act
HERE	Hotel Employees and Restaurant Employees International Union
HUCTW	Harvard Union of Clerical and Technical Workers
IBEW	International Brotherhood of Electrical Workers
IBT	International Brotherhood of Teamsters
ILGWU	International Ladies Garment Workers Union
IWPR	Institute for Women's Policy Research
LCLAA	Labor Council for Latin American Advancement
NCPE	National Committee for Pay Equity
NEA	National Education Association
NYCLC	New York Central Labor Council
PAW	Pride at Work
SEIU	Service Employees International Union
UAW	United Auto Workers
UFCW	United Food and Commercial Workers International Union
UMWA	United Mine Workers of America
UNITE	Union of Needletrades, Industrial and Textile Employees
USDL	United States Department of Labor
WWD	Working Women's Department

References

AFL-CIO (2000a) Online. Available HTTP: http.www.afl-cio.org (20–5 March).

AFL-CIO (2000b) *Today's Unions: A Voice for America's Working Families*, AFL-CIO publication No. 99091-09-R-10, Washington, DC.

APRI (2000) Online. Available HTTP: http.www.aprihq.org/About.htm (12 December).

Blau, F.D. (1998) 'Trends in the well-being of American women, 1970–1995', *Journal of Economic Literature* 36: 112–65.

Bronfenbrenner, K. (1994) 'Employer behavior in certification elections and first-contract campaigns: Implications for Labor Law Reform', in Friedman, S., Hurd, R.W. and Seeber, R.L. (eds) *Restoring the Promise of American Labor Law*, Ithaca, NY: ILR Press.

—— (1998) Lifting as they climb: The promise and potential of organising women workers. A report commissioned by the Working Women's Department of the AFL-CIO. Washington DC.

Brook, N.R. and Silverstein, S. (2000) 'Top auto firms to offer benefits to gay partners', *Los Angeles Times*, 9 June.

Chateauvert, M. (1997) *Women of the Brotherhood of Sleeping Car Porters*, Urbana: University of Illinois Press.

Chernow, H. (2000) Co-Vice President of Pride at Work and Education and Training Director for the Massachusetts AFL-CIO. Telephone interview with M. Michal, 7 February.

Ciotta, R. (1994) 'A perfect strike: A women's union flexes its muscle', *Ms. Magazine* (March–April): 88–90.

Cobb, R. (1999) 'Background Memo: Unionizing the Homecare Workers of Los Angeles County'. Unpublished paper, MIT Political Science Department.

Cobble, D.S. (1991) 'Organizing the post-industrial work force: Lessons from the history of waitress unionism', *Industrial and Labor Relations Review* 44 (April): 419–36.

—— (1993) 'Introduction: Remaking unions for the new majority', in Cobble, D.S. (ed.) *Women and Unions: Forging a Partnership*, Ithaca, NY: ILR Press: 3–23.

—— (1994a) 'Making postindustrial unionism possible', in Friedman, S., Hurd, R.W., Oswald, R.A. and Seeber, R.L. (eds) *Restoring the Promise of American Labor Law*, Ithaca, NY: ILR Press: 285–302.

—— (1994b) 'Recapturing working-class feminism: Union women in the postwar era', in Meyerowitz, J. (ed.) *Not June Cleaver*, Philadelphia: Temple University Press: 57–83.

—— (1996) 'The prospects for unionism in a service society', in MacDonald, C. and Sirianni, C. (eds) *Working in the Service Society*, edited by Cameron MacDonald and Carmen Sirianni, Philadelphia: Temple University Press: 333–58.

—— (1999) 'A Spontaneous loss of enthusiasm: Workplace feminism and the transformation of women's service jobs in the 1970s', *International Labor and Working-Class History*, 56 (Fall): 23–44.

Cobble, D.S. and Merrill, M. (1994) 'Collective bargaining in the hospitality industry', in Voos, P. (ed.) *Contemporary Collective Bargaining in the Private Sector in the 1980s*, Ithaca, NY: Cornell University ILR Press.

Cowell, S. (1993) 'Family policy: A union approach', in Cobble, D.S. (ed.) *Women and Unions: Forging a Partnership*, Ithaca, NY: Cornell University ILR Press:115–28.

Crain, M. and Matheny, K. (1999) 'Labor's divided ranks: Privilege and the United Front ideology', *Cornell Law Review* 84, 6: 1542–626.

Cummings, J. (2000) 'Gore's equal-pay refrain is played for working women', *Wall Street Journal*, 28 August: A-20.

Eaton, S. (1996) 'The customer is always interesting', in MacDonald, C.L. and Sirianni, C. (eds) *Working in a Service Society*, Philadelphia: Temple University Press: 291–332.

Firestein, N. (2000) Director, Labor Project for Working Families. Berkeley, CA. Telephone Interview by D.S. Cobble, 27 March.

Freeman, R.B. and Rogers, J. (1999) *What Workers Want*, Ithaca, NY: Cornell University ILR Press.

Gerstel, N. and Clawson, D. (2000) Unions' responses to family concerns. Paper presented at the Work and Family: Expanding the Horizons Conference, San Francisco, CA, February.

Gilliam, A. (2000) Assistant President's Office, AFL-CIO. Washington, DC. Telephone Interview by D.S. Cobble, 9 June.

Gordon, L. (1994) *Pitied But Not Entitled: Single Mothers and the History of Welfare*, New York: The Free Press.

Gray, L. (1993) 'The route to the top: Female union leaders and union policy', in Cobble, D.S. (ed.) *Women and Unions: Forging a Partnership*, Ithaca, NY: Cornell University ILR Press: 378–93.

—— (2000) Professor, Cornell University School of Industrial and Labor Relations. Metropolitan Division. Telephone Interview with D.S. Cobble, 28 March.

Green, J. (1988) 'Union victory: An interview with Kristine Rondeau', *Democratic Left* (Sept.–Oct.): 4–6.

Grimsley, K.D. and Swoboda, F. (1996) 'Women say union local ignored harassment', *Washington Post*, 8 June, Financial Section: C-01.

Grundy, L. and Firestein, N. (1997) 'Work, Family, and the Labor Movement', Cambridge, MA: Radcliffe Public Policy Institute's Changing Work in America Series.

Hallock, M. (1993) 'Unions and the gender wage gap', in Cobble, D.S. (ed.) *Women and Unions: Forging a Partnership*, Ithaca, NY: Cornell University ILR Press: 27–42.

Hart, P.D. and Research Associates (1998) 'Working women's view of the economy, unions, and public policy', in Mort, J.A. (ed.) *Not Your Father's Union Movement*, New York: Verso.

Harriford, D. (1993) 'Comments', in Cobble, D.S. (ed.) *Women and Unions: Forging a Partnership*, Ithaca, NY: Cornell University ILR Press: 402–5.

Hochschild, A. (1983) *The Managed Heart: The Commercialization of Human Feeling*, Berkeley, CA: University of California Press.

Hoerr, J. (1993) *We Can't Eat Prestige: The Women Who Organized Harvard*, Philadelphia: Temple University Press.

Holcomb, B. (2000) Friendly for whose family? A Ms. special report, *Ms. Magazine* April/May.

Hurd, R. (1993) 'Organizing and representing clerical workers: The Harvard model', in Cobble, D.S. (ed.) *Women and Unions: Forging A Partnership*, Ithaca: Cornell University ILR Press.

Hunt, G. and Rayside, D. (2000) 'Labor union response to diversity in Canada and the US', *Industrial Relations* 39, 3, July: 400–44.

Katz, C. (2000) 'Amending the Family and Medical Leave Act'. Remarks at Rutgers University Conference on Family Leave Income in New Jersey, New Brunswick, NJ, 28 July.

Kelleher, K. (1986) 'Acorn organising and Chicago homecare workers', *Labour Research Review* 8 (Spring): 33–45.

Kerchner, C., Koppich, J.E. and Weeres, J.G. (1997) *United Mind Workers: Unions and Teaching in the Knowledge Society*, San Francisco, CA: Jossey-Bass Publishers.

Kilborn, P.T. (1993) 'Strikers at American Airlines say the objective is respect', *The New York Times*, 22 November: A12.

—— (1995) 'Union gets the lowly to sign up: Home care aides are frequent target', *The New York Times*, 21 November: A10.

Kusnet, D. (1998) 'The "America Needs a Raise" campaign: The new labor movement and the politics of living standards', in Mort, J.A. (ed.) *Not Your Father's Union Movement*, London and New York: Verso.

Landau, A. (2000) President of the Harvard Union of Clerical and Technical Workers. Telephone interview with M. Michal, 10 December.

Lander, S. (2000) Executive Council of Pride at Work and AFSCME Research Department. Telephone Discussions with M. Michal.

LCLAA (2000) Online. Available HTTP: / www.lclaa.org. December 20.

Lazarovich, L. (2000) 'Parents on the march', *AFL-CIO* America@Work, 19–20 September.

Levy, F. (1998) *The New Dollars and Dreams: American Incomes and Economic Change*, New York: Russell Sage Foundation.

McCreery, P. and Krupat, K. (1999) Out Front: Lesbians, Gays, and the Struggle for Workplace Rights, Special Issue of *Social Text* (Winter): 1–118.

McNichol, T. (1998) 'My supermarket, my friend', *San Francisco Weekly*, 11 November.

Malveaux, J. (2000) 'Women at work', In *These Times*, 28 November.

Meyerson, H. (1998) 'A second chance: The new AFL-CIO and the prospective revival of American labor', in Mort, J.A. (ed.) *Not Your Father's Union Movement*, London and New York: Verso.

—— (2000) 'Rolling the union on', *Dissent* (Winter): 47–55.

Milkman, R. (1985) 'Women workers, feminism, and the labor movement since the 1960s', in Milkman, R. (ed.) *Women, Work and Protest: A Century of US Women's Labor History*, Boston, MA and London: Routledge and Kegan Paul.

—— (1993) 'Union responses to work force feminization in the U.S.', in Jenson, J. and Mahon, R. (eds) *The Challenge of Restructuring: North American Labor Movements Respond*, Philadelphia: Temple University Press.

Mills, N. (2000) Comments. MIT Task Force on Reconstructing America's Labor Market Institutions Meeting, 4 February, Cambridge, MA.

Montgomery, D. (1979) *Workers' Control In America*, Cambridge: Cambridge University Press.

NCPE (2000) 'Gender wage gap update', *Newsletter*, 27 September.

Needleman, R. (1986) 'Turning the tide: women, unions, and labor education', in *Labor Studies Journal* 10 (Winter): 203–35.

—— (2000) Professor, Division of Labor Studies. Indiana University. Gary, Indiana. Telephone Interview by D.S. Cobble, October 17.

Nussbaum, K. (1998) 'Women in labor: Always the bridesmaid?', in Mort, J.A. (ed.) *Not Your Father's Union Movement*, London and New York: Verso.

—— (2000) Director, Working Women's Department, AFL-CIO. Washington, DC. Personal interview with D.S. Cobble, January 10.

O'Farrell, B. (1999) 'Women in blue-collar and related occupations at the end of the millennium', *Quarterly Review of Economics and Finance* 39: 699–722.

Reskin, B. and Padavic, I. (1994) *Men and Women At Work*, Thousand Oaks, CA: Pine Forge Press.

Roberts, P.R. (1993) 'Comments', in Cobble, D.S. (ed.) *Women and Unions: Forging a Partnership*, Ithaca, NY: Cornell University ILR Press: 349–56.

Roediger, D.R. and Foner, P.S. (1989) *Our Own Time: A History of American Labor and the Working Day*, New York: Greenwood Press.

Rondeau, K. (1991) Organizing Harvard Workers. Lecture given at the University and College Labor Education Association Annual Conference, Miami, 23 April.

Ross, M. (1999) Attorney, Leonard, Carder, Nathan, Zuckerman, Ross, Chin & Remar, Oakland, California. Interview by M. Bielski, 11 December.

Schneider, B. (1988) 'Invisible and independent: Lesbians' experiences in the workplace', in Stromberg, A. and Harkess, S. (eds) *Women Working: Theories and Facts in Perspective*, Mountain View, CA: Mayfield Publishing Company.

Sirianni, C. (1988) 'Self-management of time: A democratic alternative', *Socialist Review* (October-December): 5–56.

Spalter-Roth, R., Hartmann, H. and Collins, N. (1994) 'What do unions do for women?', in *Restoring the Promise of American Labor Law*, Friedman, S., Hurd, R.W., Oswald, R.A. and Seeber, R.L., Ithaca: Cornell University ILR Press: 193–206.

Sweeney, J.J. (1996) *America Needs a Raise*, Boston, MA: Houghton Mifflin Company.

—— (1999) 'The growing alliance between gay and union activists', *Social Text* (Winter): 31–8.

Thompson, E.P. (1963) *The Making of the English Working Class*, New York: Vintage.

Tillotson, K. (2000) 'Domestic-partner benefits increasing', *Star-Tribune* (Minneapolis, MN), 31 October.

Uchitelle, L. (1999) 'Minimum wages, city by city', *New York Times*, 19 November, Section C: 1.

UAW (2000). Online. Available HTTP: / www.uaw.com/publications/releases/mitsu626/ htm (accessed 4 April 2000).

U.S. Commission on Civil Rights (March 1982) *Nonreferral Unions and Equal Employment Opportunity*, Washington, DC.: GPO.

U.S. Department of Labor (USDL), Bureau of Labor Statistics. (2000) *Employment and Earnings*, January.

Veverka, M. (1998) 'Safeway, union should stop posturing over greeting policy', *San Francisco Chronicle*, 11 September, 1998: B1.

Walker, H. (1994) Lead Organiser, Home Care Division, SEIU Local 250, San Francisco, telephone interview conducted by J. Nagrod, 3 November.

WWD, AFL-CIO (2000) Online. Available HTTP: /www.aflcio.org/women/exec 99.htm. 31 October.

York, C. (1993) 'Bargaining for work and family benefits', in Cobble, D.S. (ed.) *Women and Unions: Forging a Partnership*, Ithaca, NY: Cornell University ILR Press: 129–43.

12 Organised labour, sexual diversity and union activism in Canada[1]

Gerald Hunt

Introduction

A growing number of unions around the world have assumed a role in combating discrimination based on sexual orientation (Hunt 1999a). Labour movements in countries such as Australia, Canada, Britain, the Netherlands and Germany now take sexual orientation issues seriously and have supported lesbian and gay rights through such things as collective bargaining initiatives, support for legal challenges, and lobbying governments for legislative change. Although labour's commitment to sexual diversity issues is uneven – still limited to a few developed countries and tending to be stronger among public sector unions – shifts towards more inclusive policies and strategies have been impressive.

In many ways, Canadian labour has been at the forefront of these developments. Unions and labour federations in Canada now have one of the most progressive records in relation to sexual diversity issues found anywhere in the world. Activists working within the labour movement have pushed it to play an active role in pressing for greater recognition of sexual diversity within the broader legal and political policy arenas, as well as in collective bargaining and arbitration processes. In this chapter I assess these developments, first by providing an overview of the many legal and constitutional changes that have taken place in relation to sexual diversity, and second by highlighting the contribution of the labour movement to these and other related developments. Subsequently, I consider Canadian labour's contribution to sexual diversity activism relative to other countries.

The Canadian context

A number of social and legislative changes have positioned Canada as one of the most progressive and liberal jurisdictions in the world in relation to homosexuality. In 1969, the Canadian government decriminalised homosexual behaviour between consenting adults, creating the pathway for a vibrant lesbian and gay rights movement. The subsequent adoption of the Canadian Charter of Rights and Freedoms in 1982 provided a legal framework for political action.

A changed legal landscape

Changes in the Canadian constitutional landscape increasingly lured lesbian and gay activists towards litigation strategies based on equal rights. As David Rayside (1998), Miriam Smith (1999) and Barry Adam (1995) all point out in their profiles of the lesbian and gay movement, the creation of a Charter of Rights offered a powerful incentive for activists to focus on rights since it regulated relations between governments or between governments and citizens, and could be used to challenge the constitutionality of anti-gay provincial and federal statutes. Although the Charter did not explicitly include sexual orientation as one of the protected grounds, from the mid-1980s some human rights tribunals and courts were beginning to rule that sexuality was sufficiently 'analogous' to those grounds that were named as to be implicitly covered. In 1993, the *Mossop* case became the first same-sex spousal rights case to reach the Supreme Court. It involved the appeal of a union-supported grievance by a man who had been denied bereavement leave by his employer, the Government of Canada, to attend the funeral of his partner's father. The case which was brought forward on the basis of discrimination on the grounds of family status lost, although the Chief Justice at the time suggested that the result might have been different if it had been framed as a Charter challenge on the basis of sexual orientation, further reinforcing the Supreme Courts preparedness to address the issue formally. In 1995, a ruling by the Supreme Court of Canada (Egan v. Canada) did agree that in principle the exclusion of same-sex relationships in legislation providing benefits for heterosexual relationships was discriminatory. Despite some setbacks, the late 1990s witnessed a high proportion of judicial and quasi-judicial cases being decided in favour of treating same-sex relationships as equivalent to common-law heterosexual relationships, the latter having long established rights very close to those accorded marital relationships.

In tandem with significant developments in the judiciary, there have been major shifts in provincial and federal legislation covering human rights. In December 1977, Quebec became the first province to amend its Human Rights Code to include sexual orientation as a protected grounds for discrimination, followed by Ontario and British Columbia in the mid-1980s. By the year 2000, all of the Canadian provinces had amended their human rights codes to include sexual orientation explicitly, although in some provinces such as Alberta, only in the face of pressure to ensure conformity with the constitutionally-entrenched Charter. Ironically, the federal government was among the last to amend its own human rights code, doing so only in 1996 after more than a decade of procrastinating.

Legal recognition for same-sex partners has come later and continues to expand. In a highly publicised 1999 decision (M. v. H.), the Supreme Court ruled that same-sex partners had the same obligations for support after the break-up of a relationship as opposite-sex couples. In the wake of this and other significant legal shifts, several jurisdictions have taken or been forced to take additional steps to remove hetero-sexual bias in other acts and regulations that affect same-sex partnerships. British Columbia, Ontario and Quebec, for example, have amended most of their provincial legislation to remove anti-lesbian and gay bias, including the right of same-sex couples to adopt children. Although the Immigration Act (1976) has not been formally changed or up-dated, same-sex immigration for alien partners can and does occur under the Act's family reunification provisions.

Developments in the Canadian military offer an example of the speed and breadth of change. Until the early 1990s, the armed forces could with impunity fire members who were found to be gay or lesbian. However, a court challenge undertaken by former officer Michelle Douglas in 1992, with the assistance of Svend Robinson, an openly gay member of parliament, and free legal assistance by a prominent Toronto lawyer, forced the military to drop the ban on homosexuals (Rayside 1998). By 1998, the armed forces were advertising in their recruiting programmes the fact that they provide the same benefits, opportunities and protections to all members and their families, regardless of sexual orientation (albeit only for those sufficiently brave to be open and disclosing at work in what many consider still to be a very machismo culture).

Work still to be done

On the down side, provincial and federal governments continue to procrastinate, rather than do the right thing and quickly remove discriminatory provisions from the stacks of legislation defining spouse in heterosexual terms. Far too many employers seem prepared to offer relationship-based benefit and pension systems only when confronted with litigation. Same-sex partner immigration remains at the whim of sympathetic officials, rather than equal footing with heterosexuals. Confusing and contradictory laws continue to govern family and inheritance law, and there is no possibility of gay marriage or partner registration for those who are drawn to this option. As well, there continue to be significant differences in what is available and tolerated between regions of the country. Even in the large, relatively progressive centre of Toronto, the suggestion of gay-positive education programming in the school system can rally formidable opposition. Nevertheless, much has been achieved in a relatively short period of time, especially in relation to many other parts of the world.

The Canadian labour movement

Over the years, parts of the Canadian labour movement have played an increasingly supportive role in bringing about legal and constitutional change in relation to sexual minorities. Some unions and federations have lobbied government for legislative change, and provided financial and professional support to many of the pivotal legal challenges that have taken place since the mid-1980s. Some unions successfully fought for non-discrimination policies inclusive of gays and lesbians, including same-sex benefit packages, long before such things were encoded into the law, and in this way created precedents that helped to change the law. As a result of these changes, unionised workers in Canada now have access to some of the most inclusive policies and benefits in the world. These developments are the product of years of activist pressure inside and outside unions, and have coincided with sweeping changes in the make-up of the labour movement itself. A labour movement that was once dominated by white males in manufacturing and craft-based jobs, has now been replaced by one that is equally female, much more racially mixed, and increasingly dominated by middle-aged, well educated public sector workers.

Labour's diversifying membership[2]

The Canadian labour movement continues to be an important force in shaping social and economic policy (Heron 1996; Peirce 2000). Union membership reached 3.6 million by the year 2000, reflecting a pattern of continuing growth throughout most of the twentieth century. Unlike most other industrialised countries, union density remained relatively stable at around 34 per cent during the 1990s (although there has been a slight pattern of decline since 1998). From the 1960s onward, union members have been increasingly drawn from the public sector (government, education and health), versus the traditional strongholds of goods producing sectors such as mining and manufacturing. Over 70 per cent of public sector workers are unionised versus just over 18 per cent of private sector workers. The highest union rates are now found among workers in the 45–54 age range and those with some university or college education. Over the years, increasing numbers of women have joined unions: in the last three decades of the twentieth century, women's share of total union membership almost tripled; during the same period, union density for men slightly declined. Union coverage for women overall in 1999 was 32 per cent versus 33 per cent for men, although the female unionisation rate is higher than men's in the public sector and lower in the private sector. In tandem with a more racially diverse population (11 per cent visible minority overall) the labour movement is also more racially mixed (about 21 per cent of male and 32 per cent of female union members identify as visible or ethnic minorities). Still another trend is the increasing number of large unions. In 1966, only four unions had memberships of over 50,000, but by 1995 18 large unions represented over half of the unionised workforce (2.2 million members) and 10 unions had over 80,000 members each. Another trend has been the decreasing numbers of international unions (i.e. those with headquarters outside of Canada) and the rise of Canadian-based unions. In 1962, more than 66 per cent of union members belonged to international unions, mostly based in the United States, but by 1995 this figure had dropped to around 29 per cent, reflecting the rise of public sector unions which are required to be Canadian-based. Nevertheless, large and powerful international unions head-quartered in the United States continue to be a significant force in Canada labour and represent large numbers of steelworkers, electrical workers, aerospace workers, and food preparation workers. As with other industrialised countries, the union movement in Canada has been confronted with increased globalisation of production, free-trading agreements, decreasing public support, and a political shift towards the conservative right.

The industrial relations system in Canada is quite decentralised. Collective bargaining units are usually established at the level of the firm, although most of the larger unions prepare master agreements that become collective bargaining templates for local bargaining (Peirce 2000). As a result, both the union headquarters and the union local are important targets for those seeking to make changes to collective agreements. Unions in Canada bargain for a wide variety of employment perks and benefits, including extended health care insurance, pensions, leaves of absence and various allowances. They can also influence policy in areas such as harassment, violence and pay equity, making them very important sites for activist initiatives.

For most of its history, the union movement in Canada emphasised wages and working conditions and fought to improve the standard of living for the working classes (Heron 1996). However, many of the changes I have just outlined – more women, more racial diversity, more public sector unions, more unionised professionals, especially in health and education – helped to create a labour mosaic where gender and diversity activism could take root, and a labour movement somewhat more amenable to the equity issues raised by women and minorities.

Gender and labour

Gender issues were the first to appear on labour's radar screen. As early as the 1970s, some unions were beginning to include gender and minority issues as part of their mandate. This was largely in response to concerns brought forward by the increasing number of union members who were women and feminists, drawn in particular from the very rapid expansion of public sector unions throughout the 1970s (Briskin 1999, this volume; Warskett 1996; Sugiman 1994; Briskin and McDermott 1993; Kumar and Acri 1992; White 1993).

Over the last three decades of the twentieth century, labour's progress around gender has been dramatic. As Briskin points out (1999: 169), Canadian unions have 'become a central vehicle for organising around women's issues and a key player in the women's movement'. All labour federations and most unions have policies on workplace equality for women in areas such as childcare, pay equity, employment equity, affirmative action, sexual harassment, and violence. Many also provide formal positions for women in senior decision-making bodies. Briskin (this volume) argues that the achievements made by women have come about largely through women's separate organising into committees or caucuses at an early and formative stage. It was in these separate spaces that women built support, articulated their concerns and goals, and developed strategies for confronting the male-dominated union leadership as a collective voice for change.

Minorities and labour

Labour's engagement with a broader set of diversity issues came later, following on the gains that had been made by women (White 1993; Genge 1998). It was the advent of feminist activism inside the labour movement that helped to create pathways to a broader-based discussion about equity. Women activists had been the first to challenge notions of union solidarity, bargaining agendas, and organising

Table 12.1 Equality structures in selected Canadian labour organisations

	CLC	OFL	CUPE	UFCW	PSAC	USWA	CAW	CSN	TU	CEP
Women										
Reserved seats*	Y	Y	Y	N	Y	N	Y	Y	Y	Y
Central Committee**	Y	Y	Y	Y	Y	Y	Y	Y	Y	Y
Central Conference***	Y	Y	Y	Y	Y	Y	Y	Y	N	Y
Central Staff Officer****	Y	Y	Y	Y	Y	Y	Y	Y	N	Y
Lesbian/gay										
Reserved seats*	Y	Y	N	N	N	N	N	N	N	N
Central Committee**	Y	Y	Y	N	Y	Y	Y	Y	N	Y
Central Conference***	Y	Y	N	N	N	N	Y	Y	N	N
Central Staff Officer****	Y	Y	Y	N	Y	Y	Y	Y	N	Y
Race/ethnicity										
Reserved seats*	Y	Y	Y	N	Y	Y	Y	Y	N	Y
Central Committee**	Y	Y	Y	N	Y	Y	Y	Y	N	Y
Central Conference***	Y	Y	Y	N	Y	Y	Y	N	N	N
Central Staff Officer****	Y	Y	Y	N	Y	Y	Y	Y	N	Y
Disabled workers										
Reserved seats*	Y	Y	Y	N	N	N	N	N	N	N
Central Committee**	Y	Y	Y	N	N	Y	N	N	N	Y
Central Conference***	Y	N	N	N	Y	N	N	N	N	N
Central Staff Officer****	Y	Y	Y	N	Y	Y	Y	Y	N	Y

Notes

Y   = YES
N   = NO
* = one or more seats on executive board reserved for this constituency.
** = centralised, formal committee or caucus dealing with this constituencies issues.
*** = at least one conference or special meeting has been held specifically for or about this constituency.
**** = a central paid staff person with specific responsibility for the issues and concerns of this constituency (this person may have responsibility for other groups as well).

(Source: Based on data collected from union websites and publications, as well as personal contacts. Many unions are currently confronting equity issues and information in this table is changing rapidly.)

strategies, and other equity-seeking groups followed their lead. Most Canadian labour organisations now have exemplary policies to do with racial and ethnic discrimination in areas such as harassment, employment and pay equity, although some fight around these issues much more aggressively than others. Some of the unions representing public sector workers, auto workers, communication workers and steel workers, for example, now have reserved seats for racial and ethnic minorities, as well as national committees to oversee and monitor racial diversity issues. Disability issues have had much less prominence in the labour movement, but even here there are signs of momentum. The Public Service Alliance of Canada was the first union to have a conference focusing on workers with disabilities, and in late 2000 the Canadian Labour Congress organised the first national congress on disability rights and labour, outlining a number of strategies to begin a more assertive engagement with disabled people.

Table 12.1 provides an overview of formal developments that have taken place in selected federations and unions in Canada in relation to gender, race, disability and sexual orientation.

Labour and sexuality

I have been following labour's engagement with sexual orientation bias for several years (Hunt 1999b; 1997; Hunt and Rayside 2000). The information I have gathered through surveys, interviews and archival research highlights the fact that activists concerned with sexuality issues were often able to benefit from the changes in attitudes, polices and structures that had been achieved by women. In many instances, lesbian and gay issues were first raised (sometimes confrontationally) within women's committees and support groups, often by lesbians who felt their concerns warranted more attention, both from women and within the broader union membership. Subsequently, these activists (using the skills and strategies they had learned within women's groups) formed separate support groups and caucuses of their own to deal specifically with issues related to sexuality. The issues they articulated included the introduction of bias-free provisions around leaves, grievances and harassment. These separate caucuses became a location for lesbians, and later on for gay men, to gain self-confidence and build political strength inside their unions, just as they had been for a previous generation of women activists. (At the same time, many of these pioneering lesbians remained active in women's issues and union caucuses dealing with gender.)

Labour's formal engagement with sexual orientation issues started to take off in the 1990s, but note has been made of such developments much earlier. Sue Genge, an early lesbian/labour/feminist activist, recalls the presence of informal groups as early as the 1970s, mainly as subgroups at women's conferences and national congresses. Genge undertook the first significant accounting of the status of gays and lesbians in the labour movement, and found that a few unions had negotiated collective agreements that included a non-discrimination clause inclusive of sexual orientation by 1980 (Genge 1983; 1998). In the early 1990s, Julie White (1993) undertook an accounting of union engagement with gender and diversity, and found that while gender issues were definitely on labour's agenda, race and other diversity issues were only beginning to emerge. She found that a couple of labour federations, along with a handful of unions, were dealing with sexual orientation, and predicted it would become a much more significant issue as the 1990s unfolded. She was right.

The pioneers

The Canadian Union of Postal Workers (CUPW)

CUPW was the first Canadian union to organise around the rights of gays and lesbians. By the late 1970s, several locals had negotiated collective agreements prohibiting discrimination on the basis of sexual orientation. A west coast local of CUPW also initiated the first arbitration case involving same-sex benefits in Canada. The case involved a lesbian wishing a special leave in order to care for her partner of sixteen years who was ill, a provision readily available to heterosexual couples. Even though her collective agreement contained a clause prohibiting discrimination on the basis of sexual orientation, the case was lost. It was, however, the first time a union had supported a challenge over same-sex benefits all the way to arbitration. After this, progress at CUPW seems to have stalled, perhaps because of an increasingly harsh negotiating environment dominated by downsizing and restructuring battles. Recently, though, the union negotiated the only collective agreement in Canada that includes 'marriage' leave for up to five days for same-sex couples. Its harassment policy is also among the harshest in the country and allows the removal of homophobic harassers to other work sites, including other cities. An informal lesbian and gay organising group does exist, but is not yet an official caucus or committee of the Union.

The Canadian Labour Congress (CLC)

By any measure, The Canadian Labour Congress, the largest and most influential central federation in the country, has been a pioneering leader in the fight for lesbian and gay rights in the union movement. As far back as 1980 the CLC passed a resolution calling for the inclusion of sexual orientation in provincial human rights codes (at that time only the Province of Quebec had taken this step), the Canadian Human Rights Act, and the Canadian Charter of Rights and Freedoms, and encouraging its members and affiliates to bargain for the inclusion of sexual orientation in the non-discrimination clauses of their collective agreements. Then, at its 1986 convention, resolutions instructing the leadership of the CLC to cooperate with other organisations seeking human rights amendments on sexual orientation, and to begin the process of preparing a policy statement on lesbian and gay rights, were passed. Following this, during its 1990 convention, a resolution calling for same-sex benefit coverage as a collective bargaining priority was passed, as were resolutions calling for lobbying to pressure the government to include sexual orientation in the Canadian Human Rights Act, and for the creation of materials to educate affiliates about issues of concern to gays and lesbians. Not long after, at the 1994 convention, the organisation overwhelmingly approved the following comprehensive policy statement:

> (T)he labour movement can and should play a key role in the achievement of lesbian, gay and bisexual rights. This is an integral part of the new approach to unionism which is essential if we are to survive as a vital force in society.
>
> (CLC 1994)

A position paper accompanying the policy directive called for workplace education about homophobic harassment, political action, public campaigning, legal action, lesbian and gay participation in union management, union participation in non-union forums dealing with homophobia, and negotiation of inclusive collective agreement language. Specific recommendations included establishing a lesbian, gay and bisexual working group with caucus status, encouraging provincial federations of labour and labour councils to include sexual orientation in anti-harassment policies, participating 'visibly' in gay pride parades across the country, preparing and distributing educational materials and offering educational workshops to CLC officers and affiliates. As well, affiliates were encouraged to recognise same-sex spousal relationships and make benefit coverage a priority at the bargaining table. The CLC also committed itself to a future evaluation of how well it had been able to implement its policies and directives.

Much of the CLC's early momentum emerged within its own internal committee structure. One insider suggests that CLC's success was the product of 'networks, networks, networks', explaining that issues were 'inched' forward by activists starting as early as the 1970s in committee meetings, caucuses and coffee conversations (sometimes involving acrimonious and divisive debate). Over the years, the foundation for a coherent and progressive policy was secured, 'bit by bit' and 'inch by inch'. As a result, when the time came to debate and formalise policy at national congresses, most of the dissent had already been worked through, and key constituents were already on side. By this point as well, there was a core group of activists ready, willing and able to stand before the mike and passionately make their case. Insiders also cite the fact that Bob White (former head of the Canadian Auto Workers, and President of the CLC at the time of these early developments) was from the beginning a strong advocate for social justice issues in language unequivocally supportive of lesbian and gay rights.

By most measures, the CLC has met its goals. In 1995, a Lesbian, Gay and Bisexual Working Group was formalised and given official status within the CLC; sexual diversity issues are now part of a senior officer's portfolio; a seminar on 'Fighting Heterosexism' travels across the country; CLC representatives visibly participate in Gay and Lesbian Pride Festivals around the country; and many of its affiliate federations and unions have adopted pro-gay policies. In 1996, the CLC lobbied the Federal Government very assertively when it was debating amendments to the Human Rights Code to add sexual orientation as a protected grounds, and intervened in a successful Supreme Court case that forced the Alberta Government to include sexual orientation as a protected grounds in its human rights legislation. The CLC also organised the first lesbian and gay labour conference held in Canada in 1997, following that up with a local conference in the prairie region, and another national conference in 2001. At its 1999 convention, the CLC passed a resolution calling for a national, public, gay-positive, anti-homophobia, education and political action campaign. As part of the campaign, in early 2000 the CLC launched an initiative to raise awareness in union and non-union workplaces about lesbian and gay rights. Also at the 1999 convention, the CLC passed a resolution to establish a review committee regarding equity issues and to give the Executive Council the authority to implement recommendations mid-convention. The committee recommended the establishment of several new vice-presidential seats, including one to represent lesbian and gay members, and one to represent workers with disabilities, and these changes were implemented in the autumn of 2000. The current vice-president for lesbian and gay issues comes from the Communications, Energy and Paperworkers Union. In the first part of 2001, the CLC published a discussion paper dealing with transgender issues in the labour movement – perhaps the first of its kind in the world – outlining the complexity of the issues involved and laying the groundwork for a set of policy directives. Collectively, these developments highlight and strengthen the CLC's position as world leader when it comes to sexual diversity initiatives.

Provincial labour federations

Labour federations in British Columbia, Saskatchewan, Manitoba, Ontario, Quebec and Nova Scotia were the first to pick-up on the CLC's initiatives around lesbian and gay rights. First on the scene and in a leadership role ever since has been the Ontario Federation of Labour (OFL). The OFL was among the first organisations in Canada to include sexual orientation in its non-discrimination policies and has led the way in terms of pro-gay education programmes and lobbying efforts inside and outside the union movement in Ontario. In 1994, the OFL became the first provincial labour federation to establish a lesbian and gay caucus, and in 1998 the group was elevated to a standing committee with its own budget.

Activists point to the rise of a feminist agenda within the Federation in the 1970s as the catalyst for change in the organisation's culture and priorities. Once gender issues were raised and legitimised, the door opened for issues brought forward by minorities in general and sexual minority activists in particular. Within this framework, activists credit the OFL's successful gays and lesbian campaigns to 'tons of backroom lobbying' at conferences and meetings, in much the same way as had happened at the CLC. Equally important, was the emergence of lesbian support networks that emerged at women's meetings and conferences. Even before such groups were formalised, they played an important role not only for support and solidarity, but in strategy formulation as well. The presence of an 'out' lesbian in a senior position who was committed to an activist agenda was also an important catalyst in bringing about change.

The current Gay, Lesbian and Bisexual Committee (GLBC) has members drawn from unions representing steel workers, auto workers, postal workers and the public sector. It meets three times a year and publishes the 'Rainbow Bulletin' which is sent to all OFL members. In 1997, the Committee convinced the OFL to approve a constitutional change establishing a position on its executive board for a vice-president to represent the interests of gay, lesbian and bisexual members. This vice-president is elected by the GLBC and the guidelines specify he or she must be 'out'. The current incumbent is a lesbian from the Communications, Energy and Paperworkers Union. In yet another creative move, the Committee initiated a 'positive space' campaign in May 1999. This campaign encouraged people to display a positive space sticker on their office door, bulletin boards and publications to indicate they were contributing to the creation of an environment welcoming of sexual diversity. In September 1999, the OFL became the first provincial labour organisation to sponsor a lesbian, gay and bisexual labour conference. It brought together a total of 200 participants from across Ontario to develop strategies for confronting discrimination in the workplace, unions and broader community.

Quebec federations

The three main provincial labour federations in Quebec have also been active in the area of lesbian and gay rights from an early period, although the Confédération des syndicats nationaux (CSN) has been involved from an earlier point than either the Fédération des travailleurs et travailleuses du Québec (FTQ) or the Centrale de l'Enseignement du Québec (CEQ). As early as 1975, union activists drawn in particularly from the hotel and restaurant sectors, were pushing the CSN to lobby for the inclusion of sexual orientation in the human rights code of Quebec. By 1988, there was a broader-based working group of gays and lesbians who became a formally constituted group in 1991. By 2000, all three federations had some form of lesbian and gay committee and issues related to discrimination based on sexuality had become an important part of their discourse. In 1997, the CSN, the FTQ and the CEQ helped to form the 'forum des gais et lesbiennes syndiqués du Québec', a broad-based labour group specifically organised to pressure the Quebec government to overhaul provincial laws and regulations discriminating against gays, lesbians and their families. In June 1999, the group celebrated success when the Quebec government modified 28 provincial statutes in areas such as family law, insurance, health benefits, estates and taxation, so that homosexual and heterosexual couples would have the same rights.

Canadian Union of Public Employees

The Canadian Union of Public Employees (CUPE), the largest union in the country, has been at the forefront of lesbian and gay/labour issues since the 1980s (Wagner 1993). Pressure for change began at the grassroots level, especially amongst library workers, and was helped considerably by a very receptive response at headquarters once issues and concerns were raised. A lesbian and gay group, 'The Pink Triangle

Committee', was formalised in 1991 and it was the first in the world to prepare an information kit on sexual orientation, covering topics such as how to negotiate inclusive contract language and deal with insurance providers. The kit, sent to all locals, has now been revised several times and has become a model for other unions around the world.

In the early days, the union's positive engagement with sexual orientation did produce some opposition. As one activist put it, 'CUPE had its share of "old liners", for whom homosexuality represented a category for contempt rather than celebration.'

In spite of some grassroots dissent, over the years, CUPE has racked up an impressive set of achievements at both the local and headquarters level. Almost every CUPE collective agreement has a non-discrimination clause inclusive of sexual orientation. Many collective agreements have provisions for same-sex benefits, and had them long before employers were required by law to take these actions. Equally important, CUPE has financially supported many of the important legal cases that have shifted the constitutional landscape to do with sexual orientation.

CUPE itself initiated one of the most important court cases in Canada. At issue was the heterosexual definition of spouse encoded in the federal Income Tax Act, and specifically its use to control pension benefits. The Act has great leverage over all pension plans in the country because the tax deductibility of pension contributions and pay-outs requires that plans be registered with Revenue Canada (and therefore meet the heterosexual-only definition of spouse). The result was that even employers, such as CUPE, who wanted to extend benefit and pension programmes to include same-sex couples were at risk of losing their income tax deductions, and were forced to implement separate plans for lesbians and gays. Nancy Rosenberg and Margaret Evans worked for CUPE itself, and convinced their organisation to lodge a challenge to the Income Tax Act when CUPE failed to get its expansively-defined pension plan registered. In 1998 the Ontario Court of Appeal ruled in their favour with a ringing declaration of entitlement to such benefits. The Court unanimously 'read' a broader definition of a spouse into the relevant provision of the Income Tax Act, a reading that the federal government acquiesced in by deciding against appealing the judgement to the Supreme Court of Canada.

Activists inside CUPE readily acknowledge how much the organisation has achieved, but at the same time are aware of work still to be done. Sinda, for example, a lesbian and CUPE member from Saskatchewan, until recently felt unsafe to be out at work, even though she was aware of CUPE's achievements.[3] That changed in 1997, after she attended the CUPE Summer School course on discrimination and harassment in the workplace and found that 'not one thing was mentioned about lesbian and gay issues during the entire five-day course. My union was silent on the matter. That was unacceptable to me.' For Sinda this was a transformational event and within a year she was serving as the CUPE Saskatchewan representative on the National Pink Triangle Committee and the Saskatchewan Federation of Labour's Solidarity and Pride Committee. She also decided to help teach the Pride in

CUPE course at the Saskatchewan CUPE Winter School, but was surprised and disappointed to find it had to be cancelled due to low enrolment. And then, at the lesbian and gay Pride March, she was shocked to see there were so few CUPE members in attendance that she had to ask a friend to help her carry the union banner. She muses that 'it's thrilling being involved in the National Pink Triangle Committee . . . CUPE is progressive and we're very much a leader in the legal fights for equality rights. But locally, we have a long way to go', highlighting the very real fact of urban–rural gaps in terms of policy, initiatives and levels of visible support.

Auto workers

The Canadian Auto Workers (CAW) is the largest private-sector union in the country. It is a more diverse union than its name implies, representing workers in fisheries, aerospace, electronics, automobile production and parts, shipbuilding, airlines, mining and hospitality. Recently, it organised several Starbucks Coffee Shops on the west coast. It was the earliest private-sector union in Canada, and probably in the world, to tackle lesbian and gay rights.

The CAW's engagement with sexual orientation began in the mid-1980s, mainly the result of activist pressure at the local level. The call for change and a more inclusive union came primarily from locals associated with the automobile manufacturing plants in southwestern Ontario, and flight attendants. One women recalls putting an advertisement in her local newspaper as a way of drawing-out gays and lesbians in her community who were members of the union. Discovering she was not alone, and that other people also wanted the union to do more around harassment and benefit issues, provided the momentum for an activist campaign. Similar to CUPE, appeals for action received a quick and principled response at CAW headquarters, helped by the presence of a sympathetic union president and a Human Rights Department that had already been mapping a strategy in the area of lesbian and gay rights.

The response among some of the rank and file about the idea of the union tackling issues associated with sexuality was less than enthusiastic. The president of the CAW indicated that in the early days he received more negative mail from members on the issue of the union's involvement in lesbian and gay rights than on any other topic. Even in the face of resistance, the union leadership persevered, and has been a very active participant in sexual diversity issues throughout the 1990s. The CAW now has a central 'Pink and Black Committee' and three regionally-based lesbian and gay groups. Over the years it has fought some very hard battles to get same-sex benefit coverage in most of its collective agreements. This was especially the case within the airline sector, a response not only to the high profile of activists in the sector, but also to the challenge of the particularly hostile and anti-gay stance that had been taken in the early days by the two major Canadian airlines. The CAW has often been at the forefront of lobbying efforts aimed at legislative change, and has financially supported many high profile and precedent-setting legal challenges. The union has also prepared and delivered education programmes designed to curb homophobia in the rank and file membership, and recently produced a very hard hitting video about a lesbian being harassed on the shop floor.

Other unions

Although CUPE and the CAW offer particularly dramatic early cases of union involvement in sexual diversity issues, a few other unions were involved from an early period. Unions such as Public Service Alliance of Canada, British Columbia Employees Government Union, Ontario Public Service Employees Union, Hospital Employees Union in British Columbia, Syndicat canadien de la fonction publique, Communication, Energy and Paper Workers Union, along with some of the teachers and nurses unions were all involved from an early date. To take one example, among the earliest cases involving sexual orientation that were taken to grievance, and subsequently to arbitration, tribunal and courts, were ones initiated by the Public Service Alliance of Canada (PSAC), Canada's main federal employees' union. Government workers' unions in Ontario and British Columbia area are also distinguished in their early attention to sexual orientation prejudice. Prior to 1992, these union grievances on benefit plan exclusions were largely unsuccessful, and might have remained so for a longer period of time, had not unions such as PSAC aggressively supported employees seeking expansive readings of anti-discrimination language.

Moving forward: labour and sexual diversity into the twenty-first century

Following on the pioneering work of a few unions and federations, more and more labour organisations have become active in the area of lesbian and gay rights. Nearly all the provincial labour federations now have lesbian and gay inclusive policies, and most have a formally recognised lesbian and gay group. The Postal Workers Union, after a period of relative inactivity, now seems poised to reengage more assertively, and unions representing workers in the services, hotel and restaurant sectors have also been nudged towards a gay-positive position. In some instances this is limited to a policy statement, in others to collective bargaining initiatives and in others to educational endeavours.

As Brown (2000) points outs in a recent analysis of 200 Canadian collective agreements, however, public sector unions, large unions, and Canadian-based unions continue to stand out amongst those actively addressing the employment-based issues of concern to lesbians and gays. Unions representing workers in the traditional, male-dominated trades, such as plumbers, carpenters, and electricians, continue to be the group that has taken little action, opting merely to comply with changing legal requirements. International unions with headquarters in the United States, which still represent many of these trades, have tended to be the least active. The Teamsters, for example, which represent nearly 100,000 workers in Canada, have undertaken no initiatives on their own. These unions fall into a smaller and smaller category of unions that do not resist change, but at the same time do little or nothing to support change in the area of gay rights.

Notably, the Canadian unit of the United Steel Workers of America (USWA) offers an example of an international union that has opted to go against the trend. Although a couple of locals were active around sexuality issues fairly early, it is only since the late 1990s that the union headquarters has become more assertively proactive. Activists had been pushing for change for a number of years and cite a dramatic speech given by the union president at a CLC conference as emblematic of a turning point. During this speech he confessed to having 'beat up fags' in the past, and acknowledged that as a common response to homo-sexuals in his union. He then talked of how his entire perspective had changed, and of his realisation that such behaviour was intolerable inside and outside the workplace.

The USWA now has a formal 'Steel Pride' caucus which co-sponsored the 1999 Ontario Federation of Labour's Behind the Rainbow Conference. The union has negotiated same-sex coverage in most collective agreements and is officially committed to enforce actively its members' rights to benefits coverage even in the face of hostile employers and in some cases unsympathetic members. The USWA union is now a visible presence at several lesbian and gay pride marches, and as one dramatic measure of developments, activists cite the fact that same-sex partners dance at union events without much overt ridicule. Interestingly, developments at the Canadian unit of the USWA have coincided with a move towards more autonomy from its American headquarters where there continues to be little activity around sexual diversity.

Labour's involvement with sexual diversity activism throughout the 1980s and 1990s has had a powerful impact on the lesbian and gay rights movement in Canada. Labour's support for more inclusive access to work-based benefits – specifically those benefits routinely accorded to heterosexual partners in both marital and common-law relationships – has been instrumental in making these benefits available to same-sex couples. Whether or not gaining such benefits is a high personal priority, being denied them is clearly discriminatory, and has provided the basis for alliances between labour and sexual diversity activists. Most labour organisations have not yet tackled transgender and transsexual issues.

Sexual diversity and Canadian labour in perspective

Since the 1980s, the Canadian labour movement has demonstrated an increasing commitment to combating sexual orientation discrimination. Labour's support for grievances based on sexual orientation discrimination, and subsequently at arbitration hearings, along with court and legislative challenges, have been instrumental in ensuring that changes in law are applied at a level which directly affects the everyday lives of workers. Union federations, large unions, especially in the public sector, along with the Canadian Auto Workers were pioneers in this work, but have since been joined by a broader base. Union commitment to this and other equity issues continues to vary across and within employment sectors, regions of the country and union categories, but the willingness of more and more unions to take up these issues aggressively is making a significant difference.

The readiness of organised labour to take up these issues and pursue them in these ways owes much to an active lesbian and gay rights movement. Labour activism has taken off in part as a response to greater sexual minority visibility generally and in the workplace specifically. But it has also taken off at a time when individual rights are more and more secured and same-sex relationship recognition and rights have moved to the foreground of activism. This highlighted the issue of inequality in employee benefits, and implicated discriminatory employer policies and biased collective agreements (precisely the location where Canadian unions have significant jurisdiction). The AIDS crisis also brought a focus to the significance of workplace issues.

The developments that have taken place in Canada reflect years of hard work by activists and allies within the trade union movement who often worked behind the scenes for many years before seeing the results of their efforts. The early recognition of the need for support by the CLC and a few influential and pioneering unions such as CUPE and the CAW has been a very important ingredient in Canadian developments. The partnerships that have emerged between labour and sexual diversity activists not only produced more inclusive collective agreement provisions, but have also helped underwrite the legal cases that have been crucial to many of the progressive developments that have taken place in legislative assemblies and courtrooms.

The attentiveness of organised labour in Canada to new constituencies such as gays and lesbians has been part of a more general response to changes in the labour movement itself. The recurrent economic crises that began with the 1970s, the threat posed by pressures towards freer trading agreements and globalisation, combined with increasing numbers of minorities and women, along with the rise in public sector unionisation, have all played a role in increasing union interest in courting new membership and generating new energy.

Issues related to minorities in general and sexual minorities in particular, have tended to emerge after feminists made inroads in union culture. Feminists inside unions were the first to challenge the orthodoxy by raising post-materialist concerns such as harassment and violence, and legitimised the notion that union cultures might be part of the problem. Once women had made gains in terms of policies, priorities and patterns of representation, the doorway was open for others. Equally important, feminists created the concept of separate organising as a way to develop skills and confidence, and articulate demands. In other words, feminists raised labour's consciousness around discrimination, difference and diversity, and developed the idea of self-organising into caucuses. Gays and lesbians benefited from these developments, and were quick to model the idea of separate caucuses as a place to find support, formulate ideas, clarify demands, and confront leadership. The active involvement of lesbian and gay activists working *within* the labour movement has also been an important component in convincing trade union leaders that they were a constituency worthy of fair and equal treatment.

The Canadian experience has some parallels in countries such as Australia, Germany, Britain, the Netherlands, and to a lesser extent the United States (Hunt 1999; Krupat and McCreery 2001). Although it is beyond the scope of this chapter to go into detail on international developments, it is worth noting that activity in these countries has followed a pattern similar to Canada. As with Canada, early union activity has tended to follow progress on women's issues, and has been concentrated in larger, public sector unions and central union confederations, subsequently fanning-out to a wider set of sectors and institutions. Unlike Canada, the political wing of the union movement has played a somewhat stronger role in countries such as Australia and Britain (Ostenfeld 1999; Smith, D. 1999).

Labour's engagement with sexual diversity is relatively new and offers a fertile location for further research. It is now a fact that many unions and federations have adopted lesbian- and gay-friendly policies, but not much is known about the consequences of these actions at the local level. It is timely to assess the impact of these policies on union culture in terms of shop floor behaviour, attitudes and decision-making.

Notes

1 Portions of this essay appeared in Chapters 2 and 15 of *Laboring for Rights: Unions and Sexual Diversity Across Nations*, edited by Gerald Hunt. Reprinted here by permission of Temple University Press copyright 1999 by Temple University Press. All Rights Reserved.
2 The sources for statistics included in this section are: Statistics' Canada (www.statcan. ca) and Akyeampong (1999).
3 Parts of this story are taken from the CUPE website at: www.cupe.on.ca.

Canadian Unions or Federations cited in the text

CAW   Canadian Auto Workers
CEP   Communication, Energy and Paperworkers Union of Canada
CLC   Canadian Labour Congress
CSN   La Confédération des syndicats nationaux
CUPE   Canadian Union of Public Employees
OFL   Ontario Federation of Labour
PSAC   Public Service Alliance of Canada
TU   Teamsters Union (Canadian division)
UFCW   United Food and Commercial Workers International Union (Canadian division)
USWA   United SteelWorkers of America (Canadian division)

References

Adam, B. (1995) *The Rise of a Gay and Lesbian Movement*, Toronto: Maxwell Macmillan Canada Limited.
Akyeampong, E. (1999) 'Unionization: An update', *Perspectives* Autumn: 45–65.

Briskin, L. (1999) 'Unions and women's organising in Canada and Sweden', in Briskin, L. and Eliasson, M. (eds) *Women's Organising and Public Policy in Canada and Sweden*, Montreal and Kingston: McGill-Queens University Press.

Briskin, L. and McDermott, P. (eds) (1993) *Women Challenging Unions: Feminism, Democracy, and Militancy*, Toronto: University of Toronto Press.

Brown, T. (2000) Sexual Orientation Provisions in Canadian Collective Agreements: Preliminary Results. Paper presented at the Canadian Industrial Relations Association (CIRA) Annual Meeting in May at Edmonton, Alberta.

CLC (1994) *Policy Statement: Sexual Orientation*, Ottawa: Canadian Labour Congress.

Genge, S. (1993) 'Lesbians and gays in the union movement', in Briskin, L. and Yanz, L. (eds) *Union Sisters: Women in the Labour Movement*, Toronto: The Women's Press.

—— (1998) 'Solidarity and pride', *Canadian Woman Studies*, 18, 1: 97–9.

Heron, C. (1996) *The Canadian Labour Movement: A Brief History*, 2nd edn, Toronto: James Lorimer and Company Publishers.

Hunt, G. (1997) 'Sexual orientation and the Canadian labour movement', *Relations industrielle/Industrial Relations* 53, 4: 731–53.

—— (ed.) (1999a) *Laboring for Rights: Unions and Sexual Diversity Across Nations*, Philadelphia: Temple University Press.

—— (1999b) 'No longer outsiders: Labor's response to sexual diversity in Canada', in Hunt, G. (ed.) *Laboring for Rights: Unions and Sexual Diversity Across Nations*, Philadelphia: Temple University Press.

Hunt, G. and Rayside, D. (2000) 'Labor union response to diversity in Canada and the United States', *Industrial Relations* 39, 3: 401–44.

Krupat, K. and McCreery, P. (2001) *Out at Work: Building a Gay-Labor Alliance*, Minneapolis: University of Minnesota Press.

Kumar, P. and Acri, L. (1992) 'Unions' collective bargaining agenda on women's issues: The Ontario experience', *Relations Industrielles/Industrial Relations* 47, 4: 623–53.

Mainville, D. and Olineck, C. (1999) 'Unionization in Canada: A retrospective', *Perspectives* Summer: 3–11.

Ostenfeld, S. (1999) 'Sexual identity and the Australian labour movement', in Hunt, G. (ed.) *Laboring for Rights: Unions and Sexual Diversity Across Nations*, Philadelphia: Temple University Press.

Peirce, J. (2000) *Canadian Industrial Relations*, Toronto: Prentice-Hall.

Pocock, B. (ed.) (1997) *Strife: Sex and Politics in Labour Unions*, St. Leonards, Australia: Allen and Unwin.

Rayside, D. (1998) *On the Fringe: Gays and Lesbians in Politics*, Ithaca, NY: Cornell University Press.

Smith, D. (1999) 'The unwanted: 25 years of campaigning for lesbian and gay employment rights', *Gay Times*, July: 64–6.

Smith, M. (1999) *Lesbian and Gay Rights in Canada: Social Movements and Equality-seeking, 1971–1995*, Toronto: University of Toronto Press.

Sugiman, P. (1994) *Labour's Dilemma: The Gender Politics of Auto Workers in Canada, 1937–79*, Toronto: University of Toronto Press.

Wagner, P. (1993) 'Coming out: Homophobia as a union issue', *Our Times* 2, 1: 26–30.

Warskett, R. (1996) 'The politics of difference and inclusiveness within the Canadian labour movement', *Economic and Industrial Democracy* 17, 4: 587–625.

White, J. (1993) *Sisters and Solidarity: Women and Unions in Canada*, Toronto: Thompson Educational Publishing Inc.

13 Sexual politics in (Australian) labour movements

Suzanne Franzway

Introduction

Women in trade unions must deal with the 'sexual politics'[1] that are central to all social institutions, including the trade union movement. 'Sexual politics' includes the complex gender relationships of power as domination, resistance, alliances and pleasures. It has been central to women's historic struggle to become members of trade unions, to gain access to the full range of occupations and to win equal work conditions (D'Aprano 1995; Mumford 1989). However, sexual politics has been largely invisible in union discourses and practices. The effect is that men's sexuality and their gender (difference) can be disregarded, and their dominance of the trade union movement, numerically, culturally and hierarchically is largely ignored. Women and women's interests, by contrast, are perceived as entirely gendered and women have long had to fight to gain recognition of their interests, to win leadership positions and to influence policy. It is men's hostility and resistance that confirm that sexual politics is at stake.

Although men do continue to dominate union leadership, we must be wary of overstating the power of unionists, even men unionists, in contrast to the power of major employers, national governments and transnational corporations. What we need to recognise is that in the sexual politics of trade unionism, the place of men and men's interests is at stake as much as the place of women and women's interests. Sexual politics shifts the focus away from 'women as the problem' and undercuts the simple binary of men/women and fixed gender roles. It opens out to the diversity of multiple and shifting gender identities of masculinities and femininities. This plurality of masculinities recognises that men are not the same as each other; male identity is no more unitary than female identity. Not all men, or masculinities, are dominant. Rather, a specific form of masculinity, of gender identity, prevails. In the Australian trade union movement, it is a white and heterosexual masculinity that is socially dominant or hegemonic (Hage 1998; Connell 1987).[2]

This chapter moves beyond the usual equation of gender with women that forms the basis of attempts to explain the problems of gender inequalities. In the discussion that follows, I examine some of the ways that women unionists are confronted by the long-standing dilemmas of sexual politics. These arise from the pleasures and the dangers of gaining and exercising power, the effects of sexual hostilities, and the conflicts among women over questions of difference, politics and strategy. I argue that meeting the challenge of sexual politics is central to the transformation of labour movement structures and practices. Without such a focus, labour movements will fail to renew their promise or revitalise their purpose.

Research methods

Based on a study of a loose network of women union officials in South Australia where I have been a participant observer for more than two decades, the research methods include: 1) pilot interviews, short questionnaires and the examination of documents such as union journals and minutes of meetings, to identify historical and social contexts, discourses and relevant themes; 2) semi-structured interviews based on structured and open-ended questions with 27 women. These range from appointed organisers to elected senior officials, including all the current women secretaries and presidents as well as several involved in the South Australian Working Women's Centre, the United Trades and Labor Council and the Trade Union Training Authority; 3) participant observation of key women's forums and activities, recorded on a set of field notes for two years. I have occupied elected union positions but I have not held any paid positions.

Australian context

Australian unionism has undergone huge changes at almost every level over the last three decades, shifting away from its foundations in a centralised industrial relations system that regulated wages and conditions. The Australian system of industrial relations was established at the beginning of the last century following the federation of six States into the Commonwealth of Australia in 1901. Both colonial and state governments had played central roles in the country since the invasion of soldiers, convicts and settlers from Britain beginning in 1788. At the end of the economic upheavals in the 1890s, trade unions and employers were prepared to accept a strong degree of state intervention, which established the machinery to recognise trade unions and conciliate or arbitrate disputes. Wages and conditions were negotiated and registered as Awards, which had the force of law; disputed outcomes for both parties were finally determined by Conciliation and Arbitration Courts. At this time, the labour movement reasoned that it would improve its situation if it won direct representation in the parliaments. It founded the Australian Labor Party (ALP) and by 1910 had won federal government. While the ALP has since governed in both state and federal legislatures, its relationships with the trade union movement – also at the state and national levels – have often been uneasy. The labour movement overall, that is, the trade unions and the ALP, likewise has had mixed responses to issues of social diversity and the interests and concerns of women in general. The short-lived Whitlam Labor Government, 1972–5 was particularly significant in encouraging political movements to focus their claims on the state. An important initiative was that federal and state Labor governments appointed women's advisers, dubbed 'femocrats', to the public sector bureaucracies to develop and implement women-oriented policies (Franzway *et al.* 1989).

Feminists made links across public sector bureaucracies, the labour movement and the broader women's movement. (Not without differences, conflicts and countless stories of causes and consequences, of course.) A relevant example of these alliances are the Working Women's Centres: The first was set up in Melbourne, Victoria with a government grant and support from trade union peak councils in 1975, and was followed by the South Australian centre in 1979 initiated by the State Women's Adviser to the Premier together with the Secretary of the State peak union council. Each centre aimed particularly to reach out to women with 'non-English speaking backgrounds' (NESB).[3] The provision of relevant information in community languages was a major priority. The South Australian Centre retains the capacity to advocate industrially for working women as well as to lobby governments, employers and unions, while the Melbourne centre has since closed. It is worth noting that it did not reopen when federal Labor Government funding established new centres in other States after the 1993 election. Funding was withheld from Victoria with its conservative Coalition government.

The Australian labour force includes NESB workers, both women and men, who are relatively highly unionised. They generally work in highly unionised industries, but their representation among union officials is quite low (Bertone and Griffin 1995). It is more difficult to generalise about Aboriginal and Torres Strait Islander workers and their relations with trade unions, partly because very little contemporary research has been done by trade unions or other researchers. They experience significant inequalities in the workplace, including at least three times the rate of unemployment of non-Aboriginal/Torres Strait Islander women, much lower levels of income, and far fewer employment options. Aboriginal women have lower incomes than Aboriginal men, but the income gender gap is less than for Australian workers overall. Some argue that, historically, trade union support for Aboriginal workers was equivocal at best (Middleton 1980: 188; Boreham *et al.* 1993: 17). At various times, trade unions have actively recruited and supported Indigenous workers, for example in the pastoral industries (Frances *et al.*, 1994). In 1993, the Australian Education Union held its first National Aboriginal and Torres Strait Islander Education Unionists' Conference Woods (2000: 89). But the national peak body, the Australian Council of Trade Unions (ACTU), elected its first Aboriginal and Torres Strait Islander representative, Ann Flood, at its Congress in 2000 (Flood and Muir, 2000).

During the period of the federal Labor governments (1983–96) a series of agreements or Accords, as they were called, were made between the government and the Australian Council of Trade Unions. Thus began the shift away from the centralised industrial system. In 1990, the negotiation of wages and conditions on an enterprise-by-enterprise basis (enterprise bargaining) was introduced. This shift was pushed much harder by the conservative Liberal-National Coalition Government in 1996 with its introduction of the Workplace Relations Act. The Act curtailed the role of the Australian Industrial Relations Commission (as independent arbiter), strongly emphasised individual agreements between employer and employee and limited the role of trade unions. This hostile industrial environment combined with extensive changes to the labour market where 26 per cent of workers are now casual, has contributed to the urgent situation in Australian unions. Membership has declined to less than 26 per cent with private sector rates now below 20 per cent (*Workers Online*: 7 March 2000).

A survey of Australian unions by Mezinec in 1998 covering 36 of the possible 48 unions and 80 per cent of union members documents these effects (see Table 13.1). Of those unions that did not respond, the most significant to women workers is the Shop Distributive & Allied Employees' Association – it has a large proportion of women members and a male-dominated, politically conservative leadership. Women make up 40 per cent of all those included in the survey, slightly less than in the workforce overall. They are concentrated in public sector unions (61 per cent) with less than one-third in private sector unions, and just over a quarter of a small number of unions that cover both sectors. However, the somewhat shorthand distinctions between public and private sectors of employment are becoming obscured by the large scale reductions to the public sector by neo-liberal govern-ments, directly through retrenchment or 'separations', and indirectly through outsourcing or privatisation of government functions, including unemployment services and utilities (such as electricity and water).

At the national or federal levels of union organisations, Mezinec found that women were fairly represented only in a minority of unions.

Table 13.1 Gender representation in Australian unions, 1998

Union*	Total members	Women members	Women members as percentage of total
CEPU	181,958	17,323	9.5
AMWU	177,000	17,000	9.6
ASU	161,266	79,012	49
AEU	160,000	104,000	65
LHMU	129,542	69,732	54
CFMEU	120,000	3,000	2.5
CPSU-SPSF	113,000	58,000	51
ANF	110,000	105,600	96
NUW	109,000	32,700	30
FSU	91,434	62,170	68

Sources: Data collated from a survey of Australian unions conducted in August 1998, results summarised in Mezinec (1999).

Notes
*Union abbreviations:
Communications, Electrical, Electronics, Plumbing & Allied Services Union
Australian Manufacturing Workers Union
Australian Services Union
Australian Education Union
Australian Liquor, Hospitality & Miscellaneous Workers Union
Construction Forestry Mining and Energy Union of Australia
Community and Public Sector Union – SPSF Group
Australian Nurses Federation
National Union of Workers
Finance Sector Union

Table 13.2 Representation of women in senior positions in Australian unions, 1998

Position	Number of women	Total	Percentage of women
Secretary	8	35	23
President	7	33	39
Senior Officials#	54	195	28
Women's Officer	5	5	100
Junior Officials*	82	198	41
All Officials	136	393	35
ACTU Congress Delegates	69	338	20
ACTU Executive Members	20	51	39

Source: Mezinec, Sonya (1999) combination of Tables 1 and 2.

Notes
Includes secretary and sec-treasurer, president, vice-president, assistant secretary and treasury.
*Includes industrial officer, organiser and specialist staff.

Asked to nominate what possible actions or policies they had undertaken to improve the situation of women workers, two-thirds of the unions reported they published information aimed at women's interests, and about 40 per cent sent women to union training programmes and had a women's committee. Approximately one-quarter provided child care for union meetings and had internal affirmative action programmes, but only 14 per cent employed a women's officer. These constitute the current conditions of sexual politics in Australian trade unions.

Sexual politics

Perhaps the most obvious aspect of sexual politics is sexuality, or more usefully, the whole complex of sexualities, sexual identities and sexual relations. Here I wish to emphasise men's sexual identities. Naming trade unions as 'men's movements' is one of the more explicit and useful attempts to do this by identifying trade unions as men's organisations that represent the interests of men (Campbell 1984; Lake 1986). Both Campbell and Lake regard the labour movement as 'a response to men's degradation as men as well as their exploitation as workers' (Lake 1986: 138). However, other feminists believe that this characterisation of the labour movement denies the achievements of trade union women (Rowbotham 1989: 235).[4] I think 'men's movement' is a useful term, because it points to an organisation that has (too often) excluded women's membership, resisted women's interests and denied opportunities for their active participation.

Nevertheless, the term, 'men's movement' is limited; it fails to specify that the men in question are heterosexual men. As I have argued already, Australian unionism is shaped by the dominance of heterosexual masculinity, or more precisely, by the dominance of a certain kind of working-class masculinity, which in Australia has been understood as the province of white, English-speaking men (Ostenfeld 1999; Williams and Thorpe 1992). What I am suggesting is that the multiple differences amongst men must be acknowledged and understood as integral to the sexual politics in trade unionism.

Framing the strategies: sameness or difference[5]

If we argue that the labour movement should accommodate the diverse needs of all workers, the very real problem is, how might this best be achieved? This question poses a critical strategic dilemma for sexual politics: in the case of women, should they seek to become the same as men, or should they seek to incorporate their differences from men within the labour movement?

No easy or straightforward solutions are available. The gender-neutral categories of 'workers', 'comrades' and 'the working class' successfully submerge men's gender difference, and at times, women have sought to achieve the same effect in order to gain equal participation in trade unions. But this requires that they emulate men since no equitable, androgynous identity is available that would place women and men on the same footing (Tax 1980; Drake 1984). Historically, material, social, political and cultural conditions were such that few women could long sustain an identity of sameness with men. Nevertheless, political strategies based on sameness appeal where traditional union discourses that value working-class solidarity seem to allow for the inclusion of women as workers. Women have won some gains, such as leadership positions, for example, but the aggravations and difficulties of gender inequalities that extend beyond the labour movement limit them. Economic inequality, the effects of physical and reproductive difference, and cultural values have denied many women this option. I suggest that a key to this, and one that is too often overlooked, is not so much the abstractions of gender difference, but rather men's continuing resistance to equitable change. One might even say it is their entrenched resistance to any amelioration of unequal gender divisions between the domestic (where women do the second shift) and the public which constitutes a powerful barrier to the achievement of women's equality through sameness with men. (See for example, Bittman and Pixley 1997.) What gains women have made in the public sphere, are largely at the price of the domestic in their own lives.

A second strategy, framed in terms of difference from men, aims to develop discursive options that grant women's difference equal value to men's difference (Briskin 1998). In Australia, this approach has led to the establishment of women's committees in individual unions and in national and state peak councils, affirmative action positions on executives and campaigns and sponsored research on pay equity, work-based child care, and family-friendly workplaces. There are difficulties with this strategy. A focus on women's difference can undermine the possibility of 'union solidarity' and may overshadow differences among women. Perhaps more importantly, a strategy that specifies women's difference from *men* fails to challenge the discourses of men as gender-neutral unionists (Jenson 1988). Man remains the normative unionist.

In ways that are familiar to feminists in other situations, union women tend to alternate same/difference strategies, depending on 'the political conditions which force women into these alternatives (of either sameness or difference)' (Bacchi 1990: 265). As I have already suggested, men's responses are crucial to the situation of women in trade unions, as in other public institutions. Cunnison and Stageman (1995: 52) observe that these range from making alliances with their sisterly comrades to the denial of gender difference to a strenuous hostility to any modifications to male domination.[6] For example, a senior elected official from my study recounts her experience of the sexual politics she encountered when she campaigned to win a better distribution of union resources for women.

> I am now described in some sections as rabid about women's issues. Now I was no more or less committed then than I had been, but once I stepped over the line of being a nice girl, once I lost it and behaved like the boys do when they feel strongly about something.
>
> (Senior official, white-collar union)

Her anger is fuelled by her dismay at the men's resistance to the progressiveness of women's claims. The results of her behaving 'like the boys do' suggest, first, the difference between acceptable behaviour for women and for men, and second, that organisational seniority does not grant women normative status. Women may occupy the same structural positions as the men, but are expected to behave differently. As the data show, women have been 'added-on' to Australian union structures, at least to some limited degree, but attempts to change structures and culture are resisted successfully by the men. In the meantime, a few women in leadership positions will not be sufficient to challenge the sexual politics of trade unionism. As Kanter argued over two decades ago, 'the problem of acceptance and effectiveness that many women encounter in managerial and professional occupations (may) derive primarily from their token status and the fact that there are, as yet, so few women in those positions' (Kanter 1980: 319).

Men's responses to women's claims are political and are therefore integral to the outcomes of these claims. It is common at this point in the discussion to suggest that we need to review our political theory, but I want to suggest that in some senses this move contradicts feminist analysis of power and gender inequality. Women do not fail in their efforts to change sexual politics simply because their strategy is flawed. If relations of male domination shape women's subordination, then successful challenges to that domination are not entirely a matter of the adequacies of theory and strategy. Feminist theories argue that relations of domination are relations of unequal power; therefore, I suggest, any challenge is likely to be strenuously resisted by significant material and discursive opposition.

I will now discuss some of the ways some union women have negotiated the obstacles that result from men's domination in the labour movement.

Naming sexual politics

Feminism has provided language for this politics so that for example, union women often refer to male unionists as 'the boys', a phrase that parallels the term, 'the girls' applied to groups of women. It expresses irony in the face of male dominance, pleasure in resistance and varying degrees of hostility towards union men.[7]

> [There's] the entrenched boys' club mentality.
>
> (White-collar official)

> The boys in the labour movement as I have always said, are the last bastions of sexism, and I truly believe that. They are a very sexist mob.
>
> (Blue-collar official)

Speech practices have long been recognised by feminists as complex and subtle sites of sexual politics, as for example in using terms like 'the boys' (Beale 1982; Spender 1981; Tannen 1991). Feminists observe that patriarchy requires that women be silent, and therefore that women 'moving from silence into speech' is critical to the liberation of oppressed and exploited women (hooks 1989: 9). However, working out how to go beyond naming the problem is always difficult. Collectively, women move into public speech and political action from unpaid work in the domestic sphere, into paid work, into joining unions and acting in them. But as one union official warned: 'We have to be very careful that the women don't reflect 'the boys' rules' since 'the boys' rules' reflect and support men's dominance. If women followed those rules, (if it were materially and politically possible for them to do so) women-oriented gains would not be made; women's interests and needs would not be identified and male domination of the unions' interests would not be challenged. If changes are to be made to meet women's interests and needs, women need to create alternatives to the 'boys' rules'.

Use of the term 'the boys' also expresses something of the disappointment, even despair, that women unionists feel at the failure of their male union 'comrades' and 'brothers' to enact the progressive political promise of trade unionism. This potential for social and political progress distinguishes it from other public male-dominated institutions. But the problem is that it has rarely 'progressed' to include feminist politics. This might be overcome in individual unions where certain preconditions exist: a significant female membership that is active, and a female leadership that is oriented towards establishing women's issues (Mezinec 1999). In such cases, as some women have found, 'the boys' rules' do not prevail. Rather, as one woman official said, 'The men there are really supportive' (White-collar official). Without such preconditions, as is the situation in many Australian trade unions, this will mean that 'men must take up the responsibility and work with women to transform the culture of Australian unionism' (Elton 1997: 127). This assumes of course that men will also be committed to the progressive possibilities of the labour movement and to transforming its present state as a 'boys' club'.

Covert sexual politics

Compulsory heterosexuality[8] and homophobia[9]

The term, 'the boys', assumes a masculine heterosexuality opposed to, and dominant, over all others, a perspective that reflects the repressive meanings of sexuality available in the wider society. The labour movement is not the only 'men's movement' since heterosexual masculine dominance is evident in 'managerial policies, everyday practices, discriminations against and dismissals of homosexual people' (Hearn and Parkin 1987: 60). Hearn describes this organisation sexuality (for men) as a mixture of 'homosociability, latent homosexuality, homophobia and heterosexual phallocentricism' (Hearn and Parkin 1987: 158). Yet, in this public world they have created, men's sexuality is often 'desperate, uncomfortable, ritualised, ambiguous' (p. 159). Homosociobility, homosexuality and homosexual desire amongst men is therefore an important constituent of the dominance of patriarchal heterosexuality. These distinctions between homosociobility, homo-sexuality and heterosexuality in relation to men are important to sexual politics in organisations, but Hearn and Parkin pay little attention to diverse sexualities among women (Hearn and Parkin 1987: 162).

This kind of neglect also appears to be the case in Australian trade unions, where the hegemonic and homophobic dimensions of trade union sexualities have been almost entirely invisible. I note that Ostenfeld argues that the Australian labour movement has proved responsive to the needs of gay and lesbian workers, particularly through the efforts of white-collar and 'left'-wing unions in opposition to the resistance by 'right'-wing unions. However, I find that there is a considerable difference between the kind of attention paid to sexual harassment (difficult and complex as it is, see below) and the general tentativeness about the politics of homosexuality, which has remained relatively marginal in Australian unions. Some of the women officials explain this in terms of the dominance of heterosexual masculinity where the male union official has 'such a macho sort of image' that men fear the potential threat from homosexuality to their own (hetero) sexuality.

Silence about the interests and needs of lesbian women workers and officials has only recently been broken by separate organising strategies among some networks of union women. These include separate committees such as GLAM (Gay and Lesbian Australian Services Union Members). A visible sign of a growing challenge to the denial of homosexuality in the sexual politics of trade unions is the participation of some unions in the annual Sydney Gay and Lesbian Mardi Gras. This union presence has developed in spite of internal conflicts that saw some officials threatening to resign. Beginning with a small 'back-of-a-ute'[10] float, in 2000 a combined unions team developed a large puppet of Jennie George, President of the Australian peak union body the ACTU[11] (Fortescue 2000). However, a recent study of the workplace experiences of lesbian, gay and transgender people, 'The Pink Ceiling is Too Low' found that few took their concerns about industrial issues and discrimination to a union (Irwin 1999).

Nevertheless, these activities provide some counter to the more common strategy described by one white-collar woman official who argues that lesbians need to mask their sexuality in order to survive. She goes on to say:

> Yes, disguises it is what I mean, a non-acknowledgement of it. The absolute prevalence of heterosexism. A very ribald, a very palpable sexuality exists in the organised labour movement, a heterosexuality, very strong, I think. . . . It's actually led to physical violence you know.

Homosexuality may be disguised, but not obliterated, the lived experience of lesbianism and female homosexual desire is denied through the travesty of a constrained caricature, a stereotype. The result is that sexual identity may be distorted not only for those who claim homosexual identity, but also for those who claim a heterosexual identity. Homosexuality remains a silent 'other'. The damaging effect of stereotypes on individual identity and on whole groups has been well documented, and it is to this that this official refers in describing her experience as a subject of violence in order to stress the damaging effects of homophobia in the sexual politics of the labour movement.

Exposing sexual politics

Sexual harassment

In contrast with issues of sexual diversity, sexual harassment has become a highly visible aspect of sexual politics in workplaces, including union workplaces. Sexual harassment names women's lack of sexual safety at work, as domestic violence names women's experience of sexual violence in the home (Hopkins and McGregor 1991). The women officials in this study share assumptions about sexual harassment more than they do on any other aspect of sexual politics. Two major dimensions confront them: sexual harassment in their members' workplaces, and sexual harassment in their own workplace, the union movement.

The remarkable emergence of sexual harassment on to political agendas is striking given that the phrase itself was not coined until the early 1970s.[12] However, the broad women's movement, and the wider community generally underestimate Australian union women's activism about sexual harassment.[13] The Working Women's Centre (Melbourne) began to campaign towards its inclusion in the Working Women's Charter, following its neglect in the original Charter of 1978 (Owen and Shaw 1979). Teachers' unions, including the South Australian Institute of Teachers, undertook activities such as day-long seminars based on recently devised union policy (SAIT 1982). In the same year, the Administrative and Clerical Officers' Association produced an informative discussion of the problem, its history, definition, social explanations and guidelines for union policy and action (ACOA 1982). However, sexual harassment continues to be a contentious issue within unions as well as workplaces.

Where sexual harassment is understood in terms of the oppressiveness of male power, it is seen as a male weapon against women workers. Women become the victims of men's harassment, and in effect, of all workplace sexuality. But this idea of women as 'always the pathetic victims of sexual harassment' (Pringle 1988: 167) denies the possibilities that women may themselves find pleasure (and power) in workplace sexuality. This is not to underestimate the damaging and disturbing effects of sexual harassment, but I suggest we need to avoid a clumsy sex/power dichotomy, where women have the sex and men have the power.

At the same time, women are the main victims. Feminist discourses of sexual harassment enable women to talk in public about the sexual hostilities they experience at work. It also shows that the effects of male dominance in the workplace extend beyond the discrimination of the sexual division of labour to the hostilities of sexual dominance, thus workplace feminists who had adopted structural explanations of sex discrimination can begin to grapple with the complex issues of the humiliations and harms experienced by women workers.

The industrial dimensions

Achieving the conceptualisation of sexual harassment as an industrial matter has been an important gain for feminists contesting the sexual politics in the labour movement and in the wider society. In traditional union discourses, issues of sexuality are related to women and as such, are disconnected from the core business of wages and jobs. Defining sexual harassment in this way also raises the possibility of pitching unionist against unionist, but the history of the labour movement shows that many issues cause conflict among unionists, such as leadership struggles and skirmishes over coverage. Somehow these do not appear to hold quite the same threat. As the recent guide published by the South Australian United Trades and Labor Council observes:

> All sexual harassment that occurs in workplaces can be difficult to address. Unions have an additional challenge to deal with sexual harassment where it occurs in a highly political environment or between elected officials. Recent events in South Australia and Western Australia have highlighted that some unions have not always been seen to be adequately addressing sexual harassment.
>
> (United Trades and Labor Council, SA 1999: 1)

Sexual harassment between union members or co-worker harassment was addressed by Australian unions as a problem of 'conflict of interest' as early as 1983 with some unions recommending that a separate union official serve the alleged offender. My own small union (of university lecturers), which had few officials, but ample funds, paid for external legal representation for alleged offenders. These responses clearly differ from those based on the view that 'unions cannot represent members clearly guilty of harassment, if that representation is taken to implicitly exonerate such conduct or minimise its seriousness' (Lawrence 1994: 139). In Australia it is further complicated by the legal principle of innocent until proven guilty, and the union's own in-principle commitment to all members. If a union decides not to represent the accused, it may be appearing to assume guilt; if it does represent the accused, it may appear to minimise the seriousness of the issue.

Co-worker harassment has a particular bite for union feminists committed to worker solidarity who find that they have to deal with sexual hostilities in their own workplaces from their (male) comrades. In this they are similar to women in any male-dominated organisations as they are more likely to be subjected to harassment than women in other organisations (Gutek 1985; DiTomaso 1989; Schultz 1992). The work environment of women officials (with the exception of women members) is constituted by a male-dominated union leadership, male-dominated employers or employer advocates, and a male-dominated industrial relations system. Nevertheless, not all the women officials saw trade unions as typical sites of sexual harassment and some cite instances where they succeeded in getting sexual harassment dealt with (eventually). For example:

> I must say that I haven't experienced any sexual harassment working in the union movement whereas I have working in other places.
>
> (Industrial officer, blue-collar official)

> I have found they don't know how to treat women any differently than the traditional way of treating women. But that's not so in our own union. That just simply would not happen because people are more aware.
>
> (Industrial officer, white-collar official)

These officials assume that union men might be expected to be more progressive on such issues since progressive views on social issues rate highly in union discourses. Traditional ideas may be replaced by progressive ideas. For example, the white-collar, public sector union (above) does not countenance traditional (i.e. non-progressive) views on women, because as this same official says she, and other union women have managed to influence the union's policies and practices. In addition, if women have union power of their own, either through a 'progressive' union or as part of a women's network, they are less likely to be harassed by male comrades. As one said, 'No I don't think they harass women [with status] but they'd do it to some others.' Yet some officials saw sexual harassment specifically as a form of calculated political intimidation by employers – usually male – designed to gain ground in an adversarial industrial situation:

> I walked into a meeting, . . . the usual thing, me the sole woman in a room with four plus men. . . . the lawyer for the employers commented on the fact that I'd put on weight. That was the first thing that he said, which all the men in the room laughed at. It was, of course, meant to put me off balance and make me a little unsure of myself, which of course it did, even though I was angry as hell and really resented that remark being made. Women understand it, it's a subtle form of discrimination but it's difficult to hang your hat on.
>
> (Industrial officer, blue-collar official)

This official interprets the denigration of her body as sexual harassment used as a political strategy. She is humiliated and angry in ways that 'women would understand'. A second official cited a similar example of sexual harassment in the context of a formal industrial tribunal hearing where she was upset to the point of tears. But 'I didn't show them, I would go off to the ladies and have a bit of a howl' and then return to engage in another round of complex and antagonistic industrial negotiations. She understood this as political intimidation, meant 'to put me off my stride'.

In other words, sexual harassment is about power, and men recognise its strategic value. It is an explicit tool of contest in which men engage, or at least they concur in its use. The Collinsons (1989) refer to such an instance that happened to a woman who was the first to be elected to her union's large executive. She was subjected to allegations that she won and kept her position through sexual relations with male union executives. With little support from other (male) colleagues, the woman official successfully resisted the attacks by the men who were drawing on 'sexuality as a means of maintaining power and control within organisations' (Collinson and Collinson 1989: 107). However, their analysis relies on the idea that it is women's 'agency and resistance' alone that may challenge men's sexuality and power in organisations. I suggest that this stress on the individual's strength leaves women with a single option – whether or not they, as individuals, have the capacity to resist men's power. Women's agency tends to be idealised in this formulation of women's political action. In the examples I described earlier, neither woman alone was in a position to actively resist, in spite of their clear understanding that sexual harassment was mobilised as a political strategy based on sexist assumptions of women's sexuality. It is not surprising that, although relevant policies and procedures have been on the books of many unions, it recently took almost a year of overcoming resistance through consultations, debates, and many drafts before an updated handbook could finally be produced by the South Australian peak council (United Trades and Labor Council, SA 1999).

Women's resistance requires organisational and collective power that is not readily achieved given the inequalities of sexual politics and the kinds of strategic dilemma, already discussed, concerning questions of sexualities, power and violence. This has complex effects on women themselves who find that questions about appropriate political processes are not readily resolved. At times, lengthy and deeply felt disputes erupt among women unionists and can become the cause of much despair. What these conflicts do signify is that sexual harassment, and therefore sexual politics, are central to the labour movement.

Conclusion

This chapter argues that sexual politics is integral to women's relations to the labour movement. The obstacles women experience cannot be explained as uninformed sexism that can be resolved by the simple expedient of adding on a few women to leadership positions. Rather, there is a sexual politics at stake that is constituted by complex gender relationships based on the dominance of white heterosexual masculinity. I have traced some of the ways women union officials contest sexual politics in the Australian labour movement through questions on strategic dilemmas, the hegemonic masculinity of the 'men's movement', and sexual harassment. The development and implementation of relevant legislation and policies is both a stage of women's challenge to male domination of the public domain and a site of contest over discourses and practices of sexualities and power.

I argue that men as workers and as unionists are not gender-neutral. The labour movement remains a 'men's movement' that represents and defends men's interests as men, as well as their interests as paid workers. What is the same about women and men is that both are gendered. However, in the sexual politics of trade unions, the meanings and effects of gender difference is critical. Women contest men's gender-neutrality, and men resist the incursions of women's difference into the domain of the 'men's movement'. It is the difference of women's gender that challenges men's gender-neutrality in the labour movement.

Creative strategies are required to tackle sexual politics; in Australia, campaigns on issues such as protection from homophobia and racism in the workplace have made some gains. For example, GLAM (Gay and Lesbian Members of the Australian Services Union) won the award for best recruitment campaign at the ACTU Congress 2000, with their slogan, 'Job security never goes out of style'. As I have noted, the trade union movement has an erratic record on tackling racism; it generally has made rather more strenuous efforts on behalf of NESB workers than for Indigenous workers. This too may be changing as women unionists acknowledge and struggle with the questions of difference among women. As Ann Flood argues, she is more likely to be discriminated against because she is black than because she is a woman (Flood and Muir 2000: 90). For her, racism is the primary issue. At the same time, the ACTU Women's Conference 2000 recognised the need for the whole trade union movement to go beyond the rhetoric of policy in its recommendations that trade unions develop and implement action plans for better representation of Indigenous people (ACTU Women's Conference Report 2000).

Clearly, labour movements are under enormous pressures from the effects of globalisation and renewed attacks by neo-liberal governments. However, this is not the moment to claim, once again, that it is 'all too hard' (*Workers Online*, March, 2000)[14] or an irrelevant distraction, to address the sexual politics of the 'men's movement'. It is absolutely critical that the small gains made so far are encouraged and supported.

Notes

1 Millett (1969) coined the term, 'sexual politics' somewhat tentatively but with considerable effect almost thirty years ago. She argued that relations between the sexes were structured within a system of patriarchy in which men oppress women and that even the circumstances and meanings of physical intercourse between males and females are shaped by patriarchal dominance.

2 In Australia, the notions 'White', 'Whiteness' are challenging the taken-for-granted notions of white persons in relation to multiculturalism, racism and ethnicity, but as Ghassan Hage (1998) notes, these are complex issues and I cannot deal with them sufficiently here. See also Pocock 1997; Franzway 1997.

3 The term, 'non-English-speaking background' abbreviated to NESB, is used in Australia to refer to mainly European immigrants and their children who grew up in households where languages other than English were spoken. More recently, it also refers to immigrants from South East Asia such as Vietnam. It does not include Aboriginal and Torres Strait Islander people who speak languages other than English.

4 For an extended debate among British feminists, see Clara Connolly *et al.* 1986.

5 'Difference' here refers to the Bacchi definitions, as in the question, are women the same as or different from men? (Bacchi 1990: x).

6 I note that men who support women in the public domain nevertheless are slow to contribute in the private domain of the domestic.

7 In Canada, Quebec feminists call the French 'Masters', Lacan, Derrida, and Deleuze, 'les boys' (Probyn 1993: 49).

8 The phrase was first used by Rich (1980).
9 Altman notes that 'homophobia', a term coined by Weinberg in 1972, refers to 'individual fear of and defence against homosexual desire (Altman 1992: 44).
10 'ute' refers to utility, i.e. a small truck or pick up.
11 Jennie George was elected the first woman President of the Australian Council of Trade Unions in 1995 and has been an important symbol for women. See Muir 1997.
12 The draft of MacKinnon's key text on sexual harassment was circulated in the United States in 1975 (MacKinnon 1979: xi), by which time the term had become sufficiently commonplace for the *New York Times* to publish an article on the subject (Bacchi and Jose 1994: 263). Farley published the first large-scale, systematic analysis defining sexual harassment in 1978 (Farley 1978), followed by MacKinnon's more widely known text a year later (MacKinnon 1979).
13 See for example, Carol Bacchi's recent survey of feminist political and legal activism which contains no reference to trade union contributions (1999).
14 The first woman ACTU President, Jennie George, has another first to her CV. She is the first President 'who was not being moved into a safe political seat' according to an editorial in *Workers Online*. There is an 'unsavoury undercurrent' to her farewells because union chiefs have found it 'all too hard' to organise.

References

Administrative and Clerical Officers' Association (ACOA) (1982) *Sexual Harassment in the Workplace: A Union Perspective*, Sydney: ACOA.

Australian Council of Trade Unions (ACTU) (2000) *Women's Conference 2000 Report* at: http://www.actu.asn.au/campaigns/women/indexw.htm (accessed 3 March 2001).

Altman, Dennis (1992) 'AIDS and the discourses of sexuality', in Connell, R.W. and Dowsett, Gary (eds) *Rethinking Sex: Social Theory and Sexuality Research*, Melbourne: Melbourne University Press.

Bacchi, Carol (1990) *Same Difference: Feminism and Sexual Difference*, Sydney: Allen and Unwin.

—— (1999) *Women, Policy and Politics: The Construction of Policy Problems*, London: Sage.

Bacchi, Carol and Jose, Jim (1994) 'Historicising sexual harassment', *Women's History Review* 3: 2: 263–70.

Beale, Jenny (1982) *Getting It Together: Women as Trade Unionists*, London: Pluto Press.

Bertone, S. and Griffin, G. (1995) 'Immigrant female workers and Australian trade unions', *Revue Relations Industrielles*, 50, 1: 117–46.

Bittman, Michael and Pixley, Jocelyn (1997) *The Double Life of the Family*, Sydney: Allen and Unwin.

Boreham, Paul, Whitehouse, Gillian and Harley, Bill (1993) 'The labour force status of Aboriginal people: A regional comparison', *Labour and Industry* 5, 1&2: 16–32.

Briskin, Linda (1998) 'Autonomy, diversity and integration: Union women's separate organizing in the context of restructuring and globalization'. Paper to 14th World Congress of the International Sociological Association, Montreal.

Campbell, Beatrix (1984) *Wigan Pier Revisited*, London: Virago.

Collinson, David and Collinson, Margaret (1989) 'Sexuality in the workplace: The domination of men's sexuality', in Hearn, Jeff *et al.* (eds) *The Sexuality of Organization*, London: Sage.

Connell, R.W. (1987) *Gender and Power*, Sydney: Allen & Unwin.

Connolly, Clara and Segal, Lynne with Barrett, Michele, Campbell, Beatrix, Phillips, Anne, Wair, Angela and Wilson, Elizabeth (1986) 'Feminism and class politics: A round-table discussion', *Feminist Review* 23: 13–30.

Cunnison, Sheila and Stageman, Jane (1995) *Feminizing the Unions*, Aldershot, UK: Avebury.

D'Aprano, Zelda (1995) *Zelda*, Spinifex Press.

DiTomaso, Nancy (1989) 'Sexuality in the workplace: Discrimination and harassment', in Hearn, Jeff *et al.* (eds) *The Sexuality of Organisation*, London: Sage, pp. 71–90.

Drake, Barbara (1984) *Women in Trade Unions*, London: Virago.

Elton, Jude (1997) 'Making democratic unions: From policy to practice', in Pocock, Barbara (ed.) *Strife: Sex and Politics in Labour Unions*, Sydney: Allen and Unwin.

Farley, Lynne (1978) *Sexual Shakedown: The Sexual Harassment of Women on the Job*, New York: McGraw-Hill.

Flood, Ann and Muir, Kathie (2000) 'Change is slow: Indigenous women and unions', *Hecate* 26, 2: 63–5.

Fortescue, Robyn (2000) 'Mardi Gras: The biggest labour festival of the year', *Hecate* 26.

Frances, Ray, Scales, Bruce and McGrath, Ann (1994) 'Broken silences? Labour history and Aboriginal workers', in Irving, Terry (ed.) *Challenges to Labour History*, Sydney: University of New South Wales Press.

Franzway, Suzanne (1997) 'Sexual politics in trade unions', in Pocock, Barbara (ed.) *Strife: Sex and Politics in Labour Unions*, Sydney: Allen and Unwin.

Franzway, Suzanne, Court, Diane, and Connell, R.W. (1989) *Staking a Claim: Feminism, Bureaucracy and the State*, Sydney: Allen and Unwin.

Gutek, Barbara (1985) *Sex and the Workplace: The Impact of Sexual Behaviour and Harassment on Women, Men, and Organizations*, San Francisco: Jossey-Bass.

Hage, Ghassan (1998) *White Nation: Fantasies of White Supremacy in a Multicultural Society*, Sydney: Pluto Press Australia.

Hearn, Jeff and Parkin, Wendy (1987) *'Sex' at 'Work': The Power and Paradox of Organisation Sexuality*, Brighton, Sussex: Wheatsheaf.

hooks, bell (1989) *Talking Back: Thinking Feminist, Thinking Black*, Boston, MA: South End Press.

Hopkins, Andrew and McGregor, Heather (1991) *Working for Change: The Movement Against Domestic Violence*, Sydney: Allen and Unwin.

Irwin, Jude (1999) *'The Pink Ceiling is Too Low' Workplace Experiences of Lesbians, Gay Men and Transgender People*, NSW Gay and Lesbian Rights Lobby and the Australian Centre for Lesbian and Gay Research, at www.rainbow.net.au/~glrl/index.htm.

Jenson, Jane (1988) 'The limits of "and the" discourse', in Jenson, Jane, Hagen, Elisabeth and Reddy Ceallaigh (eds) *Feminization of the Labour Force: Paradoxes and Promises*, Cambridge: Polity Press, pp. 155–72.

Kanter, Rosabeth (1980) 'The impact of organization structure: models and methods for change', in Steinberg Ratner, Ronnie (ed.) *Equal Employment Policy for Women*, Philadelphia: Temple University Press.

Lake, Marilyn (1986) 'A question of time', in McKnight, David (ed.) *Moving Left: The Future of Socialism in Australia*, Sydney: Pluto Press, pp. 135–48.

Lawrence, Elizabeth (1994) *Gender and Trade Unions*, London: Taylor and Francis.

MacKinnon, Catharine (1979) *Sexual Harassment of Working Women: A Case of Sex Discrimination*, New Haven: Yale University Press.

Mezinec, Sonya (1999) *The Slow Road to Fairer Unionism: Changes in Gender Representation in South Australian Unions 1991–1998*, Centre for Labour Research and the United Trades and Labor Council of South Australia.

Middleton, Hannah (1980) 'The Aboriginal national minority: Class and national forma-tion', in Boreham, Paul and Dow, Geoff (eds) *Work and Inequality: Ideology and Control in the Capitalist Labour Process*, Melbourne: Macmillan.

Millett, Kate (1969) *Sexual Politics*, New York: Avon Books.

Muir, Kathie (1997) 'Difference or deficiency: Gender, representation and meaning in unions', in Pocock, Barbara (ed.) *Strife: Sex and Politics in Labour Unions*, Sydney: Allen and Unwin.

Mumford, Karen (1989) *Women Working*, Sydney: Allen and Unwin.

Ostenfeld, Shane (1999) 'Sexual identity and the Australian labor movement in historical perspective', in Hunt, Gerald (ed.) *Laboring for Rights: Unions and Sexual Diversity across Nations*, Philadelphia: Temple University Press.

Owen, Mary and Shaw, Sylvie (eds) (1979) Working Women. Discussion Papers from the Working Women's Centre, Melbourne: Sisters.

Pocock, Barbara (1997) 'Introduction: Gender, Strife and Unions', in Barbara Pocock (ed.) *Strife: Sex and Politics in Unions*, Sydney: Allen and Unwin.

Pringle, Rosemary (1988) *Secretaries' Talk: Sexuality, Power and Work*, London: Verso.

Probyn, Elspeth (1993) *Sexing the Self: Gendered Positions in Cultural Studies*, London: Routledge.

Rich, Adrienne (1980) 'Compulsory heterosexuality and lesbian existence', *Signs* 5, 4: 631–60.

Rowbotham, Sheila (1989) *The Past Is Before Us: Feminism in Action Since the 1960s*, London: Pandora Press.

Schultz, Vicki (1992) 'Women "before" the law: Judicial stories about women, work, and sex segregation on the job', in Judith Butler and Joan Scott (eds) *Feminists Theorize the Political*, London: Routledge, pp. 297–338.

South Australian Institute of Teachers (SAIT) (1982) Sexual Harassment. An Issue for 1982. Seminar Papers, Adelaide: SAIT.

Spender, Dale (1981) *Man Made Language*, London: Routledge and Kegan Paul.

Tannen, Deborah (1991) *You Just Don't Understand: Women and Men in Conversation*, London: Virago Press.

Tax, Meredith (1980) *The Rising of the Women*, New York: Monthly Review Press.

United Trades and Labor Council, South Australia (1999) *Uniting to Eliminate Sexual Harassment. A Guide for South Australian Union Staff, Officials and Delegates*, Adelaide: UTLC SA.

Williams, Claire with Bill Thorpe (1992) *Beyond Industrial Sociology. The Work of Men and Women*, Sydney: Allen and Unwin.

Woods, Davina (2000) 'Education is the cure', in Bin-Sallick, Mary-Ann (ed.) *Aboriginal Women by Degrees*, St Lucia, Queensland: University of Queensland Press, pp. 77–91.

Working Women's Centre (1996) *Annual Report*, Adelaide: Working Women's Centre.

Working Women's Centre (1999) *Annual Report*, Adelaide: Working Women's Centre.

Workers Online http://workers.labor.net.au/ (accessed 7 March 2000).

14 Masculinities and emotion work in trade unions[1]

Claire Williams

Introduction

One of the defining elements of heterosexual male identity and hegemonic masculinity is men's desperate desire to prove they are *not* girls (Evans and Thorpe 1998: 19; Seidler 1989: 10). While this generalisation can be applied to any number of gendered relations, it is the contention of this chapter that a particularly pronounced form of masculine culture pervades male trade unions, and this is most noticeable in those trade unions that are associated with blue-collar occupations in male-dominated industries.

Two main strategies are deployed: first by drawing upon certain concepts of masculinity – namely 'multiple' or 'diverse' masculinities, and 'hegemonic' or patriarchal masculinity (Buchbinder 1994; Connell 1995) and second by giving voice to trade union men who articulate 'gay' and 'green' discourses that challenge taken-for-granted masculine norms. Drawing on these counter-stories, and from a study of timber (lumber) production in South Australia, this chapter explores those masculine elements that are problematic, yet central to trade union cultures.

At the same time, while this increased attention on men as men in workplaces is vital for gender analysis to go forward, such attention can become a 'more sophisticated means of forgetting women' (Collinson and Hearn 1994: 8). Thus another section of this chapter considers how women trade unionists, who are still marginalised in the timber industry, have unsettled trade union masculinism. Finally, from these considerations and others, investigation is necessary of some of the ways in which patriarchal or hegemonic masculinity limits emotional expression and hence the repertoire of appropriate emotion work strategies that are increasingly vital for the well being of human service organisations – trade unions not least.

The chapter comprises three parts. The next section will draw particularly on Connell's writings on gender and masculinity to form a theoretical framework for the empirical discussion in later parts. In the next section, features of 'patriarchal masculine culture' specifically applied to trade unions will be set forth. This will be followed by a brief review of relevant literature which speaks to the relationship of class to this 'masculine culture'. Finally two empirical examples will explore the themes outlined in the introduction. The first of these is an account of a sexual harassment strike led by women workers supported by executive leadership and joined, albeit reluctantly, by their male trade union co-workers because of unequivocal support from the male union executive. This is followed by detailed recounting of experiences by two male trade union organisers, one heterosexual and one gay, from within the citadel of trade unions. Both men felt marginalised in terms of their masculinities, identities and subjectivities by the roles and styles they observed or felt obliged to mimic. Ultimately their presence disturbed the established contours of hegemonic masculinity within their unions but both felt the need also to leave the citadel.

The fear of femininity central to heterosexual male identity poses serious problems for trade unions. Firstly, the concerns of women trade unionists and women workers about sexual harassment could remain trivialised under such a male gendered regime. Second, this dominant and non-inclusive trade union practice actually rests on the troubled relationships of men with other men, in the hidden processes by which heterosexual homosocial male bonding and ultimately, working-class male fraternity, is generated. Infused in all this is a policing strategy by which dominant masculinity is maintained and reproduced. Thus it leaves little scope for those marginalised men who are required to implement official views about trade union policies. Most obviously, this deeply affects how gay men (as one form of marginalised and subordinated masculinity) operate within the Australian trade union movement. But it also affects heterosexual trade union leaders when they challenge this taken-for-granted patriarchal and fraternal world. Thus the focus on *diversity* is in terms of sexuality and politics but not non-dominant race/ethnicities among union cultures. While the latter is an important question, there is an urgent need to deconstruct the sexual politics among the Anglo group of men who are hegemonic in trade unions in particular countries including Australia.

Gender regimes and masculinities

Connell's concepts of masculinities, located as they are within his concepts of gender regimes and structures, speak directly to the following discussion. In reflections arising from his book, *Gender and Power*, he is concerned to do a number of things. Gender is a social practice that refers to bodies and what bodies do. Bodies are inflected with social processes and drawn into history. Gender regimes describe the patterning of gender structures in particular institutions such as trade unions. 'Acceptable' masculinity and femininity within trade unions are part of this. They link to the gender order of society where certain patterns of culture and personal life are more acceptable than others. For example, a strong cultural opposition between masculinity and femininity is characteristic of patriarchal gender orders. However, gender identities are not fixed and are subject to change. This structure of gender is based on power, production and emotional attachment. The latter includes desire (Connell 1996: 159–60).

A central and useful concept is the 'patriarchal dividend' (Connell 1996: 162). This refers to benefits which have accrued to men from unequal shares of the products of social labour. This includes trade union men opposing equal pay for women workers so men can receive higher wages than women. The Australian trade union movement, with a few notable exceptions, has a long history of opposing equal pay for women workers (Thomson and Pocock 1997: 71–5). This was directly related to the history of Australian trade unionism which developed around the concept of the working man's welfare state in the early twentieth century. The male breadwinner ideal was enshrined as a cultural goal until the uneven successes of equal pay cases for women workers in 1969 and 1972.

Connell locates dominant masculinity, which he calls 'hegemonic', and other kinds of masculinities as configurations of practice within this structure of gender. Thus masculinity is institutionalised while being an aspect of individual character and personality (1996: 163). Moreover, there is rarely one masculinity – rather multiple masculinities which coexist. In his schema, the most important subordinated masculinities are gay masculinities.

Another useful concept is 'marginalised masculinities' which refers to masculinities which share features in common with the dominant masculinity but are socially de-authorised. Here we can locate working-class Australian masculinity. According to Connell, marginalised masculinities which have been organised around the acceptance of the patriarchal dividend are complicit masculinities (1996: 164). However, the engagement with hegemonic masculinity can be widespread but not final. In the current period, men on the economic margins have missed out on the economic gain over women that accrues to men in employment with better job classifications who still have access to masculine authority based on economic power.

Others have given an account of the way employment and workplaces have shaped and provided meaning to the marginalised masculinities of working-class men and their male identities. Buchbinder (1994), in discussing Australian masculinities, describes how employment became a key feature of the model of masculinity that associates the aggressive, self-contained, independent man with this idea of masculinity in Anglo cultures and sub-cultures. Australia's fledgling trade unions in the nineteenth century were derived frequently from such cultures and sub-cultures through British models. Workers will often use the occupational setting and the relationships at work to create more than a job and from which a sense of identity is formed (Morgan 1993: 77). Heavy and dangerous work go with many other aspects of masculinity such as group solidarity, swearing, drinking, fighting and strict sex segregation. But this sex segregation is the result of the orchestrated removal of women from such occupations. Protection policies, in countries like Britain, North America and Australia, restricted women from night work and non-traditional occupations such as mining and working with lead. These deliberately prevented the development of more androgynous concepts of femininity and masculinity, and maintained the fiction of the invulnerable male body (Williams 1997).

Buchbinder (1994) gives one of the most compelling accounts of how men's masculinity is policed by other men, and such controls are integrally related to the workplace. While women confirm the masculinity of other men, it is actually conferred by other men. Because each man has to present a persona of emotional self-containment, and because he has to seek the companionship of other men to be a 'real man', he seeks relationships with members of his own sex. At the same time, it is these very men who constantly scrutinise his masculinity, so these relationships with other men are fraught and produce high anxiety. Furthermore, in examining the way this policing operates in organisations like trade unions we can make use of one of Sedgewick's (1985) ideas – male homosocial desire. This refers to social bonds between persons of the same sex. The term derives from an analogy with 'homosexual' and is particularly useful for describing activities such as 'male bonding', and working-class male fraternity which are accompanied by intense homophobia, or the fear and hatred of homosexuality.

The concept of hegemonic masculinity and masculinities has increasingly come under attack (Whitehead 1999) although queer theorist Judith Halberstam (1998: 40, 118) assumes it still has considerable currency. Hearn (1996: 209) warns that it may be ethnocentric, even Eurocentric. Therefore it may not even be relevant or meaningful in particular societies. To illustrate this point, he elaborates on the nineteenth century British concept of 'manliness' which was distinguished from 'masculinity'. What is interesting here and pertinent to the later examination of trade union men reflecting on how they had to operate as working men and later within trade union structures, are the characteristics which make up 'manliness' that seem more relevant. Hearn describes 'manliness' as a 'middle-class-based concept referring to the transition from Christian immaturity to maturity, demonstrated by earnestness, selflessness and integrity in the early Victorian period' changing to 'neo-Spartan virility, as exemplified by stoicism, hardness and endurance' in the late Victorian period. Writing about Scandinavia, Rantakeisu *et al.* (1997) point to the way the growth of the working-class movement itself in Europe created new concepts of honour related to respect for work. As part of a quest for respectability, values about skill, doing a good job and paying one's way became part of honour and pride for working-class men.

The 'patriarchal masculine culture' of trade unions

One of the problems with trade unions as organisations (like other male bastions such as the police and the armed forces) is how little the patriarchal masculine culture has been deconstructed successfully and changed. Drawing on Roby and Uttal's (1993) work on rank and file union activists, Cobble (1993) observes that union activism transforms women more than men. Women union officials themselves become more 'non-traditional', rather than unions moving towards women members in their style. As Franzway has shown, this impoverishes the family life of women union officials much more than it does their male counterparts (1997: 133).

The foregoing discussion sets out some important characteristics of dominant masculinities and their permutations. As noted earlier, the male breadwinner ideal is one of the foundational values in Australian trade unions which were directly influenced by British precedents. This has now declined but it has left a deep institutional legacy. It was enshrined in the Australian arbitral system and in trade unions. It is still influential because it privileges men as primary in wage negotiations and job classifications at the expense of equal pay for women (Pocock 1997: 9). Even after equal pay was achieved in 1974, and percolated through the Australian award system in the decades to follow, skills in the work women do continue to be regarded as 'other' and inadequately recognised.

Some commentators have distinguished the main features that constitute the hegemonic masculine culture of trade unions. For example, Cunnison and Stageman (1993) emphasise the following attributes which will be deployed in the empirical analysis to follow. Such attributes continue to be significant in marginalising women as potential and effective members. Firstly, there is an 'anti-femininity' and 'anti-emotions' agenda (where both are conflated) which is antithetical to the appropriate expression of emotions. Second, the preferred negotiating style is one based on mental and physical toughness, competition, aggression and, in some circumstances, violence. Women trade union members are uneasy with this. Third, the masculine culture has made women feel out of place or deviant within the union movement. Finally sexual harassment is at the heart of this culture. It is framed by both formal and informal discrimination on the grounds of sex, and rules and customs about hours of work, promotion, training and eligibility for different types of jobs (Cunnison and Stagemen 1993: 194). At the same time, by stressing their persistence, we need to minimise a tendency to regard trade union culture as *a* culture of masculinity. The latter strategy essentialises the differences between the sexes instead of emphasising cultures and masculini*ties* (Collinson 1994: 303). Agostino (1997) in her study of the Australian navy points to the way apparently fixed constructs of both femininity and masculinity are formed by multiple and contradictory gender and sexual discourses.

Class and 'masculine culture' in trade unions

Atkin (1991), Donaldson (1991), and Collinson (1992), provide contrasting gender and class accounts of the relationships between working-class men, masculinity and trade unions. Atkin's study, which foregrounds gender rather than class, examines the history of Australian meatworkers, leaving no doubt that unions were central in reinforcing the hegemony of patriarchal masculinity in blue-collar industries. For example, the union was instrumental in redefining the physical and degrading nature of meatwork towards an ideal of working-class masculinity. Meatworkers were encouraged to create a work culture which empowered men as a defence against the low regard that the public assigned to them (Atkin 1991: 14). In the face of high labour turnover related to the smell, the sight of blood and the anguish of the animals, the union presented a positive counter-image that meatworkers had special qualities of dexterity and strength to cope with the brutal and disturbing work. The union created a bond between all meatworkers that the trade was unsuitable for more sensitive and feminine types. The male versus female axis of patriarchal masculinity was mobilised in campaigns, first to bar and then to minimise, the employment of women by claiming the killing and processing of meat as a male prerogative. They sought to ban women from using knives, the instruments intrinsically linked with power and control in the meat industry (Atkin 1991: 20). This exclusionary practice helps to explain why there are almost no women butchers in Australia, except in a few supermarkets (Pringle and Collings 1993). Thus butchery continues to be founded on patriarchal masculinity. Women butchers challenged these masculine foundations by their mere presence and the reworking of the rules about weight by enlisting help from other workers, but made little headway in rewriting the dominant male/female gender script, to paraphrase Halberstam (1998: 118).

Atkin extends his analysis from the meatworkers' union to the creation of a taken-for-granted 'masculine culture' at the heart of Australian trade unions. Unions in postwar Australia reinforced a distinctive ethos based on constant resistance to employers, and the celebration of the 'union man'. The danger always existed that the trade unions were contributing to romanticising the degrading conditions rather than fundamentally scrutinising and agitating to reform them. Solidarity based on homosocial relations, and symbiotically related to working-class masculinity served to exclude, by definition, those outside the frame of patriarchal masculinity, and those different to Anglo white men as potential union members.

Donaldson (1993) argues that gender relations are bisected by class relations and vice versa and that the salient moment for analysis is in relations between the two. They are preoccupied by their bodies because the repercussions are dire if they lose the strength their bodies possess. However the very destruction of their bodies can be the method of attaining, demonstrating and perpetuating the socially masculine (Donaldson 1991: 19, 30). Collinson (1992), in a British study of shop stewards, is concerned to distance his analysis from class based accounts that romanticise the resistance of working-class men. Many of the hallmarks of their masculine identities as working men: the elevation of the practical; an oppositional identity around independence, freedom and manhood; emphasis on production; domestic sovereignty of the privatised male breadwinner; the insistence of a highly rigid and inflexible mental/manual division of labour – all limit the effectiveness of resistance.

Emotions in masculinity and trade unions

The 'anti-emotions' agenda of trade union men, like that of Anglo men, is based on the common sense views of emotions which come from the way the latter have been falsely regarded in Western thought as dysfunctional diseases of the mind and therefore to be feared and minimised. Recent scholarship emphasises instead that emotions orient us towards things that matter. In an age of information overload, we need emotion to help us orient to what is important and to set priorities (Planalp 1999: 38). Historically, emotion and reason have been separated and regarded as opposites. It is now recognised reason and rationality contain emotions and that emotions have rational aspects. In fact emotion is essential to reason. It tips the balance between competing motivations (Planalp 1999: 37).

Unfortunately, masculinity rules and values have been central in both giving and withdrawing permission about what kinds of emotional expression are allowed in particular societies. This control and censorship of emotional expression is a defining feature of patriarchal or hegemonic masculinity which requires Anglo men be emotionally invulnerable (Buchbinder 1994: 39–41). All men in such cultures are supposed to be stoical and bear misfortune with dignity and reserve. Only anger and aggression are appropriate 'manly' feelings. This creates problems for women with trade union men because whereas both genders express anger about injustice and the denial of legitimate employment rights in trade union struggles, men's limited allowable expression of emotions pushes their anger too often in the direction of aggression and even violence.

It is worth comparing trade unions as workplaces with those occupational enclaves where masculinity similarly enshrines the bifurcation of emotions and reason. Research into these highly masculinised, male dominated occupations, such as medicine, suggests that physicians have developed some of the least satisfactory ways of dealing with their own emotions in relation to their client groups. Medicine has opted to locate its occupations entirely on the reason side of the reason–emotion binary. This has not eliminated emotions, merely camouflaged and manipulated them under what has been called the 'cloak of competence' (Haas and Shaffir 1977) and involves the careful denial and dissimulation of emotions that are actually felt, including profound anxiety and insecurity. Physicians' training encourages the objectification of patients, the separation of the patient from their disease and, as a result, the patient's emotions are commonly regarded as an unnecessary hindrance to the process of treating the disease (Smith and Kleinman 1989; Baker *et al.* 1996). Likewise, the masculine culture of trade union leaders and organisers in male dominated sectors in particular, is likely to have minimised the development of appropriate emotion work skills as part of this labour process. In subscribing to the 'reason' divide of the of reason–emotion binary, men as doctors and as trade union leaders subscribe to a chimera of the way men are supposed to be. In this, they remain bound together as a gender class which has power over women (Hearn 1996: 211). It is to this power and the resistance to it that we now turn.

Case studies

As part of the exploration of the question of trade unions and masculinity, the author carried out in-depth interviews with two well-known trade union organisers who had challenged traditional unionism during the time they were working for unions. The first man is openly gay and displayed this identity in the nurses' union. The second, heterosexual man had been supportive of campaigns to incorporate women and different values into the timber or lumber union and this profoundly challenged the problematic patriarchal masculine culture. However, equally importantly, he had been decisive in introducing environmental values into the union. Such 'green men', as Connell calls them, are particularly interesting in the Australian context, because his research suggests that such men have changed their masculinity the most in the face of feminism (1995: 141).

The case study of the timber industry also draws upon a written account by a woman organiser of a sexual harassment strike in which she was a central actor. This strike occurred in the period when the author was studying the timber industry in South Australia. The latter involved interviews with trade union elected officials, paid organisers, shop stewards and a survey of the membership.

The timber or lumber industry is one of the oldest male occupations in the Western world. In Australia, it is an archetypal blue-collar industry, with ubiquitously hazardous, sometimes fatal working condition both outdoors and inside mills and factories, with regular exposure to dangerous machinery. In parts of the industry such as pine falling (industry slang for people who cut down trees) in the extensive, and sometimes remote, plantations, it is characterised by rugged individualism and male job exclusivism; it thus offers opportunities for men to achieve in terms of the main canons of hegemonic masculinity. The way change has been introduced in this industry allows us to examine claims that have been made about the place of masculine culture in traditional trade union enclaves, and the way this can be successfully challenged to facilitate a more inclusive unionism. In the period described, 5 per cent of the union membership were women and by 1998, the union nationally comprised 14 per cent women.[2]

The two men confirmed in their working lives the way patriarchal masculinity is reproduced at the workplace through brutal initiation ceremonies, now well documented in blue-collar workplaces such as in mining where rites of passage commonly involve water, grease and mild electric shocks to the genitals (Couch 1991).

As a male nurse in a psychiatric hospital in the early 1980s, the organiser recalled his initiation with patriarchal masculinity. A male patient had gone berserk. Three male nurses restrained the patient while the woman nurse stood by. One male nurse was hitting the patient. It was made clear to the gay man that he was expected to 'get in and help' and be part of the beating, and that if he refused, there would be trouble from the other male nurses. Witnessing the incident was a woman nurse who stood by as an observer and a new recruit, a young male nurse, who fled once the beating started. There was talk that 'they would go after him (the young male nurse), and beat him up to give him a lesson'. The gay man thought that they saw themselves as doing him a favour that they would not extend to the new recruit. Because he was gay and more suspect at doing the 'tough male stuff', they were helping him and 'giving him another chance'. The gay informant said it was a message that he never forgot.

Masculine culture in an archetypal blue-collar union

At this point, the chapter will examine examples in relation to the timberworkers' union. It will raise questions about ways that the 'masculine culture' may inhibit potential styles of more inclusive unionism. The union organiser presented the following picture.

The timberworkers' union took its image from the 1929 strike which was lost but became mythologised as an heroic if doomed struggle. The union had been part of something significant and even though they had been defeated they had fought to the end. As a result, a highly masculine culture of unionism had been handed down. The union was seen to be left-wing, tough, and with a particularly aggressive stance towards management. The union organiser added that,

> [W]hat was important was to get people out on strike; not other strategies that might have been clever and would get the same result. This was seen as

caving in. Other strategies might take longer and be less painful for workers but this was seen to be weak. Strike action was seen to be the only tool. Really sticking it up the boss was seen to be associated with masculinity. There was an expectation that you have to be tough, strong in the union movement, live and die for the cause, have total commitment. If you can't be on the picket line for 24 hours a day, tough it out in negotiations; if you can't cut it out there, if it's too hot in the kitchen, then it was made clear you should get out.

(Organiser, ATWU, interview May 1998)

Thus the profile of an 'acceptable' union leader was a hard-headed macho person, a 'tough nut'. Another related masculine value and emotional style was detachment. Identifying with other people's emotions such as empathy to union members was regarded as unacceptable. This latter position underscores the typification of 'manliness' noted previously. In this blue-collar union there were strong expectations to attend extreme homosocial social functions such as lunch at topless waitress bars. Heterosexual men seek pleasure in each other's company where the presence of the topless women actually reinforces the explicit heterosexual status of these working-class men (Couch 1991).

A union culture such as this one was aggressively heteronormative. It rested uneasily with a trade union politics gaining momentum in other quarters, coming from gays and lesbians who successfully lobbied the political arm of the Australian labour movement, the Labor governments, to challenge the monopoly of hetero-sexuality at work and in the political system.

The challenge of the politics of sexuality and alternative gay masculinities

In fact, in Australia, it has mostly been these Labor (ALP) governments that have provided the breakthroughs in redressing discrimination against gays and lesbians (Ostenfeld 1999: 182), while unions of white-collar public servants, teachers, social workers and blue-collar unions of the Left have lobbied governments in general. One of the most entrenched sources of serious opposition to gays and lesbians has come from blue-collar union masculinity, under scrutiny here, as well as the conser-vative influence of the Catholic Church (which has had a powerful relationship to both the Australian labour movement and the ALP). Lesbian unionists in other unions have reported on the burden of masking their sexuality in the face of the powerful heterosexism in this threatening environment (Franzway 1997: 146–7). The transgressive masculinities of gay men have the potential to challenge this culture in trade unions. In the blue-collar heartland union I have been describing, the potential challenge of gay men is repulsed successfully by homophobia intrinsic to heteronormative masculine culture. Gay men can only exist in this context by obliterating any vestiges of their gay identity. At the time of writing, this has not been possible because their 'difference' leaks out in the atmosphere created by the heterosexual, homophobic gaze.

It has been recognised that there are different kinds of masculinities among gay men (Gough 1989). The nurses' union organiser described himself as an 'out' gay man and gay activist since the early 1970s. He regarded himself as having a 'camp' manner and style. He had become a nurse in the 1970s. This occupation had appeal because it was non-traditional for men. 'For a middle-class, tertiary-educated man, it was challenging what a man should do.' As a nurse, and later working for their union, he was initially perceived as an overt homosexual. He refused to act 'straight' and 'pass'. It was always important to him to present himself as a gay man. As he stated:

> It's a gay liberation attitude. We are not apologists; they'll accept us warts and all. I'm *out* and not afraid of being out. People come to respect me. I have to work at it. There is a certain reserve you have to conquer with people. I win through as a person. I'm a reasonable person. They [fellow workmates and union members] come to know you as a person.
>
> (Organiser ANF, interview March 1998)

He described an incident when he was working for the union when he had to address a union meeting at a hospital which housed the 'criminally insane'. The male nurses here tended to be isolated and developed a particular culture because the work attracted men who saw themselves as tough males. He described how their patriarchal masculine gaze put him under pressure to present himself in ways that were less confronting to patriarchal masculinity so he would be more acceptable to these members as their union person. These strategies are illuminating. He tried to make his body look larger and stronger, swore, and adopted the trappings of a confrontationist, negotiating style towards the bosses redolent of the designated masculine culture described elsewhere in this chapter. He gave an account of how he managed this as follows:

> They saw me as a big queen. They really attacked me verbally. They could speak to you in a really abusive way because I was overtly gay. I tried to look big and strong, put in a few 'fucks', talked tough and ridiculed the bosses. Women were easier to deal with.
>
> (Organiser ANF, interview March 1998)

He himself had a sophisticated negotiating style which included work feelings. He thought that counselling was important with members. He prepared them by being 'encouraging, supportive and very patient. You have to counsel them carefully. This is what I'm going to say; this is what you will say. My mental health training was very useful.' Sometimes he thought you had to be reasonably tough with management and other times play to their emotions. Sometimes you had to be honest and let barriers down. You had to know the sort of manager, read the individual and work out the best way to appeal to them. At times, being too assertive and too aggressive would close off some individual managers. You could appeal to their reasonableness.

The challenge of women and feminism

The masculine in trade unions is defined partly against women members. Cunnison and Stageman suggest that women members problematise hidden dimensions of unionism such as negotiating style which are based on masculine culture. In their view, some union men are openly questioning the culture of patriarchal masculinity and its consequences for the unions (1993: 185). As pointed out already, they also identified important flashpoints for change such as campaigns around sexual harassment. In addition, they claimed a culture of femininity had the potential to set new priorities because women's lives are grounded in working-class community as well as in paid work and in caring for others. Women's agendas have always been wider than men's (Cunnison and Stageman 1993: 242).

The history of the timberworkers' union in Australia recently provides an opportunity to consider the impact of the entry of women's issues, campaigns around sexual harassment and the emergence of women union leaders on a non-inclusive unionism which had developed, symbiotically, over a long period of time, around working-class patriarchal masculinity. It needs to be emphasised that this was the first blue-collar union to develop equal opportunity and sexual harassment policies. So it is possible for even the most exclusively male worksites to move in less sexist directions.

During the 13 years of federal Labor Governments (1983–96), an Accord was entered into with the unions and, during the first phase, an exercise in 'Award Restructuring' was championed in an attempt to modernise and make the arbitral industrial relations system more flexible at the workplace level. This exercise included simplifying the plethora of job classifications while opening up a limited career structure. Concurrently, the Labor Government had officially endorsed Affirmative Action and Equal Opportunities policies as part of the industrial relations system. This career structure had to include women workers too.

Women timber workers in veneer factories and timber mills had been second class citizens; now they were required to be integrated into the seven rungs on the ladder and given opportunities to progress in the 'career structure'. At the same time, a process was developing, however tentative, to bring women into the leadership of the union. The union leadership introduced Affirmative Action and Equal Opportunity principles into the award or conditions of employment. Sexual harassment was addressed directly. The union was making an attempt to modify the male culture of the union and the industry. This occurred at a time when other nationalities such as Vietnamese and Cambodians were entering the timber industry. Because the equal opportunity policies were in the award, the union was justified in running courses on equal opportunity and sexual harassment. Grants were obtained from the government to pay for the training. Organisers were trained first. They had a history of frequently patronising women members, calling them 'luv' and 'dear'. They would use them, rather than regard them as union members who would grow and develop as a result of facilitation and learning. In the period from 1987 to 1990, training was initiated for job representatives at the workplace, drawing on government grants available for the process. At first, the job representatives would not attend the training but, because it was in the award, it could be justified. The owners and managers had the same male culture so the union actually initiated joint training and workers and managers were trained at the same time. Serious conflicts erupted inside the training rooms. Women confronted male shop stewards. At times the conflicts were so intense, individuals would not remain and the training was not completed. Finally the women at a timber mill in the major regional city, Mt Gambier, went on strike about sexual harassment.

The account of that strike is taken from the first woman organiser who has since died. She emerged as a union person from this regional area. She was training to be an organiser at the time. She describes how the management of this timber mill, presented the workplace as 'one big happy family'. The events occurred in November 1989 when a woman union member refused to passively accept the sexual harassment of a fellow worker. The women typified the unacceptable behaviour as 'crude remarks and filthy sneering'. The woman working with him approached other women who had been 'putting up with the same behaviour for two years'. They complained to management and asked to have the man shifted to another part of the mill, away from the women. Management told the women to go back to work and to stop being silly, as 'he was only having a joke with them'. They had no access to their shop steward who had recently resigned over problems with management, so they rang the regional union office and asked for the woman organiser to discuss the problem and sort it out. As she put it:

> I approached the women one by one and they all reported the same filthy and disgusting comments made by this man every time they had to pass his machine, and the response that they had received from Management.

The organiser approached Management who were then prepared to reprimand the man but not shift him because he would leave. She continued:

> Well, the women were furious at this and asked what action they could take. As a Union organiser I told them that they could walk out the gate to make Management realise that they were serious. Also that it was time to stand up and be counted and that they did not have to tolerate this harassment any longer. All 20 women agreed with this.

The women voted to go on a 24-hour strike the next day. The union organiser told management that they had until 4.20 p.m. that day to shift the man otherwise the women would strike and she would be asking the male union members to support them. Management still refused to shift the man and continued to treat the issue as a joke. At the union meeting with the men only one man out of 70 supported and joined the women in their action. The two regional union leaders then approached the man unsuccessfully to see if they 'could talk him into shifting to another machine'. The women decided to set up picket lines on all eight gates until action was taken. The man concerned passed the picket line laughing at the women. Management figures smiled and whistled all day. The striking women managed to stop all trucks going in and out including vital materials necessary to enable the mill to continue to run. The next day, the male union leader approached the male union members but they still refused to support the women. The woman union organiser and two of the women from the picket line then approached women union members at a veneer factory called IPL in one of the nearby timber towns. One of the striking women repeated to the women union members 'some of the things said to them by this man'. The women union members at IPL were outraged at this and the fact that the men had not supported the women. They then joined the women union members at the picket line the next day. Men had begun to join the women also. By this time an influential male shop steward had also joined the women. A further meeting was held at the timber mill and this time the 'blokes decided to walk out but none stayed back to help on the pickets'. Management were now ready to talk. The union demanded that the man be dismissed because he had continued the sexual harassment (making the same crude remarks) to the women on the picket line. Management agreed and a number of other changes were put into effect from the dispute. Two women also came forward to be shop stewards alongside two shop stewards who were men.

This strike confronted the taken-for-granted 'masculine culture' both of working-class men and the union, and effected a profound change. As part of my study, 50 working-class men, many of them timberworkers, were interviewed a couple of years later. All of them had a sophisticated understanding of sexual harassment, women's viewpoints and the law. In a regional area where social change is slow and where patriarchal masculinity, particularly in the domestic sphere can be more readily justified because the work is so physically hard, the impact of these events is profound. The union leaders were placed in a position of having to defend women members for the first time, and to do this they confronted male union members. As a result of these activities (between 1987 and 1990) a woman obtained an important post in one state branch; there were now four research officers who were women and many more shop stewards than before.

When the ATWU amalgamated with the Pulp & Paper Workers Union in 1992, and the Miners Union and the Construction and Building Workers Union in 1994 to become the Forestry Division of the Construction, Forestry, Mining and Energy Union (CFMEU), it was different from the voters in having a number of women as officers in appointed position at the state and federal level. By 1994/5 there were a number of elected women officers, including a gay woman as Branch Secretary in Victoria. She was described by a previous woman research officer for the ATWU as highly respected, a cabinet maker who understood the area, open about being a lesbian ('all the members knew it'), a strategic thinker and fighter who 'had a great way of dealing with sexism in employers and members that seemed to retain their sympathy and admiration'.

The latter account of events suggests that in a period of change significant inroads were made in dismantling the 'masculine culture' of a male-identified blue-collar union through a combination of formal government policies supporting equal opportunity and affirmative action, the entry of women and women's issues on the union agenda, and the support of male union organisers and officials who were openly questioning the 'masculine culture'. As Cunnison and Stageman predicted, the campaign over sexual harassment in particular confronted the heart of the culture of masculinity and was able to deconstruct and change it. Notwithstanding the relaxation of the masculine culture towards women, there is still a fair way to go in breaking down the rigid and narrow emotional range permitted by adherence to masculine identity as the next section discusses.

The camouflage of expressive emotions in trade unions and the potential for emotional labour

Neither in the women-controlled nurses' union, nor the blue-collar timber workers' union was there acknowledgement of emotional skills as part of the legitimate array of skills that a trade union organiser or leader needed. Stoical values prevailed in the handling of members and negotiation. Showing emotions was discouraged in the public realm.

The gay organiser had originally created his identity to have space to express his non-reserved nature in the public world. As a man on the threshold of creating diverse masculinities, he felt confined in being expected to disguise his open, emotional nature according to the dictates of both heterosexual masculinity and Anglo-Australian cultural reserve. He put it this way:

> I was seen as an emotional person, seen as highly strung. I'm not afraid to show gayness or emotions. I show emotions and show anger. Initially it was the style of person I was. Not being manly, I accommodated 'flamboyant' showing your emotions and feeling comfortable about showing emotions. Even exaggerate it a bit. This is legitimate. I'm challenging the traditional image of what a man should be. It's a good thing to do.
>
> (Organiser ANF, interview March 1998)

He has even been told in feedback after a job interview that his gesticulations were bizarre. As someone with strong empathetic and counselling skills, he found the public world of the nurses' union a demanding and stressful environment for men and women. 'Showing emotions was not encouraged; instead there was an expectation of being in control and being businesslike.' Such trade union feeling rules mimic instrumental and bureaucratic rationality, objectify emotions and amplify the mind–body dualism (Mumby and Putnam 1992). This man's effeminate gay persona deeply subverts the latter and suggests the potential of alternative gay masculinities to challenge the reason–emotion binary implicit in the public world and in trade unions in particular.

In the timberworkers' union, only anger was acceptable provided it was directed towards authority and the boss. The norms surrounding emotions followed closely the norms of patriarchal masculinity that a man was not allowed to show weakness; weakness was synonymous with emotion: 'It was almost like you were not allowed to show emotions unless they were strong. You were a tough cookie.' Such feeling rules left individuals to keep legitimate and deeply felt emotions hidden. The ATWU organiser describes the emotion work he engaged in to hide the true range of his feelings when recalling the events which led to the union moving its position towards policies of more sustainable forestry practice. In the course of his union duties, he had come upon a group of 20 forestry workers cutting trees illegally. He had told them to stop it immediately. One held a chain saw to his throat, called him a 'fucking greenie and to fuck off out of the area'. The situation was so personally dangerous, that he had to walk backwards to his car. At another time, on his first visit to an 'old growth' forest area, he came to realise that the 300- and 400-year old trees were not being used for furniture and building manufacture as he believed but were being wood-chipped and this engendered intense feelings in him:

> I remember going back to the hotel and breaking down. I couldn't come to terms with going to a meeting that night about raising their [member's] rates of pay. I was crying my eyes out. I was shaking with fear and anxiety at facing the fallers [those who fell trees]. I was expected to fight for them for a wage increase to continue doing what they were doing. I steeled myself; I couldn't eat. I was going to the meeting a shaking wreck. In the end I was able to be present at the meeting; they didn't know how I felt. However I wasn't able to talk to anyone (in the union) about it. I asked myself 'What am I doing here? What am I fighting for?' Then you become hardened to it. It becomes part of your culture. My role was to put policy in place to reduce the amount of timber that is going to these places and save some of the forest area. I had to convince the major part of the national council of the union. The first time it came up I was really isolated. I recognised that unless something was done, the union was going to die. You weren't able to show emotions.
>
> (Organiser, ATWU, interview March 1998)

Here, the organiser is making explicit the way the hidden 'feeling rules' of masculinity impel him to present himself as estranged from himself and disembodied, as personally invulnerable. This is necessary if he was to retrieve his masculinity and to restore his identity as a legitimate trade union organiser.

The strong, yet hidden presence of patriarchal masculinity in trade unions as organisations has prevented the development and acknowledgement of emotional skills to the extent required in this kind of work which has a strong human services dimension. The timber industry union organiser highlights the need for trade union employees to be able to obtain institutional support and counselling for the difficult situations they were required to deal with routinely. Debriefing after tough negotiations was essential. The gay organiser underscores the failure to acknowledge the emotional aspects of dealing with union members; emotional labour and emotion work feature in both the unanswered needs of members and in the lack of emotional support for employees of trade union themselves.

The ATWU organiser describes the impact of the taken for granted 'masculine culture' on union meetings which were dominated by strategies and control. This was contrasted to a listening stance where the union person was responsive to union members:

With the male culture of unions, you have an agenda or the leadership has an agenda. Men are action-oriented; men had ideas; men were considered leaders; men were perceived to have all the knowledge. We played the role. The male culture disempowers people. Instead of having meetings where you would have all the strategies and control, I had to learn to give up control. I had to learn quickly that was not the way to work. I had to tap into other people's feelings, emotions, ideas and points of view. Everything they had to contribute was valuable. I had to learn listening skills, tolerance and respect. In the past, I would throw caution to the wind; didn't care if I hurt somebody; if they didn't go along – fuck 'em. Working with women and feminists and the gender balance in the union was bringing in the emotional aspects of life. I learned a far greater appreciation of life. There was more to life than work.

(Organiser, ATWU, interview March 1998)

With great insight, he describes the preoccupation with control implicit in the masculine project common to all classes, but also its alternative in non-masculine ways of doing trade unionism.

Conclusion

This chapter has explored the relationship of patriarchal or hegemonic heterosexual masculinity implicit in the gender regime of certain Australian trade unions which are infused with masculinist practices that parallel those in other sex-segregated employment enclaves. Historically, these dominant masculinities have taken their supreme cultural form in the elite parts of bio-medicine such as surgery; in the police; the armed services; and in a group of manual occupations in industries such as coal mining, lumber or timber; on the docks or wharves; on ships; shearing, meat-work and construction. For working-class men these occupations, which were usually physically hard and frequently dangerous, came to be associated with toughness and hardness in the men themselves: heavy drinking, swearing and, most of all, the exclusion of women workers. For the same reasons they were often the heartlands of trade unions with high union densities (Cunnison and Stageman 1993; Pocock 1997; Briskin 1993; Lawrence 1994). Such a 'masculine culture' was central to post-World War II Australian unions which celebrated the 'union man'; conflated militancy with virility; and linked mateship to solidarity. However any roman-ticisation of working-class men's resistance is problematic and paradoxical.

The chapter also reviewed the possibilities presented by women, gay men and critical heterosexual men to bring about changes in the taken for granted masculine heterosexual culture which still defines trade unions. The effect of women and feminist policies entering the timberworkers' union was shown to confront the 'masculine culture' implicit in the union, but also in male union members and management. Out of this struggle, the union showed itself open to equal opportunity and affirmative action policies which were translated into union policies sensitive to feminist issues. The accompanying activism of newly recruited women union leaders led to a major industrial dispute over sexual harassment. In the climate created by these feminist changes, for the first time union leaders defended women union members. The 'masculine culture' was successfully changed. This served to legitimate the presence of women's issues as central union issues, and women union leaders as a normal and less deviant part of the union. While the challenge is far from over, this was an admirable beginning for a union within a conservative rural and patriarchal heartland. At the same time, while it has shown movement in relation to women, the pervasive hold of hegemonic masculinity in unions remains unforgiving to men who step outside the norms, including in a feminised union – the nurses.

The two interviews with male union organisers have raised issues which need to be investigated further. They struggled with the expected performances of dominant masculinities which they were only too aware over-emphasised control and estranged them from their bodies and emotions. They were highly sceptical of the circumscribed emotional range permitted to them in the public world of the trade unions.

In the blue-collar union, there were rigid notions of negotiations permitted by patriarchal masculinity. Strike action was the *only* permitted strategy; union leaders and organisers had to act tough and, above all, be detached from members. Other strategies, which might be smarter, were treated with suspicion as a sign of masculine weakness. Gay union men have a furtive existence inside the blue-collar enclave. A strong expectation persists that personal identity must be based on patriarchal masculine heterosexuality and this is policed by homosocial social activities. Male bonding is a source of pleasure and it is equated with solidarity in leaders and members, but is based on anti-femininity and homophobia. The presence of a gay woman official in another state implicitly challenges the latter.

While the presence of gays and lesbians was celebrated in the nurses' union leadership, heterosexual men members scrutinised the masculinity of the gay organiser featured here, with their patriarchal masculine heterosexual gaze. For them, 'masculine culture' was central to 'correct' trade unionism. Even in this union, the 'cloak of competence' about real trade unionism rested squarely in the reason half of the reason–emotion binary. Nineteenth-century manhood values, discussed earlier, prevailed. Assumptions of detachment dictated the permitted emotional range for union leaders and organisers in relation to members. Like other men in contemporary management and organisational work (Kerfoot and Knights 1996: 19) they were expected to exhibit an instrumental form of 'rational control' (be in control and businesslike).

Trade unions as organisation are deeply marked by the influence of patriarchal heterosexual masculinity in ways that have only begun to be deconstructed. So far, most of the gender change in union leaders has come from women taking on the burden of a more non-traditional persona, and we know this has meant an inhuman sacrifice in non-work life. Men in unions have a great deal to gain as individuals in developing more inclusive organisations which would affirm the spectrum of human identities, sexualities and identities.

Notes

1   I would to thank the editors for their helpful comments. I also thank Dr Bill Thorpe for his stylistic suggestions and intellectual input.
2   Thanks to Sonya Mezinec, Department of Social Inquiry at Adelaide University for access to these figures.

References

Agostino, K. (1997a) 'Masculinity, sexuality and life on board Her Majesty's Royal Australian Ships', *Jigs* 2, 1: 15–30.

Ashforth, Blake, E. and Humphrey, Ronald H. (1993) 'Emotional labor in service roles: the influence of identity', *Academy of Management Review* 18, 1: 88–115.

Atkin, D. (1991) 'Aristocracy of muscle: Meatworkers, masculinity and trade unionism in the 1950s', *ASSLH Labour History Conference* July.

Briskin, L. 1993, 'Union women and separate organizing', in Briskin, Linda and MacDermott, Patricia (eds) *Women Challenging Unions. Feminism, Democracy and Militancy*, Toronto: University of Toronto Press.

Buchbinder, D. (1994) *Masculinities and Identities*, Carlton: Melbourne University Press.

Baker, P.S., Yoels, W.C. and Claire, J.M. (1996) 'Emotional expression during medical encounters: Social dis-ease and the medical gaze', in James, Veronica and Gabe, Jonathon (eds) *Health and the Sociology of Emotions*, Oxford: Blackwell.

Cobble, D.S. (ed.) (1993) *Women and Unions: Forging a Partnership*, Ithaca, NY: ILR Press.

Collinson, D. (1992) *Managing the Shopfloor: Subjectivity, Masculinity and Workplace Culture*, Berlin and New York: Walter de Gruyter.

Collinson, D. and Hearn, J. (1994) 'Naming men as men: Implications for work, organization and management, *Gender, Work and Organization* 1, 1 January.

Collinson, M. (1994) Review, *Work, Employment and Society* 8, 2 (June): 302–4.

Connell, R.W. (1995) *Masculinities*, St. Leonards: Allen & Unwin.

—— (1996) 'New directions in gender theory, masculinity research and gender politics', *Ethnos* 61, 3–4: 157–76.

Couch, M. (1991) 'Production and reproduction of masculinity in a mining community'. Paper presented at a Conference on Research on Masculinity and Men in Gender Relations, Sydney, June.

—— (1999) 'Men sticking together: Homosociality and Broken Hill', in Palmer, D. Shanahan, R. and Shanahan, M. (eds) *Australian Labour History Reconsidered*, Unley, South Australia: Australian Humanities Press.

Cunnison, S. and Stageman, J. (1993) *Feminizing the Unions*, Aldershot: Avebury.

Donaldson, M. (1991) *Time of Our Lives: Labour and Love in the Working Class*, North Sydney: Allen & Unwin.

—— (1993) 'What is hegemonic masculinity?', *Theory and Society* 22, 5: 644–57.

Dowsett, G. (1993) 'I'll show you mine, if you'll show me yours: Gay men, masculinity research, men's studies, and sex', *Theory and Society* 22, 5: 697–709.

Evans, Raymond and Thorpe, Bill (1998) 'Commanding men: Masculinities and the convict system', *Journal of Australian Studies* 56: 17–34.

Franzway, S. (1997) 'Sexual politics in trade unions', in Pocock, B. (ed.) *Strife, Sex and Politics in Labour Unions*, St Leonards: Allen & Unwin.

Gough, J. (1989) 'Theories of sexual identity and the masculinization of the gay man', in Shepherd, S. and Wallis, M. (eds) *Coming on Strong: Gay Politics and Culture*, London: Unwin Hyman.

Haas, J. and Shaffir, W. (1977) 'The professionalization of medical students: Developing competence and a cloak of competence', *Symbolic Interaction* 1: 71–88.

Halberstam, J. (1998) *Female Masculinity*, Durham: Duke University Press.

Hearn, J. (1996) 'Is masculinity dead? A critique of the concept of masculinity/masculinities', in Maz, M. and Hill, G.M. (eds) *Understanding Masculinities*, Oxford: Oxford University Press.

James, N. (1989) 'Emotional labour: Skill and work in the social regulation of feelings', *Sociological Review* 37, 1, Feb.: 15–42.

Kerfoot, D. and Knights, D. (1996) ' "The best is yet to come?": The quest for embodiment in managerial work', in Collinson, D. and Hearn, J. (eds) *Men as Managers, Managers as Men*, London: Sage.

Lawrence, E. (1994) *Gender and Trade Unions*, London: Taylor & Francis.

McNaught, Brian, (1993) *Gay Issues in the Workplace*, London: St Martin's Press.

Matthaei, J. (1997) 'The sexual division of labor, sexuality and lesbian/gay liberation. Toward a marxist-feminist analysis of sexuality in U.S. capitalism', in Gluckman, A. and Reed, B. (eds) *Homo Economicus, Capitalism, Community, and Lesbian and Gay Life*, New York and London: Routledge.

Morgan, D. (1993) ' "You too can have a body like mine": Reflections on the male body and masculinities', in Scott, S. and Morgan, D. *Body Matters: Essays on the Sociology of the Body*, London: Falmer Press.

Morgan, D.H.J. (1992) *Discovering Men, Critical Studies on Men and Masculinities*, London: Routledge.

Morris, J.A. and Feldman, D.C. (1996) 'The dimensions, antecedents, and consequences of emotional labor', *Academy of Management Review* 21,4: 986–1010.

Mumby, D.K. and Putnam, L.L. (1992) 'The politics of emotion: A feminist reading of bounded rationality', *Academy of Management Review* 17, 3: 465–86.

Ostenfeld, S. (1999) 'Sexual identity and the Australian labor movement in historical perspective', in Hunt, G. *Laboring for Rights: Unions and Sexual Diversity Across Nations*, Philadelphia: Temple University Press: pp. 157–90.

Planalp, S. (1999) *Communicating Emotion: Social, Moral, and Cultural Processes*, Cambridge: Cambridge University Press.

Pringle, R. and Collings, S. (1993) 'Women and butchery: Some cultural taboos', *Australian Feminist Studies* 17, Autumn: 29–45.

Pocock, B. (1997) *Strife, Sex and Politics in Labour Unions*, St Leonards: Allen & Unwin.

Rantakeisu, U. Starrin, B. and Hagquist, C. (1997) 'Unemployment, shame and ill health – an exploratory study', *Scandinavian Journal of Social Welfare* 6: 13–23.

Roby, P. and Uttal, L. (1993) ' "Putting it all together?" The dilemmas of rank-and-file union leaders', in Cobble, D.S. (ed.) *Women and Unions: Forging a Partnership*, Ithaca, New York: ILR Press.

Sedgwick, E.K. (1985) *Between Men: English Literature and Male Homosocial Desire*, New York: Columbia University Press, (esp. Introduction).

Seidler, V.J. (1989) *Rediscovering Masculinity: Reason, Language and Sexuality*, London: Routledge.

Smith III, A.C and Kleinman, S. (1989) 'Managing emotions in medical school: Students' contacts with the living and the dead', *Social Psychology Quarterly* 52, 1: 56–69.

Stenross, B. and Kleinman, S. (1989) 'The highs and lows of emotional labor: Detectives' encounters with criminals and victims' *Journal of Contemporary Ethnography* 17, 4: 435–52.

Thomson, C. and Pocock, B. (1997) 'Moving on from masculinity? Australian unions' industrial agenda', in Pocock, Barbara, *Strife, Sex and Politics in Labour Unions*, St Leonards: Allen & Unwin.

Whitehead, S. (1999) Review Article: 'Hegemonic masculinity revisited', *Gender, Work and Organization* 6, 1, Jan.: 58–62.

Williams, C. (1997) 'Women and occupational health and safety: From narratives of danger to invisibility', *Labour History* 73, November: 30–52.

Index

Creese, G. 29
Crompton, R. 188, 189
Cunnison, S. 280, 296, 302
Cully, M. 190

demarcation 9, 11, 12
democracy – *see* trade union democracy
developed world 10, 77, 215
developing countries 1, 20, 23, 55
Dickens, L. 155, 159, 162, 193–4
difference; *see* diversity
disabled 1; rights 207; trade union members
    15, 159, 164; trade union structures 16,
    128, 154, 159, 160, 162, 164, 178, 266; *see
    also* disabilities
disabilities 12, 16, 39, 128
disability movement 5
diversity 2, 4, 5, 22, 31, 38–40, 48, 64, 115,
    128, 261, 263, 293; groups 128; and
    separate organising 38–40; sexual 7, 128,
    139, 293; in trade unions 137, 138;
    among women 136, 139, 280
domestic division of labour 101, 102, 103,
    104, 109, 110, 135, 220
domestic violence; *see* violence against women

economic development 73, 75
Economic and Social Research Council 163
electronics sector 3, 75, 77, 79, 80, 81, 84, 86,
    87, 88
El Savador 42
emotion work 12, 245, 297–9, 305–6
employer partnerships 19–20
employers 10, 51, 81, 87, 89, 100–1, 104,
    189, 232, 245, 249, 259, 268
employment rights; *see also* by country
engineering workers 192
equal opportunity 58, 83, 97, 115, 125, 131,
    143, 154; activists 154, 156, 181; business
    case 158; legislation 134, 146, 147;
    liberal approach 159, 163, 164, 166;
    mainstreaming; *see* mainstreaming;
    networks 145; quotas 115; radical
    approach 159, 160, 163, 164, 166; social
    justice 158; *see also* affirmative action
equal rights; *see* equal opportunity
equality – *see* equal opportunity
ethnicity 7–8, 15, 16, 73–4, 75, 87, 88, 89,
    96, 115, 249–50, 260; Aboriginal 8, 34,
    30, 38; adivasis (Scheduled Tribes ST) 96,
    98; African 208, 213; African-American
    20, 15, 236, 242, 249;
    Afro-Caribbean 156; Asian 10;
    Bangladeshi 90, 156; Black 208, 236;
    Caribbean 10; caste 96, 98, 108; Chinese
    75, 87; Coloured 208, 213; dalits
    (Untouchables, Scheduled Castes) 96, 98,
    100; and demarcation 12; differences in
    Malaysia 74, 83; First Nations 30, 31;

Hispanic 242; Indian 74, 77, 79, 87, 213;
    indigenous 8; and integration 64, 65, 66;
    intra-ethnic competition 82, 91; Latina
    15, 236, 242, 249; Malay 75, 79, 83, 87;
    minorities 128; Non-English speaking
    backgrounds (NESB) 277, 288; Pakistani
    156; people of colour 38; Torres Strait
    Islander 8, 277; untouchability 96; visible
    minority 30, 33; white 8, 208, 213, 236,
    239, 279; women of colour 236, 242, 249;
    see also by country *and* immigrants
Europe 3, 8, 15, 20
European Commission 114
European colonialism 7
European Trade Union Confederation
    (ETUC) 10
European Union 21, 156; equal opportunities
    policy 143; gender mainstreaming 21, 143
exclusion 8, 9, 10–11, 12, 80, 123, 134, 140,
    155, 159, 294; *see also* strategies, *and* trade
    unions
Export Processing Zones 20
export sector 37, 67, 73, 77, 80
expulsion of women 123

fair representation 159, 160; *see also*
    UNISON
family 20, 52, 76, 79, 85, 103, 107, 109, 114,
    134, 147, 211, 221, 234, 239–42, 245,
    250; *see also* collective bargaining
'family friendly' 17, 195, 241, 245
feminism 53, 119, 120, 121, 123, 196;
    academic 2; bourgeois 52, 119, 121, 123;
    and industrial relations 2; labour 233,
    234; party and union 146; pragmatic 125;
    radical 122, 123; second wave 1; socialist
    52, 142–3; union 118;
feminist 6, 59, 123, 223, 272; activism 154,
    261; agenda 201, 266; analysis 6;
    anti-feminist 140, 144; critique 155; equal
    opportunity 143; extreme-left 123;
    feminist-socialism 142–3; humanist 53,
    57, 66; movements 98, 110, 113;
    paradigm 193;
    pragmatic-feminists 125; radical 123;
    research 2; socialist 52; studies 4; trade
    union 119, 120, 121, 144; vanguard 22;
    wage earning 59, 67; working class 53
flexibility 126
flight attendants 15, 233, 245, 246
formal sector 10, 15, 96, 97, 98, 99, 109,
    213
Franzway, S. 295
Free Trade Zones (FTZ) 81, 83, 84, 85, 86,
    90

the Gap 42
garment workers 108
gay 4, 12, 16, 20, 39, 139, 214, 248, 257–73,

white 208; craft unions 212; intellectuals 213; heterosexual masculinity 275; masculine tradition 1; trade union women 215; workers 157, 208, 211, 212

Whitstone, C. 157, 197

Witz, A. 9, 17, 188

women; academic 143; dual role 52; diversity/difference among 136, 139, 280; double disadvantage 34; education levels 220; health dangers 79; political styles 17; professional and highly qualified; *see* professional; resistance 84; and trade union structures, *see* trade unions; and training 105–6, 107; networking 20, 21, 178, 195; vanguard 22, 154, 158; in the workforce 29

women's autonomous organising 10, 15, 22, 98, 101, 104, 108, 119; *see also* separate organising

women's movement 20, 41, 98, 139, 146, 223, 233; *see also* by country

women in trade unions 31, 33, 58, 59, 84–8, 116, 117, 118, 119, 121, 130, 154–5, 159, 213–17, 260; absence in union leadership; *see* women in trade unions: leadership positions; activists/activism 17, 120, 127, 158, 177, 181, 215; agenda 17, 85, 174, 193, 201; black women 215; career 140, 191; career paths 140; childcare provision 197; in decision making; *see* women in trade union leadership positions; democratic deficit 7; education levels 208, 209, 210, 215, 220; empowerment 37; 'the girls' 281; leadership positions 10, 11, 58, 60, 61, 80, 99, 101–2, 104, 117, 121, 123, 126, 132, 134, 144, 191, 194, 206, 217, 218–9, 221, 222, 233, 235–6, 279; marginalised 217, membership 31, 58, 84, 85, 116–17, 133–4, 137, 165, 196, 218, 228, 232, 234–7, 260, 278; networking 194, 195; proportional representation 60, 163, 192; *see also* UNISON, Proportionality,

GPMU, GPR *and* women's trade union structures; self-organisation; *see* self-organisation *and* women's trade union structures; shop stewards 218; solidarity 798; strategies; *see* strategies; training 124, 279; under-representation 19, 126, 219, 225; white 215; workplace representation 80, 84, 116, 126

women's trade union structures; *see also* by country; 12, 16, 17, 18, 22, 35, 39, 53, 60, 120, 122, 126, 127, 134, 139, 142, 143, 144, 145, 146, 159–60, 164, 165–6, 168, 172, 190–1, 195, 197, 225, 279, 280; affirmative action seats 33, 280; bargaining 144, 145; committees 53, 80, 84, 120, 122, 126, 127, 141, 145, 166, 168, 172–3, 190, 191, 194, 223, 224, 225, 280; conferences 145, 160, 166, 195, 197; congress 54, 60, 80; council 53, 54; departments 12, 139, 145; education courses 59, 119, 195, 197, 224; fair representation 163, *see also* UNISON; forums 120, 122, 223, 224–5; networks 145–6; officers/officials 60, 145, 191, 192, 195, 197, 218; proportionality 17, 60, 165, 192, 196, 201; quotas 17, 115, 123, 142, 143, 144, 165, 225–8; rejection of 139; reserved seats 17, 160, 162, 191; self-organisation 194

women's studies 141

Women Working Worldwide 21, 95, 110

worker control 211

working time 130, 239, 240

work-life balance 19, 21, 52, 239–40

World Trade Organisation 110

works councils 139, 140, 144, 145

young workers 76, 79, 127, 134, 138, 213, 214

young members' structures 134

Yugoslavia 8

Yuval-Davis, N. xv, 20